URBAN AND RURAL DECAY PHOTOGRAPHY

J. Dennis Thomas

URBAN AND RURAL DECAY PHOTOGRAPHY

HOW TO CAPTURE THE BEAUTY IN THE BLIGHT

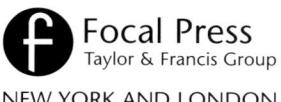

Focal Press
Taylor & Francis Group

NEW YORK AND LONDON

First published 2014
by Focal Press
70 Blanchard Rd Suite 402, Burlington, MA 01803

Simultaneously published in the UK
by Focal Press
2 Park Square, Milton Park, Abingdon, Oxon OX14 4RN

Focal Press is an imprint of the Taylor & Francis Group, an informa business

© 2014 J. Dennis Thomas

The right of J. Dennis Thomas to be identified as author of this work has been asserted by him in accordance with sections 77 and 78 of the Copyright, Designs and Patents Act 1988.

All rights reserved. No part of this book may be reprinted or reproduced or utilized in any form or by any electronic, mechanical, or other means, now known or hereafter invented, including photocopying and recording, or in any information storage or retrieval system, without permission in writing from the publishers.

Notices
Knowledge and best practice in this field are constantly changing. As new research and experience broaden our understanding, changes in research methods, professional practices, or medical treatment may become necessary.

Practitioners and researchers must always rely on their own experience and knowledge in evaluating and using any information, methods, compounds, or experiments described herein. In using such information or methods they should be mindful of their own safety and the safety of others, including parties for whom they have a professional responsibility.

Product or corporate names may be trademarks or registered trademarks, and are used only for identification and explanation without intent to infringe.

Library of Congress Cataloging in Publication Data
Thomas, J. Dennis.
  Urban and rural decay photography : how to capture the beauty in the blight / J. Dennis Thomas.
    pages cm
  ISBN 978-0-415-66321-2 (pbk.) — ISBN 978-0-203-38105-2 (ebk.) 1. Architectural photography—Technique. 2. Abandoned buildings—Pictorial works. 3. Abandoned houses in art. I. Title.
  TR659.T48 2013
  778.9'4—dc23   2012045980

ISBN: 978-0-415-66321-2 (pbk)
ISBN: 978-0203-38105-2 (ebk)

Typeset in Trade Gothic
By Cenveo Publisher Services

Printed by 1010 Printing International Limited

Dedication

For H. Lynn Jones, teacher, mentor, and most of all a good friend.

Contents

Introduction — ix

Chapter One	About Decay Photography	1
	Key photographers	3
	Urban decay	7
	Rural decay	10
	Safety issues	13
	Legal issues	16
Chapter Two	Equipment	21
	Cameras	22
	Lenses	33
	Tripods	40
Chapter Three	Composition and Technique	45
	Quality of light	46
	Rule of thirds	49
	Balance and symmetry	51
	Leading lines and patterns	52
	Textures	55
	Color	56
	Isolating the subject	60
Chapter Four	Shooting Digital	71
	Sensors	72
	Exposure	76
	Using histograms	81
	Shooting RAW	83
	White balance	83
	Noise and noise reduction	84
Chapter Five	Shooting with Film	93
	Film types	94
	Film processing at home	102

Chapter Six	Shooting in Low Light	109
	Settings	111
	Digital	116
	Film	122
Chapter Seven	Digital Post-Processing	127
	Finding the keepers	130
	Metadata	131
	Tonal adjustments and color correction	133
	Black-and-white conversions	135
	Color conversions	138
	TtV: melding film and digital	144
Chapter Eight	High Dynamic Range	153
	Bracketing	154
	Tone mapping	157
	Exposure blending	161
	Software	162
Chapter Nine	Decay Portraiture	173
	Gear and settings	174
	Lighting tips	175

Index — **183**

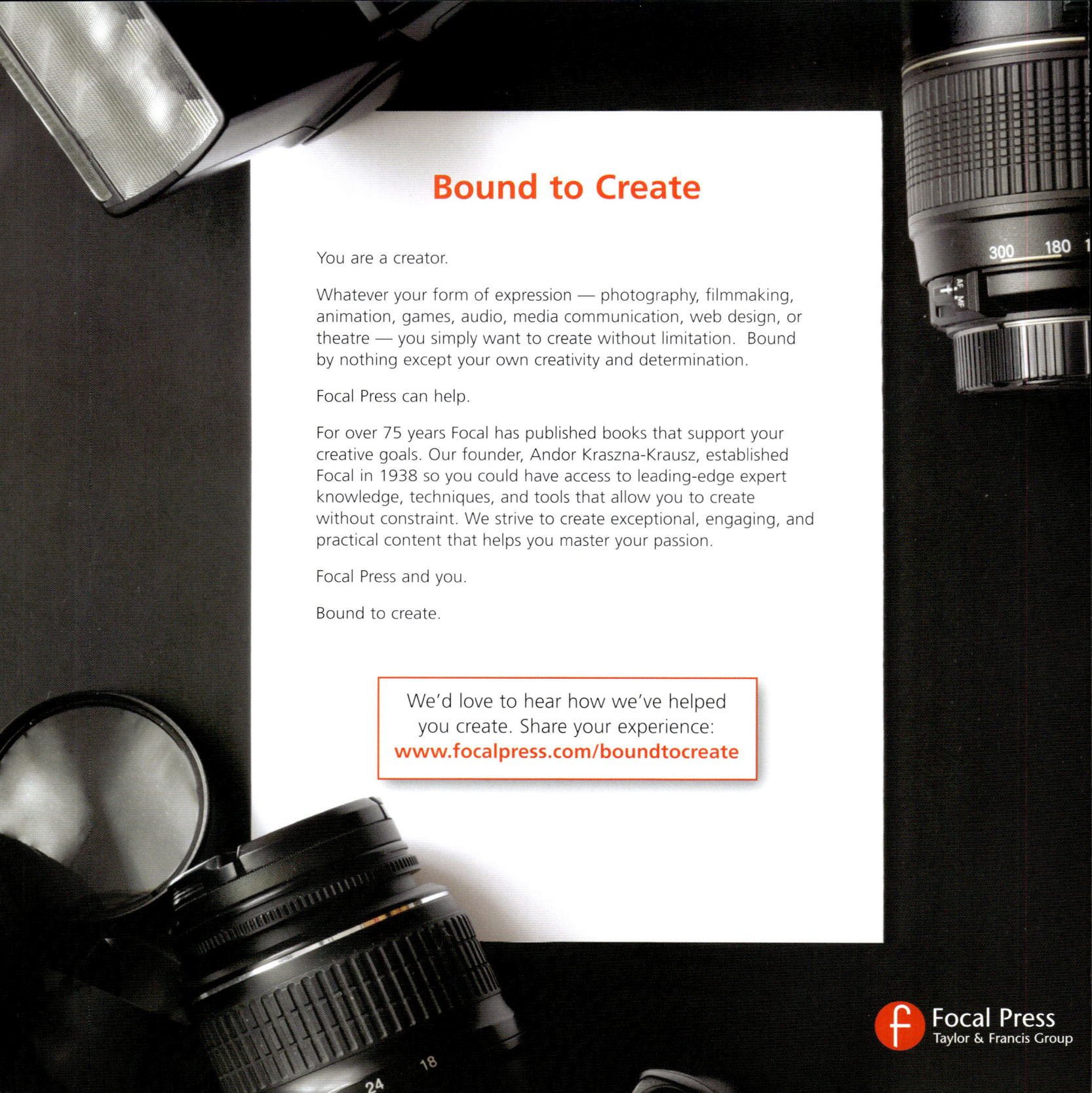

Bound to Create

You are a creator.

Whatever your form of expression — photography, filmmaking, animation, games, audio, media communication, web design, or theatre — you simply want to create without limitation. Bound by nothing except your own creativity and determination.

Focal Press can help.

For over 75 years Focal has published books that support your creative goals. Our founder, Andor Kraszna-Krausz, established Focal in 1938 so you could have access to leading-edge expert knowledge, techniques, and tools that allow you to create without constraint. We strive to create exceptional, engaging, and practical content that helps you master your passion.

Focal Press and you.

Bound to create.

We'd love to hear how we've helped you create. Share your experience:
www.focalpress.com/boundtocreate

Focal Press
Taylor & Francis Group

Introduction

I don't know what it is about decay that attracts us as photographers. Maybe it just reminds us of our own mortality and our fleeting time on this planet. Maybe it's just the simple beauty we as photographers can dig out of the ugliness of a collapsing and deteriorating structure. I've been attracted to decay photography for as long as I can remember being attracted to photography itself. One of the things that always struck me is that I wanted to know the stories about the people that inhabited or worked in these places. I wanted to know why they left behind the things that they did and what drove them away. Photographing what is left gives us a connection to people whose stories we many never know, but that we can try to illustrate by using images.

I always looked to the wrong side of tracks to find subjects for my art, I always strived to find the inner beauty in things that others found repulsive or insalubrious. You, dear reader, must also follow this path or you wouldn't have picked up this book.

This book wasn't written by me alone, but by a team of people all pitching in in their own way. I want to thank Stacey Walker for approaching me with the subject, and Deirdre Byrne for taking over right at the point where things started getting complicated. I want to thank Kate Iannotti for organizing promotions and contests. I pretty much want to thank the whole team at Focal Press for believing in photography and their willingness to publish niche books that may not appeal to the broadest market share, but are important subjects just the same. Thanks to Chris Folsom for providing another point of view on the subject and for contributing some great art. I'd also like to thank all of the contestants for participating and the winners for providing some great images to work with.

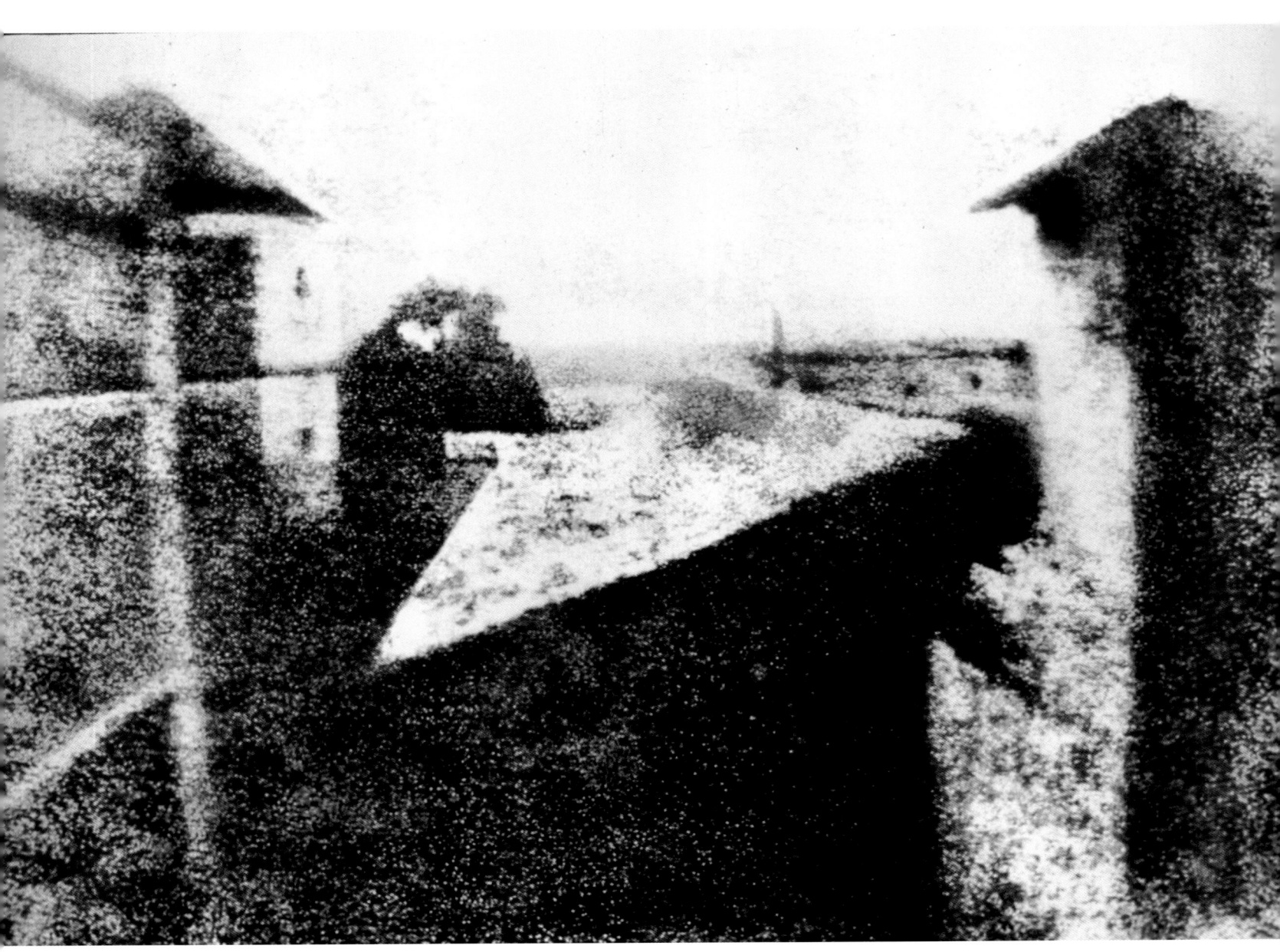

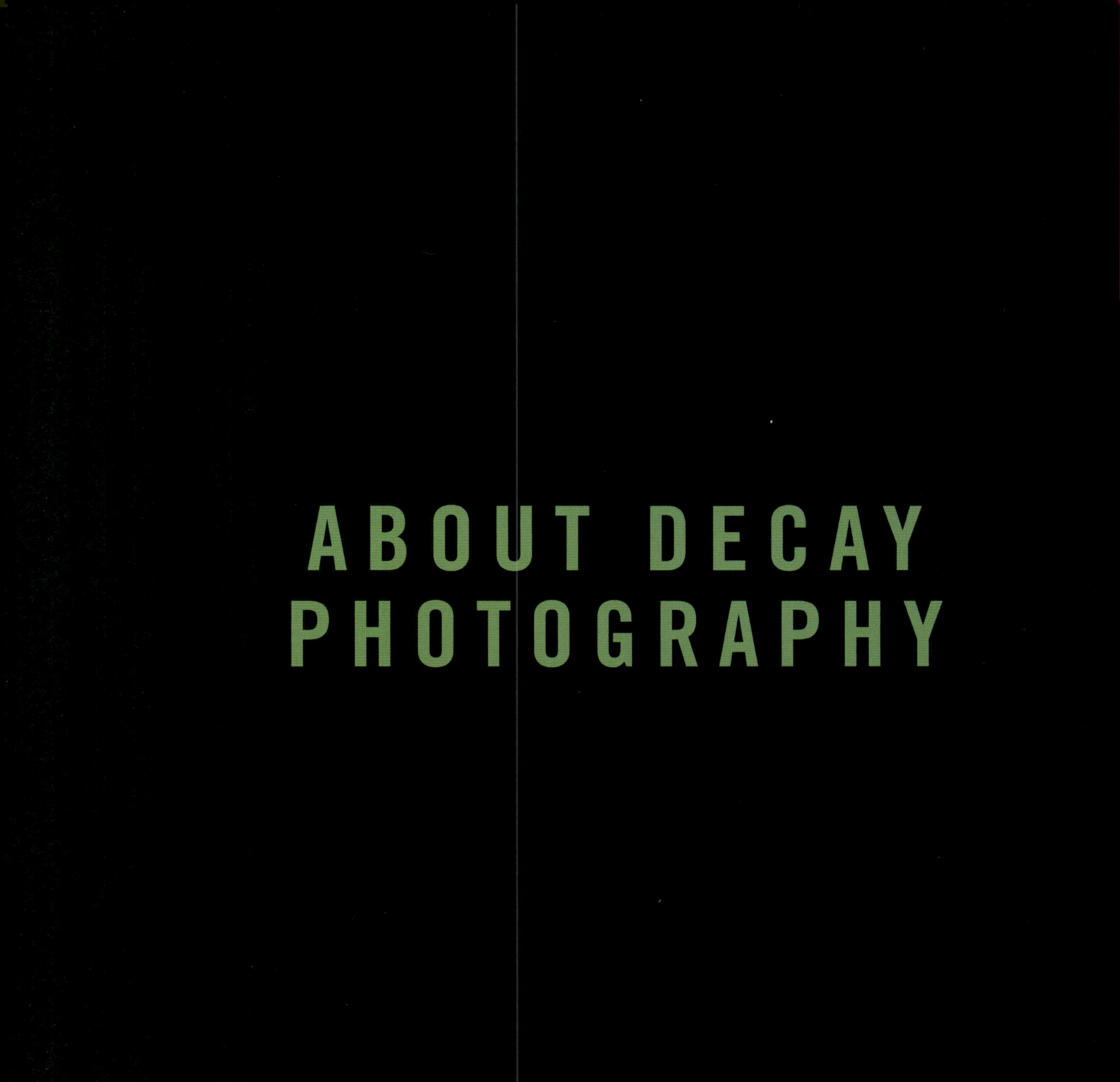

ABOUT DECAY PHOTOGRAPHY

One

FIGURE 1.1 View from the Window at Le Gras. Long before photography was purportedly invented in 1839, Joseph Nicéphore Niépce created this image (which he termed a heliograph) in 1825

Arguably, decay photography has been around as long as photography itself. The first photograph ever taken by inventor Joseph Nicéphore Niépce in 1825, "View from the Window at Le Gras" could conceivably also be the first photograph of urban decay. It simply shows a back alley in France. Coincidentally, this photograph is housed in Austin, Texas at the University of Texas and I have actually had the chance to view it in person.

Not much information is available on the actual history and derivation of decay photography. It's almost impossible to pinpoint when it became an art form in and of itself rather than a form of photojournalism. You can find decay photography both on the front page of the daily newspaper and hanging in art galleries all across the world, but one thing is for sure, decay photography has become a viable form of fine art as well as a form of social documentation.

Decay photography means a lot of different things to a lot of different people. To me, decay photography is the ability to find the beauty in the blight. Finding interesting patterns, textures, and colors, and creating captivating compositions from scenes of collapsing architecture is a challenge that has started to attract the attention of many photographers and has even transformed people who were solely urban explorers (urbexers, as they refer to themselves) into photographers themselves. It's funny to imagine a deteriorating building as being the catalyst for someone finding a new passion in life, but it has happened!

Decay photography is a medium that allows the photographer to document a moment in time, because every single minute the earthly elements of weathering and chemical reactions are changing sometimes seemingly unchangeable structures made from iron, steel, and concrete. Some photographers have even been known to return to the same

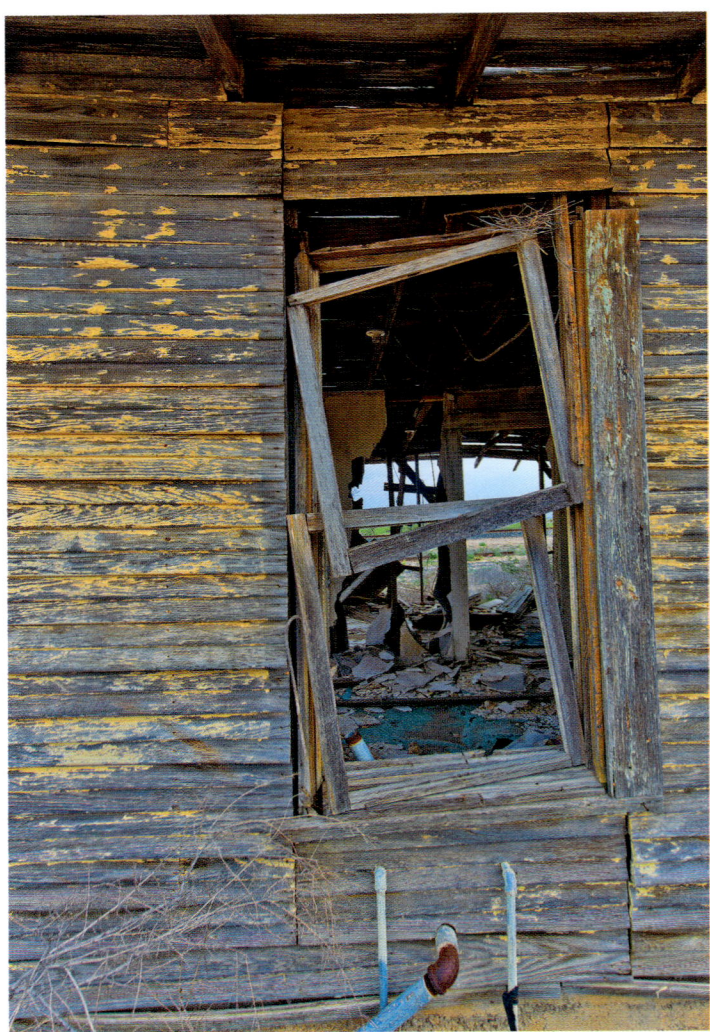

FIGURE 1.2 Putting together color and texture, and framing the image just right is what makes decay photography a challenging subject. **Nikon D800 with Nikon 14–24 mm f/2.8G at 20 mm. 1/60 sec. @ f/6.3 ISO 100**

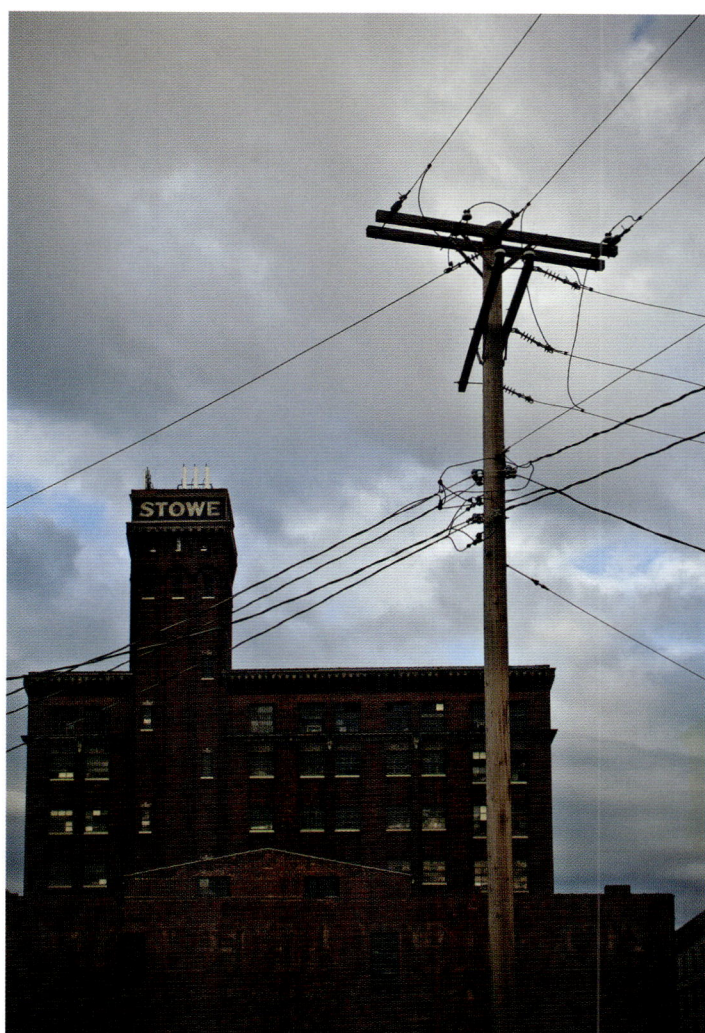

FIGURE 1.3 The historic Stowe building at the West Bottoms area of Kansas City, MO. Nikon D70 with Tokina 19–35 mm f/3.5–4.5 at 35 mm (52 mm equivalent). 1/400 sec. @ f/6.3 ISO 200

scene for many years to document how time, weather, and even man have taken a toll on the landscapes and structures of an area.

It's easy to find the beautiful parts of a city: the fantastic new skyscrapers gracing the skyline, the recently erected modern city buildings, and the hip high-rise condos are all designed to be pleasing to the eye; yet to some of us the shiny facades of these structures only solicit yawns. We are the urban explorers that cross over to the *wrong side of the tracks* to find the collapsing structures that may have once held magnificent interiors with chandeliers and ballrooms, the discarded industrial buildings where workers once toiled. We are the travelers that take the back roads to our destinations in hopes of discovering an abandoned dwelling where people used to live, work, and play. We stop and document the things left behind, sometimes wondering what these lives were all about, why they've gone, and what made these long lost people, these veritable apparitions, leave their possessions behind. We are the decay photographers.

Key photographers

Probably the first photographer to recognizably portray urban decay photography was Jacob Riis, although Riis' goal wasn't to find the beauty in the decay, but to portray the squalor in which people were living in the tenements in New York City. His photographs were ultimately used in a book called *How the Other Half Lives*, published in 1890. The darkness of the tenements ultimately resulted in him helping to pioneer the use of a flash in photography. Riis' ultimate goal was to use his images as a tool for social change, but in doing that he also created some of the first urban decay photographs.

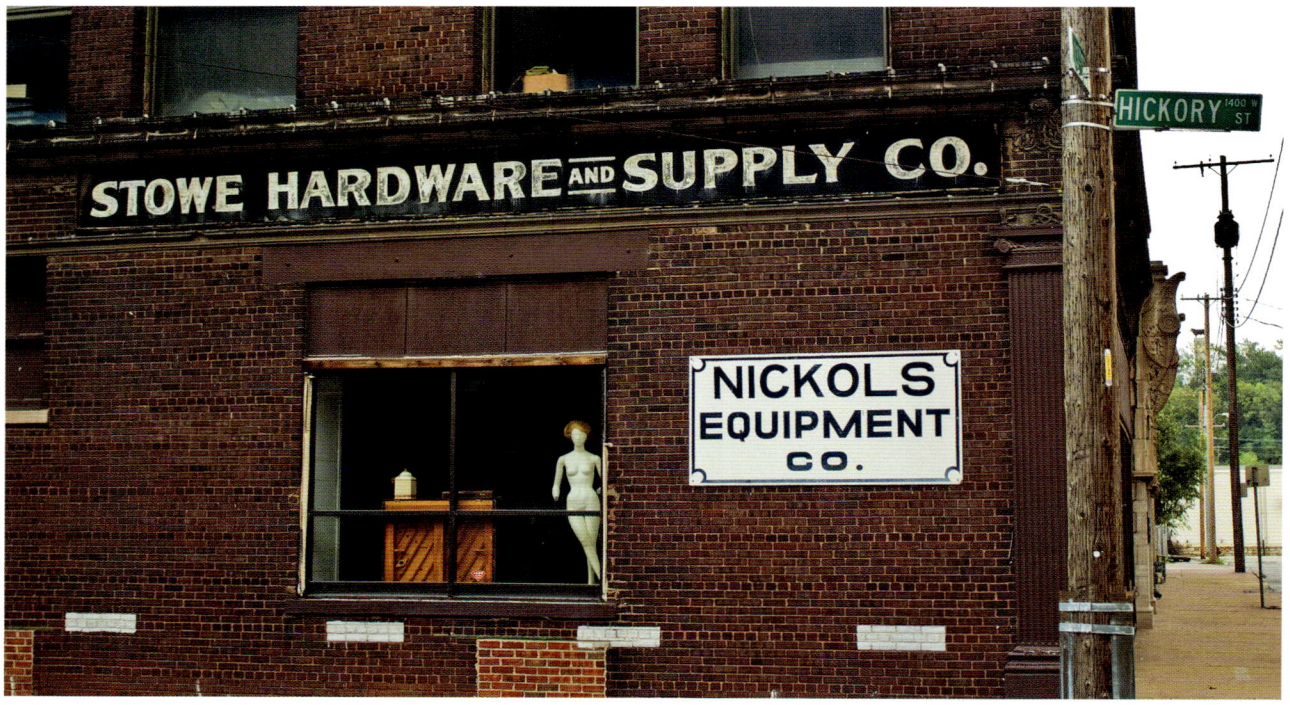

FIGURE 1.4 In this photo you can see the ground floor of the Stowe building as it appeared in 2004; since then the ground floor has been converted into a reception hall for weddings and looks very different. Decay photography can document the history of a building.   Nikon D70 with Tokina 19–35 mm f/3.5–4.5 at 35 mm (52 mm equivalent). 1/125 sec. @ f/4.5 ISO 200

Flash forward about 45 years to the Great Depression. The Farm Security Administration, better known as the FSA, commissioned a slew of photographers to document the plight of the farmers that were suffering under the worst drought in American history. These photographers by definition weren't rural decay photographers, but by necessity captured many photographs of rural decay. A few of these photographers were Dorothea Lange (although she was more well known for her portraits), Walker Evans, Arthur Rothstein, and Carl Mydans; there were many more. As they documented the poor conditions of the farmers they were also unwittingly creating rural decay photography as well as urban decay photography by documenting the farm workers as they moved to the cities and urban environments.

In the 1970s and 1980s urban and rural decay photography had a bit of a resurgence, perhaps in part due to the fact that most buildings at that time were built in an earlier era, and due to the economic problems of the period, buildings were falling into disrepair. Unlike previous eras, however, the intention of many of these photographers was,

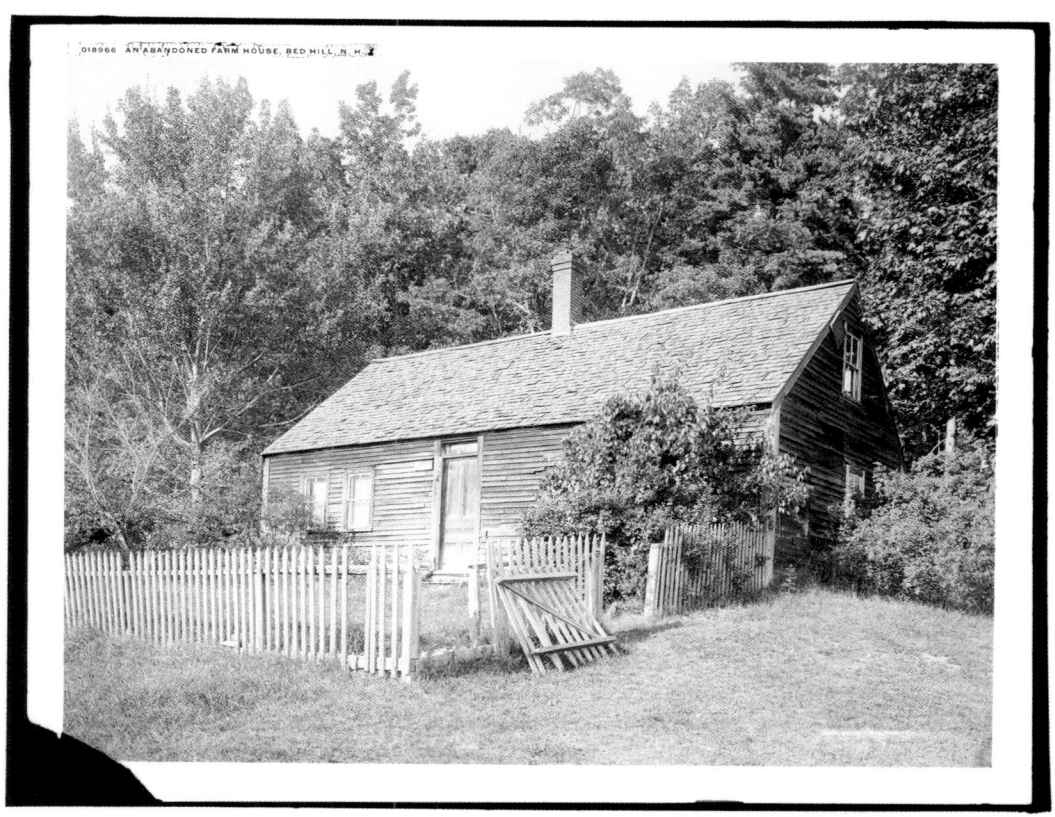

FIGURE 1.5 Photographers have almost always been attracted to photographing decay. This photograph of an abandoned farmhouse was taken circa 1906 in Red Hill, New Hampshire. Library of Congress, Prints and Photographs Division, Detroit Publishing Company Collection

for the first time, to create art rather than journalism or social change.

Edward Burtynsky is one of the photographers that looked at decay photography as an art form and preferred a more industrial climate over that of inner cities or rural communities. His favorite subjects were scrap piles, industrial wastelands, quarries, and any type of landscape that had been altered by industrialization. His photographs are vast, sweeping landscapes, usually shot at ultra-wide angles to accentuate the scene.

Another great photographer of this period is Camilo José Vergara. He is famous for what is known as *rephotography*, in which he would go back to the same place months and years later and document the changing landscape from the same

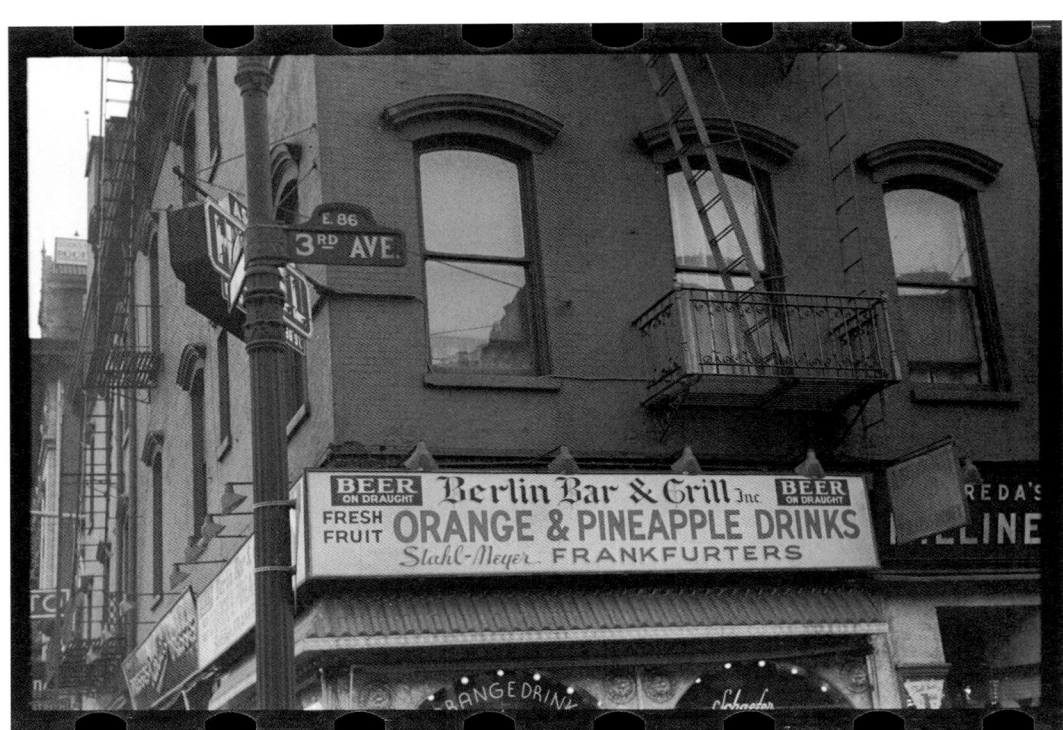

FIGURE 1.6 Signs, Yorkville, NY, by Arthur Rothstein. Library of Congress, Prints and Photographs Division, US Farm Security Administration

vantage point, using the same lens and film format. The result is the documentation of the change of the scene, be it for better or for worse. He also captured crumbling inner-city tenements, fallen buildings, and structures in disrepair. I think that, out of all urban decay photographers, his style is copied the most, even though the bulk of photographers probably don't realize it. His style is very intuitive.

These days, with the advent of digital photography, there are hundreds of thousands of photographers out there documenting urban and rural decay, and making great art from it. At the same time, most major American cities are cleaning up and removing the infrastructure from urban decay. Just a decade ago most cities were rife with dilapidated structures, but most are disappearing, whether for safety reasons or to rid the city of what most people see as an eyesore; therefore, it is a good time to get out there and start shooting. Document what you can before these beautiful scenes of decay disappear for good, being replaced by shiny new modern buildings.

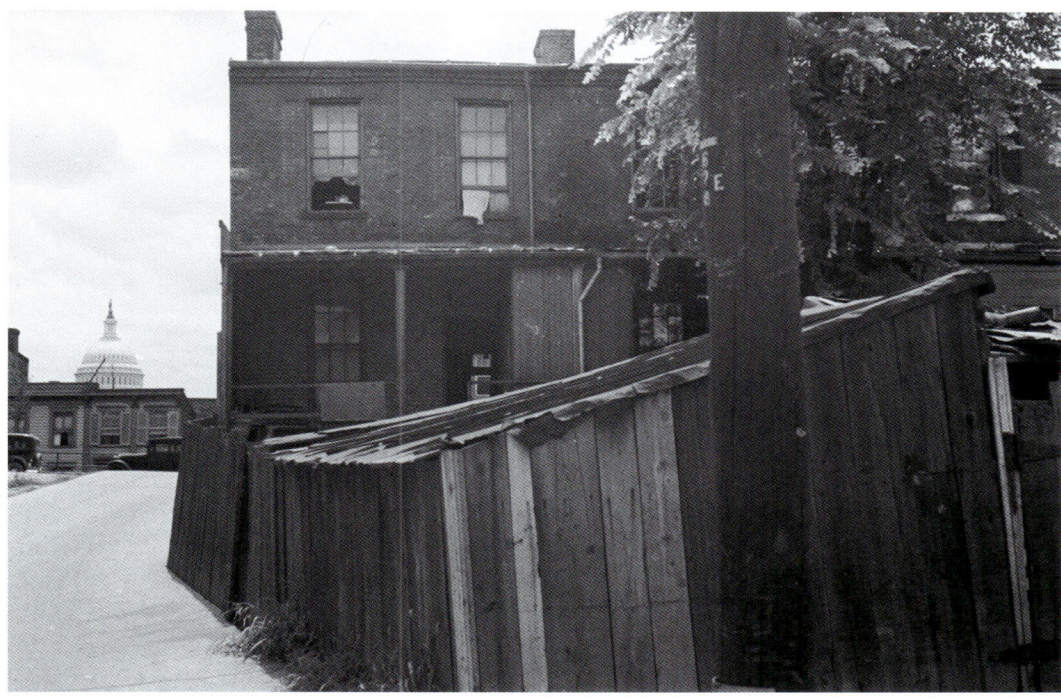

FIGURE 1.7 An image of urban decay from Washington, DC circa 1935, taken by Carl Mydens. Library of Congress, Prints and Photographs Division, US Farm Security Administration

Urban decay

Images of urban decay can be found almost anywhere that has been visited by man, both in and outside of cities. Oftentimes these scenes include sights of industrial ruin as well as exterior and interior shots of buildings that have fallen into disrepair. Abandoned homes, hospitals, hotels, industrial facilities, jails, power plants, and prisons are but a few of the many places that may serve as sites for scenes of urban decay. The key to finding these scenes is to keep a sharp eye open at all times. Whenever I'm traveling I instinctively keep my eyes open for interesting architecture and possible opportunities for photos of decay. It may take some time to train yourself to do this, but after a while it becomes second nature and you won't even realize you're doing it until you see a location.

In urban decay photography there are lots of different subjects that can be utilized; the subject doesn't have to be a falling-down building or a ravaged building interior. It can be something as simple as a fire hydrant, a piano that has been dumped in the middle of a roadway, or simply a vehicle abandoned in the street and left to rust. Old cemeteries are another place to get great decay photographs.

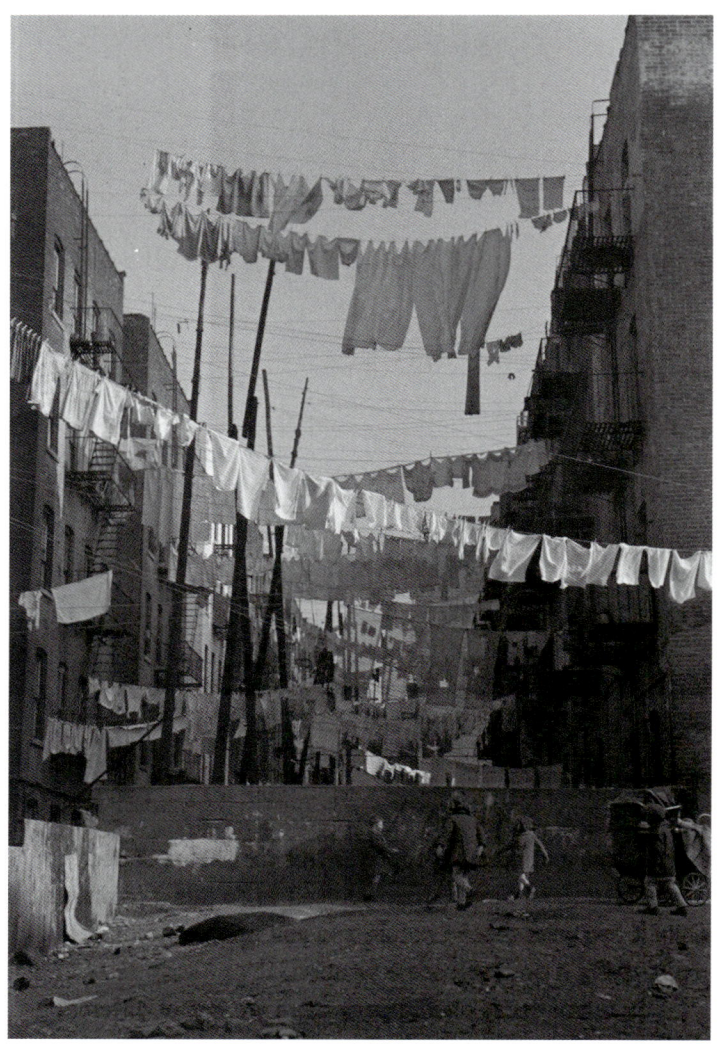

FIGURE 1.8 An early example of urban decay photography. An avenue of clothes washings between 138th and 139th Street apartments, just east of St. Anne's Avenue, Bronx, New York, by Russell Lee, circa 1936. **Library of Congress, Prints and Photographs Division, US Farm Security Administration**

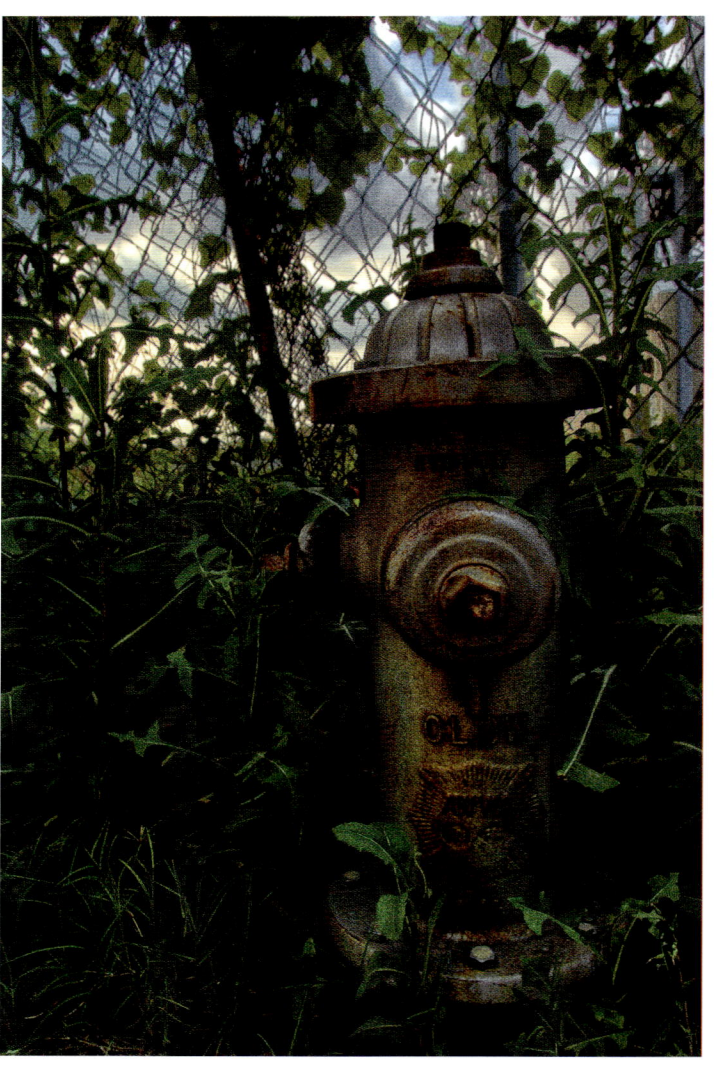

FIGURE 1.9 Even a simple fire hydrant sitting among the overgrown weeds of an abandoned construction site can make a good subject for urban decay photography. **Nikon D2H with Sigma 17–35 mm f/2.8–4 at 17 mm (25 mm equivalent). 1/100 sec. @ f/5.6 ISO 200**

To find great subjects for urban decay photography, many photographers gravitate to the run-down sections of town, but you can find suitable subjects in almost any urban environment just by doing a little scouting around or by doing internet searches using key terms such as "urban decay photography Austin, TX" (obviously you would use your own locations in the search). Sometimes the best places to start are the simplest and oftentimes the most obvious locations. Back alleys in the center of the city are often very run-down looking, even in the upscale locations. Junkyards and empty lots with detritus strewn about are great places for detail shots.

If I'm in a new city and I have some free time, I'll wander the downtown areas, randomly ducking into alleys looking into corners and crevices, peering down stairwells and looking up at buildings. As I mentioned earlier, keep your eyes open and the subjects will often make themselves clear to you.

City officials usually post *No Trespassing* signs and fences around abandoned buildings in and around the city to prevent unwanted visitors from entering the property and getting injured and/or squatters from taking over the place. Disregarding a *No Trespassing* sign and/or forcing entry can

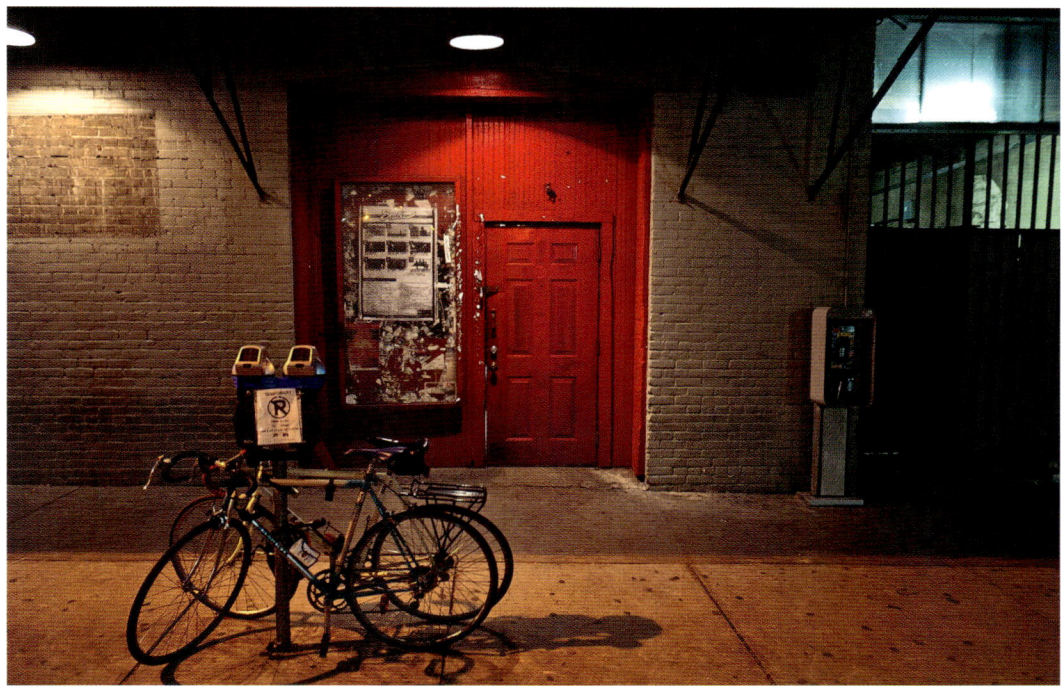

FIGURE 1.10 This empty building in Austin's famous Red River district once housed Austin's most renowned and revered rock and roll club, Emo's, and was abandoned to move to a newer and fancier location. This punk rock Mecca will soon be razed to make room for a boutique hotel. Nikon D2H with Sigma 17–70 mm f/2.8–4 OS at 17 mm (25 mm equivalent). 1/6 sec. @ f/2.8 ISO 640

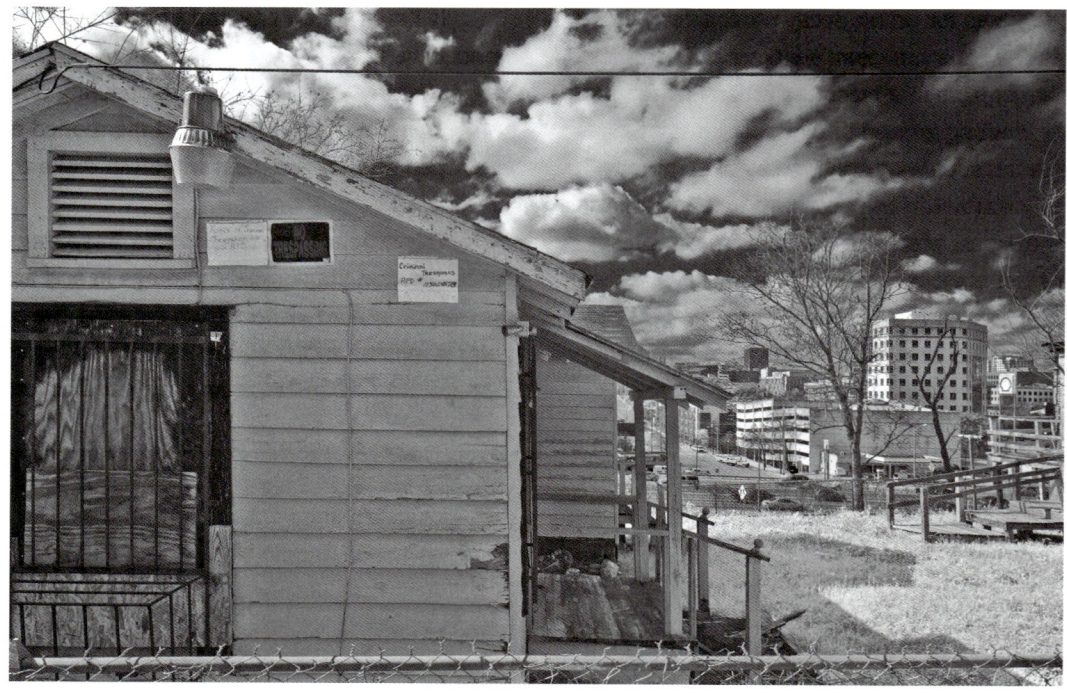

FIGURE 1.11 This abandoned house sits on a lot just across the highway from Austin's booming entertainment district. All around it sit brand-new condominiums. I did not attempt to enter the property due to the numerous *No Trespassing* signs. **Nikon D700 with Nikon 24 mm f/2.8D. 1/200 sec. @ f/9 ISO 200**

easily lead to serious legal entanglements, especially when dealing with city police.

Rural decay

Although more widely spread out, I would venture to say that rural decay photography is more prevalent than urban decay in a lot of areas these days. As a matter of fact, I would go so far as to say that most decay photographs that you are likely to come across on the web are more likely examples of images taken outside of the city center. "Urban decay photography" has become almost a catch-all phrase to describe just about any photograph depicting anything in ruins that isn't from an ancient era. Examples of rural decay can be found along major highways and back roads alike, and can consist of many different types of subjects, such as abandoned farmhouses or barns, homes, and the occasional industrial building. Often, vehicles are left to rust in fields, and I've even seen old boats just languishing in a field, rotting away. Ghost towns often found in desert areas are also a great place for rural decay photography.

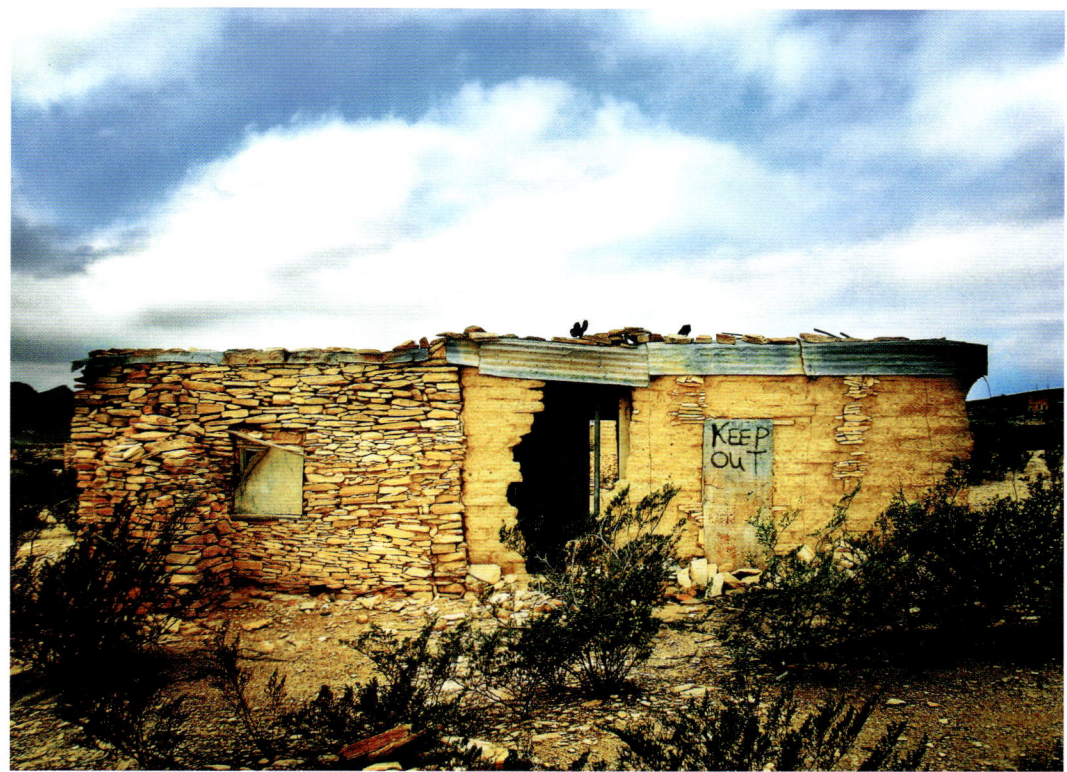

FIGURE 1.12 This is one of many building at the ghost town in Terlingua, TX. Although there are many *Keep Out* and *No Trespassing* signs, you're pretty much free to wander around. Nikon D200 with Nikon 17–55 mm f/2.8G at 55 mm (82.5 mm equivalent). 1/200 sec. @ f/5.6 ISO 200

Places in rural areas are generally easier to gain access to than urban decay sights in the midst of a city, because a lot of times the abandoned properties are easily accessible and can often be without *No Trespassing* signs. This doesn't mean you have the right to explore or enter the property, but it's easier to talk your way out of getting into serious trouble if there are no clear indicators that you're on private property.

Abandoned and decaying buildings and structures in more densely populated areas are more likely to be off-limits, often fenced in and locked up. Many places may have security guards or regular police patrols. Keep in mind that these measures are not put in place to hinder your artistic endeavors, but to protect the public (yes, this means you as well) from danger and harm.

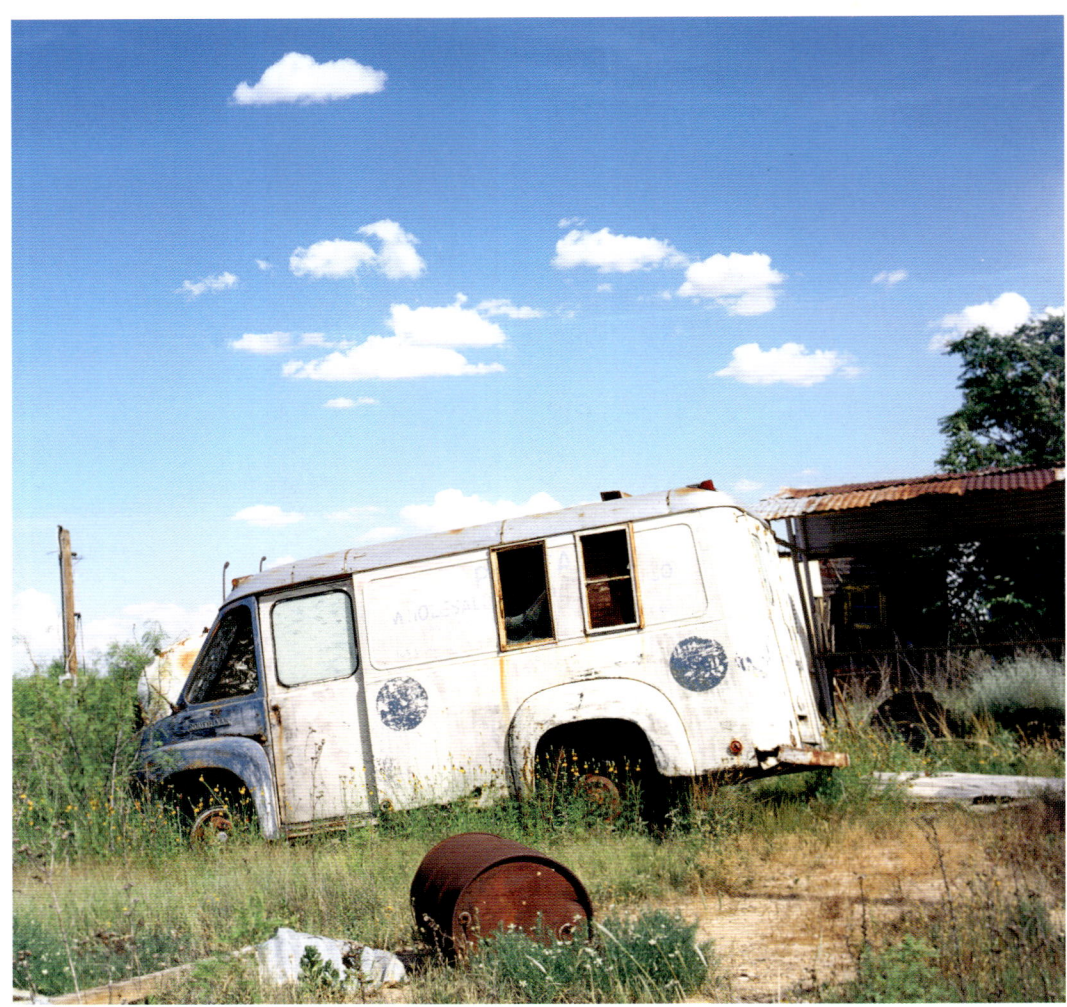

FIGURE 1.13 Driving out on old country roads will often lead you to discovering scenes like this one in Pecos, TX. Bronica SQA-I with a Zenza Bronica 80 mm f/3.5. Agfa Optima 1/250 @ f/16 ISO 200

Safety issues

This section isn't here to frighten you away from doing decay photography, but there are very real dangers associated with this type of activity. I have run across almost all of these scenarios, and these warnings are included so that you know that decay photography isn't necessarily a walk in the park. You can get hurt, and many photographers have.

Subjects of urban decay are often found in disreputable parts of town. This means there may be some dangerous elements lurking about. I recommend taking someone along with you, as the last thing you want is to be walking around with thousands of dollars worth of camera gear with no one to watch your back as you stare through the viewfinder, oblivious to what is going on around you. If you feel unsafe, by all means beat a hasty retreat. And although I don't recommend any type of violence, but having a means of protection such as pepper spray is a good idea, especially if you're in an area you're unfamiliar with. Although some people carry knives for utility purposes you may want to leave yours at home, as this may only lead to trouble in the case of police involvement.

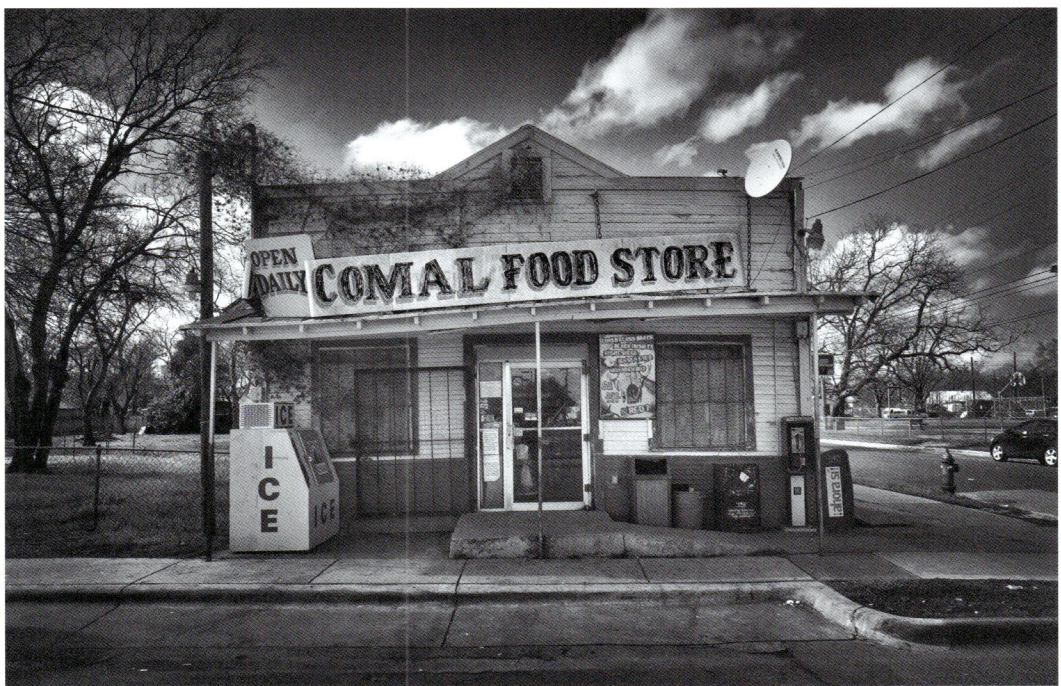

FIGURE 1.14 This little corner store isn't in one of the best neighborhoods. Although relatively safe in the daytime, at night you may want someone watching your back.   Nikon D700 with Nikon 24 mm f/2.8D. 1/125 sec. @ f/8 ISO 200

Abandoned buildings can also harbor more than the element of human danger. There are many buildings that have been abandoned simply because of health hazards such as asbestos, which can ultimately cause a rare form of lung cancer called mesothelioma if inhaled for long periods of time. Some buildings may contain cancer-causing PCBs (polychlorinated biphenyls) or any number of other carcinogenic substances. Man-made contaminants aren't the only dangers that can be present in abandoned buildings; droppings from pigeons, bats, or raccoons can also cause diseases such as histoplasmosis, hypersensitivity pneumonitis, or other ailments. Bringing along a mask or respirator is highly recommended if you plan on entering any buildings, especially in any type of industrial area.

You may run across all sorts of dangerous critters such as rats, spiders, scorpions, or snakes. Wearing protective clothing such as long sleeves, pants, and boots is highly recommended to prevent yourself from being bitten or stung. You may even encounter rabid animals in these areas (I recently ran across a rabid squirrel); if you even *suspect* that an animal is rabid vacate the premises immediately.

Long sleeves, pants, and boots are also recommended when out exploring through the decay to protect yourself from

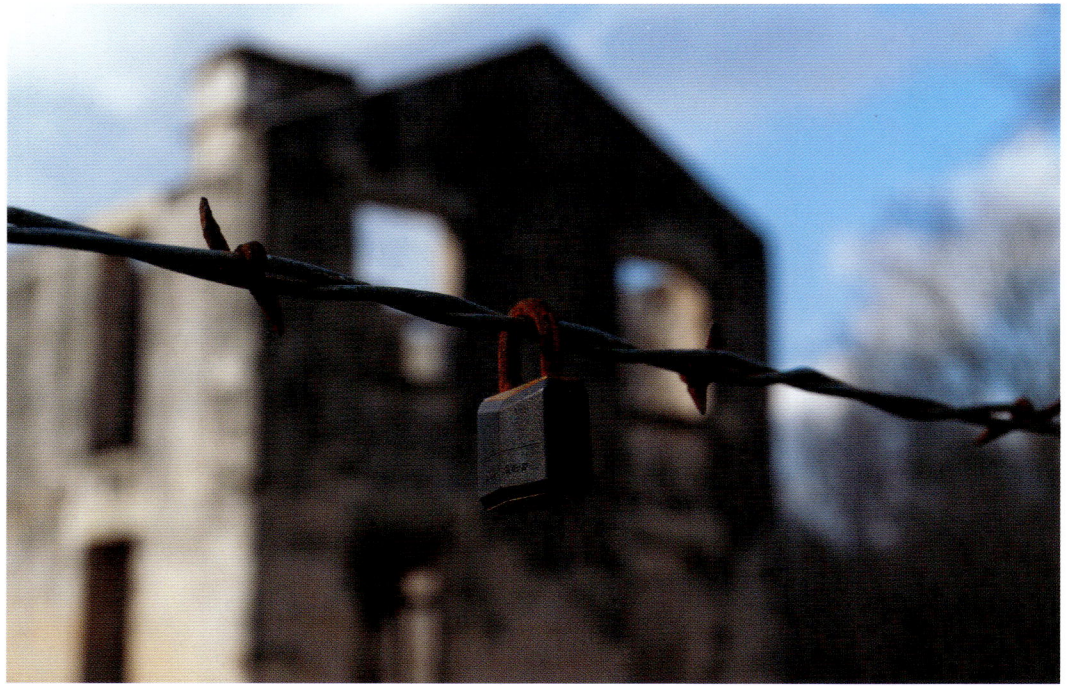

FIGURE 1.15 Barbed wire surrounds the ruins of the McKinney homestead just outside of Austin, TX. Nikon D300s with Tamron 17–50 mm f/2.8 at 50 mm (75 mm equivalent). 1/160 sec. @ f/11 ISO 200 −2/3 exposure compensation

the aforementioned critters as well as thorns, barbed wire, rusty nails, broken glass, and things of that nature. Some places may even have used syringes and other nasty things lying around. As the risk of sounding overly cautious, it's a good idea to make sure you're up to date on your tetanus shots as well.

Tip: A good thing to keep in your camera or kit bag is a packet of antiseptic wipes. If you get scratched, poked, stabbed, or stuck by something, getting the wound disinfected quickly is a very important step in preventing infection.

It is also very important to remember that these buildings are collapsing and are likely to have structural elements that are weakened or failing, as well as other dangers such as broken boards with rusty nails, floors with undetectable weak areas, lead paint, loose handrails, crumbling concrete, and many other things. Tread lightly in these areas; testing out the weight limits of wherever you are placing your feet is very important. If out exploring by yourself in a remote abandoned area there's a real possibility that you can be seriously hurt and nobody will find you.

Note: Probably the number one injury to decay photographers is puncture wounds from rusty nails. It's best to wear a good pair of steel-shanked construction boots. You may also want to pay a visit to your physician to be sure you're current on your tetanus shots.

Keeping a fully charged cell phone on you is a necessity, and if you're out in a remote area with limited reception you need to be extra careful, especially if you're on your own. Another very handy tool is a flashlight; LED flashlights are especially nice as they are a lot brighter than a standard flashlight of the same size. It's also a good idea to keep a spare set of batteries in your bag. Flashlights can not only be used to

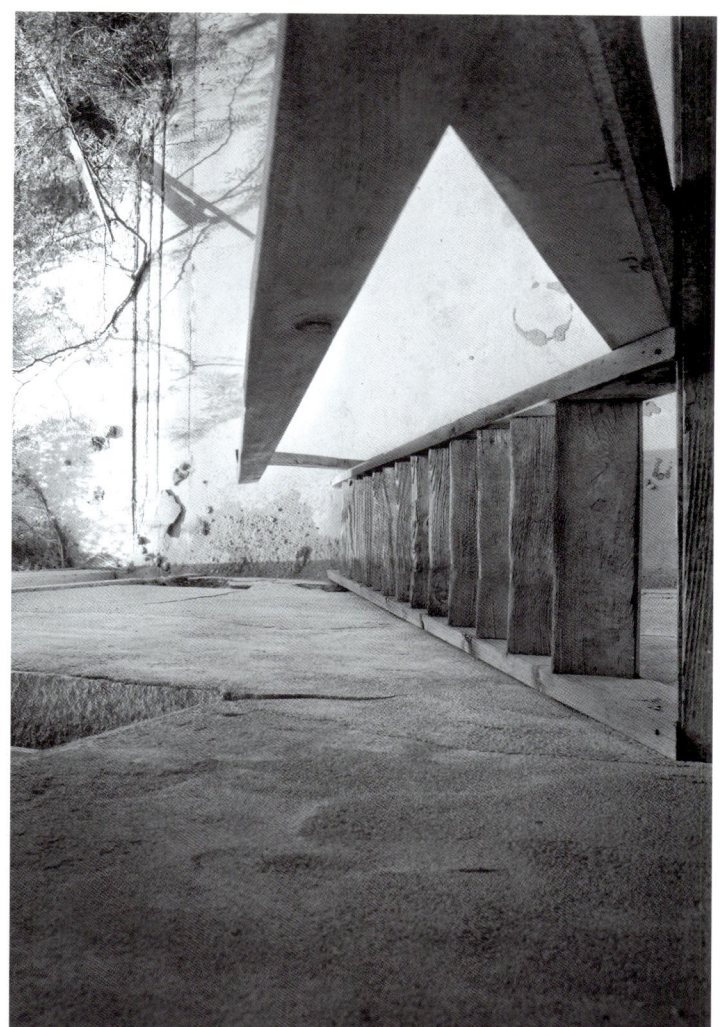

FIGURE 1.16 At first glance it may not be apparent, but on the right side of this image is a rickety old "staircase" made out of 2 × 4 planks. I climbed up this only to discover a platform that was nearly collapsing under my weight. **Nikon D800 with a 28–70 mm f/2.8D at 31 mm. 1/400 sec. @ f/11 ISO 200**

light your way, but can also be used to illuminate shadowy areas in the scene while doing long exposures.

At the very least if you go out on your own, let someone know where you're going to be and when you expect to return.

Legal issues

First and foremost, I am not a lawyer. None of this information should be construed as strict legal advice. If you should get into a legal entanglement, hire a lawyer. That being said, as a photographer you do have rights, whether you're a photojournalist, an artist, or just taking pictures for fun.

One of your biggest concerns when doing decay photography is trespassing. If you're photographing the building or subject from or on public property that is readily accessible, such as a city street or road, then you have no fear. It's legal to photograph a building or subject that can easily be seen from a public thoroughfare or from public property.

Once you step onto private property, however, you run the risk of being prosecuted for trespassing. As I mentioned earlier, if there's no clear indicator such as a *No Trespassing* sign, it's much

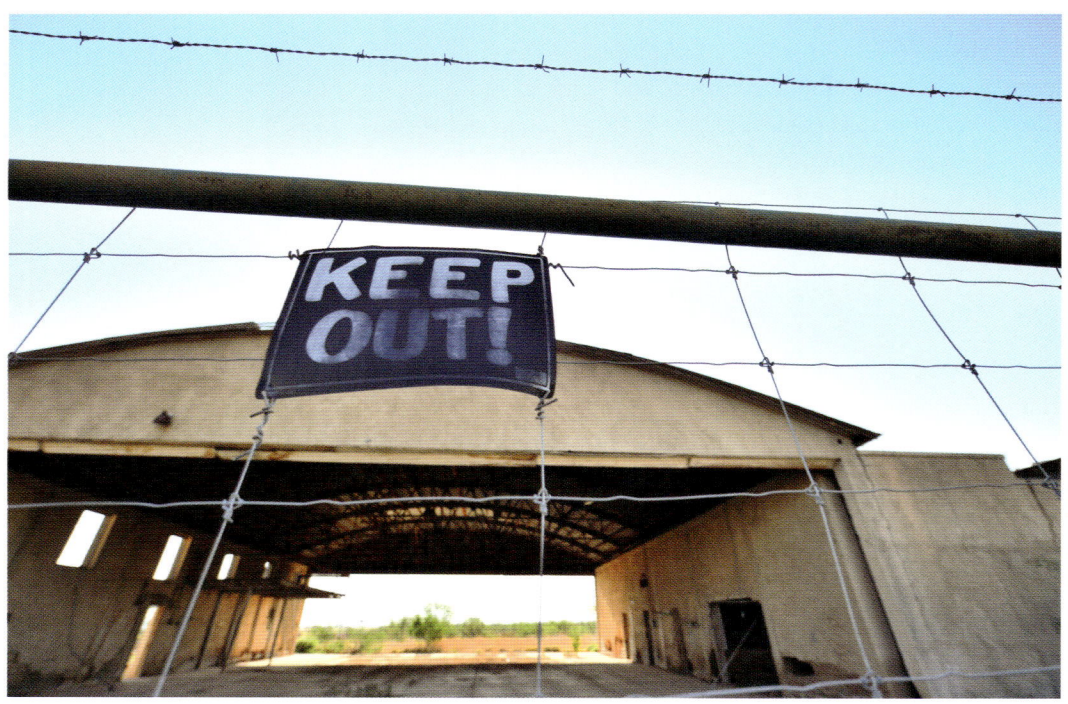

FIGURE 1.17 This is a common sight at a lot of abandoned sites. This *Keep Out* sign was found at an abandoned airplane hangar in west Texas. **Nikon D800 with a 14–24 mm f/2.8G at 16 mm. 1/8000 sec. @ f/2.8 ISO 180**

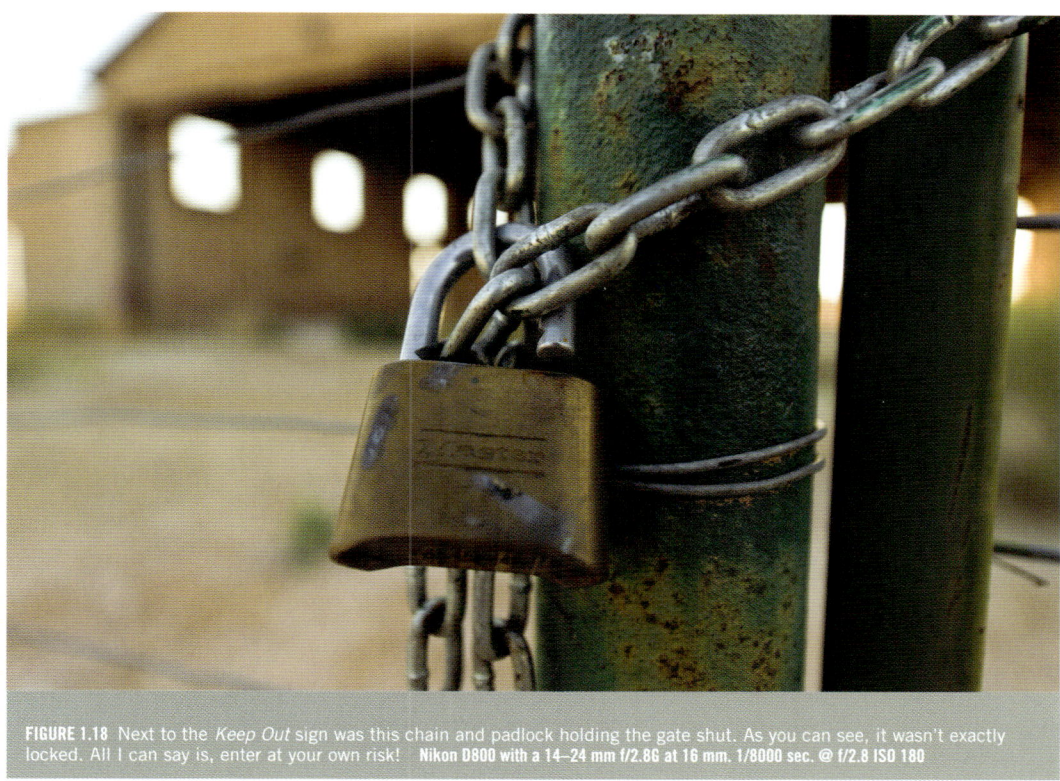

FIGURE 1.18 Next to the *Keep Out* sign was this chain and padlock holding the gate shut. As you can see, it wasn't exactly locked. All I can say is, enter at your own risk! Nikon D800 with a 14–24 mm f/2.8G at 16 mm, 1/8000 sec. @ f/2.8 ISO 180

easier to talk your way out of a ticket than it is if the property is clearly delineated with a fence-line and *No Trespassing* signs.

Sometimes you may run into a property owner or concerned neighbor. Just explain what you're doing, show them some images if you're shooting digital, and often they may not be bothered, or sometimes they may just ask you to leave. Respect their wishes and go.

You may, however, run into law enforcement officers. In this situation it's best to be as polite as you possibly can, and once again explain yourself and your intent to make artistic photos.

If you willfully disobey a *No Trespassing* sign or forcibly enter a property you can, and most likely will, be charged with criminal trespass or breaking and entering, which can lead to serious consequences such as fines or even jail time. Basically, what I'm recommending here is that you don't break the law. I know that it can be very enticing, but you can get into serious trouble.

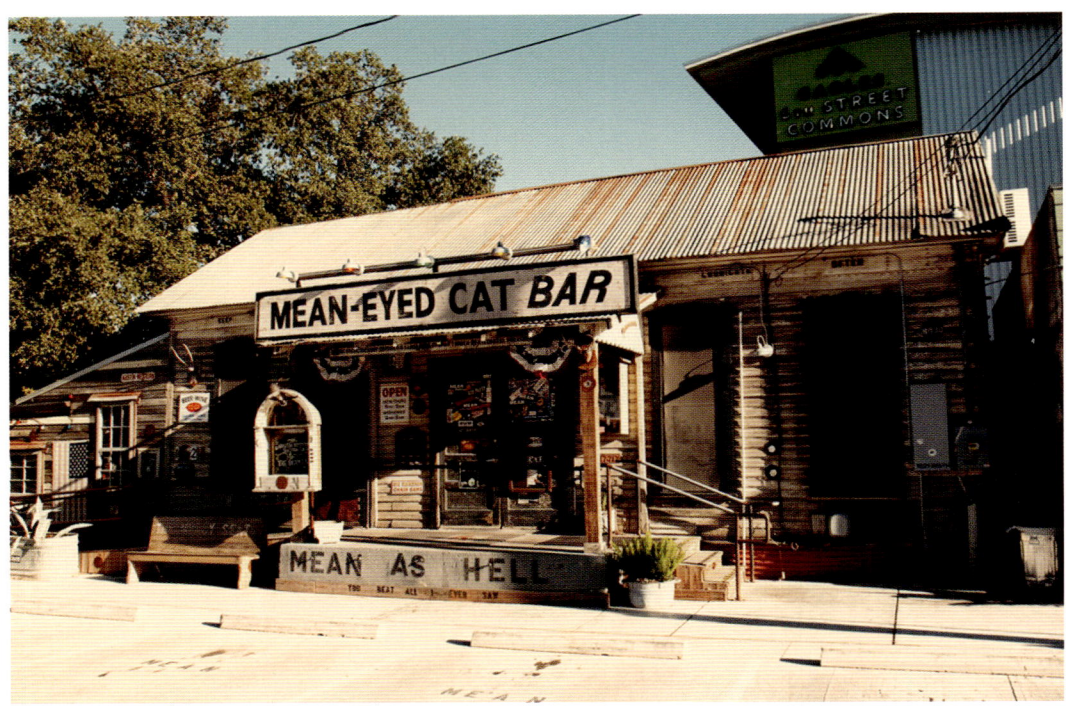

FIGURE 1.19 A building doesn't necessarily need to be abandoned to qualify for decay photography status. At one time this building was a dilapidated chainsaw store that grew to fame in the *Texas Chainsaw Massacre* film. It has since been turned into a thriving trendy neighborhood bar. The Mean-eyed Cat Bar still maintains an urban decay feel to it. **Nikon D300s with a 14–24 mm f/2.8G at 16 mm. 1/8000 sec. @ f/2.8 ISO 180**

Photographer's rights

As I mentioned at the beginning of this section, you as a photographer DO have certain rights under the law. Here are a few of the most important ones.

- If you are on public property you *can* take photographs of private property; for example, you can take pictures of a building from a sidewalk, street, or road. This also includes bridges, highway overpasses, roads, and other infrastructure, and also includes public transportation and utility buildings including airports, train stations, and power plants. However, if you are on private property and asked not to or to stop photographing, you *must* comply; this includes any signage that prohibits photography. One caveat to this is government buildings and installations if photography is considered a threat to national security. Most government buildings like capitol buildings, courthouses, or city halls are usually fair game.

- You do *not* have to hand over your camera and/or film to anyone. Law enforcement officials need a court order to confiscate your property, unless you are being arrested. Security guards or private citizens have no right to take your property and can be charged with theft or coercion if they take your camera by force or threaten you into handing it over.
- You do *not* have any obligation to explain why you are taking photographs, nor do you have to present identification to a private citizen or security guard. Certain states, such as Texas, do require you present an ID when asked by a law enforcement official. However, as you may guess, being polite and explaining what you're up to is usually a better way to go as you can garner more favor by being nice.
- Private individuals cannot detain you against your will and can be criminally charged, including the charge of kidnapping, if you are held against your will.

The best thing to do if you are confronted is to remain calm, be polite, and respectful (especially in the presence of law enforcement). If the person is not a law enforcement official and tries to attack, detain, or confiscate your equipment, call the police. Be sure to get their name and employer and ask them what legal grounds they believe they have for taking this action.

Please note that these suggestions apply to the United States, but laws from county to county and state to state may vary and laws in other countries may be completely different.

Note: For more details there is a book called the *Legal Handbook for Photographers* by Bert Krages, who actually is a lawyer and specializes in this type of law. See also http://www.krages.com/phoright.htm.

One thing I'd like to make perfectly clear is that damaging property is definitely unacceptable. This not only means willful vandalism to property, but also includes breaking locks, windows, or kicking in doors to gain access to areas that are closed off to the public. Even if a door has been forced open or a window broken by another person to gain access, there's no guarantee that *you* won't be charged for creating the damage should you happen to be caught on the property.

Keep in mind that although a door may have been open, providing easy access to the premises, you are still trespassing on another person's property unless you have gotten specific permission. If there's an inaccessible property you feel you *must* photograph you may be able to find the owner's information through city, county, or state tax records.

There's an old, oft-repeated adage: *take only pictures, leave only footprints.* This is a great saying that can be applied to nature photography as well as decay photography. Leave things as you found them for other photographers and explorers to enjoy. The less of an impact photographers and people make on a scene, the less likely that the building will be locked down. Discretion is paramount.

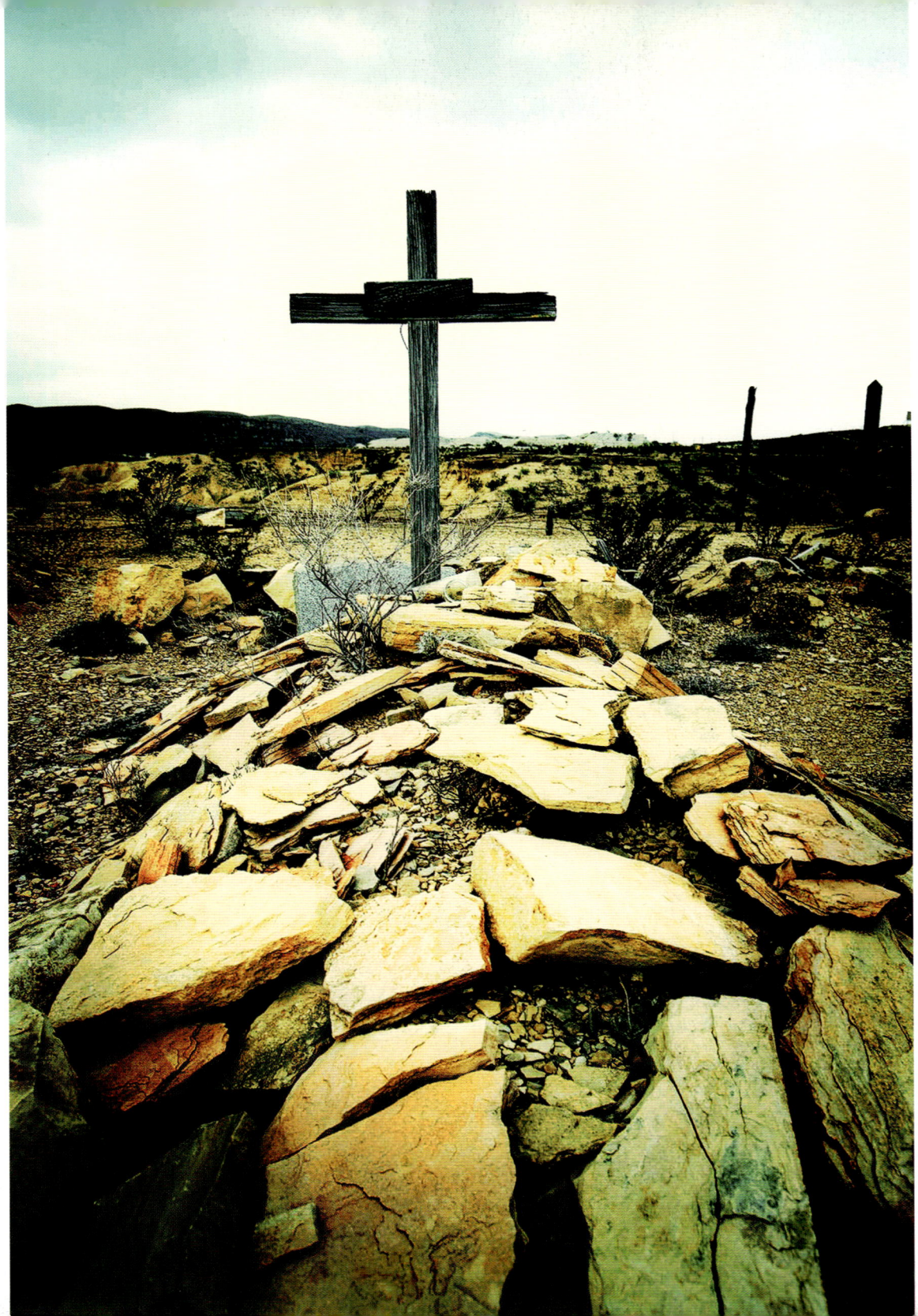

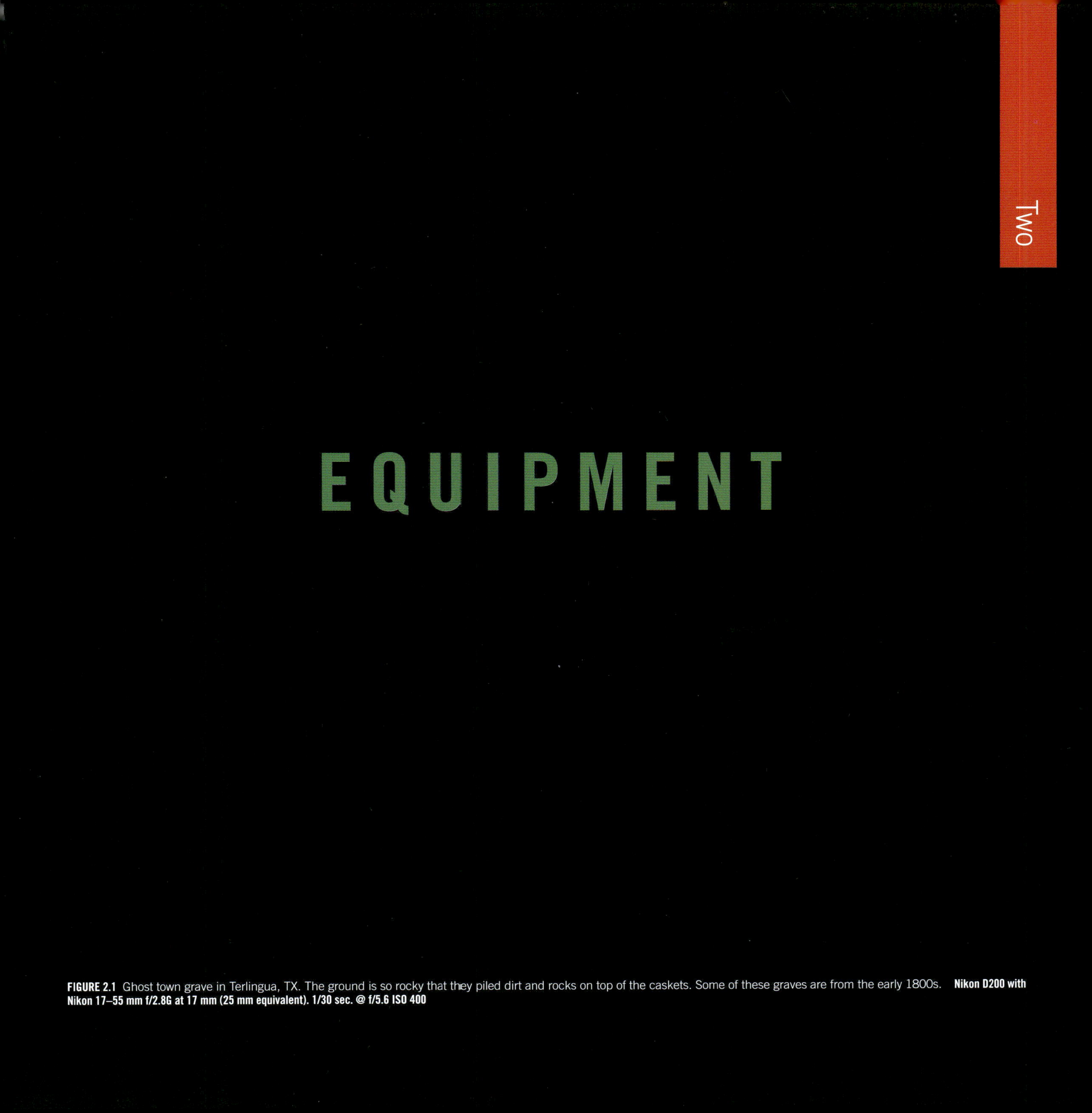

Two

EQUIPMENT

FIGURE 2.1 Ghost town grave in Terlingua, TX. The ground is so rocky that they piled dirt and rocks on top of the caskets. Some of these graves are from the early 1800s. **Nikon D200 with Nikon 17–55 mm f/2.8G at 17 mm (25 mm equivalent). 1/30 sec. @ f/5.6 ISO 400**

Cameras

The great thing about decay photography is that almost any camera or camera system can produce good images. It's more about the subject than the format, although different formats can have an effect on how your photographs turn out. You can use a vintage camera and film to capture an authentic retro scene, or shoot digitally and use Photoshop filters to add a similar vintage effect. There's also the possibility of using software to add a hyper-realistic look, such as high dynamic range (HDR) photography. Really, the possibilities are almost limitless, which is one of the great aspects of this type of photography.

For all practical purposes, it doesn't matter what type of equipment you use. I've successfully made decay photographs from the cheapest plastic toy cameras to very expensive medium-format film cameras to top-of-the-line DSLR cameras. One of the things I love about urban and rural decay photography is that you are not limited to a specific format or system. It's almost an egalitarian type of photography.

In later chapters I'll go in depth more on the different types of photographic formats, mainly the differences between film and digital. For now, I'm going to cover the different types of cameras that are available to you.

SLRs and DSLRs

SLR stands for *single lens reflex*. This means that the camera uses one lens, a reflex mirror, and a pentamirror or pentaprism to reflect the image into the viewfinder (the pentamirror or pentaprism is used to invert the image so that it's not upside-down in the viewfinder).

These are by far the most common type of camera that professionals and amateurs are likely to be using these days.

DSLR cameras (digital single lens reflex) act, for the most part, like their film counterparts. The only major difference is that DSLRs capture images using an electronic sensor, rather than film. DSLR cameras have also benefited from continued innovation in metering and focusing technologies that the film SLRs of yesteryear never had access to.

The concept behind these cameras is simple; you look through the viewfinder, focus, and release the shutter, thus capturing the image. Since the image is coming in through the lens, what you see is what you get. These cameras are also interchangeable-lens cameras, so you can choose and attach different lenses with varying focal lengths to capture your vision in your own way.

SLR cameras come in at many different price points; from a vintage film SLR you may find on eBay for $20, up to a professional DSLR that can cost as much as $8,000 without a lens. There are literally hundreds of options available, but the best option with the quickest way to process is a standard DSLR, which generally costs anywhere in the $500–$3,000 range, depending on the feature set you're looking for.

Full frame vs. crop sensor

In the earlier days of DSLR photography this was more of a consideration than it is today. Initially, the main problem was that DSLR cameras came with sensors that were smaller than a single frame of 35 mm film (24 × 36); most of these sensors were APS-C sized (16 × 24 for Nikon and 15 × 23 for Canon). This left no true option for ultra-wide-angle lenses due to the reduced field of view of the smaller sensors. This is no longer an inconvenience since most camera manufacturers have revamped their lens line to cater to the APS-C size so that obtaining true wide-angle lenses is easy. For example, Nikon and Canon have a 10–24 mm and a 10–22 mm, respectively

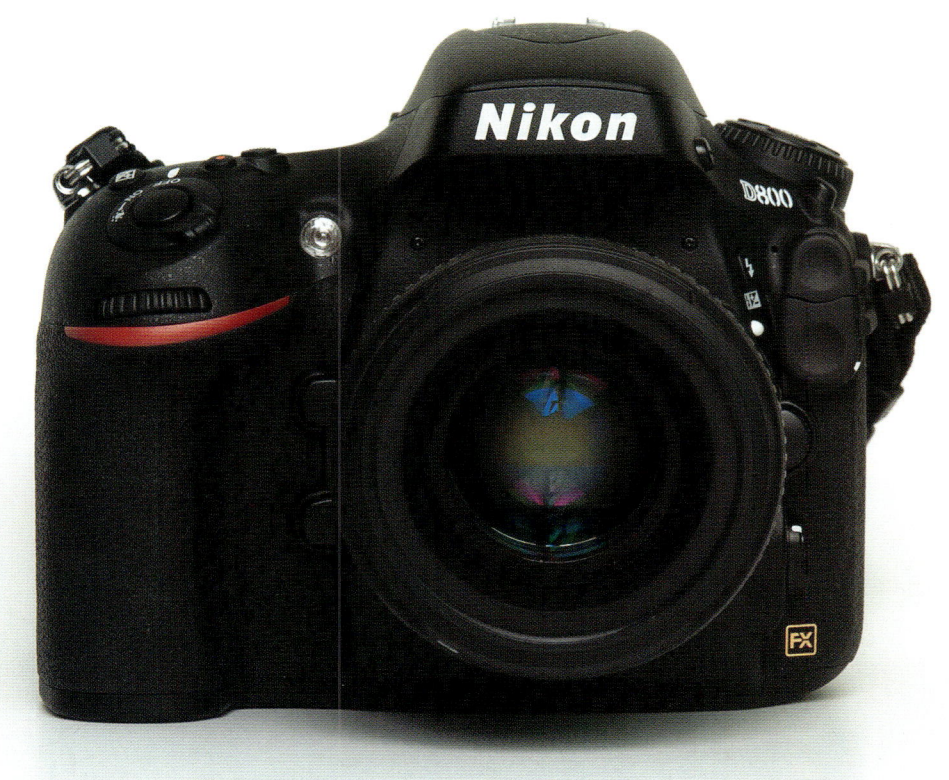

FIGURE 2.2 The Nikon D800 is a semi-professional DSLR camera. The high resolution of this camera makes it very good for capturing fine detail

(15–36 mm and 15–33 mm equivalent), and Sigma has even developed the ultra-wide 8–16 mm, which is equivalent to a 12–24 mm full-frame lens (Sigma also has a full-frame 12–24 mm lens, which is the widest production zoom lens available).

The term *crop factor* is often used when talking about crop sensor cameras. Crop factor determines how much of the frame is "cropped out" as compared to a frame of 35 mm film. Crop factor values for DSLR cameras are 1.5× for Nikon and 1.6× or 1.3× for Canon, depending on the model.

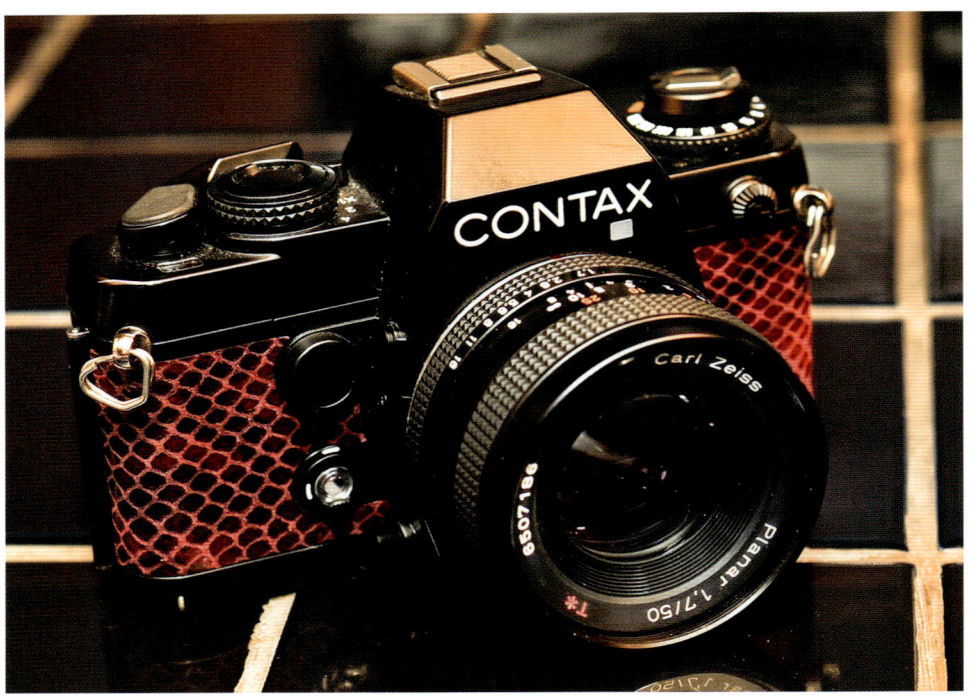

FIGURE 2.3 Film SLRs are compact and affordable and offer an easy way to get into processing your own film

Multiplying the focal length of the lens by the crop factor gives you the focal length equivalent to 35 mm film.

Note: Nikon terms their APS-C sized cameras as DX and their full-frame cameras as FX.

There are a few advantages to crop sensor cameras. First and foremost they are less expensive than their full-frame counterparts; the crop sensor lenses are less expensive, smaller, and lighter; and because of the crop factor with longer lenses, your telephoto lenses get more "reach" – for example, a 70–200 mm lens gives the equivalent field of view of a 105–300 mm lens.

More and more camera manufacturers are using full-frame sensors in their professional lines of cameras. These cameras tend to be much more expensive and the lenses are more expensive as well. At this time there are rumors of entry-level full-frame cameras circulating, and in the future I expect that full-frame cameras might become the norm.

One major advantage of having a full-frame sensor is that the pixel pitch is larger in comparison to a smaller sensor with

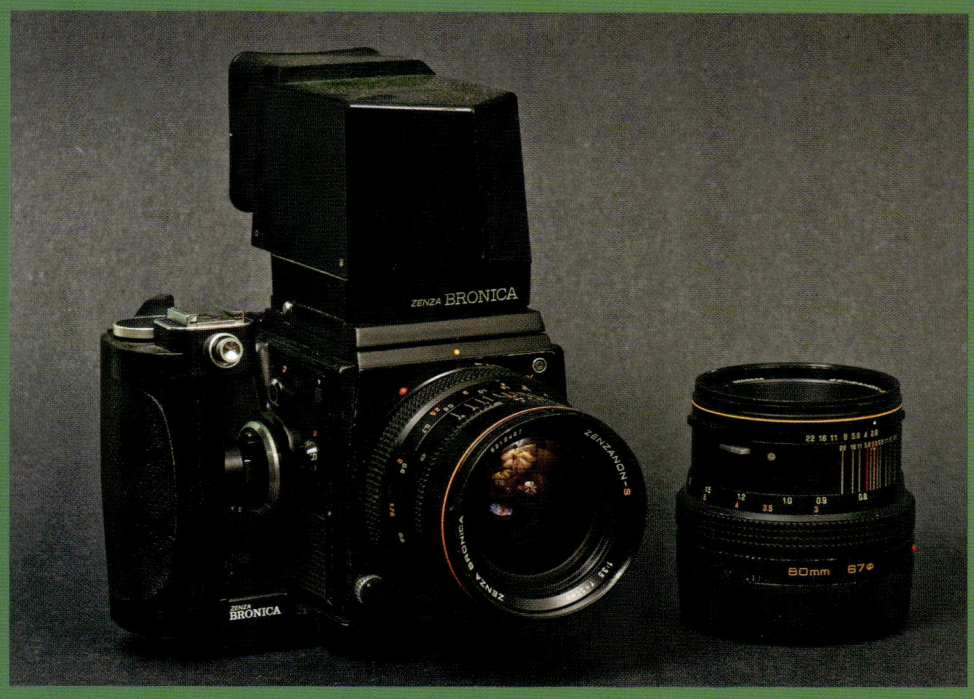

FIGURE 2.4 For high-resolution film photography, medium-format cameras like this Bronica are great and can be found used for not much money

Medium-format SLRs

SLR cameras also use what is known as medium format. In these cameras, the film or sensor is larger than in your standard SLR camera. These cameras are pretty flexible and can be pieced together to use different formats – for example, an old Hasselblad medium-format camera can be fitted with a back that takes 120, 220, 35 mm or Polaroid film. That same camera can also use a digital back that uses the same digital technology as your standard DSLR camera, although these digital backs can cost anywhere from $10,000–$40,000.

These cameras can also be fitted with different types of viewfinders; a waist-level viewfinder (WLV) or a prism type viewfinder that acts much like a standard DSLR. As with their smaller counterparts, these cameras also have interchangeable lenses.

These camera bodies also come with a variety of frame sizes ranging from the standard 6 cm × 4.5 cm (also known as 645 or 2:3), 6 cm × 6 cm (square format or 1:1), and 6 cm × 7 cm (4:5).

My personal medium format system is a Bronica SQA-i, which is a square-format camera. I also bought a pistol grip/winder, WLV, prism finder, sports finder (a prism finder with a larger view), normal and wide lenses, and a 220 back for about $400. For not much more I bought a 120 back (120 film is easier to find) and a Polaroid back. In the pre-digital days of photography this setup would have cost thousands of dollars.

the same number of megapixels. Larger pixels are more effective at capturing light, which allows the sensor to produce images with less noise.

Rangefinders

Smaller than their SLR counterparts, these types of cameras were traditionally preferred by reportage and street photographers due to their small size and quiet operation. Rangefinder cameras have viewfinder optics that are separate from the lens and lack a reflex mirror. Different cameras operate in different ways, but generally their operation consists of looking through the viewfinder (which bifurcates the image into two separate parts). You manually turn the focus ring on the lens until the two segmented halves come together and appear as one.

Most rangefinder cameras are older and almost all of them take 35 mm film, although this style of camera is making an astounding comeback here in the digital age, most notably with the Leica M8 and M9 and the Fuji X100 and X100s X10, and X-Pro 1. The Leicas are very expensive cameras starting at about $8,000, but are known for having excellent optics in a wide range of focal lengths, including the 50 mm f/0.95 Noctilux, the fastest production lens available (and costing an exorbitant $10,000 as well). The Fuji X100 and X100s and X10 cameras have fixed lenses; the X100 and X100s come with a 23mm f/2 prime lens, while the X10 has a zoom; the X-Pro 1 has an interchangeable lens system.

Note: One caveat to the rangefinder system is that when focusing close-up the camera can suffer from parallax error, which impedes proper composition.

TLR

TLR stands for *t*win *l*ens *r*eflex. As you may have surmised, this type of camera has two lenses, both of the same focal length. One of the lenses is used for viewing, with the reflex mirror reflecting the scene up to a waist-level viewfinder, and the other lens projects the image to the film. To my knowledge there has never been a production model digital TLR. There was a miniature digital replica of the venerable Rolleicord 2.8, although it was no more than a point-and-shoot camera, and the second lens was for appearances only, with the camera having an electronic viewfinder.

All TLR cameras come with a fixed lens that is usually between 60 mm and 80 mm, which is a normal lens in the medium-format system. I'll get into more about lenses further along in this chapter.

There are a few manufacturers that still make TLR cameras, Seagull and Lomo to name a couple. Your best bet is to find a used one – they are easily found relatively inexpensively on eBay or mail-order camera stores that deal in used equipment.

Most TLR cameras use easy-to-find 120 film and are square format, but some of the smaller cameras use 620 film which is pretty difficult to find, so I'd suggest making sure you buy a camera that uses 120 film.

Toy cameras

Toy cameras have become a catch-all name for any number of different cameras made by a plethora of manufacturers. The first names people think of when they hear the words toy camera are inevitably Holga or Lomo, but there are literally dozens of different makers.

Toy cameras aren't necessarily *toys*, but derived their name because they are usually cheaply made (mostly plastic) and have subpar optics and anomalies such as light leaks, color shifts, images that are in and out of focus along the image plane, and many more abnormalities.

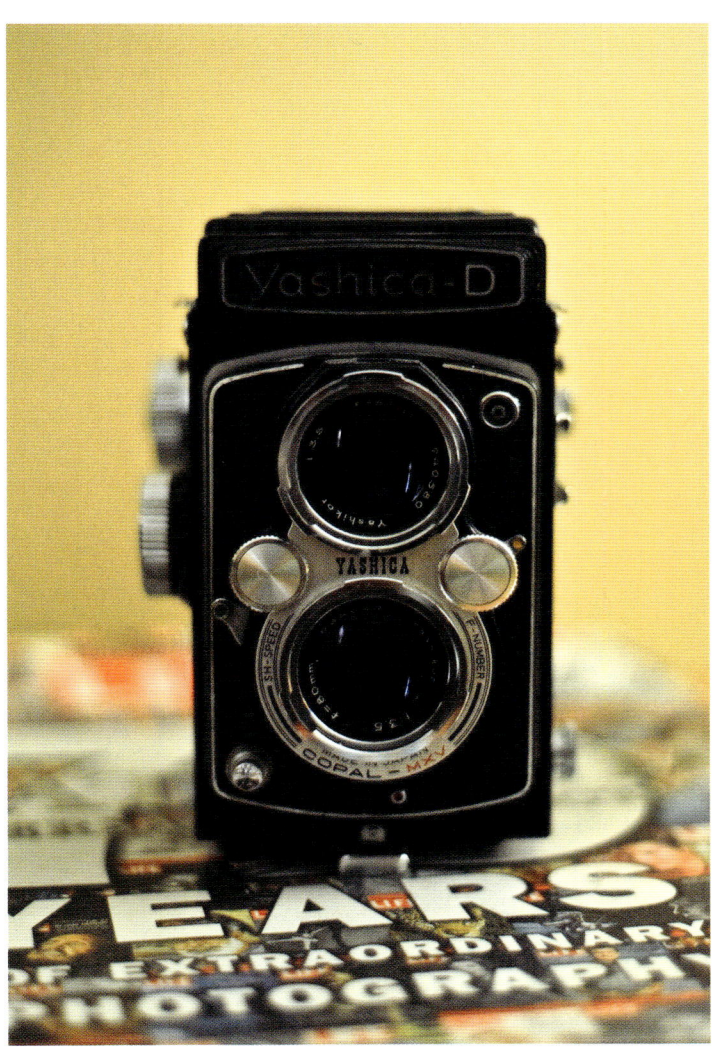

FIGURE 2.5 TLR cameras are a great way to get into medium-format photography without having to invest in a whole system of lenses and viewfinders. These cameras can be found relatively inexpensively at second-hand stores or eBay

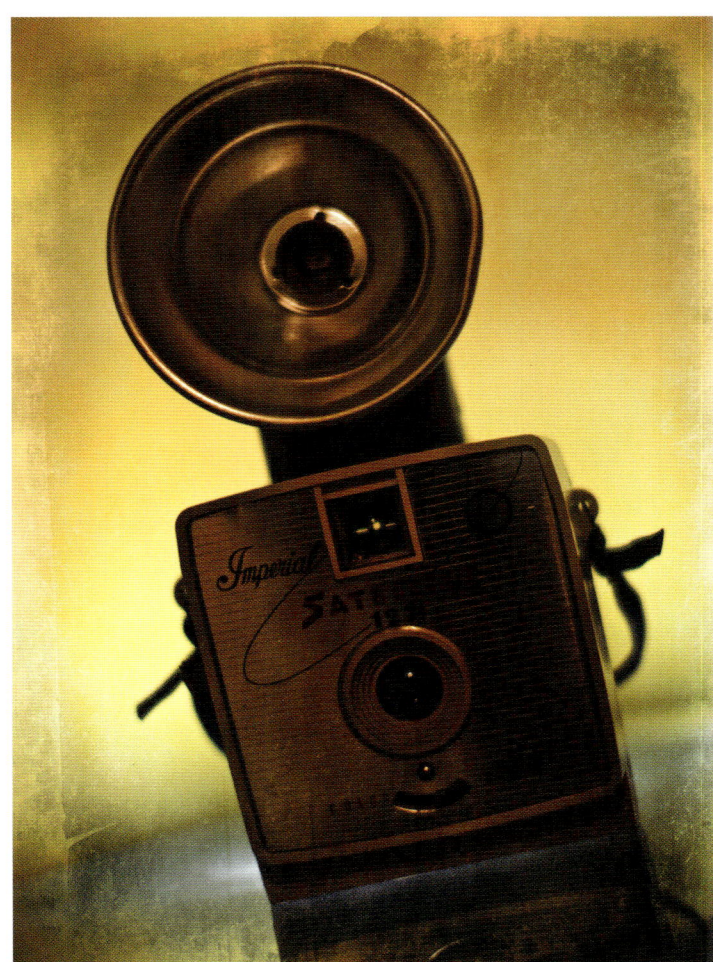

FIGURE 2.6 This Imperial Satellite is a toy camera from the 1950s that I modified to take 35 mm film

These cameras are cheap, use film, and produce images with rather low quality.

Right about now you're probably asking yourself "Why on earth would anyone want to shoot with a camera that produces pictures with all of these terrible qualities?" Well, the unpredictability of these cameras is *exactly* what draws photographers to these types of cameras. As a matter of fact, most of the top-selling photography apps for smartphones are actually supposed to mimic images made by toy cameras.

Toy cameras take all different kinds of film, but are usually 35 mm or 120 film based. Some people modify cameras to use different types of film than they were intended for. For example, I found that with almost no modification my Imperial Satellite 127 could be adapted to use 35 mm film. The resulting pictures were grainy, soft, and sometimes scratched, which adds to the *decay* theme. Since 127 film was larger than 35mm the whole piece of film is exposed, including around the sprocket holes. Lomo also makes a camera that exposes 35 mm film this way. The camera is called the "Sprocket Rocket." Following is a list of some of the most popular film cameras.

- **Holga:** The Holga is by far the most well known of the toy cameras. They come in 35 mm and 120 film formats. The 120 cameras can be masked to shoot 6 × 4.5 or 6 × 6. There's also a pinhole version as well as versions with and without flashes.
- **Lomo LC-A:** Originally manufactured in Russia by the Leningrad Optical Mechanical Amalgamation (LC-A stands for Lomo Compact – Automat), this was a fully automatic point-and-shoot 35 mm camera known for its soft edges and high-contrast images. In 2005 Lomo ceased production of the LC-A and the Lomographic Society purchased the brand and moved production to China. It rebranded the camera as the LC-A+ and added some features as well as other cosmetic flourishes to give the camera more mass appeal. Most people agree that the original Russian LC-A is preferable to the newer ones for build and lens quality.
- **Lubitel:** This is another camera also originally manufactured by Lomo in Russia (Lubitel means *amateur* in Russian). This was the entry-level model of a TLR camera and shared many image qualities with the LC-A. The Lubitel came under a few monikers, the most common being the Lubitel-166. These were produced until 1988. In 2008 the Lomographic Society also resumed production of these in China under the name Lubitel-166+.
- **Diana:** Probably one of the least known toy cameras, the Diana is actually a precursor to the Holga and shares many similarities. The Diana was originally made in Hong Kong and exported to the US and UK for very nominal sums. The Diana all but disappeared in the late 1970s and was revived once again by the Lomographic Society and marketed as the Diana+, with added accessories and features to make it more marketable.

There are many, many more types of toy cameras out there. They can be found for a fraction of the cost of some of the more popular cameras listed previously. eBay is a great resource for finding these cameras. Flickr groups are also a great resource for information on different toy cameras with links to resources and mods.

Note: Holga and Diana lenses that mount on your DSLR are also available. This allows you to get the lo-fi look without the time and expense of processing film.

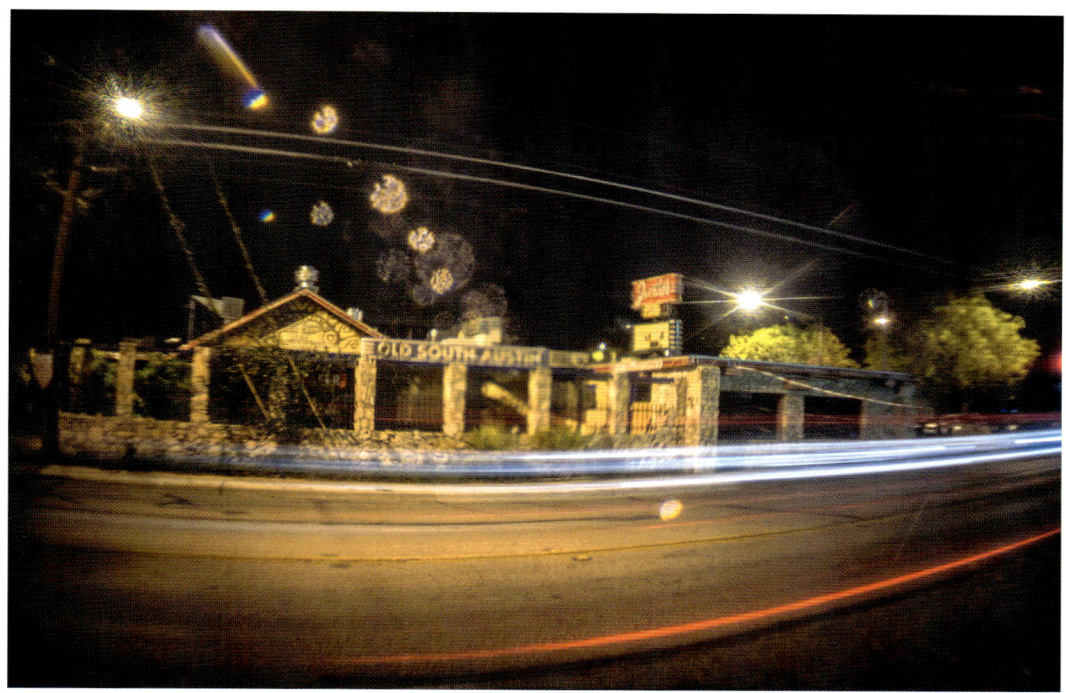

FIGURE 2.7 This photo of one of Austin's now-defunct Mexican restaurant and music venue Jovita's was taken using a Holga lens with a Nikon mount. This allows you to get the lo-fi Holga effect on you digital camera. This particular image also uses the Holga fisheye filter to add more distortion. The soft focus, vignetting, and prevalent lens flare is one of the hallmarks of the Holga lens. Nikon D600 and Holga HL-N with fisheye adaptor 30 sec @ f/8, ISO 400

Smartphones

Yep, that's right. Your camera phone is a great way to capture decay photography. Chances are you almost always have your phone with you, and most cameras in phones these days are pretty good. If you see something cool, don't hesitate to use your camera phone just because it's not a *professional* camera. Work with what you have. There are so many different apps out there that can make your photos interesting that it would be a shame *not* to use your smartphone, even concurrently with another camera. Now, I wouldn't recommend using a smartphone as the only camera you bring on an urban exploration trip, but camera phones definitely provide a great option when used as an adjunct to a dedicated camera.

A lot of smartphones can be fitted with different lenses and other accouterments as well, so you can have almost the same versatility as a regular camera. There are too many types of phone out there to even begin to delve into which camera phone is preferred for this type of photography.

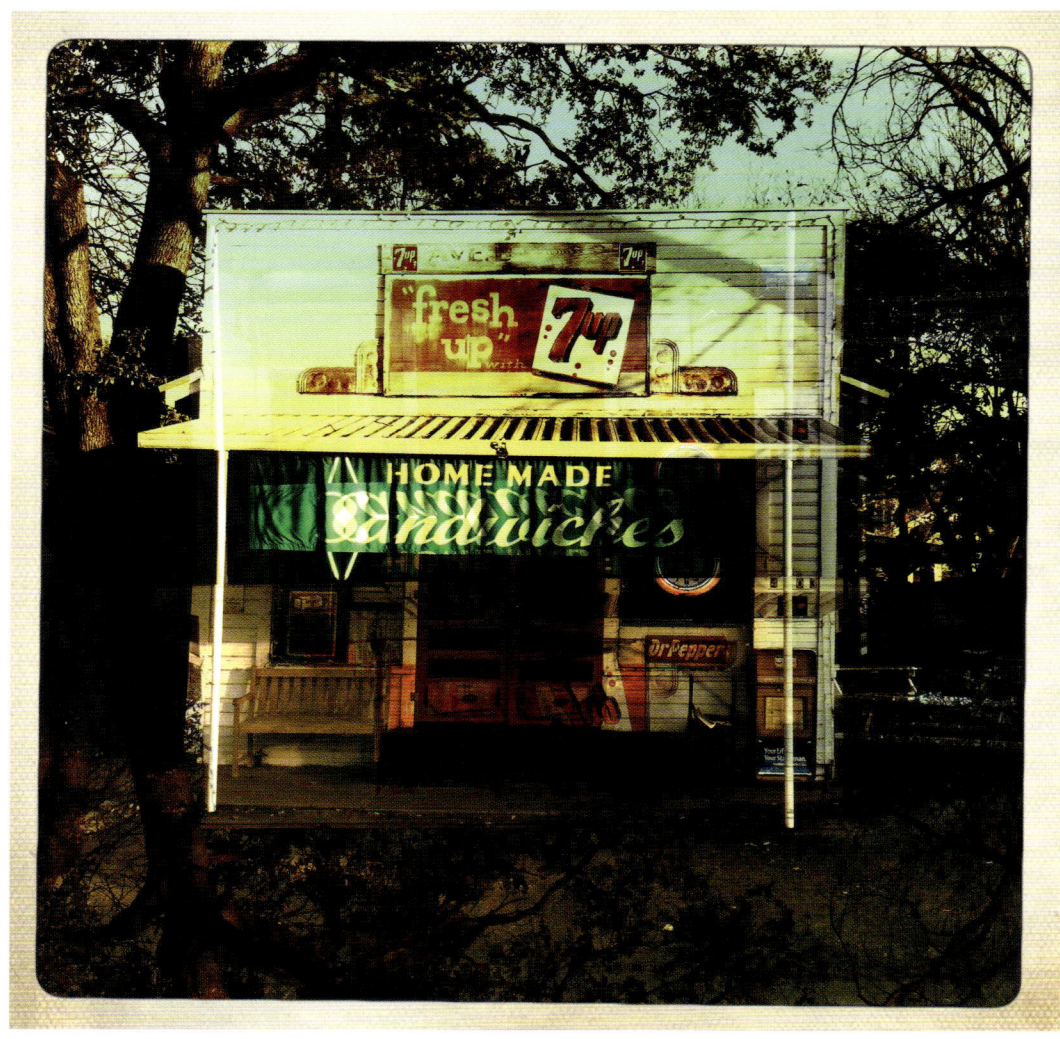

FIGURE 2.8 I took this photo of Ave. B Grocery in Austin, TX with my iPhone and the Hipstamatic app

Another great thing about using a smartphone is the ability to upload your decay photographs in real time as you go to photography social networking sites like Instagram and photo-sharing sites such as Flickr.

The main reason I like shooting decay scenes with a smartphone is that there's little post-processing involved, yet there are thousands of different effects that are available to you through the world of apps. These days the most popular apps are the ones that simulate film and emphasize the lo-fi imagery. This lo-fi look complements decay photography exceptionally well. There are literally thousands of photography apps out there, but although I have nearly 100 of them on my iPhone, I find that I only use a handful. Some I use because I like the effect produced, some I use not for the effects alone, but for the social networking aspect as well. Here's a list of some of my favorite apps.

- **Instagram.** This wasn't my favorite app when it was first introduced, but I have found that it has become the app I use most for almost all my decay photography and everyday iPhone photography. The filters are simple and not overly processed, which is a nice feature. There is also a blurring filter that allows you to simulate shallow depth of field. I also like that you can take photos with the app or you can import photos from your phone. Where the app stands out is its seamless ability to integrate your photos with other social networking sites such as Twitter, Facebook, Tumblr, and Flickr. It's also a standalone mobile social networking tool, so you can connect with friends and other urban explorers even if you don't subscribe to any of those other sites.
- **Hipstamatic.** For a while Hipstamatic was the definitive lo-fi photography app for smartphones such as the iPhone. Hipstamatic is a very versatile app that allows you to create

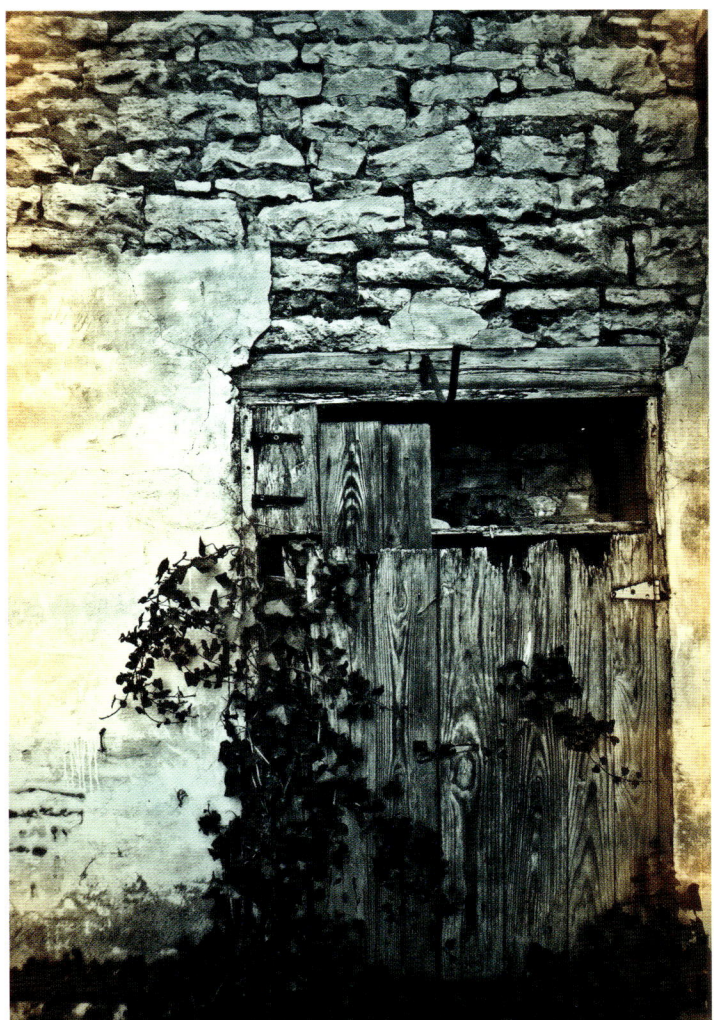

FIGURE 2.9 This photo of the dilapidated entryway of an old general store in Hico, TX was taken with my iPhone and processed with the Plastic Bullet app

many unique effects by using different combinations of "films, lenses, and flashes." This app is very cool if you have time to experiment with the combinations, but in the field the app is very cumbersome to use. There are so many variables involved in using this app I have found that I use it less and less as time goes on, preferring to use simpler apps, even if they don't produce as nice an image as Hipstamatic. The other drawback is that the Hipstamatic app doesn't let you import photos from your phone. You must shoot the picture with the app to get the effect. The bottom line is that you can use this app to create great images if you have the time and the patience to work with it.

- **Plastic Bullet.** This is one of my favorite apps. The effects it applies to your images are excellent. If I was to have to pick one and only one photo app, this would be it. Plastic Bullet generates random frames, textures, contrast levels, colors, simulated light leaks, and more to create a unique image every time you use it. No two pictures look alike. This app comes as close to replicating the look of film as any other app I've used.
- **Photo55.** This simple app simulates Polaroid Type 55 and Type 665 black-and-white instant films. It's a straightforward no-frills app that allows you to get a cool vintage Polaroid look, complete with frame and emulsion smears on the edges.
- **Flickr.** Users of the popular photo-sharing website Flickr can now use the Flickr app not only to browse the Flickr site, but also to use the camera to take photos, apply filters, and upload the images straight to Flickr. It's a good app to have, especially if you're an avid Flickr user.

Compact cameras

Compact cameras are very common these days. Almost everyone has one and they're small enough to fit in a pocket, purse, or small camera bag. These are often great cameras for capturing decay photography at unexpected times, or when you want to travel light. There are many different styles of cameras and many different feature sets, from fully automatic cameras to cameras with some of the same shooting options as DSLR cameras.

Point and shoots

The compact cameras often referred to as *point and shoots* are small cameras with built-in zoom lenses, oftentimes with limited or no control for the photographer, and tiny little sensors. These are by far the most common cameras you'll find in the hands of everyday people. Camera manufacturers make a huge variety of these cameras and usually update them every six months or so. These cameras are great for daytime work with a deep depth of field (the smaller the sensor, the deeper the depth of field at any given aperture), but lack the quality in low-light situations that you find with cameras that have larger sensors. Some of these cameras are water-proof, shock/drop-proof, and freeze proof, which makes them a good candidate for decay photography in less than ideal situations, such as rain, snow, or damp places, such as along a riverbank (I kayak, so having a water-proof camera is great for me).

Mirrorless cameras

In the past few years camera companies have recognized a void in the market for small cameras with more versatility and larger sensors for better image quality, and have stepped up to the plate with some amazing cameras that are not only compact, but also have interchangeable lenses like DSLR cameras. These smaller cameras started out with a relatively small sensor termed Micro Four Thirds or sometimes M43. These cameras have a sensor size of about 17 × 13 in a 4:3 ratio, hence the term "four thirds." Micro Four Thirds cameras include the Panasonic Lumix G-Series and the Olympus PEN series.

More recently, camera manufacturers have started putting APS-C sized sensors in these compact cameras, which along with the versatility of the interchangeable lenses gives these cameras image quality comparable to a DSLR. Some of the notable cameras in this series are the Sony NEX series, Canon EOS M series, Samsung NX series, and the Pentax K series.

Nikon went a different direction and designed an all-new sensor size near the 4:3 ratio, but on a smaller scale (13.2 × 8.8). Nikon refers to this as CX.

The main difference these mirrorless cameras have from DSLR cameras is the lack of a large mirror box to reflect the image from the lens up to the viewfinder. The image is projected straight from the lens to the sensor and is viewed electronically on the LCD screen (like a point and shoot).

The versatility of these cameras along with the superb image quality has made them a favorite among quite a few urban explorers and decay photographers.

Lenses

Although I touch on a few different types of cameras, I am going to assume that most of my readers today are going to be using DSLR cameras, therefore, this section is going to cater more toward coverage of standard DSLR lenses (and for the most part applies to film SLR cameras as well).

Usually, I point out at the beginning of any lens discussion that the lens is the most important part of your camera system and that investing in high-quality lenses is often the best use of your money. In the case of decay photography, I'm going to amend this statement because, as I stated in the section on toy cameras, sometimes a cheap $25 lens does a better job at achieving your artistic vision than an ultra-sharp $2,400 lens will. Of course, this depends on the photographer's goal and intended outcome of the image. If one has the penchant for hyper-realistic HDR photos, then a more expensive lens is going to be a necessity, but if the photographer is aiming for a more lo-fi approach, an inexpensive lens will certainly suffice. Personally, I fall

GPS and geo-tagging

One great technology to have when out exploring and photographing decay scenes is a Global Positioning System (GPS) device. GPS devices that add metadata tags to your images with latitude, longitude, altitude, and time codes are now available relatively inexpensively, and most current DSLRs have an input for a GPS device. Canon was the first company to add a built-in GPS system to a DSLR camera with the 6D, although a few manufacturers have had built-in GPS in compact cameras for a few years. GPS isn't absolutely necessary in a lot of cases, but for those who travel extensively the ability to import your images to your computer and have the precise location already attached is great.

Why is it great? If you've ever traveled through deserts of the western US or if you've taken a trip to numerous cities and photographed dozens of different buildings over the course of days or weeks, you know that it can become easy to forget exactly where you took the shot if it's not an instantly recognizable landmark. Geo-tagging is a quick and inexpensive way to keep track of the locations of all your shoots.

Software such as Adobe's Lightroom 4 has the ability to show the images on a map upon importing the geo-tagged photos. The popular photo-sharing website Flickr will automatically map your images according to geo-tagged information as well.

somewhere in the middle – I like the lo-fi approach, but I also like sharp images as well, so I often shoot the same subjects with different lenses.

The great thing about interchangeable lens cameras is that you can use different types of lenses to portray an otherwise normal scene in a way that others can't see it. Essentially you are using the lens as *your* eye, allowing the viewer to see things from your unique perspective.

Aside from lens quality, the two major features to look for when selecting a lens are focal length and aperture. Focal length determines the *angle of view* of a lens, or in lay terms, how much of the scene you can see in the frame. Wide-angle lenses have lower numbers and fit more of the scene into the frame, while higher numbers have a narrow angle of view and allow you to focus on a smaller part of the scene and help to pull far-off subjects close into the frame. From wide-angle to normal to telephoto, each type of lens has its uses. I cover the different focal length categories individually in following sections.

The aperture of the lens determines how much light can get through the lens and subsequently to the sensor. More light equals means lower ISO settings and/or faster shutter speeds to keep the noise down and the subject sharp, respectively. Zoom lenses come in two distinct types, fixed aperture and variable aperture. A fixed aperture zoom lens maintains the same aperture as you zoom in and out. These lenses are usually more expensive and generally have apertures of either f/2.8 or f/4.

Variable aperture lenses have a lens opening that gets smaller as you zoom in to longer focal length settings. This is very important because your exposure changes as you change the focal length and may impact your image quality. Almost all *kit lenses*, or lenses that are bundled with cameras, are variable aperture and usually start out at f/3.5 at the wide end and wind up at f/5.6 on the long end. While f/3.5 is a relatively fast aperture, when you zoom in to longer focal lengths, shooting at f/5.6 can cause quite a problem due to the longer shutter speeds and higher ISO settings required to get the exposure settings needed, although this is really only a problem if you are handholding the camera in low light.

Zoom vs. prime

The difference between a zoom lens and a prime lens is that the prime lens has a fixed focal length while the zoom lens has a variable focal length that can be changed. Prime lenses are available in all types, from ultra-wide to super-telephoto, and everything in between. Prime lenses are often sharper than zoom lenses, but in recent years zoom lens technology has grown by leaps and bounds, so a lens such as the Nikon 14–24 mm f/2.8G is actually sharper than either the Nikon 14 mm f/2.8D or the 24 mm f/2.8D prime lenses, for example.

One of the main advantages of a prime lens, however, is that it can be made with faster apertures than zoom lenses since there are fewer lens elements and so can be made in a smaller package. This means you have the opportunity to get a lens that allows you to shoot in low-light situations, in a small package, for not a lot of money.

I generally tend to prefer zoom lenses for most of my work since it's easier to work with getting the right composition, but in the case of decay photography I kind of hang in the middle. When shooting digitally, I tend to use zoom lenses for the most part, simply because I have a plethora of top-quality lenses, but I do on occasion use a prime. Almost all of my film cameras are fitted with prime lenses. Medium-format cameras use mostly prime lenses, but there are a few zooms out there, although they can be hard to find and usually aren't as sharp as the prime lenses.

I think starting out using prime lenses causes a photographer to concentrate more on the composition since you can't just zoom in and out, you are forced to move in and around the environment and consciously make decisions about the composition of the image.

Wide-angle lenses

Wide-angle lenses allow you to fit a lot of the scene into the frame due to the large angle of view. The focal lengths of wide-angle lenses usually run from about 10–24 mm on a crop sensor camera and from about 14–35 mm on a full-frame or 35 mm film camera, and from 35–50 mm for medium format. There are also fisheye lenses which run anywhere from 8–10.5 mm on crop sensor and about 15–16 mm on full-frame or film. Fisheyes are special types of wide-angle lenses that aren't corrected for the lens distortion and appear to be very bowed, especially at the edges of the frame. Most standard wide-angle lenses are considered *aspherical*, and have special lens elements designed to correct for most of the lens distortion.

Note: Lenses from 10 mm to 14 mm on a crop sensor and 14–20 mm on full-frame and film are considered ultra-wide lenses.

Wide-angle lenses can give your images very dramatic looks because of the distortion they can impose on the image. There are two types of distortions that are typical of wide-angle lenses. The first type is *perspective distortion*; this type of distortion causes things that are close to the camera (foreground) to look disproportionately larger than things that are farther away from the camera (background). Although this effect is traditionally terrible for portraits, it can be used effectively in decay photography by making small spaces look very spacious (real-estate photographers use this trick to make rooms look larger than they really are). Using this special distortion allows you to convey emptiness to an otherwise small or cramped room.

The second type of distortion is a symptom of the aspheric elements in wide-angle lenses that are used to stop

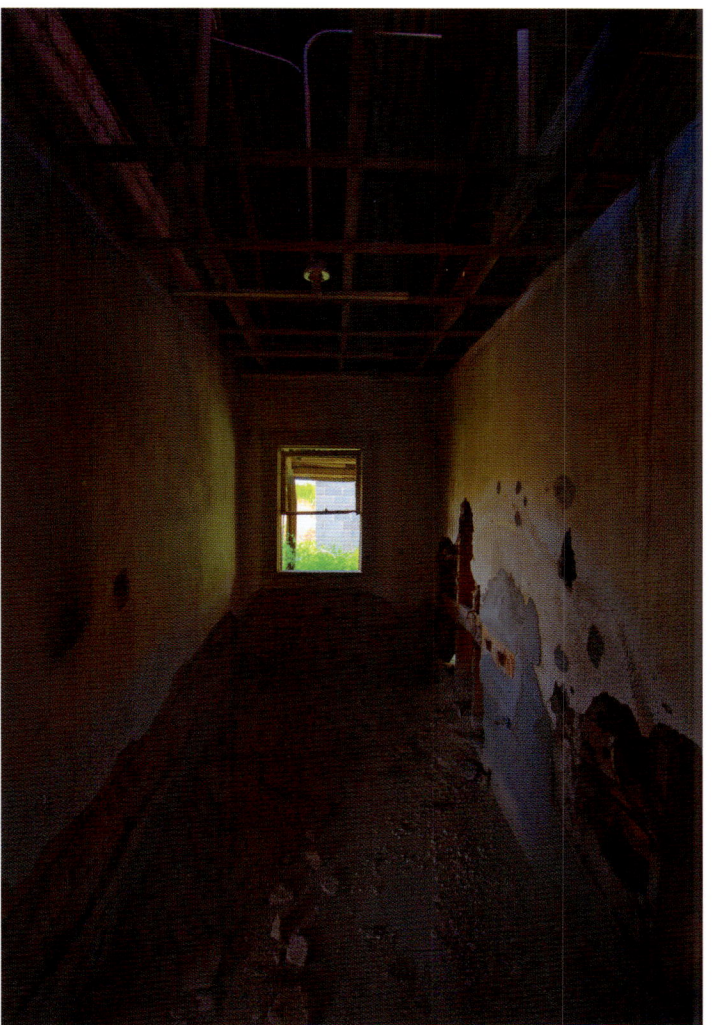

FIGURE 2.10 Using an ultra-wide lens causes this small, cramped room to look much more expansive than it really is. Nikon D800 with Nikon 14–24 mm f/2.8G at 14 mm. 1/20 sec. @ f/5.6 ISO 200

the images appearing bowed out near the edges (like you would see in a fisheye). The byproduct of these aspherical elements is that near the far corners of the frame things start looking as if they are stretched out. When shooting a landscape photo this may not be readily noticeable, but when introducing any type of architecture this becomes very noticeable. Since decay photography is a highly abstract form of photography, this effect can also be used effectively to make your images more compelling.

When shooting decay photography I usually find myself drawn to using wide-angle lenses to take advantage of the distortion and the surrealism that it adds to the composition.

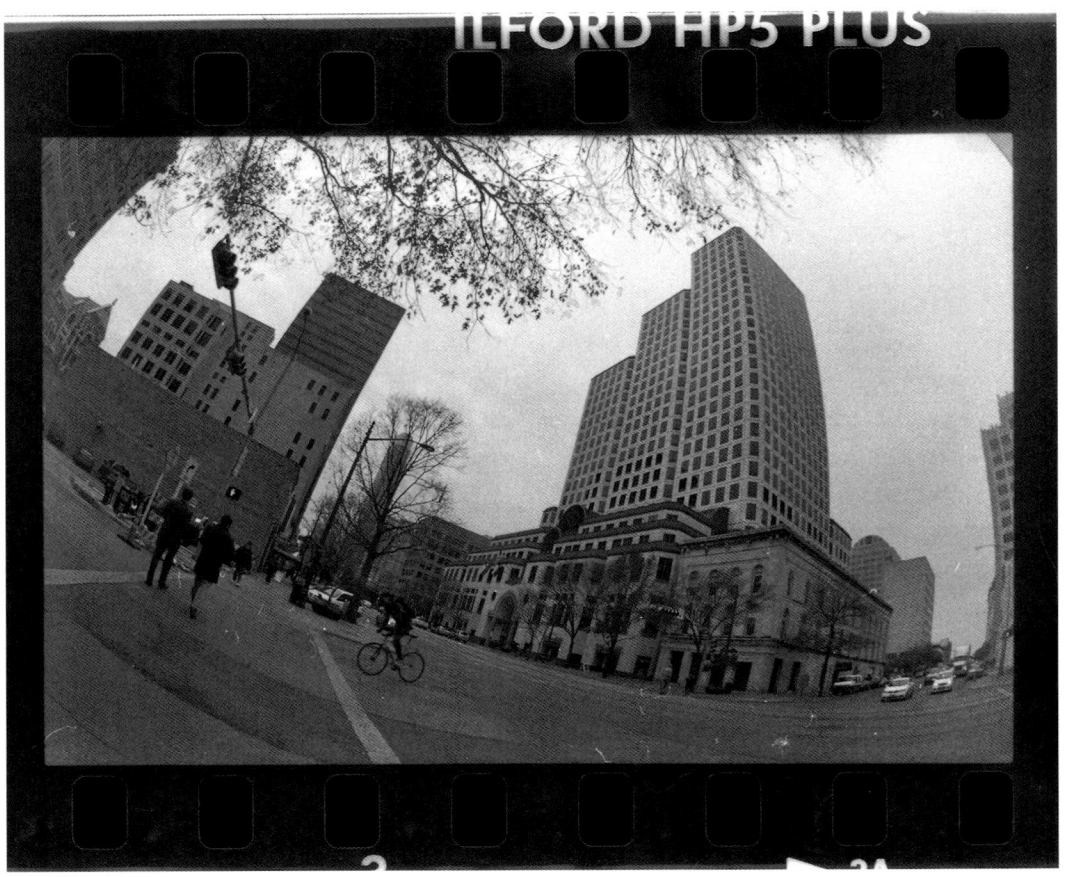

FIGURE 2.11 Fisheye lenses have massive distortion that gives images a very distinctive look. Nikon F90X with Zenitar 16 mm f/2.8 exposure unrecorded

One thing to remember when using a wide-angle lens is to fill the frame with the subject. Most of the time, if the subject is very small with a lot of distracting space surrounding it, your image can lose impact. Don't be afraid to get right up close into the subject. Finding an interesting focal point and getting right up close to it is one of the keys to making your image dynamic and interesting to the viewer.

On the other hand, with certain subjects, placing it in the middle of an expansive space can lend the image a feeling of isolation and desolation. This, too, can be an effective tool for engaging the viewer.

Mid-range, standard, or normal

A mid-range or standard zoom lens is the lens with the focal length that you'll find bundled with a camera kit. These lenses usually have a focal length that starts out marginally wide and zooms in to a short telephoto lens. Typical focal lengths go from 17–50 mm for crop sensor cameras and 24–70 mm for full-frame cameras.

For prime lenses this is usually called the "normal" lens, because it's supposed to coincide with about the same field of vision as your eyesight. Focal lengths for a normal prime lens are from about 28–35 mm for crop sensors and from about 40–60 mm for full-frame digital cameras or 35 mm film cameras and 80 mm for medium format.

These types of lenses are extremely versatile since they give you the choice of going from wide to short telephoto. This means you can work with the wide-angle distortion or stand back and get a more normal look.

If you can only afford one good lens, I'd make it this type of lens. Odds are you're going to be doing more than decay photography and this lens is more useful for many other applications, as well as decay photography.

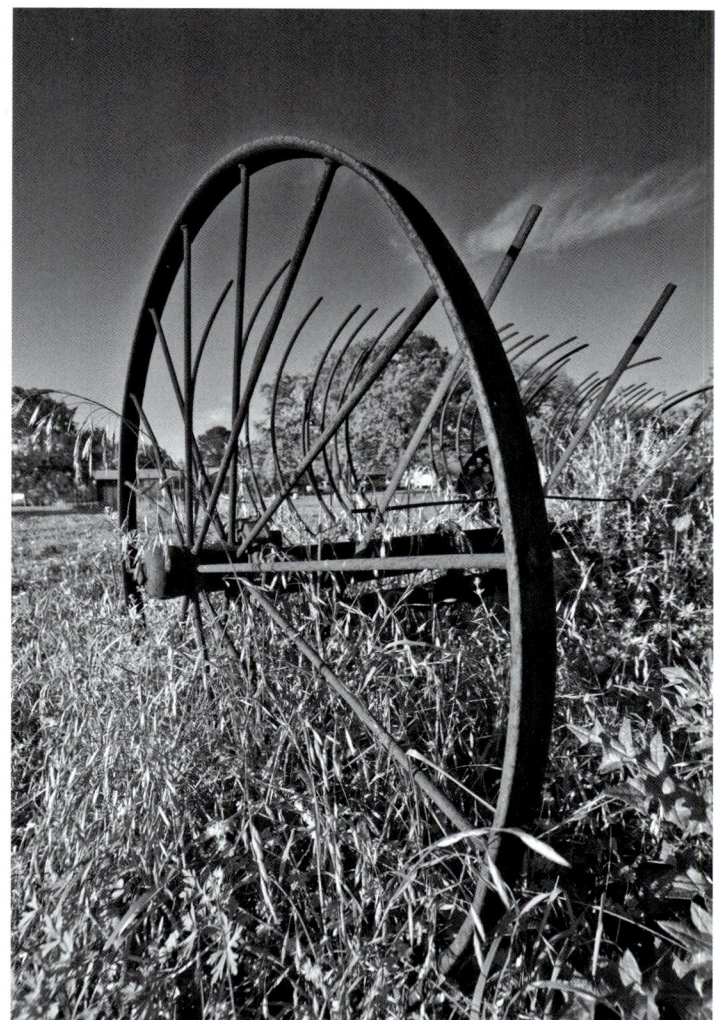

FIGURE 2.12 Using a wide-angle lens and getting up close brings the viewer right into the scene of this abandoned farm machinery. Nikon D800 with Sigma 17–35 mm f/2.8–4 at 17 mm. 1/200 sec. @ f/7.1 ISO 100

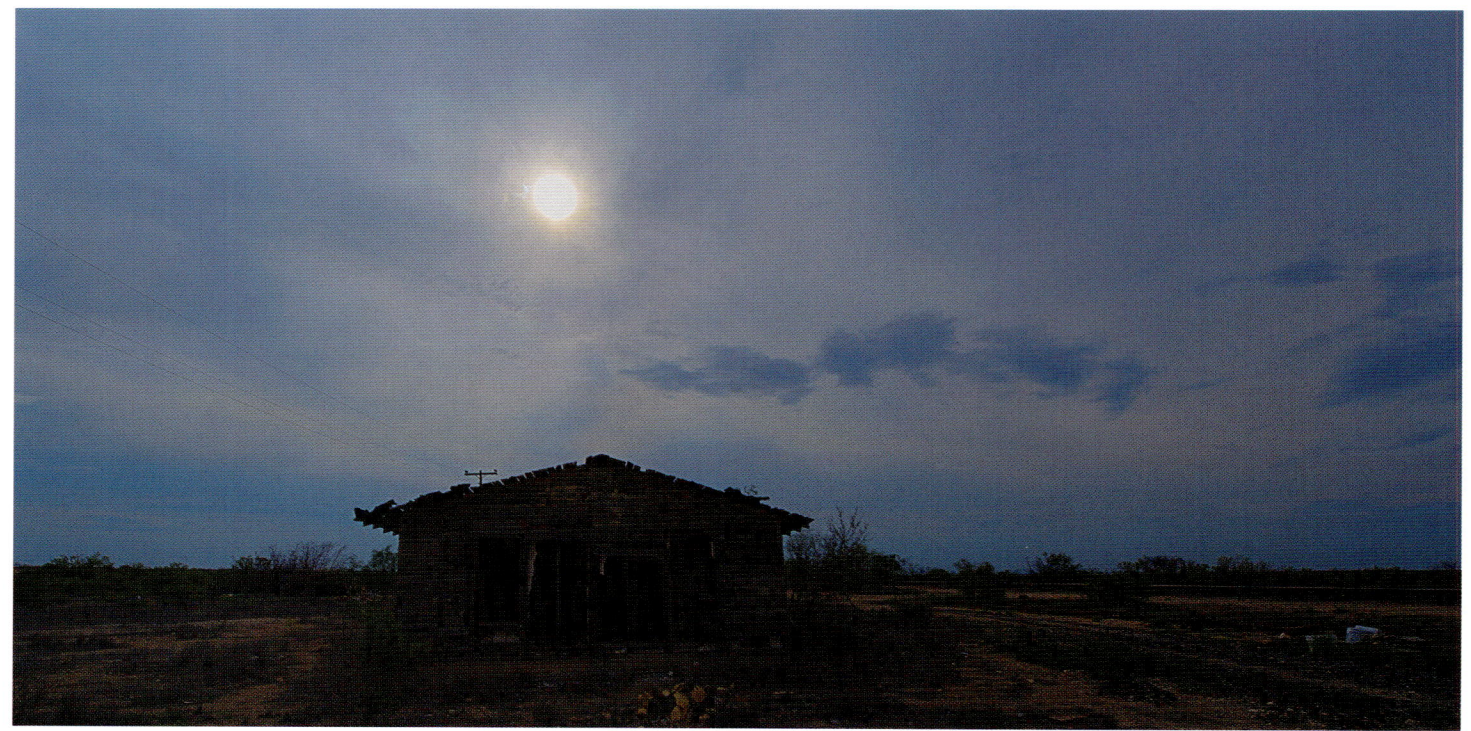

FIGURE 2.13 Using a wide-angle lens and giving the subject space lends a feeling of isolation to the shot of this abandoned home in west Texas. Nikon D800 with Nikon 14–24 mm f/2.8G at 14 mm. 1/640 sec. @ f/7.1 ISO 100. Bracketed three stops (one stop over, one stop at exposure, and one stop under) and merged to HDR using Photoshop CS5

Telephoto lenses

Telephoto lenses have long focal lengths and act sort of like a telescope to pull your subject in and allow you to fill the frame even though you may be quite far away. The typical range for a fast telephoto zoom is 70–200 mm. There are telephoto zooms made specifically for crop sensor cameras which cover the 55–200 mm range, but most of these are variable-aperture lenses. Medium-format lenses are usually about 150 mm, and are rarely much longer due to the size of the lens. Lenses longer than 200 mm are usually prime lenses. To make some of these longer lenses more affordable and portable, oftentimes they are offered with a fixed f/4 aperture.

You'll probably find yourself using a lens with this type of focal length the least. You won't really need a lens this long unless you cannot gain access to a particular subject, which can happen in some circumstances.

IS, VR, OIS, and more

Most camera and lens manufacturers these days have some sort of mechanical device that either shifts the lens elements or in

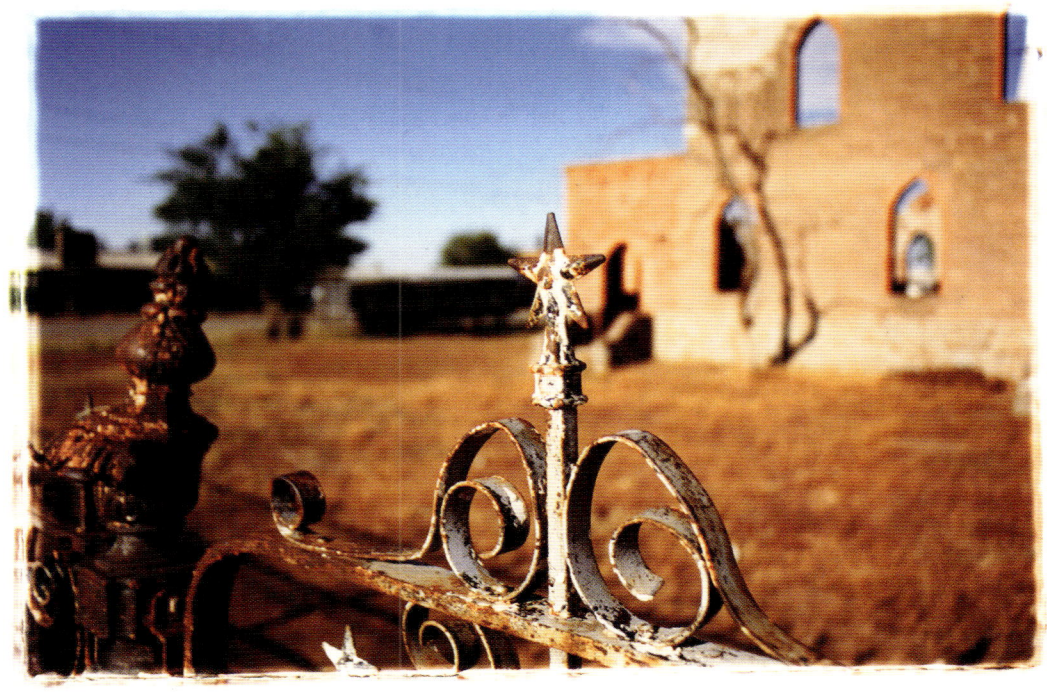

FIGURE 2.14 I used a normal prime lens to capture the detail of this gate at the ruins of an old church in Van Horn, TX. Pentax Spotmatic with 55 mm f/1.8 Super-Takumar and Agfa RSX II. 1/500 sec. @ f/4 ISO 100. Scanned from a color print on Kodak Endura paper

some cases shifts the sensor inside the camera body to reduce the amount of apparent motion from camera shake. Camera shake is most evident at slower exposure times and is magnified exponentially as longer focal lengths are used. This technology goes by many different names. Canon uses the term Image Stabilization (IS), Nikon terminology is Vibration Reduction (VR), Sigma uses Optical Stabilization (OS), and Tamron calls their technology Vibration Compensation (VC).

Note: Sony has the "Steady Shot" system, but it is built into the camera body rather than the lens system.

This technology helps you get steady images at longer exposure times than you would normally be able to when handholding a camera. There is a rule of thumb that most photographers refer to when doing day-to-day photography. This rule is known as the *reciprocal rule*. The reciprocal rule states that your shutter speed setting should be at or near the reciprocal of the focal

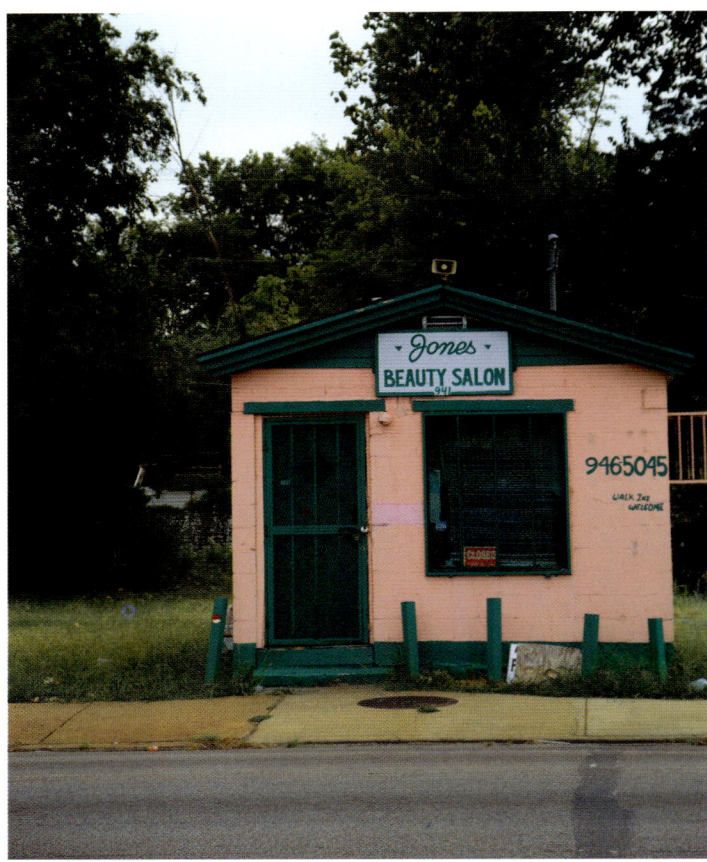

FIGURE 2.15 I snapped this shot near the Stax Museum in Memphis, TN using a slight telephoto setting on my zoom lens. Nikon D3100 with Sigma 17–70 mm f/2.8–4 OS at 50 mm (75 mm equivalent). 1/500 sec. @ f/4 ISO 100

camera. As focal length increases, the lens not only magnifies the scene but also any camera movement. This is a good guideline to follow for most photography. Stabilization technology allows you to handhold the camera at shutter speeds up to four times longer than would normally be recommended. Of course, in the real world this is subjective because not everyone's hand is as steady as the next person's.

For decay photography this technology can be a real advantage, as sometimes you may be entering dark places or small places that you can't get your tripod into. This can allow you to get a nice sharp shot in situations where you normally couldn't.

Tripods

A good tripod should be a part of every photographer's kit. If you're going to be shooting in dark, abandoned places, or at night, handholding the camera usually isn't an option. Even in the daytime a good tripod can let you capture images with deep depth of field using small apertures at low ISO settings. And of course, if you plan on doing HDR photography a tripod is an absolute necessity to keep your images lined up.

The main thing to look for when buying a tripod is that the tripod should be able to adequately support your camera and the heaviest lens you're going to use with it. A tripod that can't support your camera is pretty useless.

Tripods come in many styles and price points. The cheaper ones are usually lightweight and come with a built-in head. The more high-end tripods can cost anywhere from $100 for a standard aluminum one up to $700 for one with carbon fiber legs. With the more expensive tripods you may also

length of the lens you're using, so at 50 mm your shutter speed should be about 1/50 (or the more common full stop setting of 1/60). What the reciprocal rule is designed to deal with is reducing blur from camera shake when handholding the

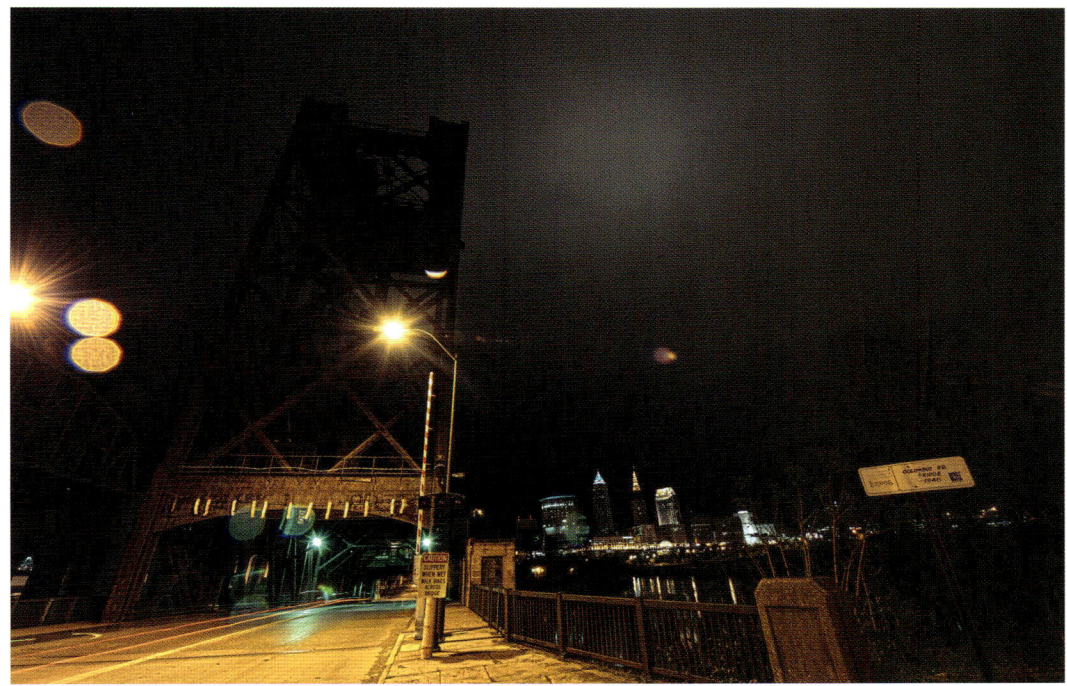

FIGURE 2.16 This shot of the Columbus Rd. Bridge would have been impossible to capture without using a good sturdy tripod to support my camera, battery pack, and lens, which weighs about 6 lb altogether.   Nikon D700 with Nikon 14–24 mm f/2.8G at 14 mm. 10 sec. @ f/8 ISO 200. Manfrotto 190XB tripod with Manfrotto 322RC2 pistol grip ball head

have to buy the tripod head separately, which can range anywhere from $50 for a standard head to $300 for a pistol grip ball head, up to $600 for a fluid head (these are mostly used for video work). I have about $300 invested in my tripod; early on in my career I tried the cheap tripod route and was always frustrated, but once I got a nice sturdy tripod and a pistol grip ball head I was much more satisfied. The ball head makes composing much quicker.

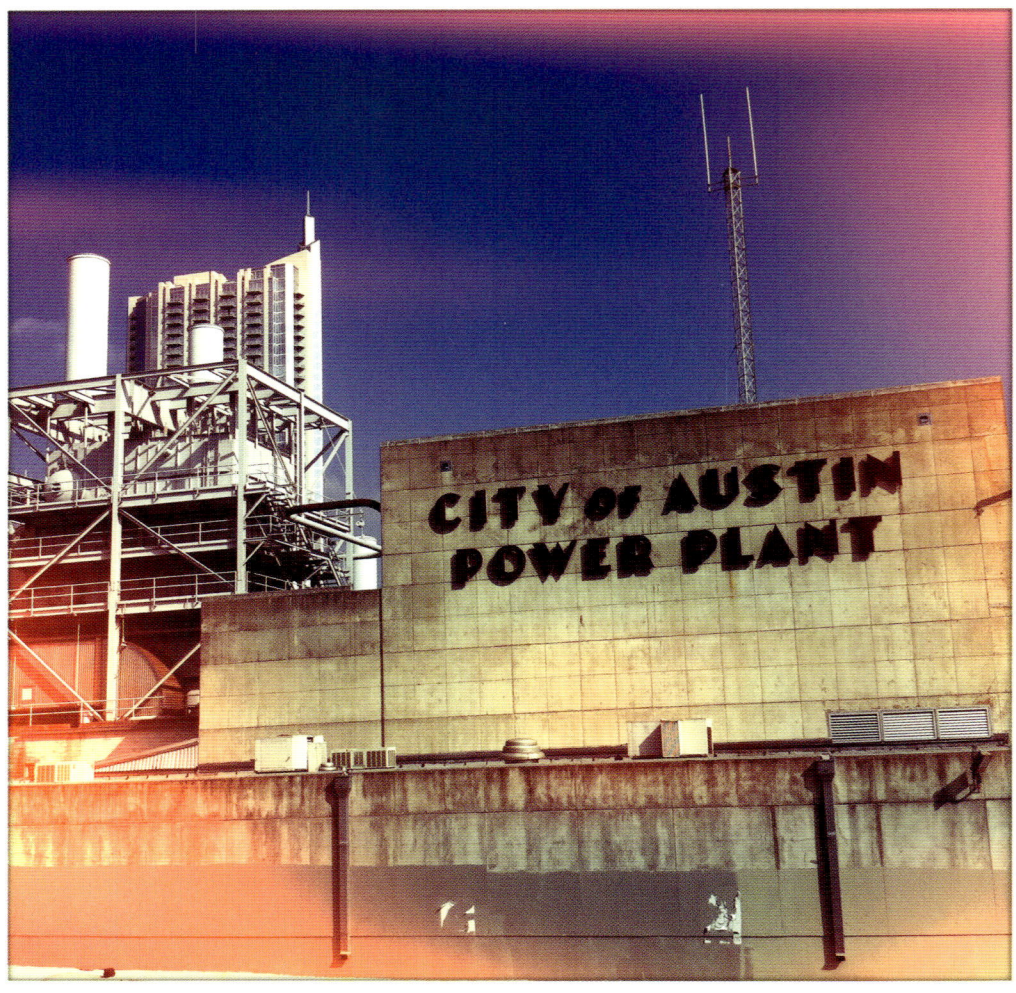

FIGURE 2.17 A shot of the City of Austin Power Plant taken using the Hipstamatic app for the iPhone

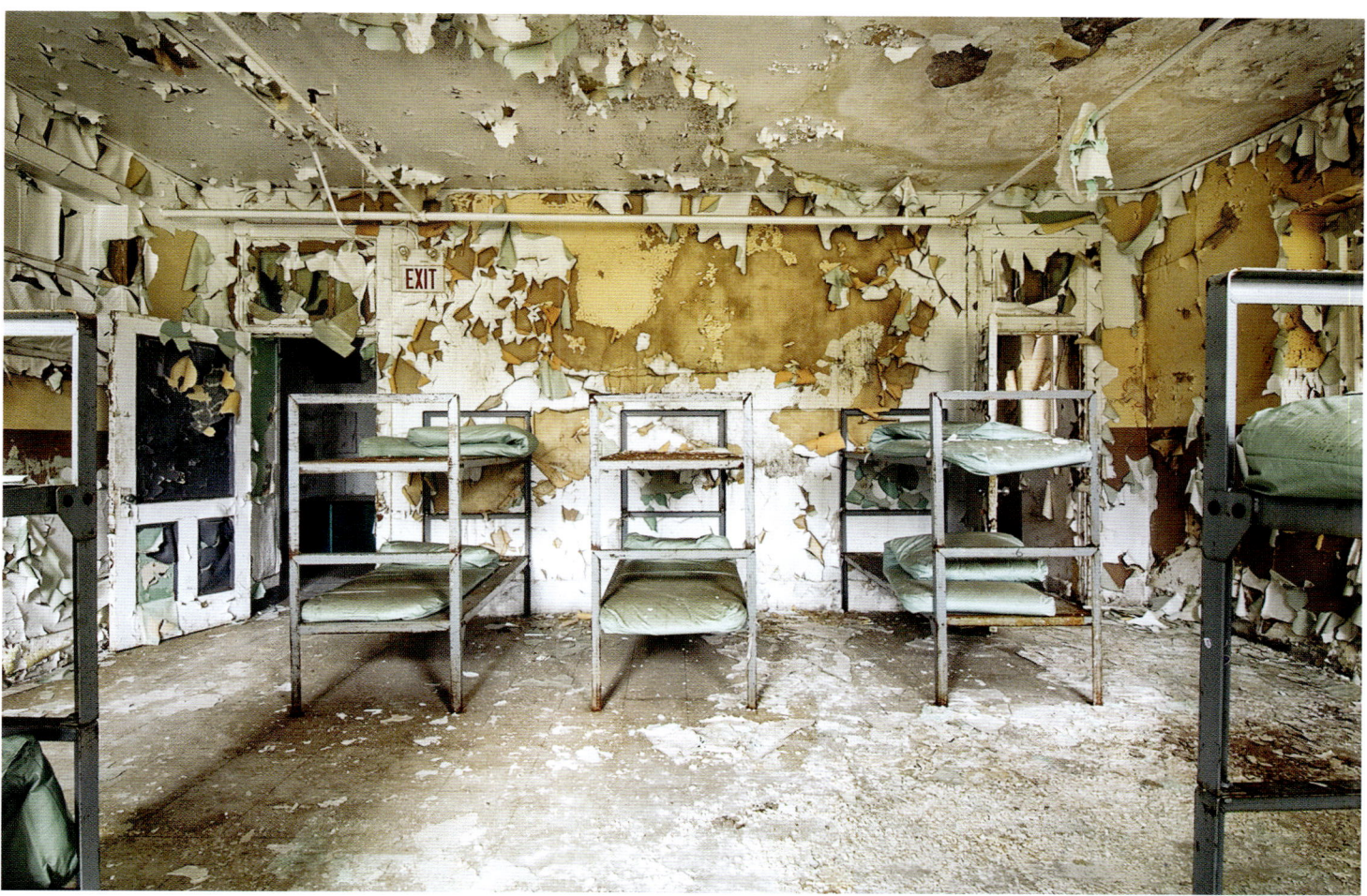

FIGURE 2.18 From the photographer: This image was taken in what was once the infirmary of the Essex County Penitentiary in New Jersey. I thought these bunks, still arranged as they were when they were used by the inmates, told a particularly human story amidst all of the rubble and decay of the now demolished building. Nikon D200, Nikon 12–24 mm lens. 1.3 seconds at f/18. ISO250 © Leslie Granda-Hill

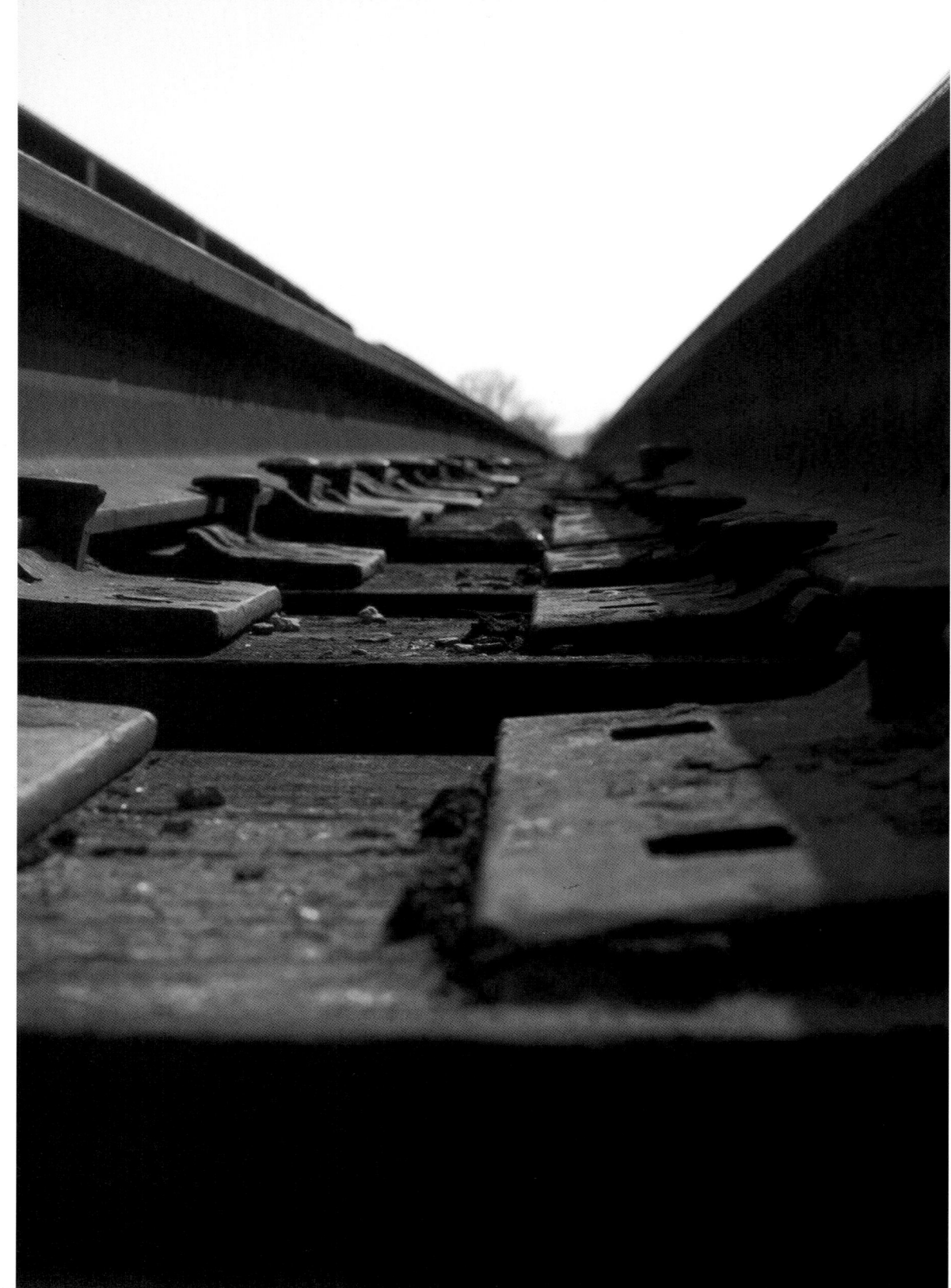

Three

COMPOSITION AND TECHNIQUE

FIGURE 3.1 Detail of railroad tracks. You can combine a number of different composition guidelines in one image.   **Nikon D300s with Nikon 35 mm f/1.8G. 1/160 @ f/11 ISO 200**

One of the most often overlooked aspects of decay photography, and photography in general these days, is composition and technique. Since very few contemporary photographers are classically trained, quite often the first and foremost thing on a photographer's mind isn't composition, but exposure and whether the image is properly exposed. Then composition comes, sometimes as an afterthought.

While exposure is definitely a very important factor in setting the tone and mood of a decay photograph, composition is also a very important part of it as well. It's nearly, if not as, important as exposure.

One of the single most important challenges a photographer faces, regardless of the subject, is finding the perfect composition to complement the scene. The key to making any photograph successful is to find a composition that works well with the subject. There is, however, no single composition that works in every situation, but therein lays the beauty of decay photography. Each and every photographer gazes upon every scene of decay with his or her own eyes and using their different life experiences interprets it with a unique mindset. Decay photography is a highly individual art form and every scene has a distinct story to tell to each and every person that comes across it. You can send three photographers to the same location and each one will undoubtedly come back with vastly different images.

An oft-repeated adage is that there are no rules when it comes to photography. I find this statement can often be a hiding place for photographers who are unwilling to learn the compositional skills or to accept that within any art there are disciplines that are sometimes helpful to adhere to. Ansel Adams, possibly the most famous photographer of all time, once said "There are no rules for good photographs, there are only good photographs." Even Ansel Adams' photographs follow at least one of the major guidelines of photographic composition, as do the majority of the most famous photographs throughout history.

Although there may be no hard-and-fast rules in photography, there are plenty of guidelines (often referred to as *rules*) to help you make your images more interesting to the viewer. Learning these guidelines will help you make your images more interesting.

All artists, not just photographers, but also painters, printmakers, sculptors, and many other artisans, have used these rules and guidelines throughout the centuries. There's a reason these guidelines are referred to over and over – because they work.

While learning the basic rules of composition is an important first step toward better photography, it is just as important to learn when it is best to break those rules as well. Don't be afraid to try many different compositions to see what works best for your particular subject and situation!

Quality of light

Quality of light is a term that photographers and artists use to define the type of light that illuminates the subject. In this sense *quality* doesn't mean that the light is *good*, but it defines the interaction of the light with the subject. In photography there is no good light or bad light, only the *right* light for your image. Even then the *right light* is a subjective term, because it depends solely on your artistic vision what the right light is.

For all practical purposes, in photography the quality of light is divided into two types: hard light and soft light. Hard light comes from a light source that is small in relation to the subject, is very directional, meaning that it is easy to determine where the light is coming from, and has a very defined shadow edge transfer, which means the lines from the shadow to the highlight areas are very sharp. Hard light images are high contrast.

Note: Shadow edge transfer is a term that describes the transition of light to dark or from shadows to highlights. The shadow edge transfer is the principal point of reference in determining the quality of light of an image.

Conversely, soft light emanates from a light source that is large in relation to the subject; it's often harder to determine what direction soft light is coming from, and the shadow edge transfer is very gradual, meaning the transition from the shadow to highlight is less abrupt.

For the most, part decay photography is done using *available light*, or light that occurs naturally in the scene. This generally means sunlight in the day, but at night depending on the location you may be using moonlight or an artificial source such as a streetlight. I don't often recommend using a flash, but an off-camera flash can add some directional light to a scene if needed, especially when photographing indoors in a dimly lit environment.

The sun as a light source can be both hard and soft; when the sun is out on a cloudless day it is going to be a hard light source. Although the sun is massive compared to the Earth, our distance from it makes it small in relation to the subject and that gives the sun a very directional appearance with hard shadows and high contrast. During the late morning and early evening your shadows are going to be longer than they are during the afternoon when the sun is high in the sky. The lower the sun is in the sky the softer the light gets as well. This is due to the fact that as the sun sinks the light has more atmosphere to pass through, and as it passes through the gases

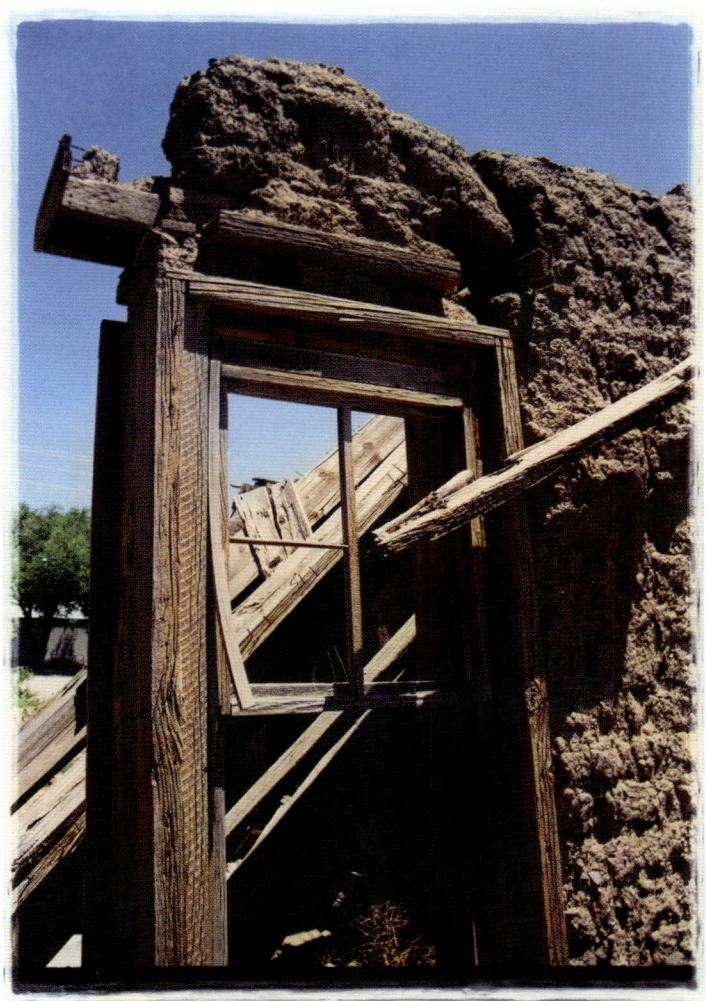

FIGURE 3.2 This photo of a collapsed adobe house taken somewhere in New Mexico in an example of hard light from direct sunlight. **Pentax Spotmatic with a Super Takumar 50 mm f/2. 1/125 sec. @ f/16 using Kodak Ektar ISO 100 film, scanned from a print on Kodak Endura metallic paper**

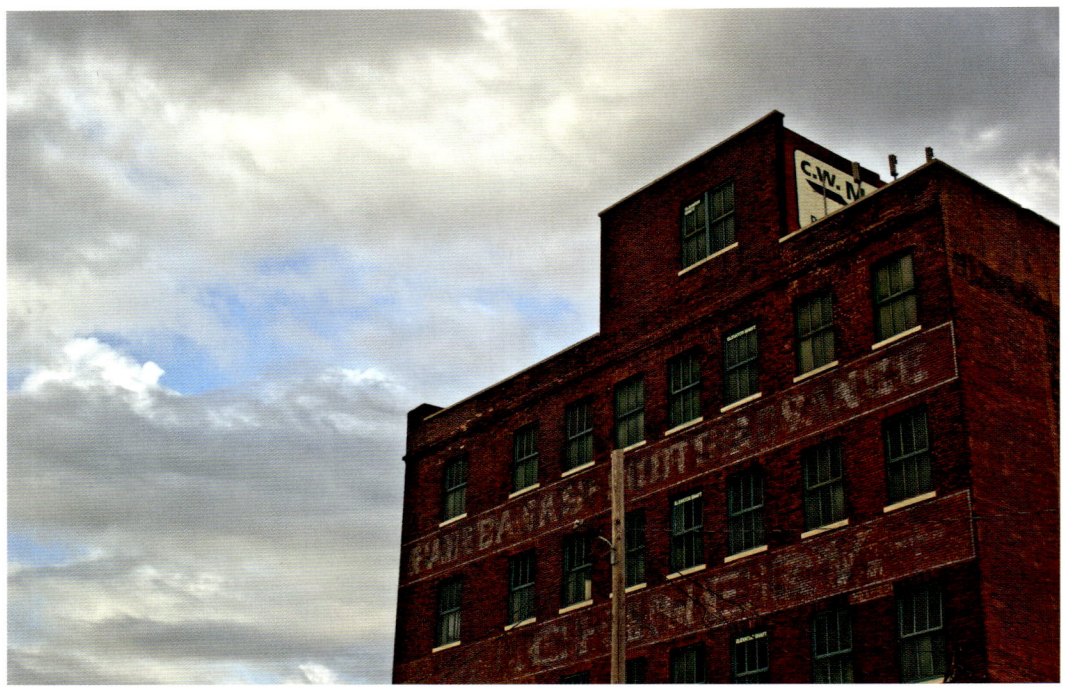

FIGURE 3.3 On a cloudy day the light is diffused and appears softer, as in this picture of an abandoned machine shop in Kansas City.   Nikon D70 with Tokina 19–35 f/3.5–4.5 at 35 mm (52 mm equivalent). 1/1250 sec. @ f/4.5 ISO 200

in the atmosphere it is subject to a phenomenon known as Rayleigh scattering. Rayleigh scattering is also responsible for the color of the sky.

Tip: Photographing early in the morning around sunrise and late evening around sunset usually yields the best results for photography. Most photographers refer to this as the "Golden Hour."

On cloudy days, the clouds act as a diffuser and they scatter the sun's rays, making for a larger light source. This makes the light very soft and even. Even when the sun is bright you will find soft light in areas of open shade.

At night, your light is nearly always going to be hard. The moon is simply reflecting light from the sun back at the Earth. You may think that since it's being reflected (i.e., bounced) back it should be softer, but the moon and the sun are relatively similar in size when viewed from the Earth due to the vast distance differences, so the moon is actually a pretty hard light source. Streetlights, porch lights, headlights, flashlights, etc., are all also going to be very small directional lights.

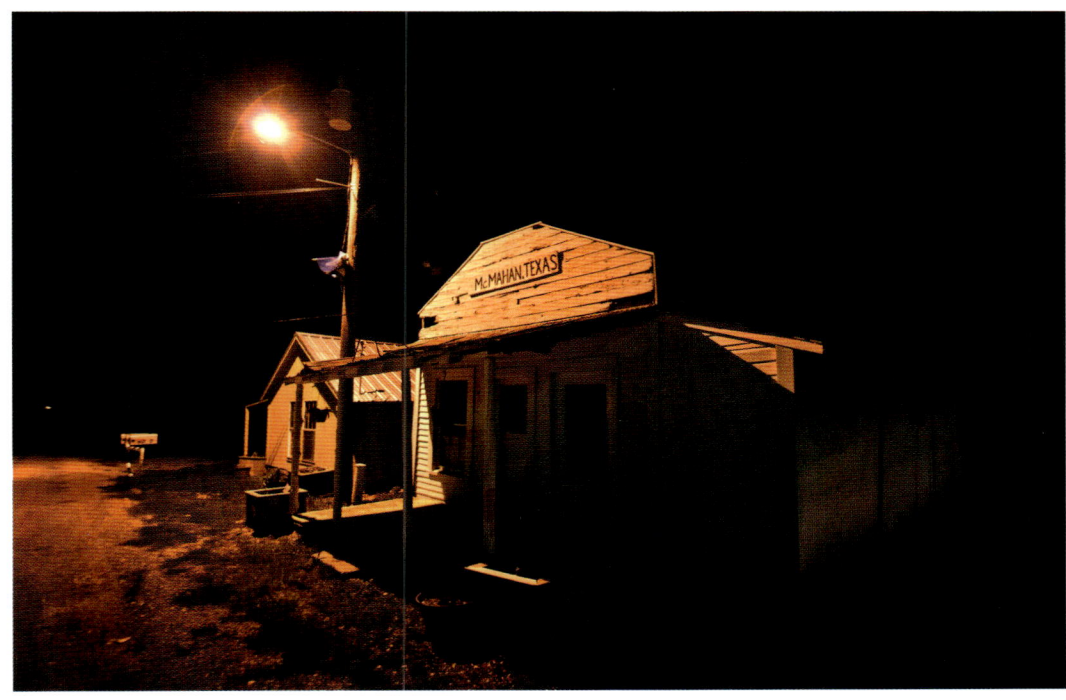

FIGURE 3.4 When doing photography at night, the light is often hard because of the small light sources. **Nikon D800 with Sigma 17–35 mm f/2.8–4 at 17 mm. 1/30 sec. @ f/2.8 ISO 6400**

Hard light and soft light can also appear in the same scene. Finding a scene where a beam of sunlight is cutting across a room is a perfect example of this. The sun shining directly in a window into a dark room, or a swath of light beaming across an area of open shade, are also similar examples. The key to finding this is to keep your eyes open and aware of these scenarios. This can also be achieved by adding off-camera flash to the scene. Beware of using on-camera flash as it will only serve to flatten the lighting in the scene because of the light being frontal. Lighting the scene from the side adds dimension and keeps texture.

Rule of thirds

The tendency for most inexperienced photographers is to place the subject directly in the middle of the image, thus making for a relatively uninteresting compcsition. The rule of thirds conveys that an image is generally more compelling when the subject is framed off-center. This is probably the most well-known guideline. Still, like all "rules", feel free to compose your image based on the subject and your vision. More often

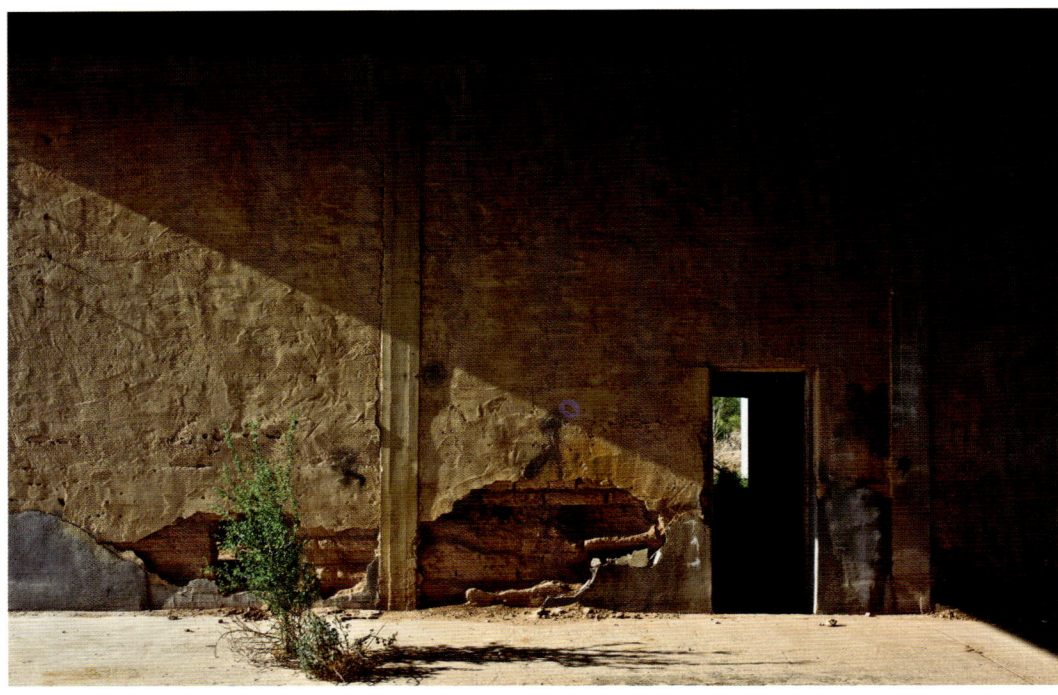

FIGURE 3.5 This photo shows an example of both hard light and soft light in the same image. As you can see, the area in the shade has much less shadow definition than the area where the sun is hitting. Nikon D800 with Nikon 28–70 mm f/2.8D at 45 mm. 1/400 sec. @ f/8 ISO 200

than not, this rule will help you transform a simple snapshot into a well-composed photograph.

Tip: Most cameras have an option of superimposing a grid in the viewfinder or on the LCD to help with composing.

To put the rule of thirds to use, simply divide the image into nine equal parts using two imaginary horizontal lines and two vertical lines. You then place the subject at or near the intersection of one of these lines. If a horizon appears in the image then generally it should be placed either in the top two-thirds or the bottom two-thirds, but not in the middle.

This is a very useful concept, but as was mentioned previously, this is not a hard-and-fast rule. Sometimes the horizon can be placed right in the middle if there is another element in the image that is placed off-center and dominates the frame.

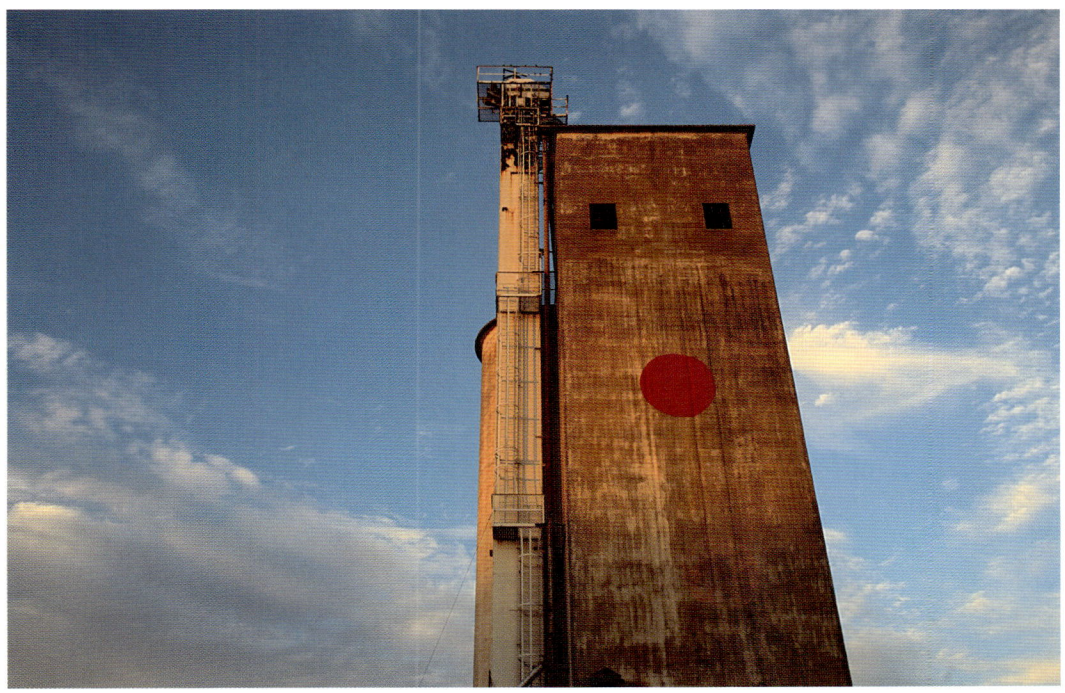

FIGURE 3.6 The main subject appears in the frame according to the rule of thirds and makes use of complementary colors, as well as keeping the subject simple.   Nikon D600 with Sigma 17–35 mm f/2.8–4 HSM 1/40 sec. @ f/8 ISO 160 +1EV

Balance and symmetry

Humans have a propensity to find things that are balanced and symmetrical aesthetically pleasing. It's a proven fact that the faces that people find most attractive are symmetrical, and the same concept can also be used for photographic images. Whereas placing the subject off-center can make an image more dynamic and interesting by adding tension to the composition, balance and symmetry can be used to make an image that allows the viewer to feel relaxed and harmonious when looking at the photograph.

Using the rule of thirds can sometimes cause your image to feel unbalanced, especially if one side of the scene has too much *negative space*, or space around the subject that is empty. To counteract this, compose the image with a subject of lesser importance that acts as a *counterweight* to achieve a more balanced image by filling the void on the opposite side of the subject (see Figure 3.9).

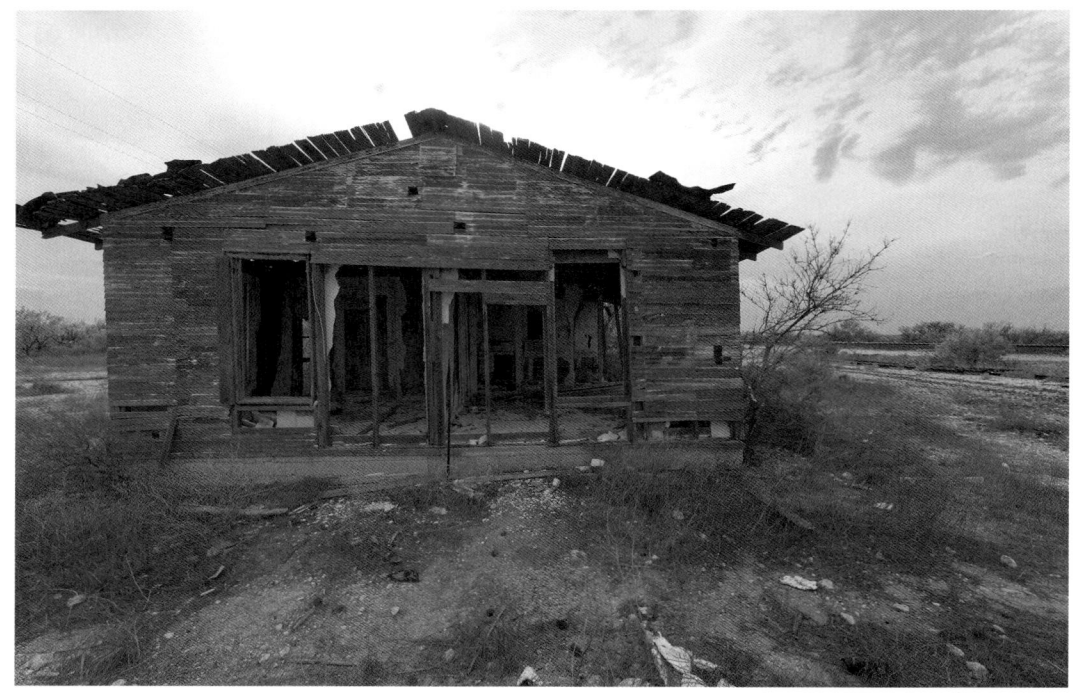

FIGURE 3.7 In this image the horizon is placed in the center, but the shack, which is the dominating feature of the image, is placed according the rule of thirds.   **Nikon D800 with Nikon 14–24 mm f/2.8G at 14 mm. 1/640 sec. @ f/6.3 ISO 100**

You may come across subjects that may work very well by simply placing them directly in the center of the frame. In contrast to the rule of thirds you can balance the image by using symmetry. In this situation, when the image is divided in half both sides are exactly the same (see Figure 3.10). Symmetrical subjects create a natural and equal balance which is quite different to adding a counterpoint to create a balanced image.

Leading lines and patterns

Using leading lines is a great way to draw the viewer's eye through the composition so that the whole image is seen, or they are a great way to lead the viewer's eye to the main subject of the photograph. Leading lines can be one straight line, two or more parallel lines, a curve, an S-curve, or even a meandering line that wanders up through the image.

The odd rule

One little talked about composition "rule" is the odd rule. This states that compositions work better when including an odd number of subjects rather than an even number. I generally find that one or three subjects usually work best.

One is a simple subject and three makes it easy to form a triangular pattern which is pleasing to the eye or creates a fulcrum or middle point that ties the image together; as opposed to an even number of subjects, which can cause the eye to separate the image into sections. When combining more than three subjects the image starts to get overcrowded and busy. When composing your images keep an eye out for the "odds."

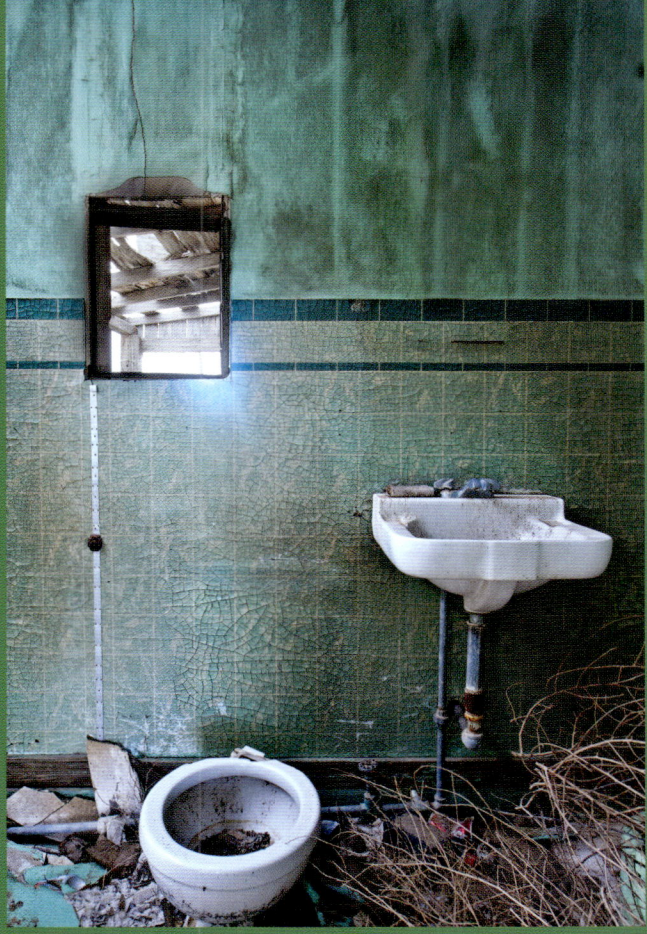

FIGURE 3.8 The three main elements in this image – the window, the sink, and the toilet – create a triangular shape, which leads the eye through the image. **Nikon D800** with Nikon 14–24 mm f/2.8G at 20 mm. 1/60 sec. @ f/6.3 ISO 100

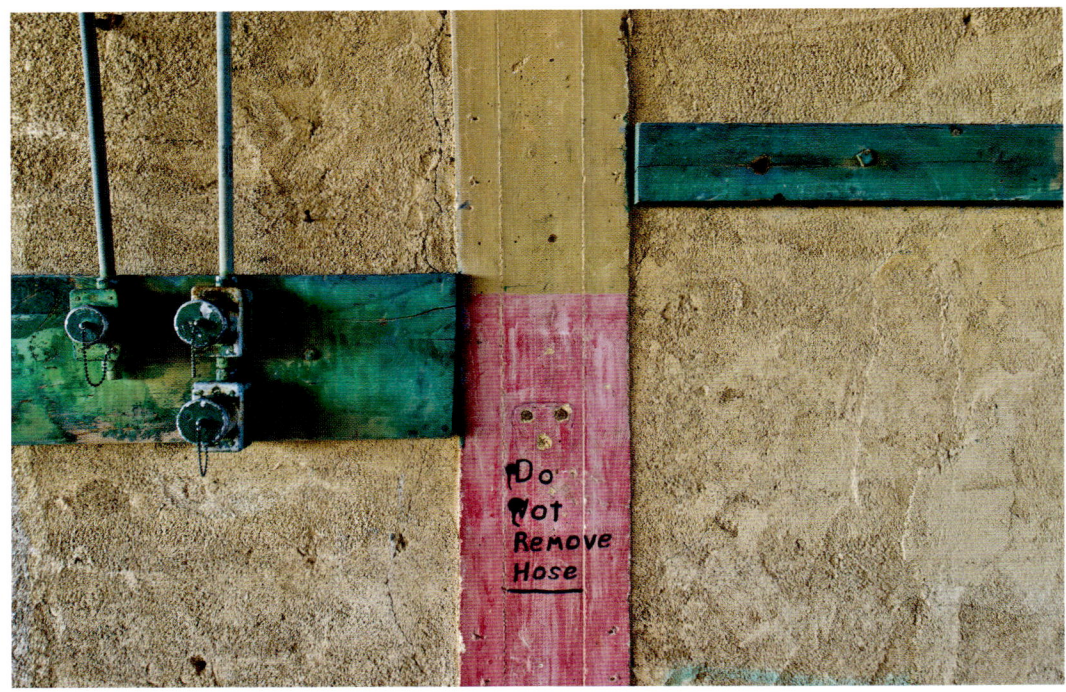

FIGURE 3.9 In this image the strong contrasting colors as well as the negative space work together to create balance. Nikon D800 with Nikon 14–24 mm f/2.8G at 20 mm. 1/60 sec. @ f/6.3 ISO 100

As a general guideline leading lines work best when composed going from left to right; this is due to the fact that most cultures read from left to right, making this a natural path for our brain to lead our eyes.

Another way that leading lines can be used to make a photograph more interesting is by recognizing repeating patterns and using them to create dynamic tension in your image. The human eye is naturally drawn to repeating patterns and this helps to lock in and hold the viewer's attention within the image.

Patterns don't have to be repeating to be used as an effective subject. Random patterns with strong geometric shapes can create a very compelling subject as well, especially when complemented by a relatively sparse background the

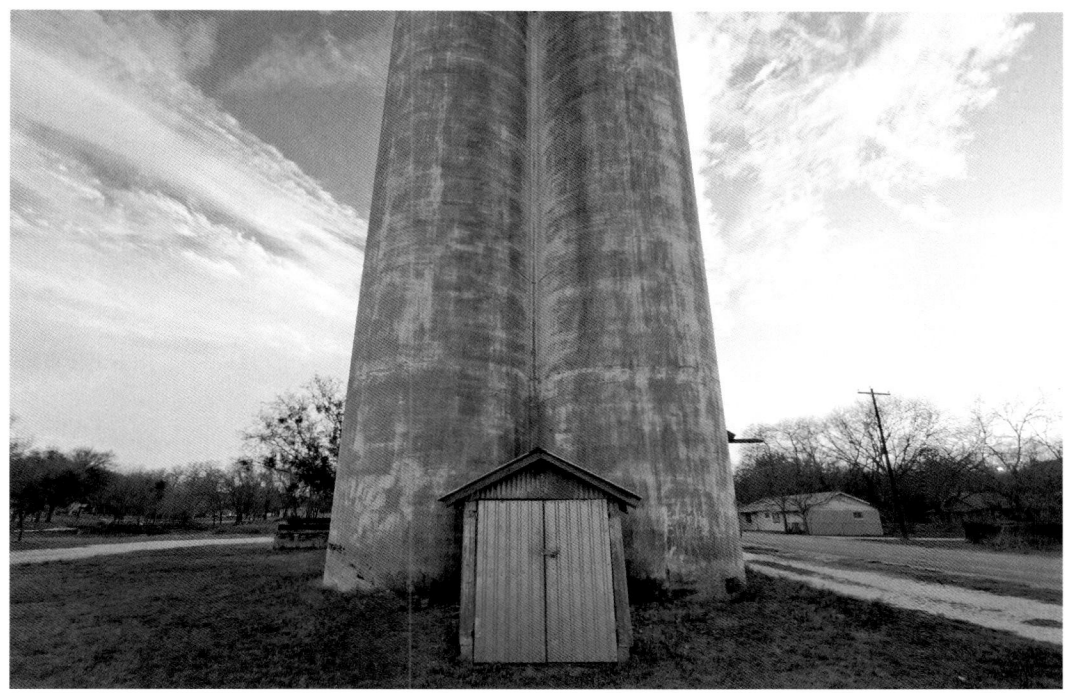

FIGURE 3.10 When placing a subject in the middle of the frame, look for a strong pattern that divides the frame equally. Having a competing element on either side can throw off the balance of a symmetrical subject. **Nikon D200 with Sigma 17–70 mm f/2.8–4 at 70 mm (105 mm equivalent). 1/640 sec. @ f/8 ISO 720**

creates well-defined negative space. The sky usually works well for this.

Textures

Like patterns, textures are another great way to keep the viewer's attention on the image. Textures are created by the surface details of a subject, and can be small or large. Textures create patterns and can help to add dimensionality to the subject; in other words, it can help a two-dimensional photograph appear to be three-dimensional.

Whereas a lot of times photographers search out softer light, textures are best photographed using hard light to really accentuate the shadow and highlight contrast. Using side lighting plays up the detail of a textured subject by casting distinct shadows.

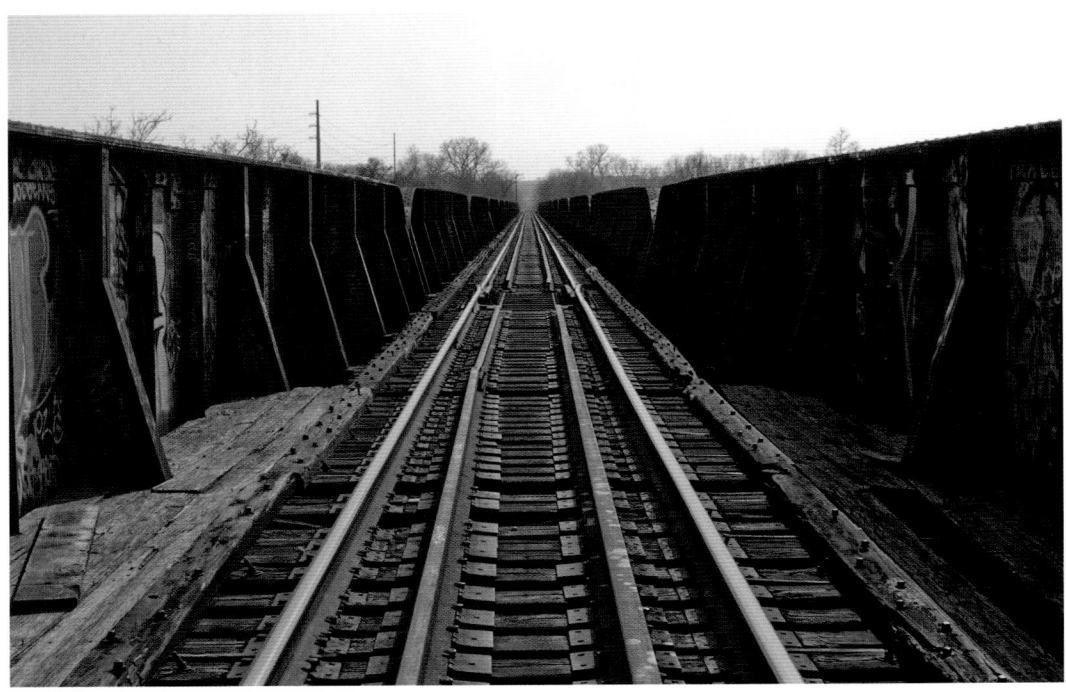

FIGURE 3.11 The strong parallel lines lead your eye up through the image. Railroad tracks are a great place to get started with leading lines.   Nikon D300s with Nikon 35 mm f/1.8G. 1/400 sec. @ f/10 ISO 200

As with patterns, texture can also create interesting leading lines. Some great examples of textures are peeling paint, rust, the grain of an old wooden plank, or dried cracked mud.

Color

The way color is used (or not used) plays a very important role in the composition of photographs as well. Colors can evoke different feelings in viewers. Cool colors such as blues, greens, and purples tend to evoke calm and tranquil feelings, while reds, oranges, and yellows tend to make images more lively or energetic. Converting to black and white can lend your images a loneliness or solemnity, or can evoke a nostalgic feeling. You can also convert to monochrome and leave your images with a color cast such as cyan or sepia (cool and warm, respectively).

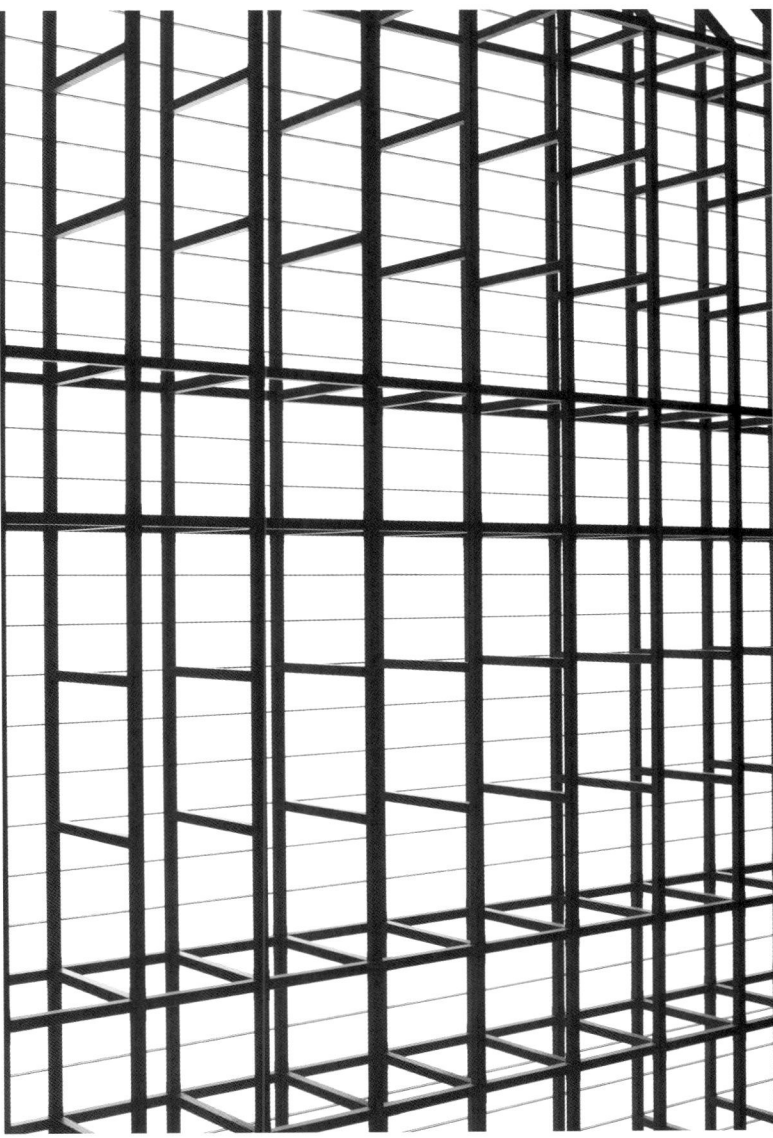

FIGURE 3.12 The roof beams from this roofless warehouse made for a very strong pattern. Nikon D800 with Nikon 14–24 mm f/2.8G at 20 mm. 1/60 sec. @ f/6.3 ISO 100

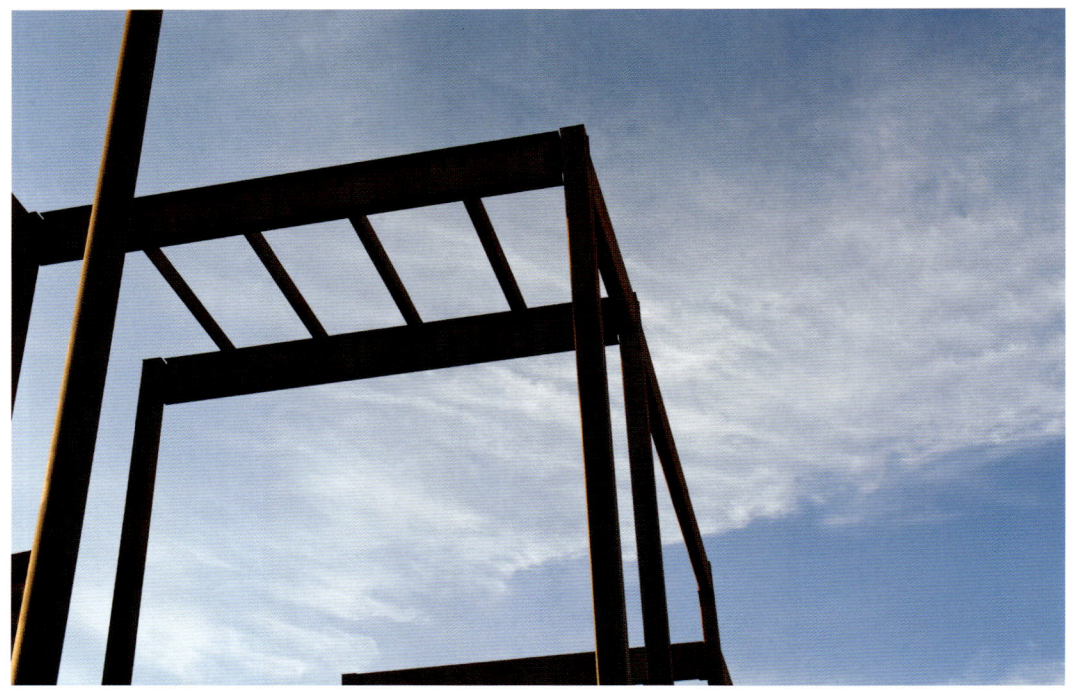

FIGURE 3.13 The rusty structural beams from this abandoned construction project make a strong geometric pattern. **Nikon D800 with Nikon 50 mm f/1. 1/250 sec. @ f/13 ISO 200**

Bold, bright, highly saturated colors can be used to attract the viewer's eye to the image, or to a specific part of the image, or muted subtle tones can be used to evoke a mood or feeling.

Colors can be used in different ways to attract and hold a viewer's attention. For example, you can use a pallette of similar colors, such as an image with nothing but shades of reds, blues, or greens, making your image almost monochromatic. Using *adjacent colors* also works to evoke a specific mood or feeling. Adjacent colors are next to each other on the color wheel (see Figure 3.16).

You can also use *complementary colors* to offset each other to make the image more dynamic. Complementary colors are opposite or near opposites on the color wheel. Complementary colors make each color stand out more; examples of these colors are red/green, yellow/violet, and blue/orange. Strong primary colors also work well together.

Composition and Technique 59

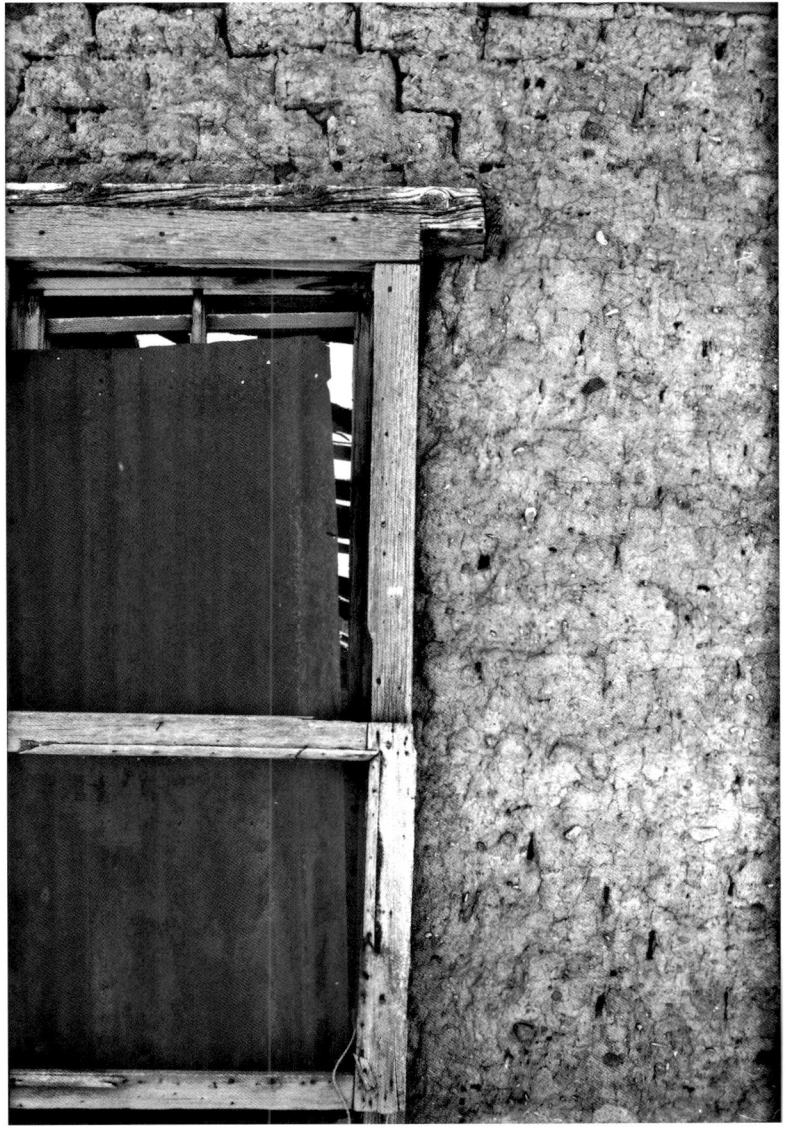

FIGURE 3.14 High-contrast black-and-white images like the one of this old adobe house help to accentuate texture. **Nikon F90X with Nikon 50 mm f/1.8D. 1/125 sec. @ f/16 using Fuji Acros ISO 100 film**

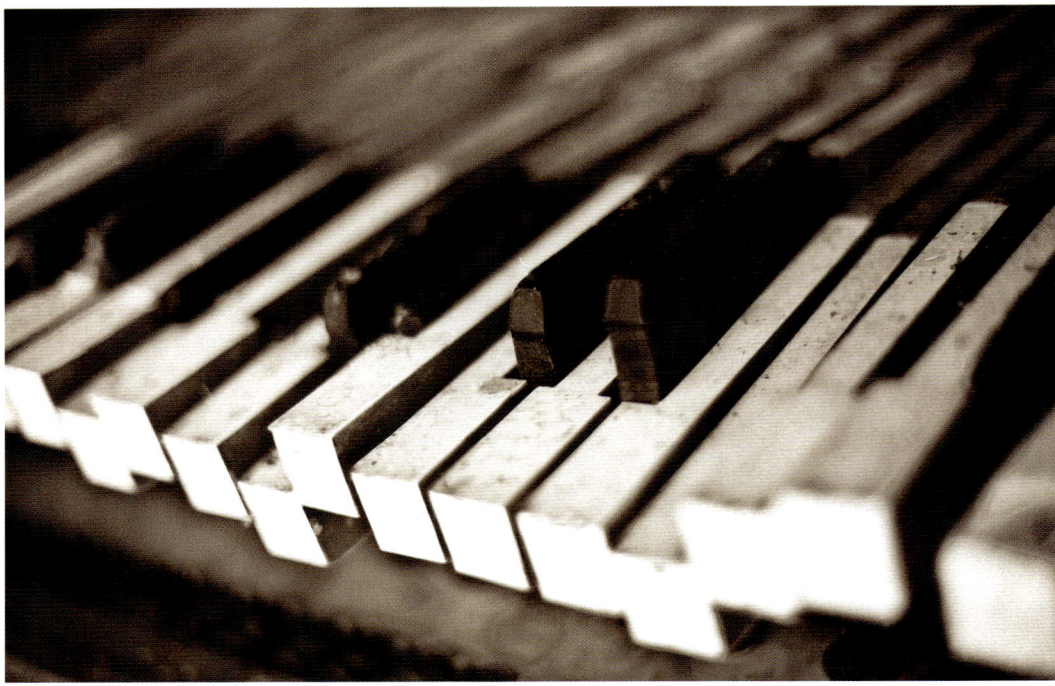

FIGURE 3.15 Adding a sepia tone lends an old-timey nostalgic feel to this broken and discarded piano. Nikon D700 with Nikon 50 mm f/1.4G. 1/160 sec. @ f/1.4 ISO 200

Isolating the subject

A common problem in decay scenes is that there are often many different colors, patterns, textures, and light sources competing with each other for attention. This can make it difficult for the viewer to determine what the most important subject in the scene is. It's the photographer's job when composing the image to try to make it apparent what the subject is and to draw the eye to it. This section deals with some of the different techniques that photographers can implement to make sure the subject stands out in the composition.

There's an acronym that a lot of photography instructors like to use: KISS. This stands for Keep It Simple, Stupid. Kelly Johnson, the lead engineer at Lockheed Martin's "Skunk Works," which designed the spy planes the U-2 and the SR-71, coined this acronym. Johnson wasn't implying that the engineers were stupid, but should be translated more like

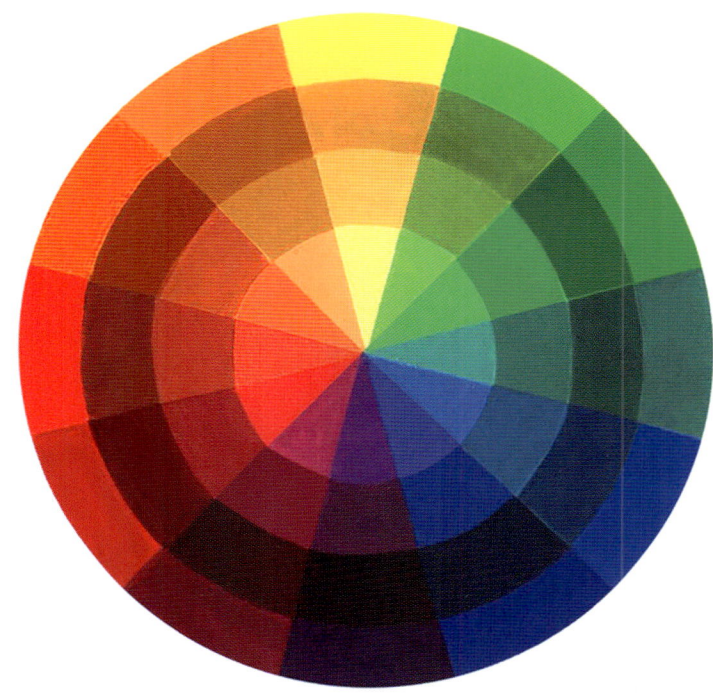

FIGURE 3.16 The color wheel

"keep it simple *and* stupid," implying that a design is much better when it's not too complicated. This is a great design principle to apply to your decay photography (or any photography, really). The simpler the subject the easier it is for the viewer to comprehend the image. Here are a few different tips on how to isolate the subject to simplify the composition.

- **Selective focus.** This is one of the easiest and most artistic ways to isolate your subject. You do this by using a wide aperture to create a shallow depth of field. This allows your subject to be in focus while the background elements fade to an indistinct blur. This is one reason to get a lens with a fast aperture (f/2.8 or better).
- **Fill the frame.** This is another easy trick to do. Simply get close up or zoom in on your main subject. Or pick out one small detail of a larger subject and fill the frame with that. When the subject dominates the frame the viewer easily takes notice.
- **Perspective.** Shoot from an angle that places your subject against a plain background. Oftentimes when outdoors, shooting from down low allows you to use the sky as a background. When indoors, you can sometimes use a wall, ceiling, or floor as a backdrop. Move all around and shoot from many different angles; straight on, from up high, and from down low.
- **Selective lighting.** In low-light environments you can add lighting to the subject to brighten it up and bring it to the forefront of the composition. When using long exposures you can use a flashlight to "paint" light onto the subject. You can also use off-camera flash directed at a subject to make it pop out from the scene. This technique works best when using a relatively slow shutter speed to capture the ambient light as well. You will need a tripod to use these methods.
- **Add something different.** Adding something pretty into a decay photo is a nice twist upon the theme – for example, including flowers into the composition can accentuate the decay while adding a bit of beauty.

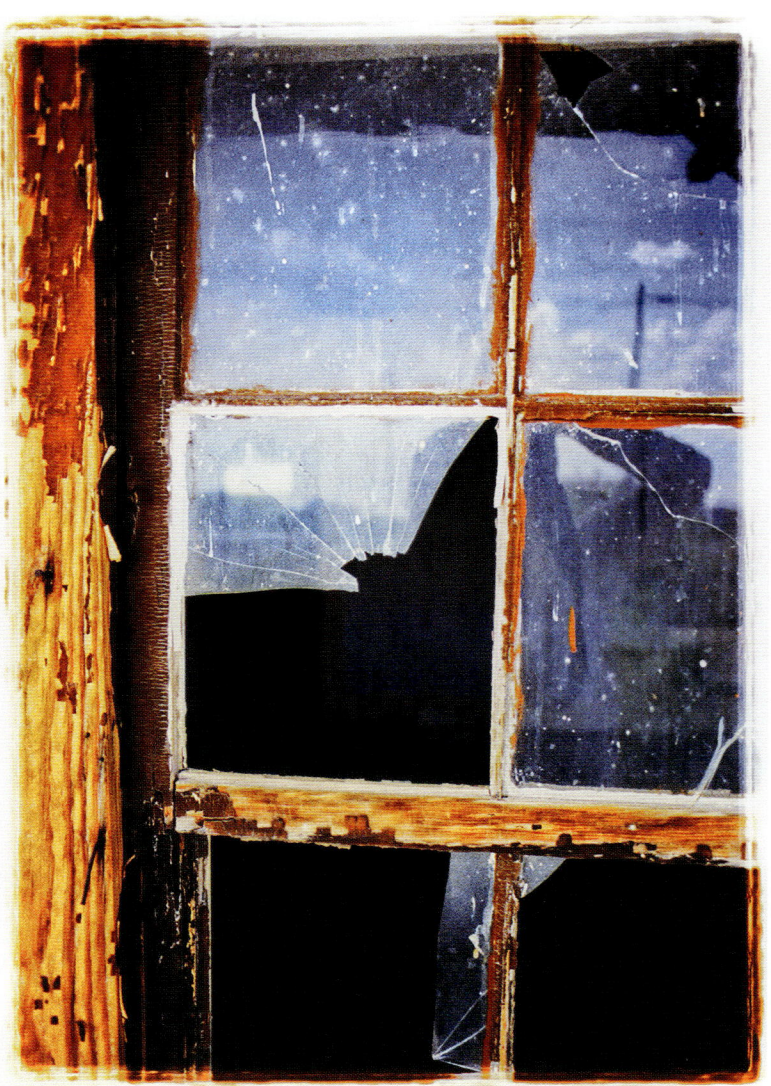

FIGURE 3.17 The strong complementary colors of blue and orange make the image "pop." Pentax K1000 with Pentax 50 mm f/2.8. 1/125 sec. @ f/4 using Kodak Ektar ISO 100 film, scanned from a print on Kodak Endura paper

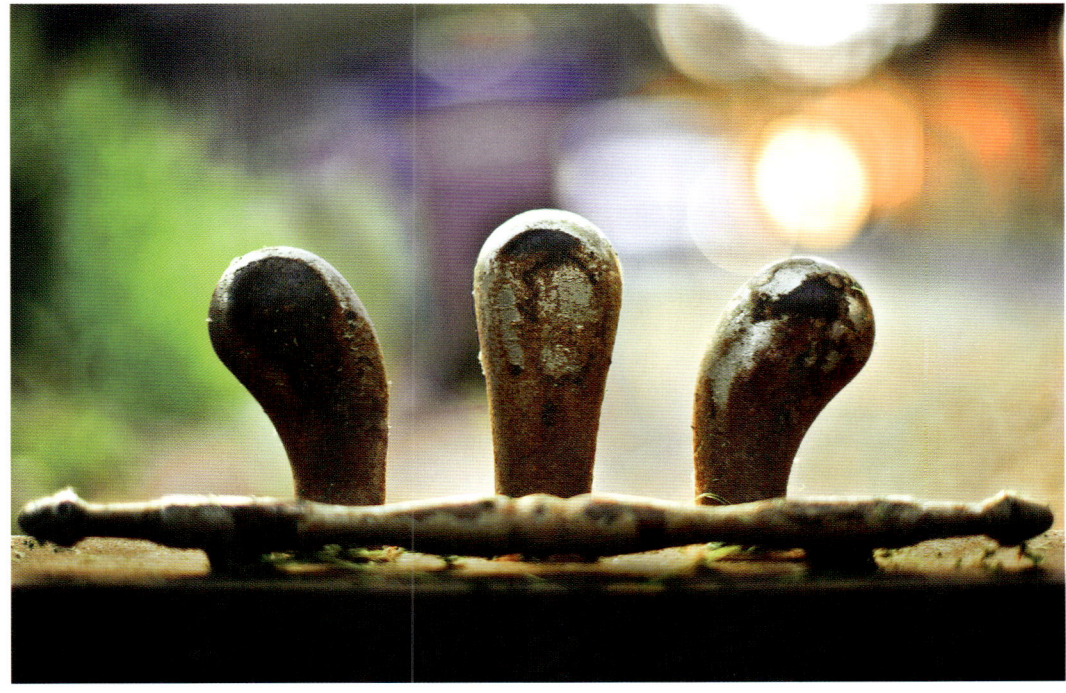

FIGURE 3.18 Detail of piano pedals. Here I used an extremely shallow depth of field to isolate the subject from the background. Nikon D700 with Nikon 50 mm f/1.4G, 1/400 @ f/1.4 ISO 200

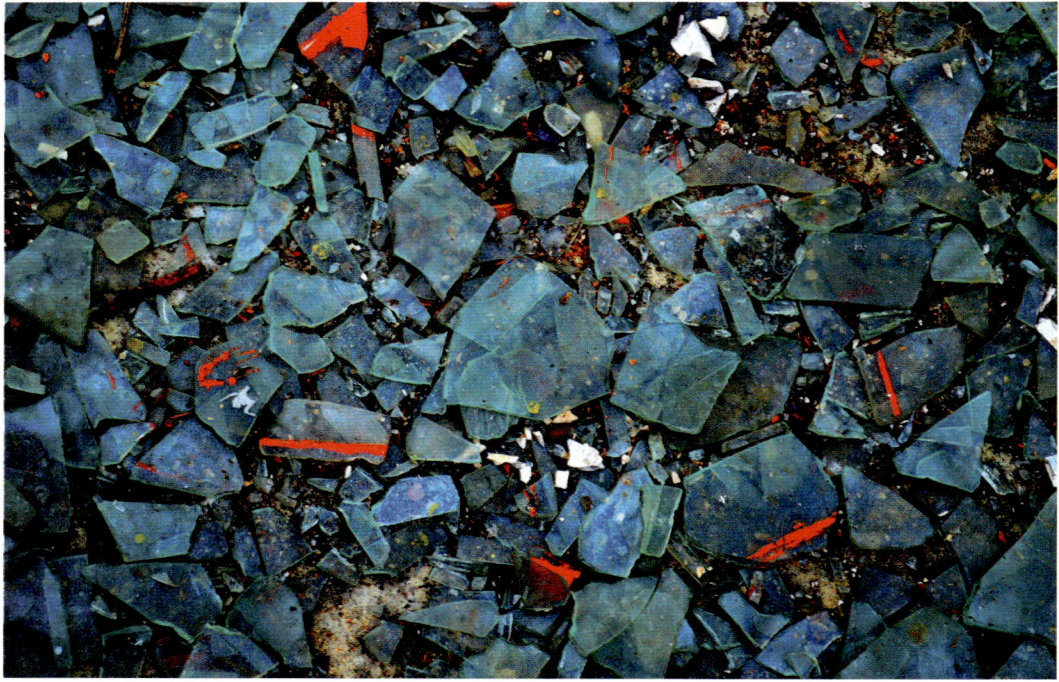

FIGURE 3.19 This image shows that filling the frame is easy and keeps the eye focused in the image. The photographer also notes: "My intentions were to show that there are interesting and beautiful things to look at a lot of the time in places where we don't often look. That beauty can come from chaos. A lot of times when we explore abandoned buildings we pay more attention to the quietness of them and not necessarily the sounds we are creating. As I was exploring these buildings I kept hearing a crunching noise I was making by stepping on the broken glass. So I looked down and saw this beautiful mosaic with all these colors and shapes and textures and lines. So I decided to capture that. I use more of the presets in case I have to get out of somewhere quickly." Nikon D3200 with Nikon 18–55 mm f/3.5–5.6G. 1/100 @ f/5.6 ISO 360 −1EV. © Chris Shipton

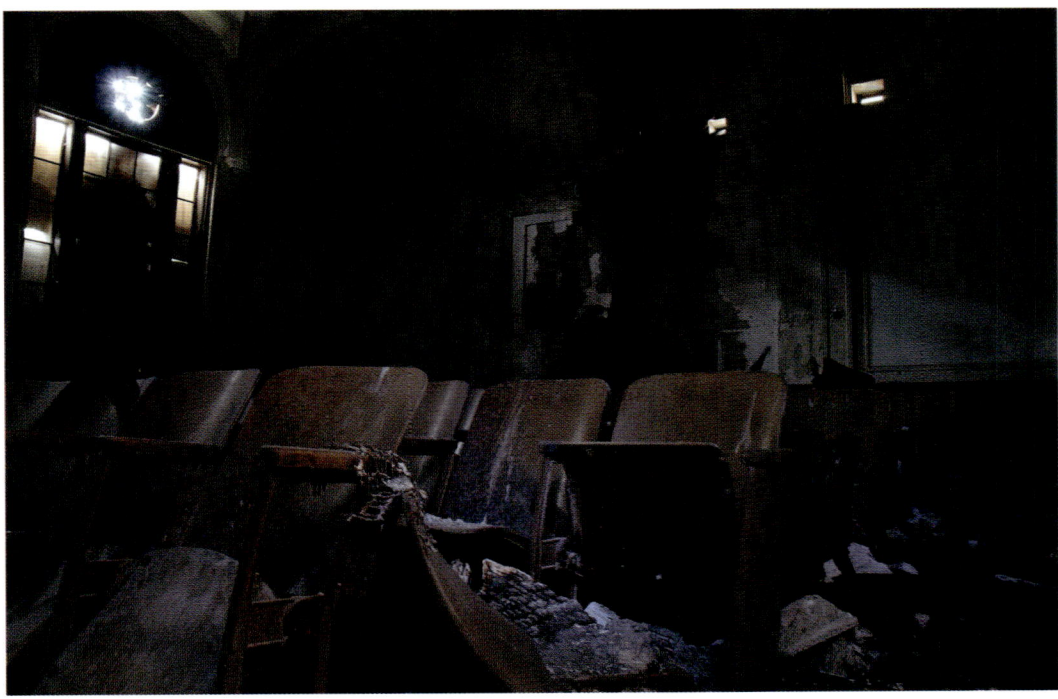

FIGURE 3.20 Light painting was used to illuminate the seats to separate them from the background. Sony a300 with lens, 30 sec @ f/8 ISO 200. © Chris Folsom

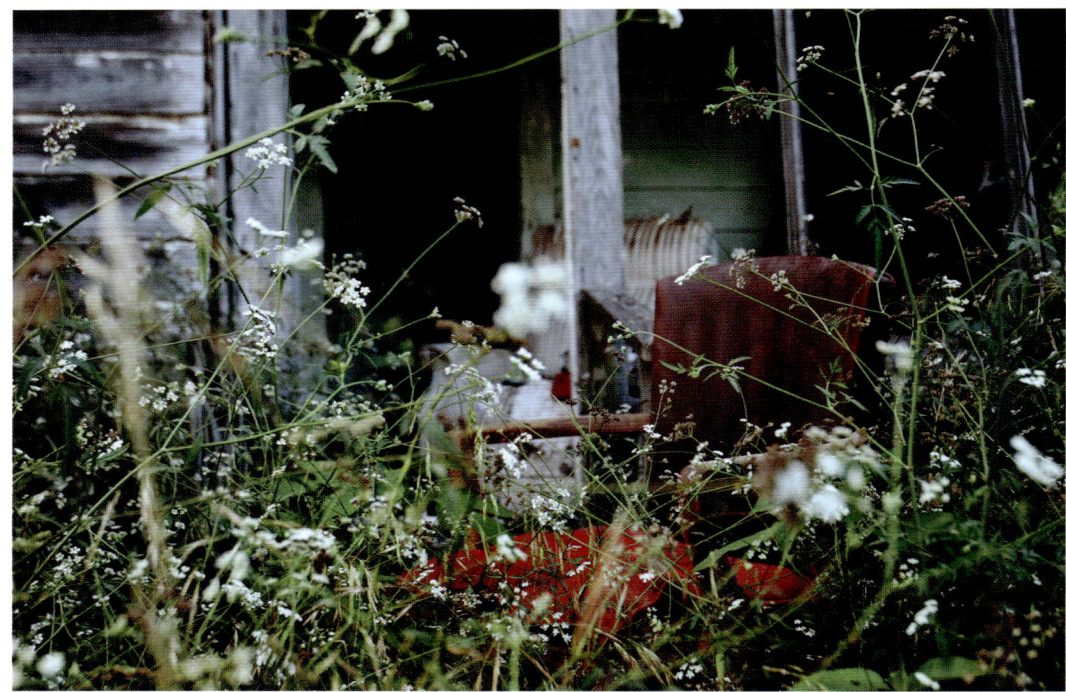

FIGURE 3.21 Decay photography doesn't necessarily have to be ugly. The flowering weeds in this image help to lend softness and serenity to an otherwise bleak scene. Nikon D200 with 18–70 mm at 34 mm (51 mm equivalent) f/3.5–4.5. 1/100 sec @ f/4 ISO 200. © Julian Humphries

Using angles to create interest

While having a nice straight horizon line often works best for a lot of images, sometimes adding a tilt to the scene helps to add mystery and tension. This technique was used a lot in the 1940s and 1950s in film noir. It's often referred to as the "Dutch angle" (a derivation of Deutsch angle because it was invented by German filmmakers in the 1930s). Adding a tilt to the scene causes the viewer to feel uneasy, which is a great effect when portraying an eerie decay scene.

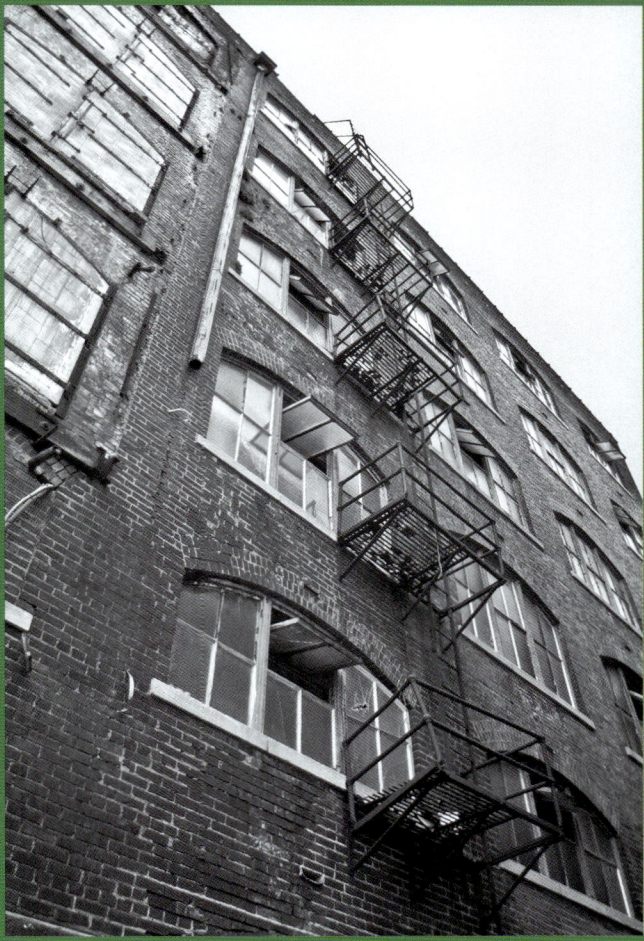

FIGURE 3.22 The Dutch angle gives this image a film noir feeling and creates tension in the image. **Nikon D70 with Tokina 19–35 mm f/3.5–4.5 at 20 mm (30 mm equivalent) 1/125 @ f/4 ISO 200**

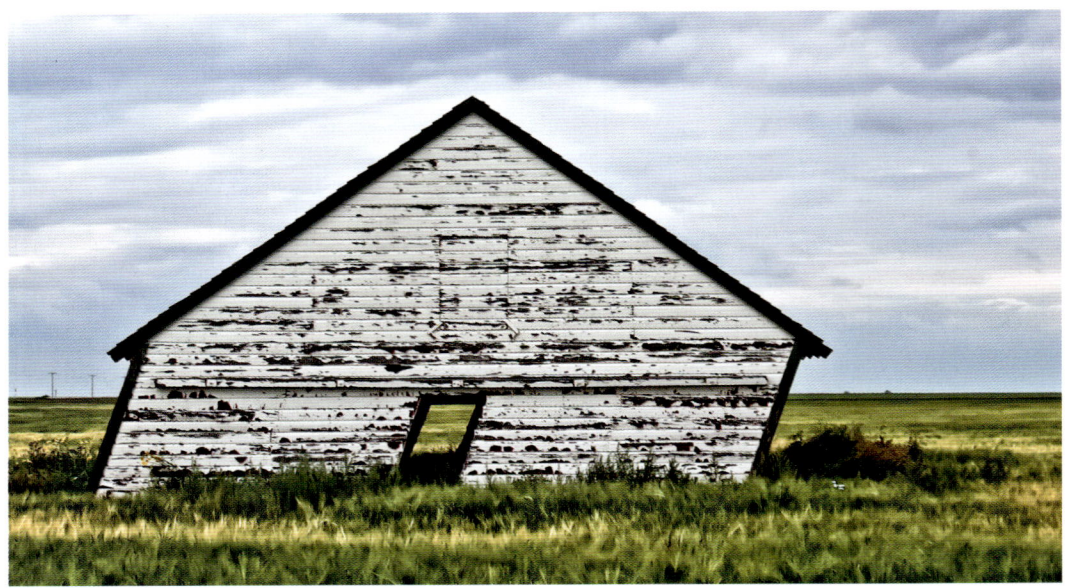

FIGURE 3.23 This is a great use of an interesting angle. The straight horizon and the perfect leaning building instantly catch your eye and hold your attention. Nikon D40 with 18–55 mm f/3.5–5.6 at 42 mm (63 mm equivalent) 1/400 @ f/10 ISO 200. © Scott Moodie

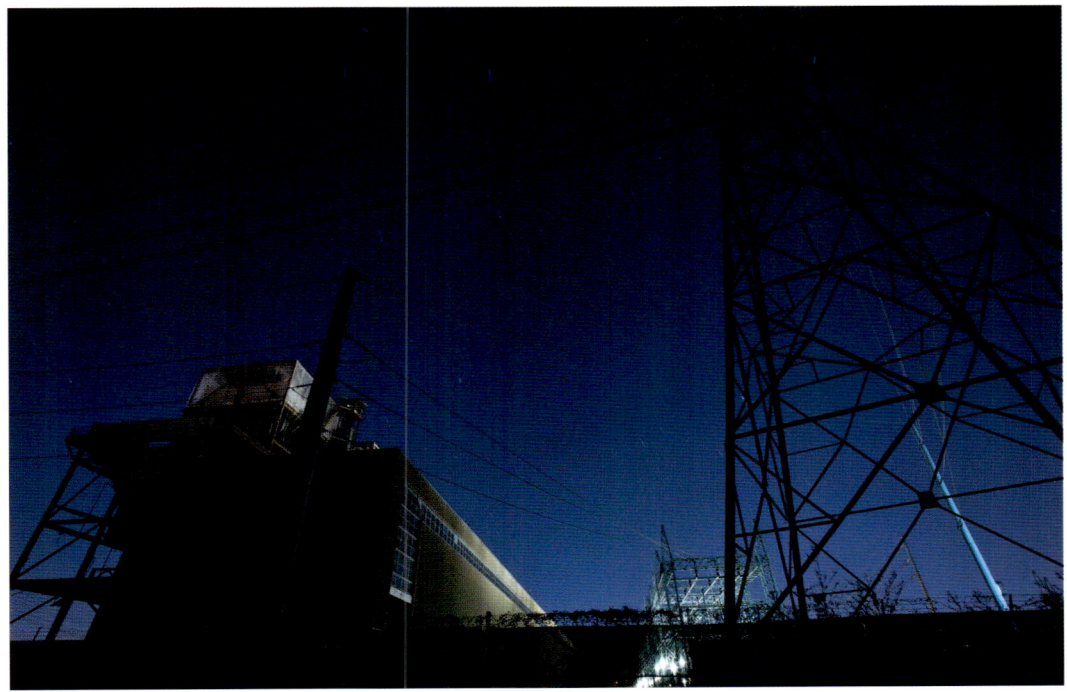

FIGURE 3.24 In this shot of the disused City of Austin Power Plant I used lines, angles, and the contrast between light and dark to give the image depth and texture. This building has been gutted and is currently being transformed into high-end condos. Nikon D700 with 14–24 mm f/2.8G at 1/80 @ f/2.8 ISO 3200

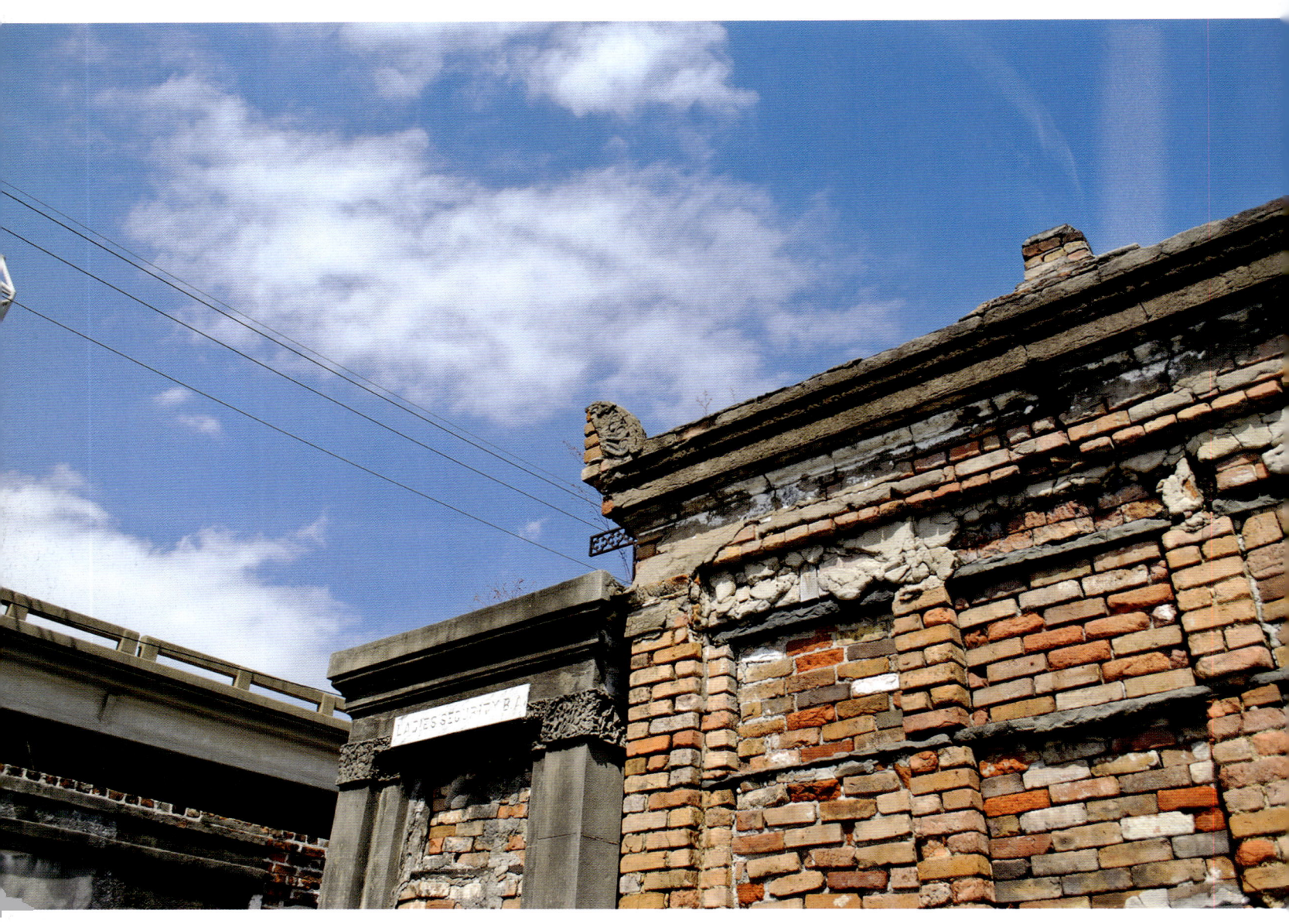

__Four__

SHOOTING DIGITAL

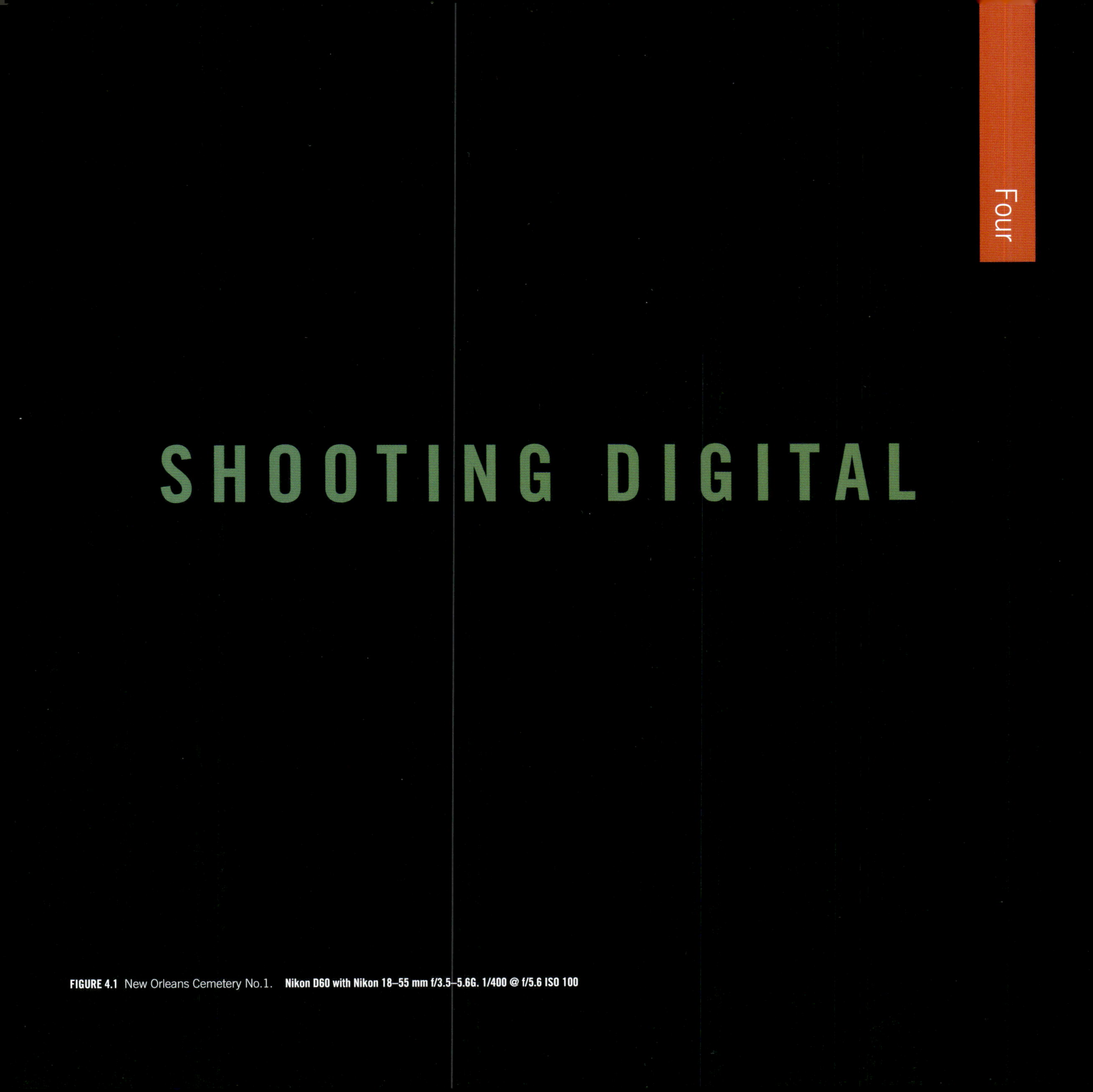

FIGURE 4.1 New Orleans Cemetery No.1. **Nikon D60 with Nikon 18–55 mm f/3.5–5.6G. 1/400 @ f/5.6 ISO 100**

Just a little over ten years ago, digital photography was a pretty new and relatively expensive format. These days it's possible to get a great-performing DSLR for well under $1,000. The image quality of these new cameras improves by leaps and bounds year after year. Image resolution and signal-to-noise ratios are reaching new heights very quickly. The result is that photographers now have access to extremely high-quality cameras, lenses, and accessories at a cost that would have been unthinkably low just a decade ago.

Digital photography offers quite a few benefits to film photography, such as instant review, instantly adjustable ISO settings, histograms, and more. But there are also some drawbacks, such as reduced dynamic range, which makes shooting digitally a little different than traditional film capture.

Of course, this is the digital age, and most photographers these days are using digital cameras to create images of the world around them, and this includes decay photographers. The reality is that digital photography is a much more convenient medium to work with than film.

In this chapter I cover some of the nuances to capturing an image digitally.

Sensors

Digital cameras use a sensor to capture and record light in order to make an image. There are very complex workings going on in the camera and, although it's not necessary to know how the sensor works in detail; knowing a little bit about how the sensor works can help you with understanding how the sensor affects exposure.

There are two different types of sensors used in modern digital cameras: CCD and CMOS. CCD stands for charge coupled device; CMOS is an acronym for complementary

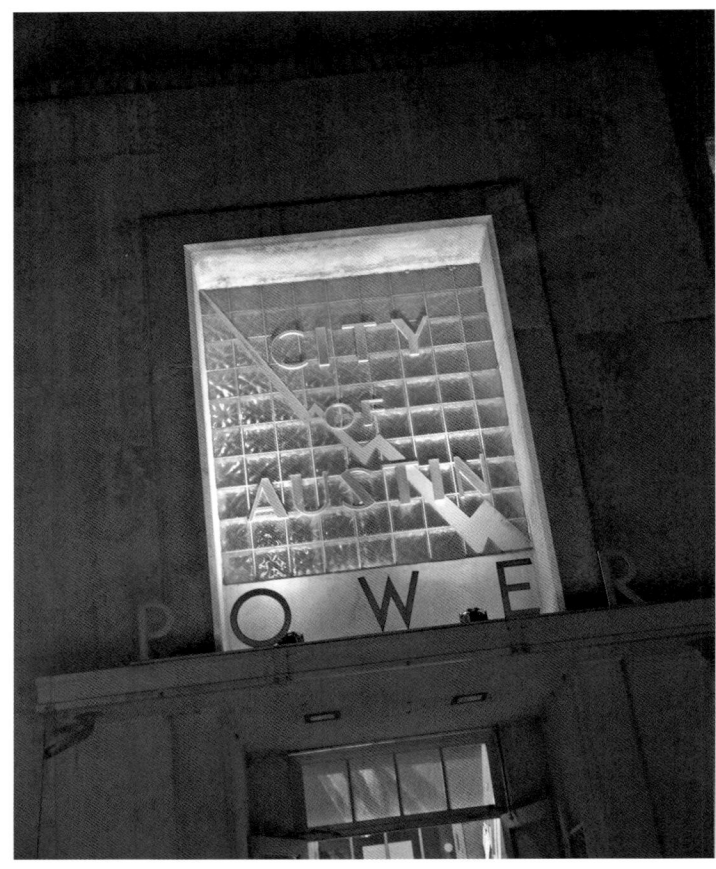

FIGURE 4.2 This shot was taken during Austin Psych Fest, one of the last events held at the abandoned City of Austin Power Plant. The illumination of the glass block windows and the darkness of the surrounding area made for a difficult exposure. In post-processing I brought detail back into the extremely dark areas, which made for a very noisy image. Converting the image to black and white allowed me to make the image usable by making the noise less obvious.   **Nikon D5100 with Sigma 17–70 mm f/2.8–4 HSM OS at 32 mm (48 mm equivalent) 1/30 @ f/3.5 ISO 1600**

metal-oxide semiconductor. Both of these types of imaging sensors do the same job; they collect photons and turn them into electrons, changing an electric charge to voltage, allowing the voltage readings to be used to determine the intensity of light so that the information can be used to create an image.

CCD technology was used in most cameras prior to 2007. CCD sensors have lower inherent noise than the CMOS sensors because all of the circuitry to record light is off the chip, allowing the whole pixel to be used to collect light; however, they are slower due to the way the charge-to-voltage conversion is handled and they also consume a lot more power. CMOS sensors have a lower signal-to-noise ratio (more noise) than CCDs, but the circuitry to do the charge-to-voltage conversion is right in the chip next to the pixel. Theoretically this makes the CMOS more susceptible to noise, but in practice the difference is unnoticeable in this day and age due to advanced image processing technology. Since the charge-to-voltage conversion is done right on the sensor, the information can be processed more quickly and the power consumption of a CMOS sensor is much lower, resulting in greater battery life for the camera. CMOS sensors are standard in most current DSLR cameras.

Analog to digital

A sensor is covered with millions of *pixels* (short for picture elements). Each of these pixels acts as a sort of bucket that collects photons. When you press the shutter release button the sensor is exposed to light; the pixels collect the photons, and once the shutter is closed the photons are converted into an electrical charge. The electrical charge or voltage is sent to an analog-to-digital converter, more commonly known as an A/D converter, which then reads the voltages of each pixel (all assigned separate X and Y positions) and determines the intensity of the light. Higher voltages result in the pixel being

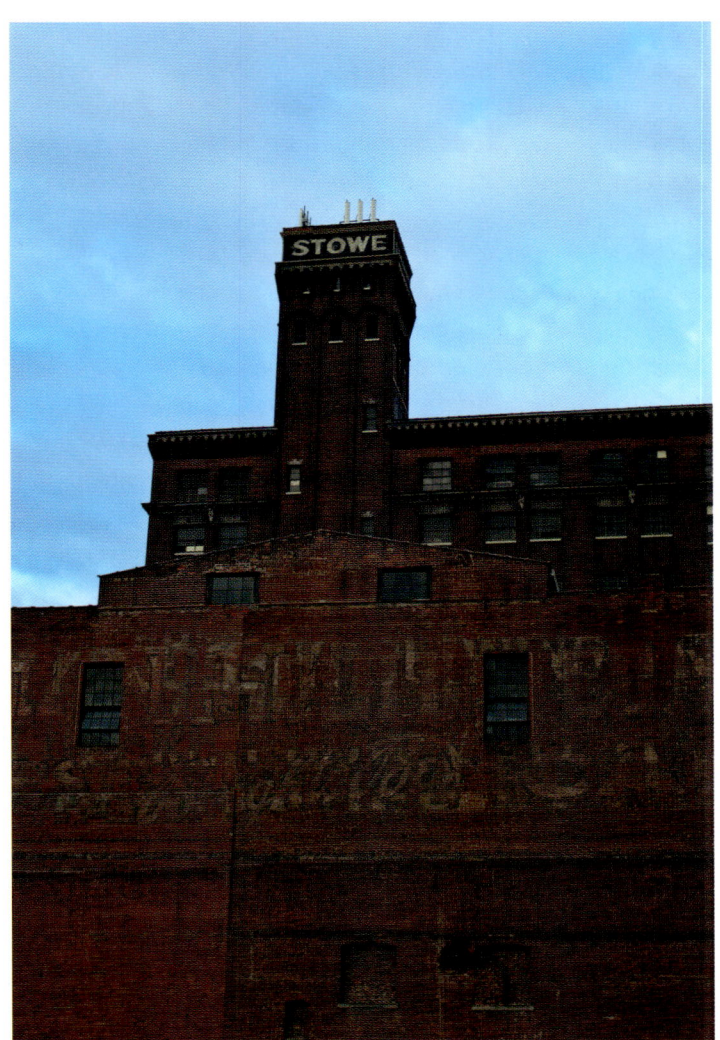

FIGURE 4.3 The Nikon D70 was Nikon's first DLSR under $1,000. It had a 6 mega-pixel CMOS sensor. **Nikon D70 with Tokina 19–35 mm f/3.5–4.5 at 35 mm (52 mm equivalent) 1/200 @ f/4.5 ISO 200**

assigned a brighter luminosity value; lower voltages mean a lower luminosity is assigned. The voltage information is turned into a binary number by the A/D converter and recorded as digital information to the memory card. Attached to these files is other image information (metadata) such as white balance, color settings, etc.

If a camera had a plain sensor, it would only be able to read the information from the A/D converter as a monochrome image. In order to get a color image the sensor is overlaid with a filter that consists of red, green, and blue elements that cover each pixel with rows that alternate between red/green and blue/green filters. This is called the Bayer array, after Eastman Kodak scientist Bryce E. Bayer. This filter allows only red, green, or blue light to be collected by any given pixel. The Bayer filter array uses twice as many green filters as red and blue to more accurately portray color as a human eye would see it, since the human eye is more sensitive to green light. Using this color information the camera uses a process called *demosaicing* to interpret the color data. Using complex algorithms the camera processors determine the correct colors for each pixel, resulting in a full-color image.

If our pixels act like buckets to collect light, just like filling a bucket of water, these pixels can get filled up and overflow. When that happens the pixel is recorded as absolute white, resulting in no detail being recorded. This is what happens when you overexpose an image. At the opposite end of the spectrum, if the sensor isn't exposed to light for a long enough time the pixels won't gather enough photons, which results in a dark or underexposed image.

Resolution

As I mentioned earlier, each camera sensor is covered with pixels. A camera's resolution is measured in *megapixels* (MPs).

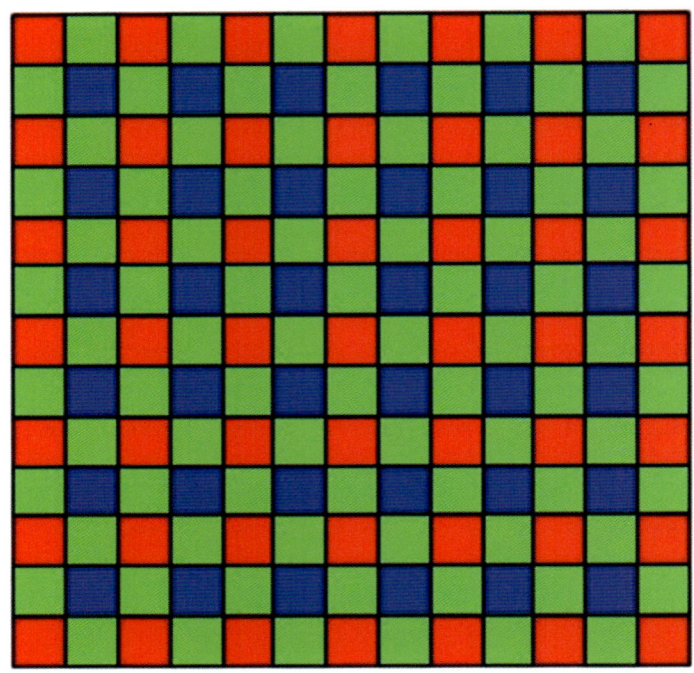

FIGURE 4.4 The Bayer array pattern

One megapixel is equal to one million pixels. Counting each pixel on the X-axis (horizontal) and the Y-axis (vertical) and multiplying the number determines the sensor's resolution. For example, a sensor that has 6,000 pixels on the X-axis and 4,000 pixels on the Y-axis has 24 million pixels or 24 megapixels.

The more pixels a sensor has, the higher the resolution is. In theory, higher resolution sensors allow you to capture more fine detail than sensors with lower megapixel counts. You'll notice I say in theory – that's because the number of pixels on a sensor is only one aspect that affects actual resolution.

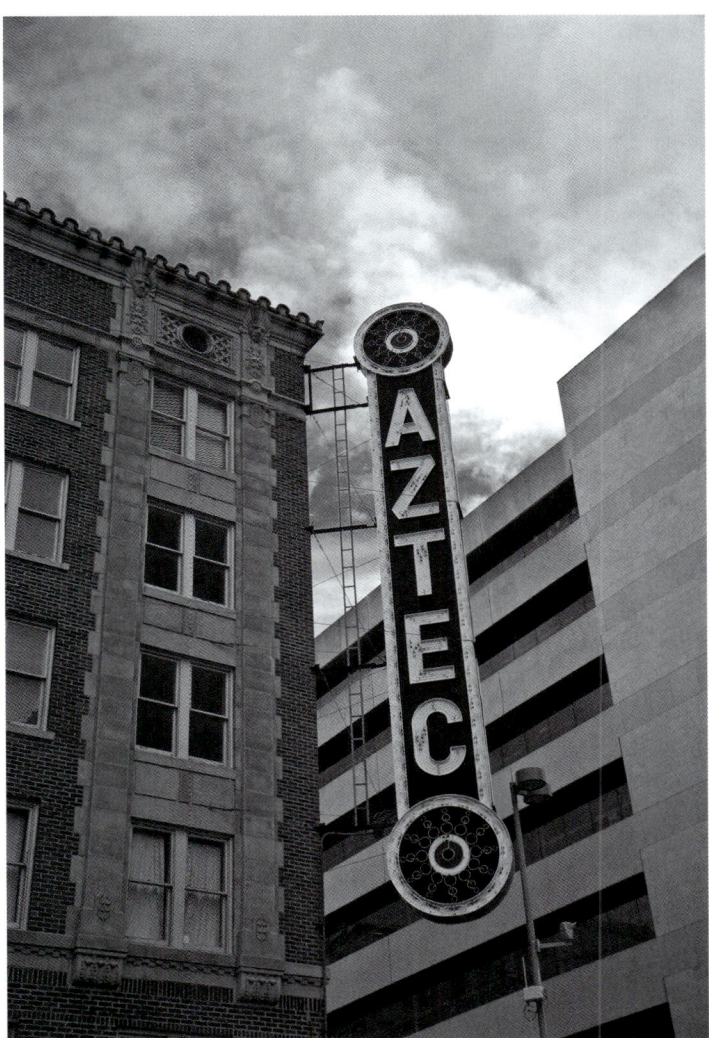

FIGURE 4.5 The 12MP D300s is 1/3 the resolution of the 36MP Nikon D800. When posting to the web or printing sizes not exceeding 8" × 10" the difference is not as apparent as one would expect. The D300, which is considered "old" by today's standards in digital photography, is a well-built professional camera that will give sharp detail to your images, as you can see in this photo of the Aztec Theater in downtown San Antonio, TX. Nikon D300 with Sigma 17–70 mm f/2.8–4 HSM OS at 32 mm (48 mm equivalent) 1/640 @ f/3.5 ISO 200

The truth is that camera manufacturers have been using MPs as a selling point for cameras for years. Actual resolution of fine detail depends on a few factors: the number of MPs, sensor size, and pixel size. More MPs doesn't necessarily mean that a camera is better. The biggest effect on resolution is sensor size. A larger sensor can hold more pixels while keeping them large enough that they are still effective at capturing light. Smaller pixels have more difficulty effectively capturing photons; therefore a small sensor actually provides less detail than a larger sensor with the same amount of pixels. Smaller pixels also mean that each individual pixel can hold fewer photons, which leads to blown-out highlights. That is why an 8MP camera phone doesn't provide an image comparable to that of an image taken with an 8MP camera. The point is that in order to take great decay photographs you don't necessarily need the newest camera with the most MPs. A camera with a modest 6MPs is absolutely capable of creating great images, which is something to consider when looking at purchasing a camera for urban decay photography. Determine what your outputs needs are likely to be before buying the latest high-megapixel camera.

Tip: Consider buying an inexpensive lower resolution second-hand camera for shooting in inclement weather or dirty and dusty conditions.

Most compact digital cameras also have sensors that are a fraction of the size of a DSLR camera, which is one of the reasons most photography enthusiasts prefer DSLRs to the smaller compact digital cameras. In the past few years camera manufacturers have taken notice of this and most major companies are addressing this issue by releasing compact cameras with larger sensors, such as the Olympus PEN, Nikon 1 series, and the Canon M series.

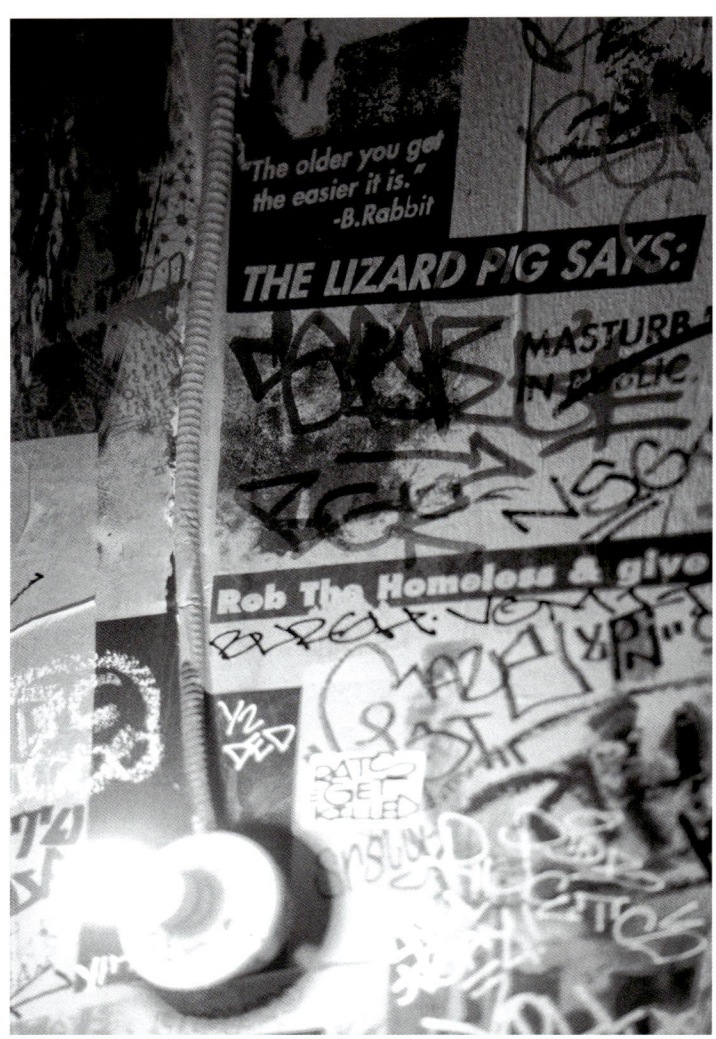

FIGURE 4.6 5MP iPhone image

Dynamic range

Dynamic range is the amount of luminosity that a camera sensor can record. The rule of thumb is that the bit depth of the camera's A/D converter is the amount of dynamic range the camera can capture. Most cameras use anywhere between a 10-bit to 14-bit A/D converter, so on paper your camera sensor should be able to record a 10–14-stop difference in brightness. In actuality, however, about 6–10 stops is the maximum tonal range you'll get from a typical digital camera, whereas film can easily resolve up to 15 stops.

Dynamic range is important in decay photography because you will often run into situations where you will have a huge amount of dynamic range. Obviously, if your camera can capture more dynamic range you will see a better reproduction of the scene you are photographing. The differences between the degree of tonal change of light and color will be much more subtle, resulting in smoother transitions. Knowing how your camera deals with dynamic range can help you to know what kind of situations your camera excels at and what kind of situations to avoid. For example, if your camera doesn't have the ability to handle a wide dynamic range, you may want to photograph the shady side of a building as opposed to the side that is brightly lit by the noon sun, which has a very high contrast ratio.

Cross-reference: Using digital imaging allows you to combine images with different exposures to increase the dynamic range of your photograph. This is known as high dynamic range (HDR). This is covered in depth in Chapter 7.

Exposure

In photographic terms, an exposure is the amount of light that is captured during a single shutter cycle. An exposure is made up of three different elements that are all interrelated: aperture, shutter speed, and ISO sensitivity. Although the numbering system of each of these is different, each change in a setting is known as a "stop." Most cameras allow each setting to be changed in increments of one-third stops for more accurate control of exposure settings. As the value of one is changed, the value of another must be changed proportionately to keep an equivalent exposure. For example, a typical exposure for taking a photo during a sunny day is 1/125 @ f/16 ISO 100, but maybe you wanted to use a wider aperture of f/4 for a shallow depth of field for selective focus; that's a difference of four stops. In order to get an equivalent exposure, you need to either use a faster shutter speed or decrease the ISO sensitivity setting. At ISO 100 you're at the lowest setting – therefore you need to use a faster shutter speed. Using a shutter speed of 1/2000 gives you the same exposure, but allows you to use the wider aperture setting to get the effect you desire.

The main goal in any type of photography is to get the correct exposure, or just the right amount of light to the sensor so that the image recorded isn't too bright or too dark. You want to try to keep detail in both the highlight and shadow areas. In addition to that, there is a very important secondary goal; getting the right exposure settings for the image. The key to that is selecting the perfect combination of settings to achieve a specific goal, such as balancing a small aperture with a slow shutter speed and a low ISO setting to get an image with low noise and a deep depth of field, or sacrificing image quality by using a high ISO, or depth of field by using a wide aperture to get a fast shutter speed so you can handhold an image while keeping it free of blur caused by camera shake. These are the types of things that must go through your mind every time you are about to press the shutter release button.

One thing I want to point out is that the principles of exposure are the same whether you're shooting digitally or using film.

Aperture

The aperture, also known as the f/stop (these two terms are interchangeable), is the opening within the lens that controls how much light enters the camera. All lenses have a diaphragm which functions similar to the iris of your eye; it opens wider to let more light in and closes to reduce the amount of light. In the vernacular of a photographer, *"opening up"* refers to making the aperture wider and *"stopping down"* refers to making the aperture smaller.

Apertures are referred to by f/numbers. Smaller numbers denote a wide or large opening and larger numbers denote a narrow or small opening. To some, especially beginning photographers, this seems completely counter-intuitive and can lead to some confusion. It only begins to make sense when explained in more detail.

The first thing you should know is that f/numbers are actually ratios, which translate into fractions. The number of the f/stop is determined by dividing the diameter of the lens opening by the focal length of the lens. The easiest way to think about it is to put a one on top of the f/number and make a fraction out of it. As an example, let's use a Zeiss 50 mm f/2 lens. Take the aperture number of f/2 and turn it into a fraction with 1 as the numerator; this comes out to 1/2. This indicates that the aperture opening is half the diameter of the focal length, which equals 25 mm. At f/4 the diameter of the aperture diaphragm is 12.5 mm. So in effect, 1/2 or f/2 is a larger number than is 1/16 or f/16. This is why the smaller

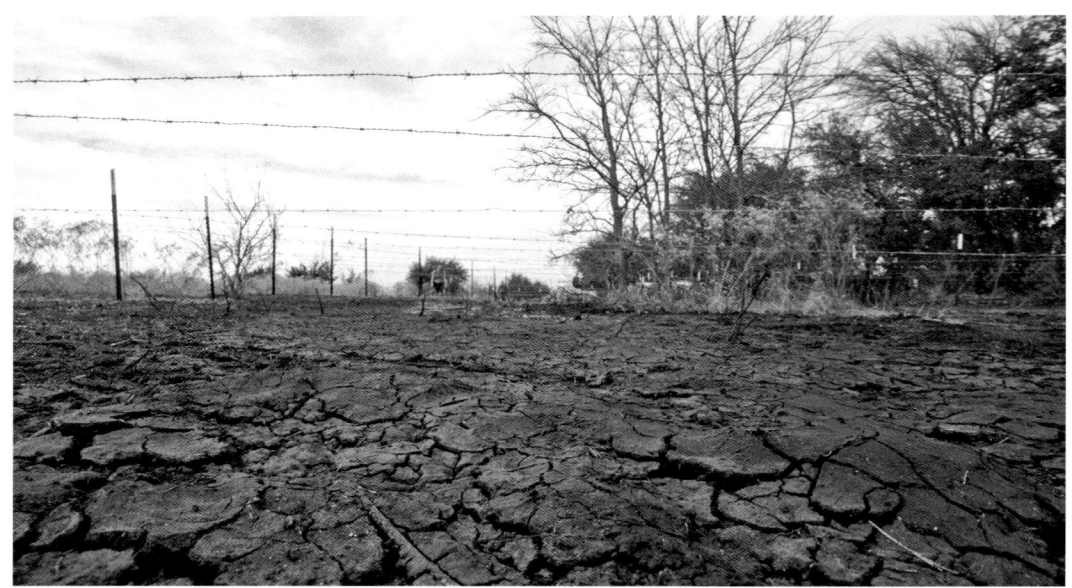

FIGURE 4.7 I used a small aperture to increase the depth of field in this image to allow the barbed wire in the background to be visible and in focus.   Nikon D600 with Sigma 17–35 mm f/2.8–4 HSM at 17 mm 1/40 @ f/16 ISO 100

numbers are larger openings and the larger numbers are smaller openings.

The most common f/numbers (in one-stop increments) are: 1.4, 2, 2.8, 4, 5.6, 8, 11, 16, and 22. At first glance these look like a random array of numbers, but looking a little closer you see that every other number is a multiple of 2. Although not obvious, if you break it down even further you will discover that each number is actually a factor of 1.4: 1.4 multiplied by 2 is 2.8, multiply 2.8 by 1.4 and you get 4 (rounded up from 3.92), 4 times 1.4 is equal to 5.6, and so on.

In photography the aperture or f/stop has two functions that are not mutually exclusive, but are tied together. Wide apertures not only let in more light, but they also decrease the depth of field so that the background may be out of focus. At the opposite end, using a smaller aperture increases the depth of field, resulting in an image that has a background that is in sharp focus.

Each of the elements of this double-edged sword can be used effectively in decay photography. You can use a wide aperture to focus on a particular subject while letting the background go out of focus so as to not be distracting, or you can use a small aperture to create depth in the scene and to be sure that multiple subjects that are at different distances are all in sharp focus.

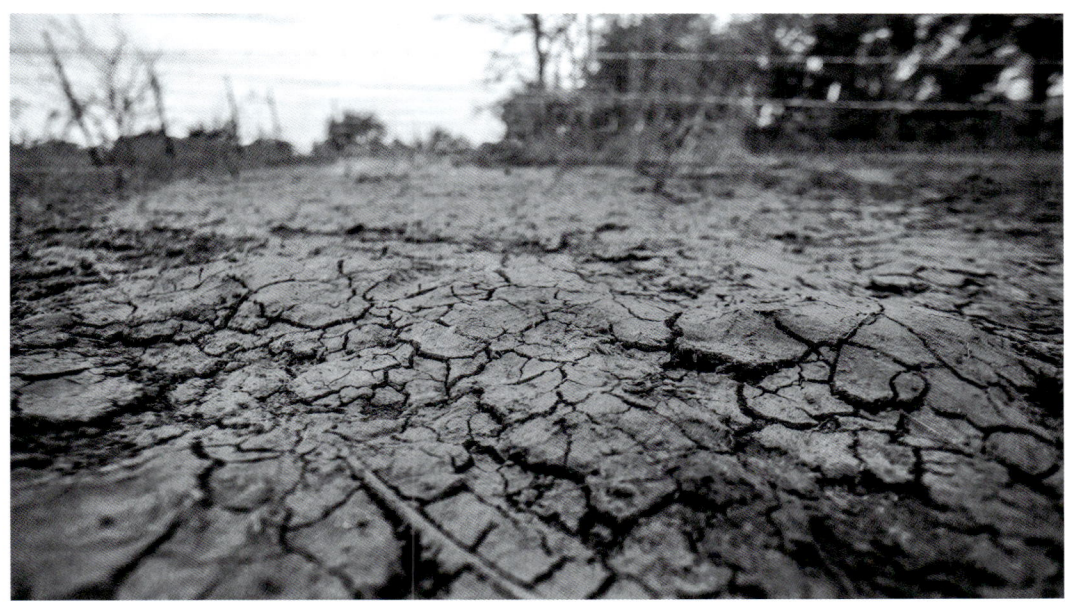

FIGURE 4.8 I used a wide aperture to decrease the depth of field in this image to blur the background and draw attention to the drying and cracked mud in the foreground. **Nikon D600 with Sigma 17–35 mm f/2.8–4 HSM at 17 mm 1/40 @ f/16 ISO 100**

Depth of field

The technical definition of depth of field, often referred to as DoF, is the distance range in a photograph in which all portions of the image are acceptably sharp. By focusing the lens on a certain point, everything in the image on the same horizontal plane is in focus as well. Everything in front of and behind that point (known as the plane of focus) is technically not in focus, *but* our vision isn't keen enough to perceive the minor amount of blurring that occurs and it still appears to our eyes as sharp. This is what photographers call *the zone of acceptable sharpness* or more commonly depth of field.

The zone of acceptable sharpness is based upon a concept known as *the circle of confusion*. The circle of confusion is the largest blurred circle that appears to the human eye to be acceptably sharp. Factors that contribute to the size of the circle of confusion are visual acuity, viewing distance, and the size of the image. A circle of confusion is formed when light passes through the body and opening of a lens. Changing the size of the circle of confusion is as simple as opening up or stopping down the aperture. Open up the aperture and you get a large circle of confusion, which translates into an image with a shallow depth of field and more out-of-focus areas. Stopping down the aperture creates smaller circles of confusion, which results in the depth of field being increased and more of the image being in focus.

Depth of field is mainly determined by aperture size, but is also greatly influenced by subject and focus distance. The closer you focus on your subject the shallower the depth of field is at any given aperture. For example, focusing on a person 12 feet away using an aperture of f/16 results in a photo where everything is sharp from foreground to background; but focus on a smaller subject just 12 inches away at f/16 and you will have a shallow depth of field.

A third element in depth of field is focal length. Shorter focal length lenses have deeper depth of field at the same focus distance as longer focal length lenses.

Shutter speed

The shutter speed, quite simply, is the amount of time that your camera's sensor is exposed to light. Most cameras have the ability to control the shutter speed from a very slow 30 seconds to a lightning fast 1/8000 of a second, and are usually able to be set in one-third stops. Your most commonly used shutter speeds are fractions of a second, although on most cameras the shutter speed number is shown as a whole number. For example, 1/125 of a second appears in the viewfinder as 125. When shutter speeds get down to one second or longer, most cameras indicate this by adding two hash marks after the number, so eight seconds appears as 8".

The shutter speed setting is used to control how motion is displayed in your photograph. Faster shutter speeds (1/125 to 1/8000) freeze motion. Slower shutter speeds (30 seconds to 1/15) allow the motion to be blurred. Shutter speeds in the mid-range (1/30 to 1/60) can go either way, depending on the motion of the subject: fast-moving subjects tend to get a little motion blur, slow subjects tend to be a little sharper.

For the purposes of decay photography, shutter speed isn't a really big concern since your subjects aren't likely to be moving. The only real issue about shutter speed is when handholding your camera. For this we follow the *reciprocal rule*. The reciprocal rule states that your shutter speed setting should be at or near the reciprocal of the focal length of the lens you're using, so at 50 mm your shutter speed should be about 1/50 (or the more common full-stop setting of 1/60). What the reciprocal rule is designed to deal with is reducing blur from camera shake when handholding the camera. As focal length increases the lens not only magnifies the scene but also any camera movement. This is a good guideline to follow, although if you're using a lens with image stabilization or vibration-reduction technology you may be able to use slower shutter speeds when handholding your camera.

ISO sensitivity

The third equation in the exposure triumvirate is ISO sensitivity, or what used to be commonly known as *film speed*. ISO is derived from the International Organization for Standardization, and also even cleverer is the fact the term *iso* is Greek for *equal*. The ISO standard makes sure the sensitivity of the sensor is equal across all platforms so that ISO 100 yields the same exposure no matter what camera you are using, or even whether it's film or digital.

ISO sensitivity controls how much the camera hardware amplifies the signal from the sensor, but for all practical purposes and for simplicity's sake, for our needs as a photographer the ISO determines how sensitive the camera sensor is to light. Higher numbers mean that the sensor needs less light to make a proper exposure. Most cameras have base ISO settings that range from ISO 100 to ISO 6400. Standard ISO settings are 100, 200, 400, 800, 1600, 3200, and 6400 in one-stop intervals. Each increase doubles the sensor's sensitivity to light. As with shutter speed and aperture, most cameras allow you to change the ISO settings in one-third stops to allow you to fine-tune your exposure settings.

Some cameras have expanded settings that allow you to go even higher – to an ISO setting equivalent to ISO 25600 in the case of some Nikon cameras. These expanded settings are exceptionally noisy and I don't recommend using them except in extreme situations.

As you increase the ISO sensitivity you amplify the signal from the sensor. Unfortunately, as you amplify the analog signal from the sensor you also amplify some unwanted signals, resulting in noise. As I mentioned earlier, this is one of the things you must think about when determining your exposure settings.

Using histograms

By far the most valuable tool you have to evaluate your exposure is the histogram; unfortunately, the histogram is also one of the most widely misunderstood features of the camera. Almost all cameras have a feature that lets you view the histogram, and I urge you to use it.

A histogram is a graphic representation of the tonal values of your image. There are two types of histograms: color and luminance. The color histogram shows the tonal values of each color channel of the image and are separated into three histograms: red, green, and blue. The second type of histogram, which is the one that's most important for evaluating exposure, is the luminance histogram. The luminance histogram shows the brightness or luminosity of the image, which is what we perceive as the exposure.

Since a histogram is just a factual representation of the luminosity values of your image there is no *proper* histogram. However, you should try to set your exposure so that the tones are spread across the whole graph. In general you usually want to watch for spikes at the extreme left and right of the graph, which indicate that there are highlights and/or shadows that are clipping.

Figures 4.9–4.11 shows the same subject shot with different exposures to convey the differences in the luminosity histograms for different exposures.

Figure 4.9a shows a severely underexposed image. For this shot, I spot metered on the brightest area of the image (the ground near the bottom of the door on the left). The highlights

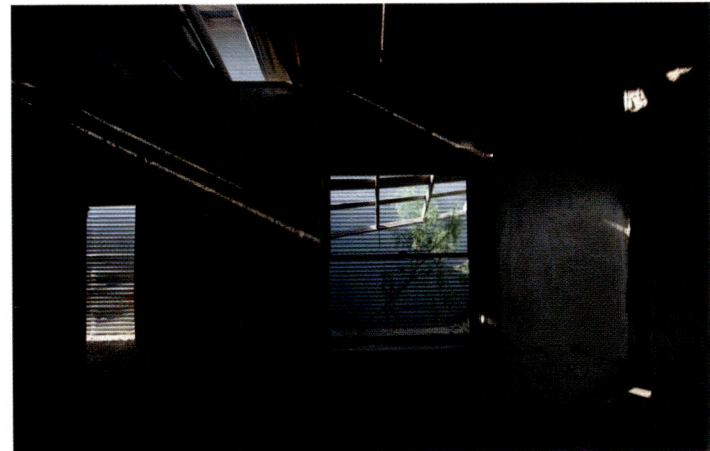

(a)

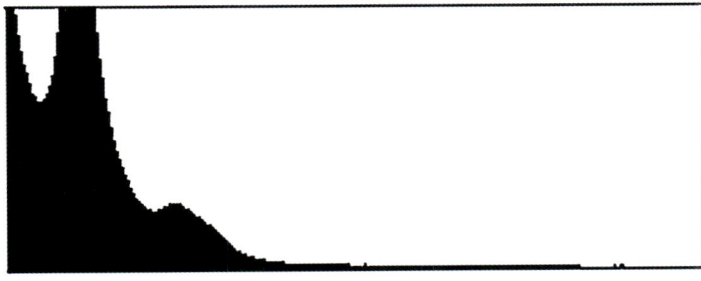

(b)

FIGURE 4.9 (a) Underexposure, (b) Histogram

are all exposed properly but the rest of the image is way too dark and the shadows are completely blocked up. This is evidenced in the histogram (Figure 4.9b) by showing the tones heavily weighted to the left. This indicates that most of the image data is in the blacks.

Figure 4.10a shows the opposite – the image is very overexposed. This shot was spot metered for the darkest shadow areas. Although the shadow areas show a good amount of detail and the image has a wider range of tones than Figure 4.10a, there are spots in the images where the highlights are completely blown-out to white. Blown-out areas are very distracting to the viewer and the rest of the image lacks drama because there are a lot of high mid-tones and little contrast.

You can see the histogram is heavily weighted toward the right and there is a spike on the far right that indicates that there is quite a bit of pure white in the image (blown-out highlights).

Figure 4.11a shows the scene with a good exposure. The image was metered using multi-segment metering. The scene has a wide dynamic range with dark shadows and bright highlights, while retaining detail in both. The image has contrast showing lights and darks with subtle mid-tones and

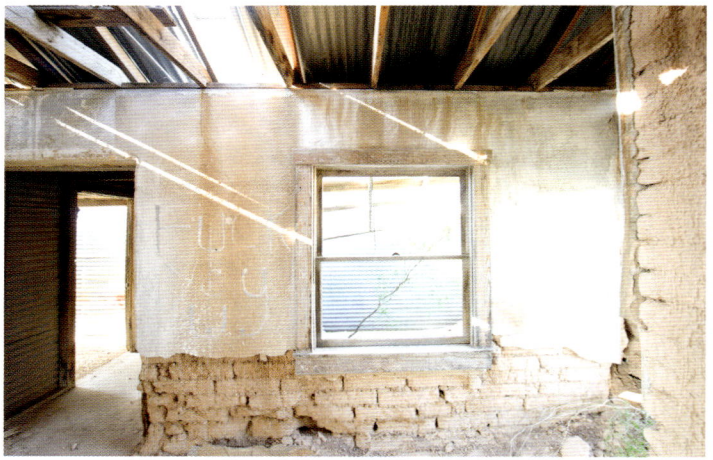

(a)

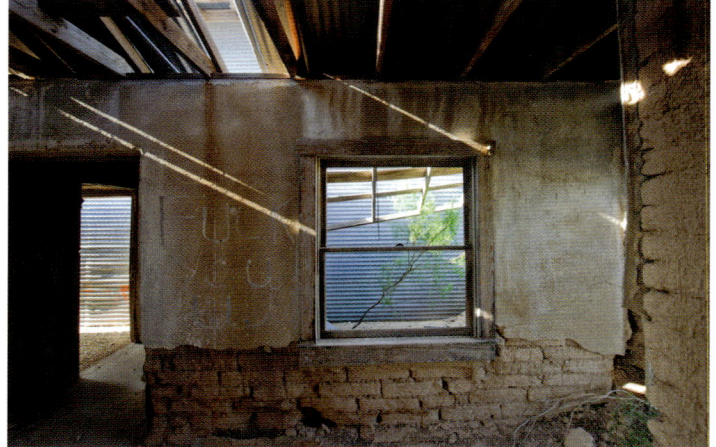

(a)

(b)

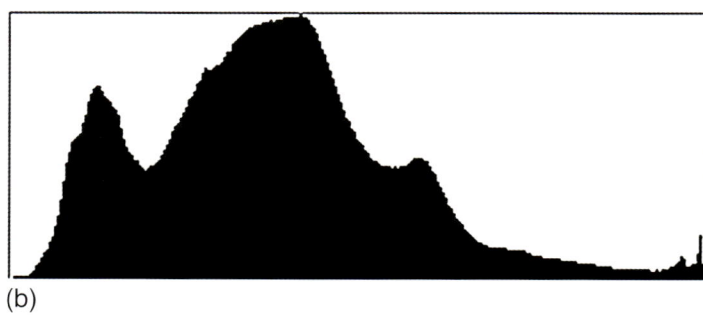

(b)

FIGURE 4.10 (a) Overexposure, (b) Histogram

FIGURE 4.11 (a) Correct exposure, (b) Histogram

lots of variation. The histogram tones are spread evenly across the board and there are no spikes at either end indicating blocked up shadows or blown-out highlights (Figure 4.11b).

By necessity, not all of your images are going to have an evenly spread-out histogram. For example, while shooting in the dead of night, your histogram will obviously be weighed toward the left side, and on a bright day the opposite is true. The key is to try to adjust the exposure so you capture detail in the darkest and lightest parts of the image.

Shooting RAW

For the most flexibility in post-processing images you should shoot RAW. Each manufacturer has its own type of RAW file: .NEF for Nikon, .CRW for Canon, and so forth. For all practical purposes these files are the same. RAW files contain all of the image data that was captured at the time the exposure was made and are usually 12- or 14-bit files, depending on the camera.

The biggest advantage in using a RAW file is bit depth. Simplified, what bit-depth breaks down into is how many separate colors your camera has the ability to capture and store in the file. An 8-bit file can record up to 256 luminosity values for each separate color channel in the file; red, green, and blue. Broken down further to the pixel level, this theoretically allows your camera's sensor to record more than 16 million different colors. A 12- or 14-bit image has many, many more colors available.

What this boils down to is that the more colors you are able to record, the smoother the color gradation you can achieve in your images. This is especially important in shadow areas where you can often see posterization or banding caused by the camera's inability to smoothly go from darker to lighter tones because of the lack of image information in an 8-bit file.

White balance

As most of us probably know, not all light sources are the same color. The human brain can be put in any type of light source and will automatically figure out what is white and compensate for it. Our cameras only see what is actually there, so they must be adjusted to compensate for different light sources.

White balance is measured in units of kelvin, which for photographic purposes is a measure of temperature in relation to a specific color. This color temperature scale was originally used in stellar astronomy to classify surface temperature. The kelvin color temperature is based on a theoretical "black body"

JPEG

Without going into the boring details about compression algorithms and quantizing coefficients, JPEGs are compressed files. Once the shutter is released and the camera's image-processing engine is finished processing the image data, any unneeded data is thrown away, leaving you with an 8-bit file in which the image data has been fixed. This allows for a much smaller file, especially when the file is compressed. Of course, some adjustments can be made using editing software, but with the limited amount of data in the file, more radical changes can cause unwanted artifacts in your image file such as posterization, banding, or fringing.

radiator which appears black at 0 K (the absence of all heat); as the black body radiator is heated it begins to glow different colors depending on how hot it is. On the kelvin scale the lowest temperatures are in the red zone, and as the temperature increases the colors shift through to orange, yellow, white, and blue. However, this is counter-intuitive to most people because humans perceive reds as "warm" colors and blues as "cold." To make understanding kelvin a little easier, remember that the white balance setting is used to counteract the color cast of the light source; for example, a standard household light bulb emits a very orange light, so in order to achieve balance the camera adds the opposite color, which is bluish.

Luckily for us, most cameras have built-in white balance settings that are preset to temperatures according to the light source, although most cameras allow you to set the white balance in kelvin as well. Personally I generally shoot in the auto setting and adjust in post-processing if needed.

One of the main reasons I recommend shooting in RAW is the ability to adjust the white balance settings without any degradation to the image quality. When the white balance is fixed in a JPEG you can make some adjustments, but the quality can really suffer.

When asked about white balance settings I use in any given situation, my answer is auto. While some hardliners still insist that you must set everything manually, I find that auto white balance works quite well in most situations, and as I mentioned in the previous section, I shoot in RAW almost exclusively, so changing the white balance is only a matter of a click or two.

The thing about white balance in this type of photography is that subtle adjustments can have a profound effect on the look and feel of your image. You can add a slight bluish tint for a cool look, which can make the viewer feel cold and lonely, warm it up by adding an amber tint for a more friendly or nostalgic feel, or make it look slightly ghastly with a greenish hue.

There isn't necessarily a *wrong* white balance for an image, but I suggest keeping it close to a neutral white balance and adding only slight tints when needed.

That being said, even when shooting RAW you may want to use the presets available on your camera to set a custom white balance. You can do this so you can preview your image to see if you are getting the effect you want. Setting the white balance close to what you think you are going to use will also give you a more accurate histogram reading so you can adjust your exposure for the right colorcast.

By using a gray card or a neutral-colored object you can set a custom white balance in-camera or you can use an accessory like the ExpoDisc or the baLens to get an accurate reading of the light in the scene.

Noise and noise reduction

Digital noise is an artifact that appears in your image as random specks of color. Noise comprises two elements: chrominance and luminance. Chrominance refers to the color of the specks (which is most commonly red and blue), and luminance refers to the size and shapes of the individual specks of noise (which increases as the sensitivity is increased). There are two types of noise: high ISO noise and long exposure noise.

Noise isn't a new thing. Before digital photography, photographers used high-speed film, or *pushed* film, with lower ISO ratings when processing to achieve more light sensitivity. High-speed films had larger particles of silver halide

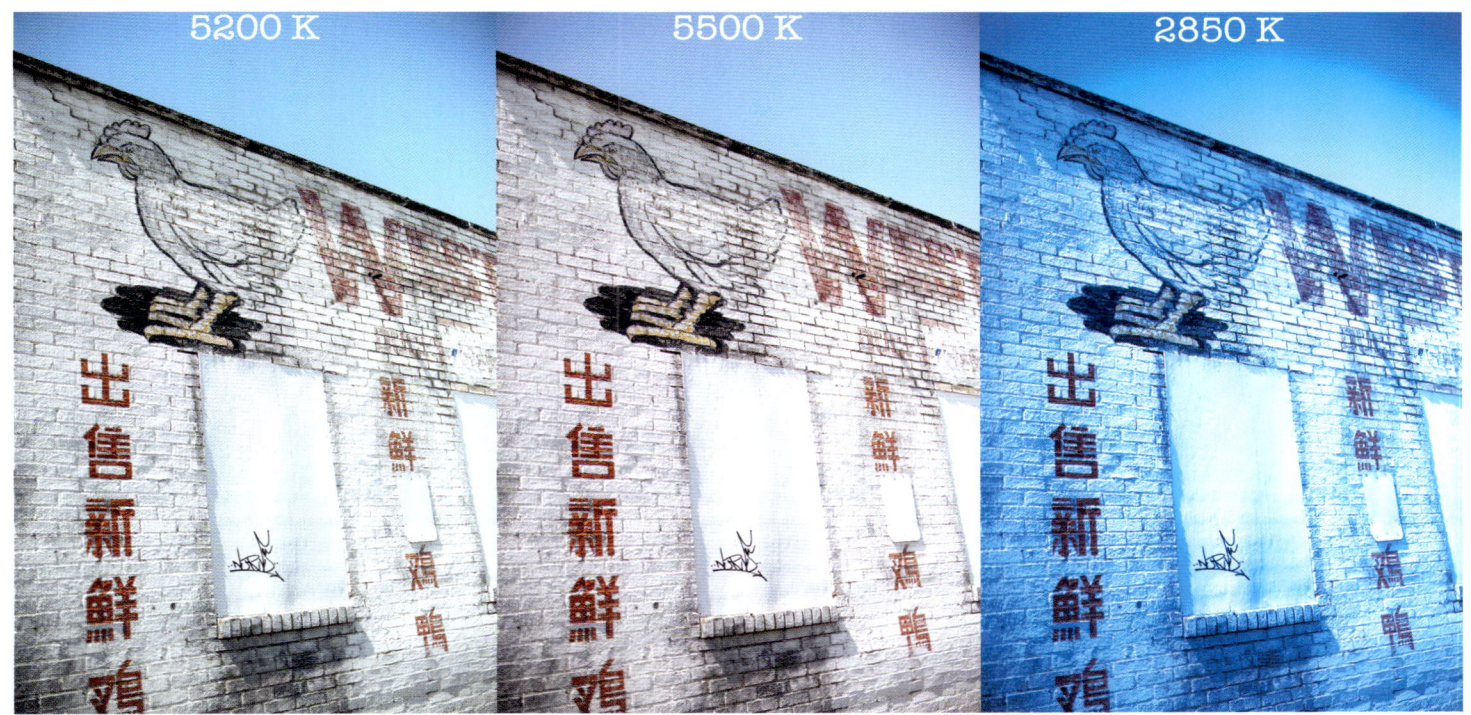

FIGURE 4.12 This figure shows the difference that white balance can make in an image. The image on the left shows the in-camera auto setting, which is 5200 K; this is a pretty good approximation of the scene as it was. The image in the center is the same picture but the white balance is set for daylight and you can see a slight difference in the color of the white wall. The image on the right shows the same scene with the white balance set for a tungsten light bulb, which gives the image a very blue cast

(the light-sensitive element in film), which resulted in images that had a grainy look. We called this "film grain." It was a necessary evil if you wanted to do low-light photography – therefore it was an acceptable part of photography.

The point I'm getting at is that film grain and noise are very similar and that some level of noise is to be expected. Noise gives your images a more natural quality at lower light levels. Over-processing to get rid of noise can often make your images look worse.

Similar to how different brands of film had different grain quality; different cameras have different amounts of noise at comparable ISO settings. So whether you need to use some sort of noise reduction or not is highly dependent on your camera (or your personal preferences).

High ISO noise

When in low-light situations, sometimes you need to dial up your ISO sensitivity settings. Increasing the ISO sensitivity is

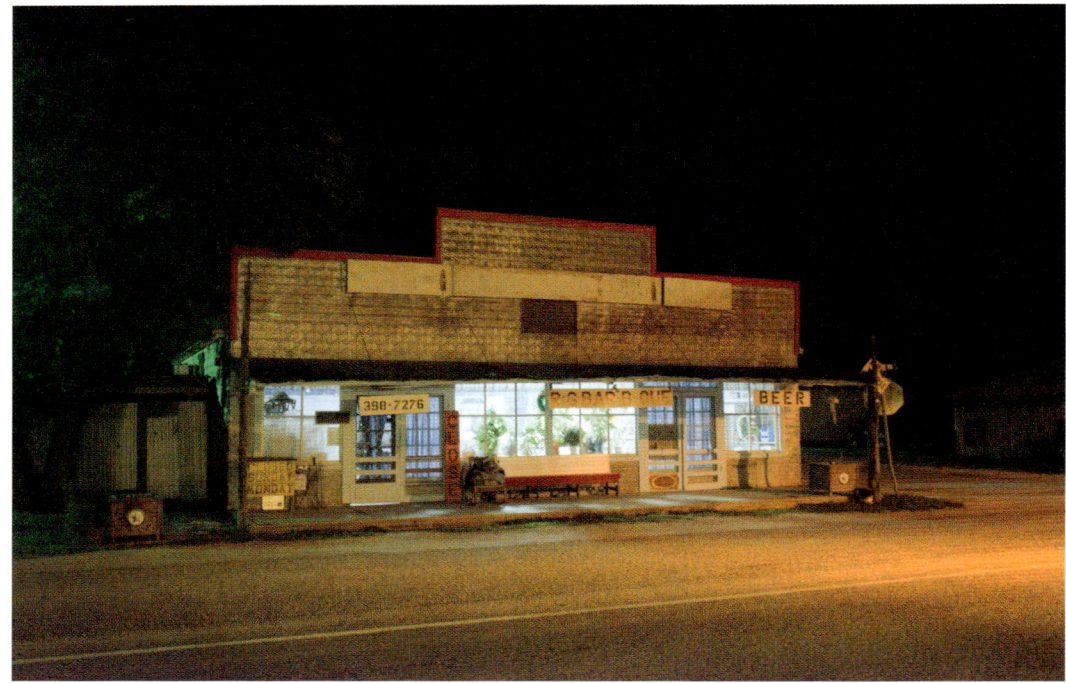

FIGURE 4.13 In this high-ISO image you can easily see the noise artifacts of colored dots. Noise is more likely to be noticeable in the shadow areas. This image was purposely shot at an ISO setting of 6400 and pushed to an equivalent of 25600 to accentuate the noise. No noise reduction has been applied to the image

nothing more than taking the original signal from the sensor and amplifying it. All electronic components inherently have background electrical noise. Generally the background noise is very small and mostly unnoticeable, but when amplifying the signal from your sensor you also amplify the background electrical noise, which show up as artifacts in your images.

Long exposure noise

This type of artifact is also known as *thermal noise* because it's produced when the sensor heats up during a long exposure. The heat knocks free extraneous electrons from the sensor, which contaminates the pixels, ultimately resulting in more noise. The longer the shutter speed the more heat is generated, which compounds the noise.

Noise reduction

Most cameras offer some sort of noise reduction technology; usually there are two separate settings for high ISO and long exposure noise. Unfortunately, when shooting in RAW these in-camera settings aren't supported unless you use your camera's proprietary software to process your RAW files.

Most RAW converters such as Adobe Camera RAW (within Photoshop) or Lightroom 4 have noise reduction modules. You can also use third-party plug-ins or other standalone noise reduction applications. The Adobe Lightroom 4 noise reduction is very good, as is Nik D-fine and Noise Ninja. D-fine and Noise Ninja are available as either plug-ins or standalone programs.

Earlier I noted that there are two different elements that comprise digital noise: *chrominance* and *luminance*. Chrominance refers to the color of the specks, while luminance refers to the size and shapes of the individual specks of noise.

All of this is increased as the ISO sensitivity is set higher and the shutter speed gets longer.

Chrominance noise is by far the most unnatural looking type of noise (when compared to film grain) and can be more detrimental to image quality than luminance noise, which looks more like traditional film grain. Chrominance noise generally comprises colored specks that appear to be mostly magenta, blue, and green. This type of noise is more prominent in the shadow areas.

Luminance noise appears as a grainy type of speckle in the image; while it can be troublesome when printing large images for display, as a whole it's not quite as unattractive as

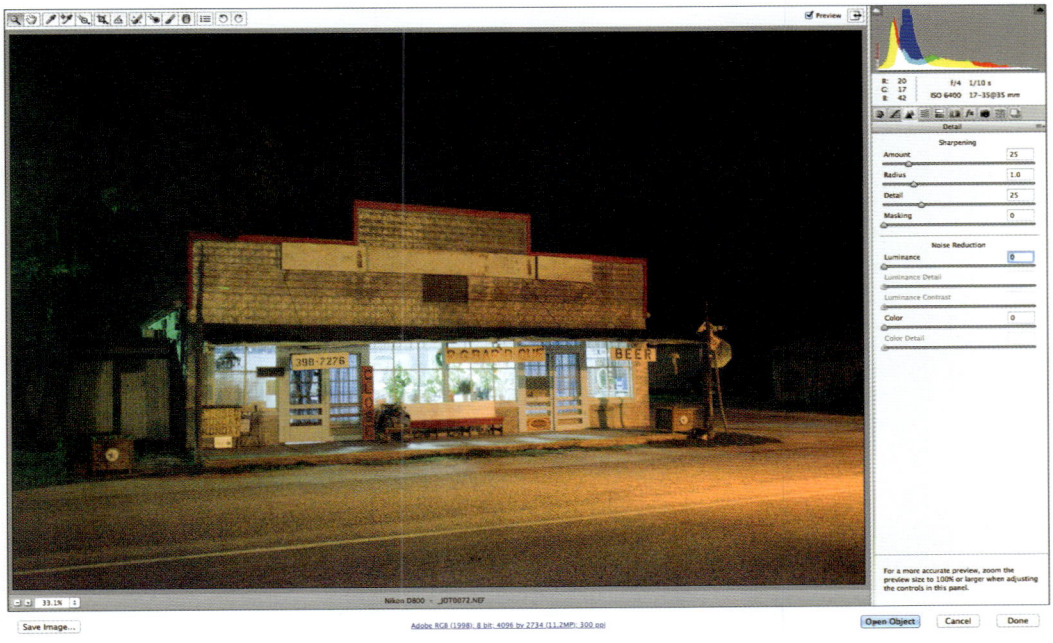

FIGURE 4.14 Adobe Camera RAW in Photoshop CS5 has a module for applying noise reduction

the chrominance noise can be. For most magazine print uses, luminance noise isn't even an issue at all, so keep that in mind when doing any type of noise reduction.

Most of the current noise reduction software deals with each type of noise separately and has separate controls that allow you to fine-tune the separate adjustments as well. Some software, such as Nik D-Fine, also uses a control point technology that allows you to pinpoint where the noise reduction is applied. This is a great feature considering most noise appears in the shadow areas and oftentimes applying noise reduction reduces the detail in the brighter areas.

In my experience the best way to approach noise reduction is to use chrominance noise reduction with moderate to high settings. Reducing chrominance noise has almost no detrimental effect to your image quality. When using luminance noise reduction a very light touch is required. Luminance reduction reduces the detail in your image at a very high rate and it's easy to overdo it, leaving your image looking smeary or *plasticky*, as I've heard a lot of people call it.

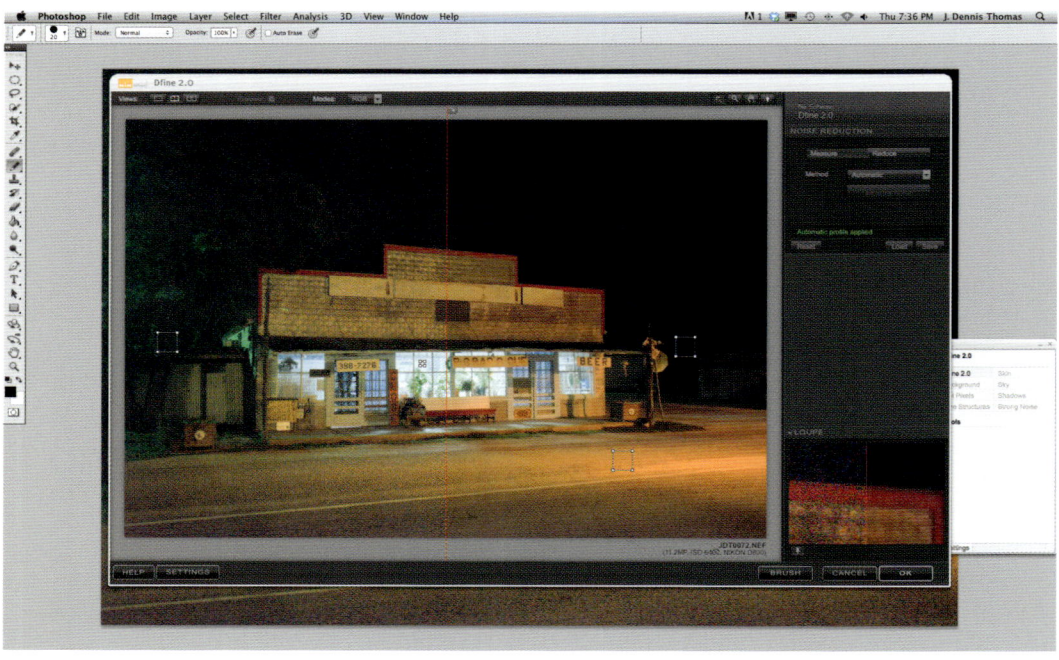

FIGURE 4.15 Nik D-Fine is a great tool for noise reduction. It allows you to choose precisely where and how much noise reduction to apply in different areas of your image. In-camera noise reduction is much more ham-fisted in its approach

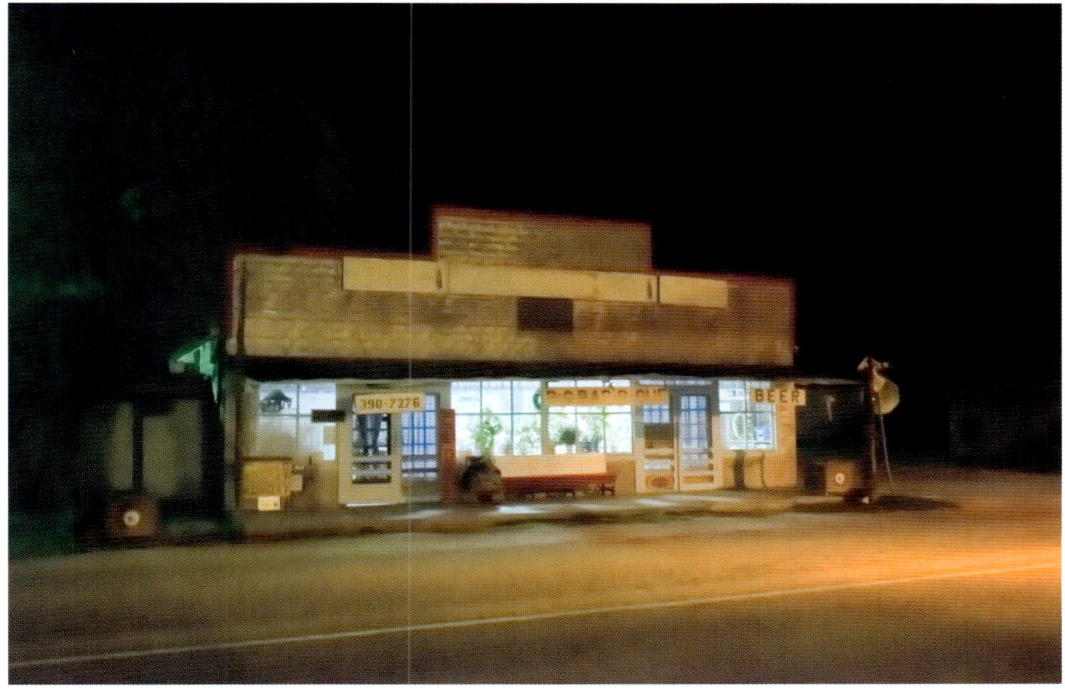

FIGURE 4.16 Overusing noise reduction can result in the loss of detail in your image. As you can see in this image, almost all of the detail has been obliterated due to over-processing with Adobe Camera RAW noise reduction

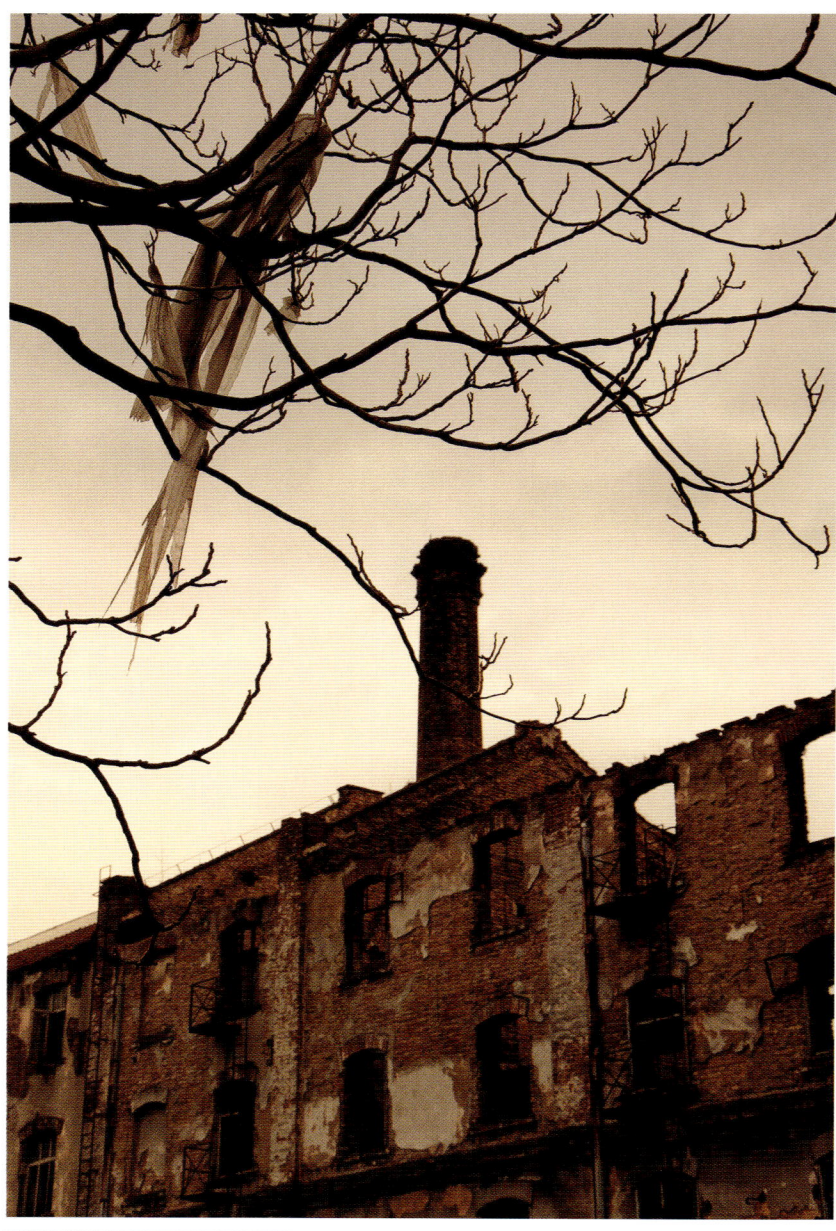

FIGURE 4.17 The warm tone of this image of an abandoned factory in the center of Belgrade, Serbia adds a nostalgic feel to the image while retaining a feeling of loneliness. **Exposure unrecorded.** © Alexander Nterilis

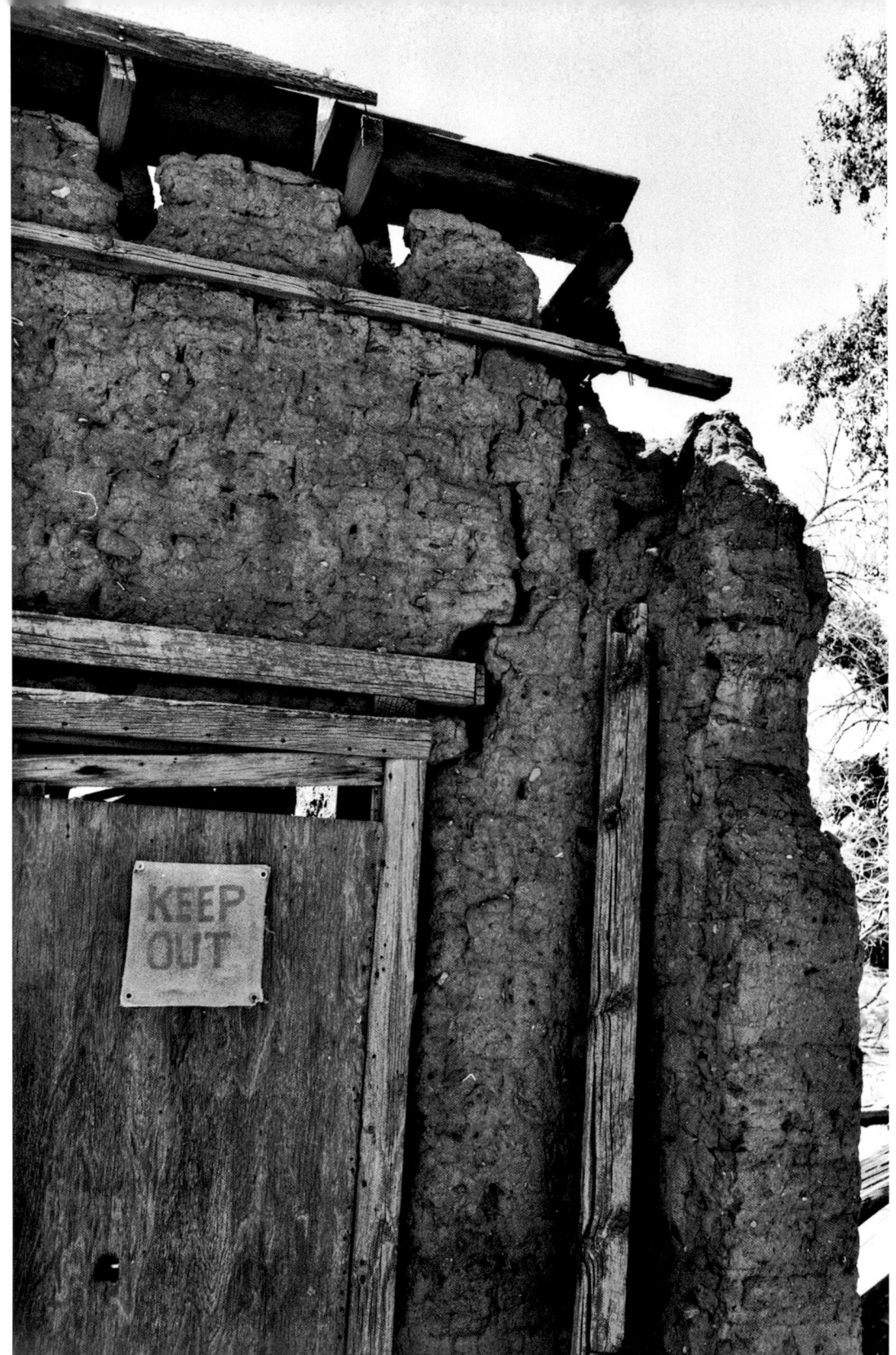

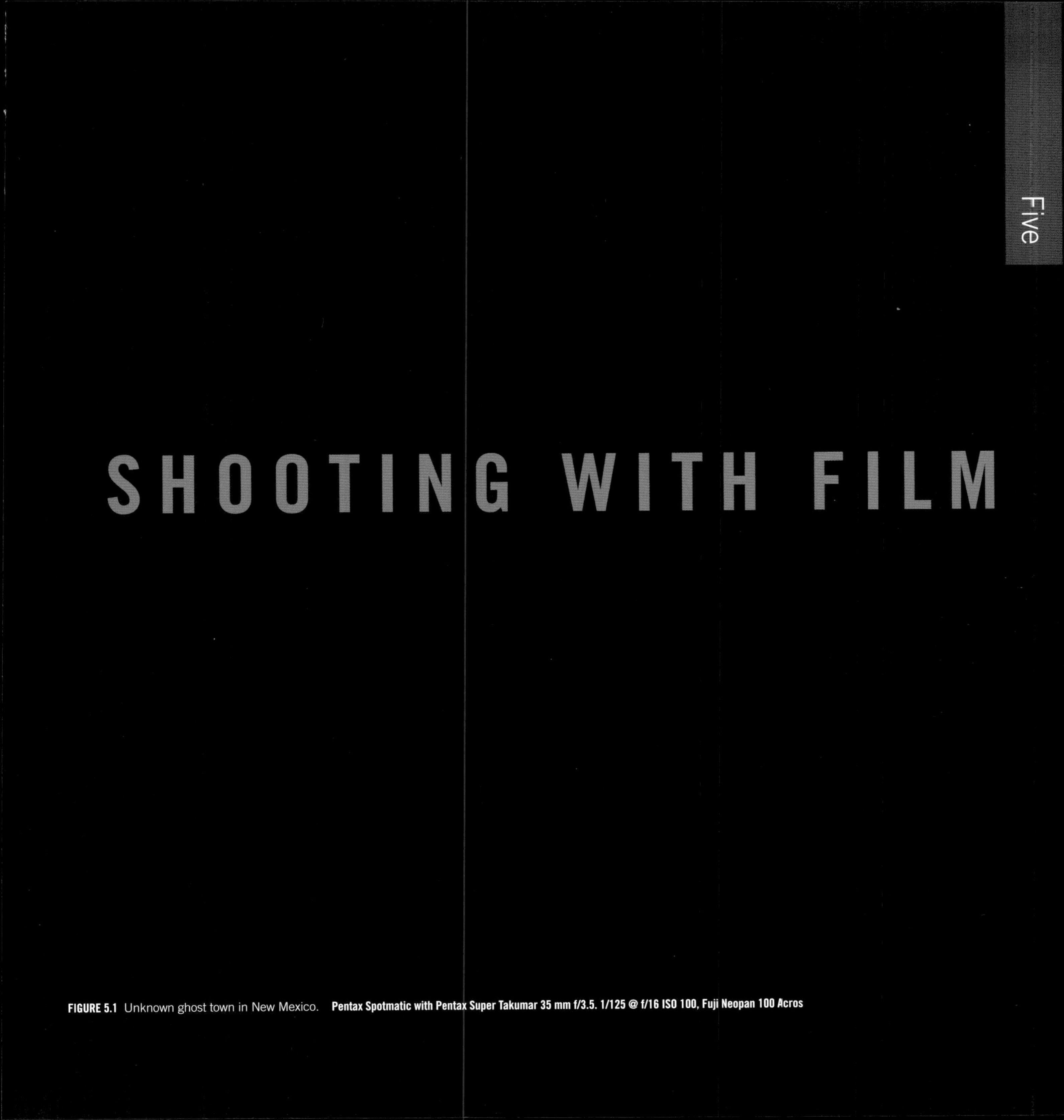

Five

SHOOTING WITH FILM

FIGURE 5.1 Unknown ghost town in New Mexico. **Pentax Spotmatic with Pentax Super Takumar 35 mm f/3.5. 1/125 @ f/16 ISO 100, Fuji Neopan 100 Acros**

Although most photographers are using digital capture these days, there are still quite a few photographers who continue to use the time-honored method of film photography. Film photography is not only used by old purists, but is steadily being embraced by the younger generations as well. In the past few years I've seen more and more people carrying around vintage film cameras.

In my opinion, one of the best qualities of using film to capture your images is that it forces you to look at the subject closer and, being that you have a limited number of shots, you take more time with focus, composition, and exposure. In the end, a film shooter tends to be more disciplined than someone who shoots solely with digital cameras. I believe that even photographers who are more inclined to shoot digitally can benefit from running a few rolls of film through an old manual camera.

As far as decay photography goes, I think film adds a certain *je ne sais quoi* to images of run-down and decaying subjects. Film, especially black-and-white film, gives the images a gritty texture and a feel that can't be replicated easily, even with expensive Photoshop filters and plug-ins.

In the end, film is very easy to integrate into a digital workflow. Most photographers that shoot film ultimately end up scanning the film and creating a digital file to share on the internet.

Film types

Although there used to be a plethora of films available to photographers, the rise in popularity of digital cameras has taken its toll on the film manufacturing industry, which has caused many of the less popular film stocks to be discontinued. Luckily, there is still a demand for film, so the most tried and true films are still readily available.

Another stroke of good fortune is that there are still plenty of labs around, so getting film processed isn't a problem. However, it is considerably more expensive than it was in the past.

For the most part, there are three major manufacturers of film these days: Kodak, Ilford, and Fuji. Each of these three companies manufactures a number of different types of film with different ISO sensitivities and grain types. These films are readily available at most professional photography stores as well as online from major photography retail websites.

Each type of film has different characteristics, as well as strengths and weaknesses. In the next few sections I'll cover some of the nuances of different film types.

Black-and-white negative

Black-and-white photography is my favorite type of photography, possibly because it was the first type of photography I became involved with when growing up. Over the years I've shot every type of subject with black-and-white film: concerts, sports, portraits, architecture, and yes, urban and rural decay. In my eyes, black-and-white film is perfect for decay photography. The stark contrast of black-and-white film strips down a subject to the basics and gives a stark representation of whatever it is you're photographing.

Another reason why I prefer black-and-white photography is the ease with which you can develop the film at home. All you need is a pitch-black room and a few inexpensive tools and chemicals and you're in business. I'll cover film processing later in this chapter.

Black-and-white films comprise three layers: a light-sensitive emulsion, a substrate (usually polyester or acetate), and an anti-halation layer. The light-sensitive emulsion comprises silver halide crystals suspended in gelatin, which

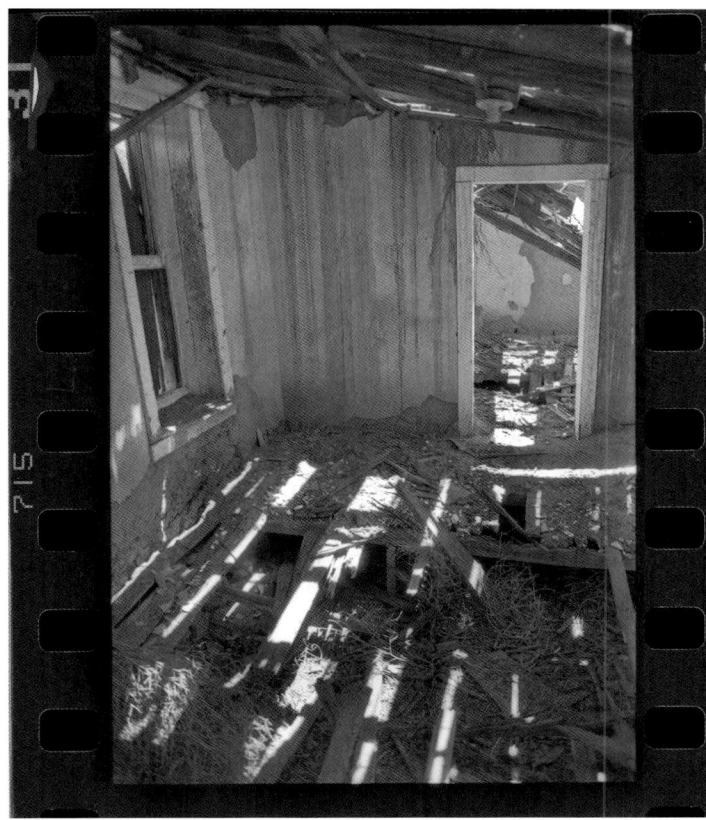

FIGURE 5.2 Unknown ghost town in New Mexico. **Pentax Spotmatic with Pentax Super Takumar 35 mm f/3.5. 1/125 @ f/5.6 ISO 100, Fuji Neopan Acros 100**

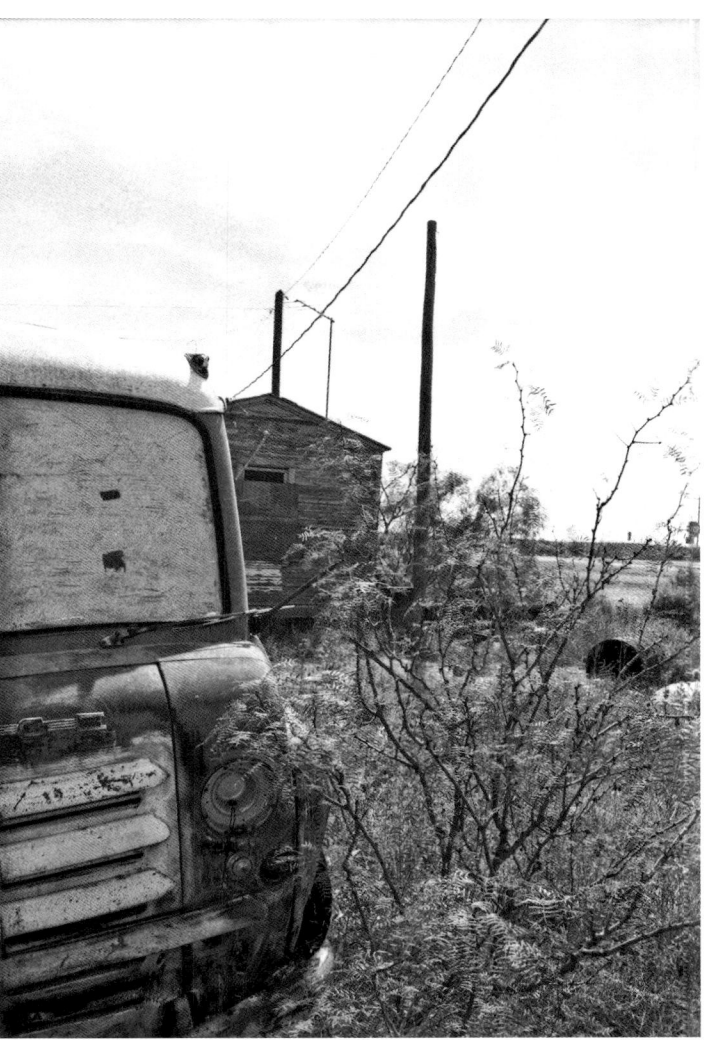

FIGURE 5.3 Abandoned farmhouse outside of Pecos, TX. **Nikkormat with Nikon 50 mm f/1.8D. 1/125 @ f/11 ISO 100, Ilford Delta 100**

coats the substrate. The anti-halation layer dulls the substrate, which prevents the light from being reflected back up to the emulsion, which would cause the film to appear foggy or blurry.

When exposed to light, the surface of the silver halide crystal is rendered into a metallic silver speck. After being exposed to light the silver in the emulsion forms what is known as the *latent image*. The latent image is invisible and indistinguishable from the rest of the emulsion until it is introduced to a developing chemical. The developer dissolves the silver halide crystals of the darker areas and turns the areas with more light into silver specks. This leaves a negative image in which the clear parts of the film are reproduced as blacks when printed, and the more dense parts of the film are reproduced as whites and shades of gray.

The size and amount of the silver halide crystals in the emulsion determine the light sensitivity of the film. The higher the sensitivity or ISO of the film, the larger the crystals, which results in the films having larger grain. As I mentioned in the chapter on digital capture, this grain is akin to digital noise. While similar to digital noise, since the silver halide crystals are organic the film grain has a more natural appearance, which is one reason why fine art photographers prefer black and white film to digital capture.

Another reason why some photographers prefer black-and-white film is not only for the aesthetic value of the black-and-white print, but because black-and-white film has the ability to record a vast dynamic range, up to 20 stops for some films, depending on the dilution of the developer, the time spent in the developer, and the temperature of the developing solution. This can be invaluable when recording scenes with a very wide dynamic range.

Some of my favorite black-and-white films for decay photography include:

- **Fuji Neopan 100 Acros.** This is possibly one of the finest black-and-white films ever produced. It has a very fine grain, which results in ultra-sharp images with excellent reproduction of fine detail. This film is great for use with subjects that have fine detail such as wood grain or paint texture.
- **Ilford Delta 100.** This is the ISO 100 film I use the most, simply because my local camera store doesn't stock the

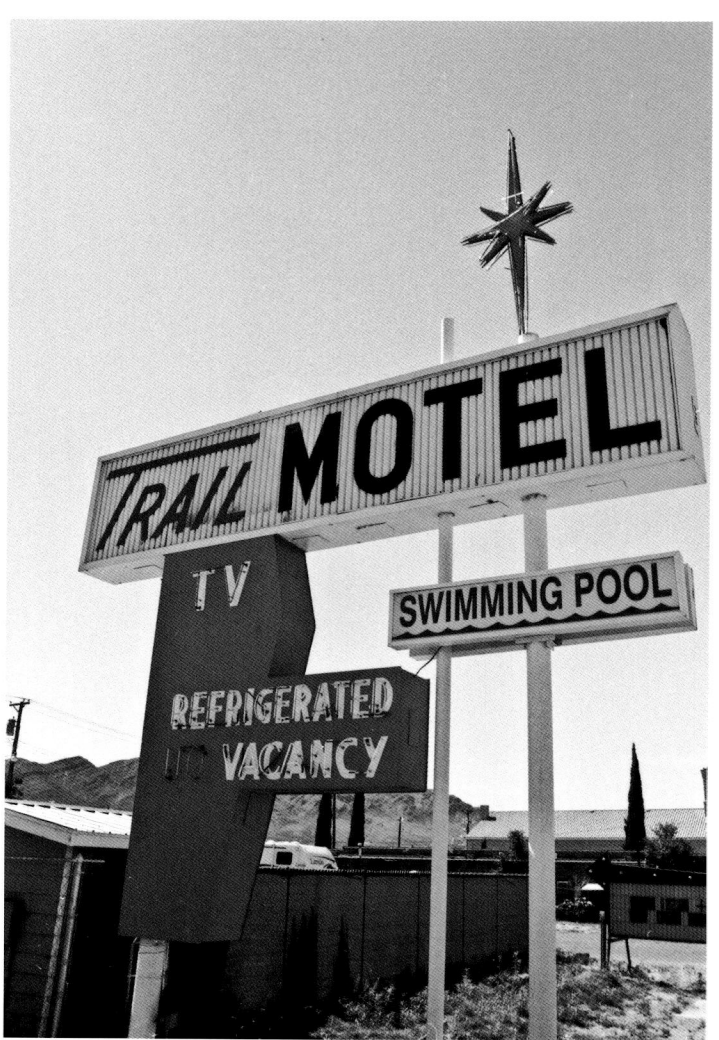

FIGURE 5.4 Trail Motel, somewhere in Arizona. Pentax K with Pentax Super Takumar 35 mm f/3.5, 1/125 @ f/16 ISO 100, Fuji Neopan Acros 100

Fuji 100 Acros. This film also has a very fine grain, but is a little less detailed than the Fuji Acros.
- **Ilford HP5 Plus.** This is a great all-round film and what I generally use for most situations. It has wide exposure latitude and the ISO of 400 is slow enough for use in broad daylight, but fast enough for most indoor work with a fast lens.
- **Kodak T-Max.** This film is available in both ISO 100 and 400. Both films have exceptionally fine grain and good detail reproduction. These films are generally my last resort, not because they aren't good, but simply because I have been working with Ilford and Fuji more often and I'm familiar with the characteristics of the films which allow me to get more predictable results. Many photographers swear by this film, so don't hesitate to give it a shot.
- **Efke.** Efke is a film manufactured in Croatia that utilizes emulsions that are chemically similar to the compounds found in films during the 1950s. The silver content is supposedly higher, resulting in a high dynamic range. The Efke film also comes in slower ISO speeds than any of the other films, such as 25 and 50. These are great for getting long exposures in the daytime and can create some cool special effects.

Color negative

This type of photography is probably less popular than black and white film photography these days. This is due to the fact that color photography is much easier to do with a digital camera than it is with film, although color negative film does have a propensity to have more dynamic range than a digital sensor (especially when it comes to highlights). When it comes to digitizing color film, having a high-quality film scanner is

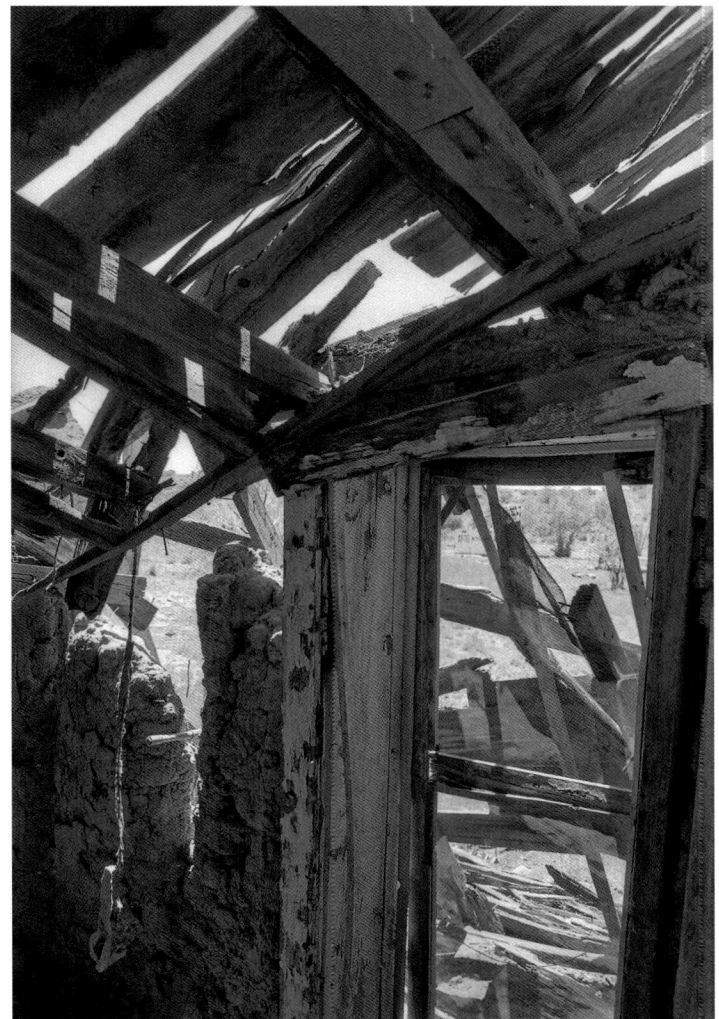

FIGURE 5.5 The ultra-fine grain of the Fuji Neopan was perfect for capturing the fine details of the wood and the texture of the adobe. Unknown ghost town in New Mexico. Pentax Spotmatic with Pentax Super Takumar 50 mm f/2 for 1/60 @ f/5.6 ISO 100, Fuji Neopan Acros 100

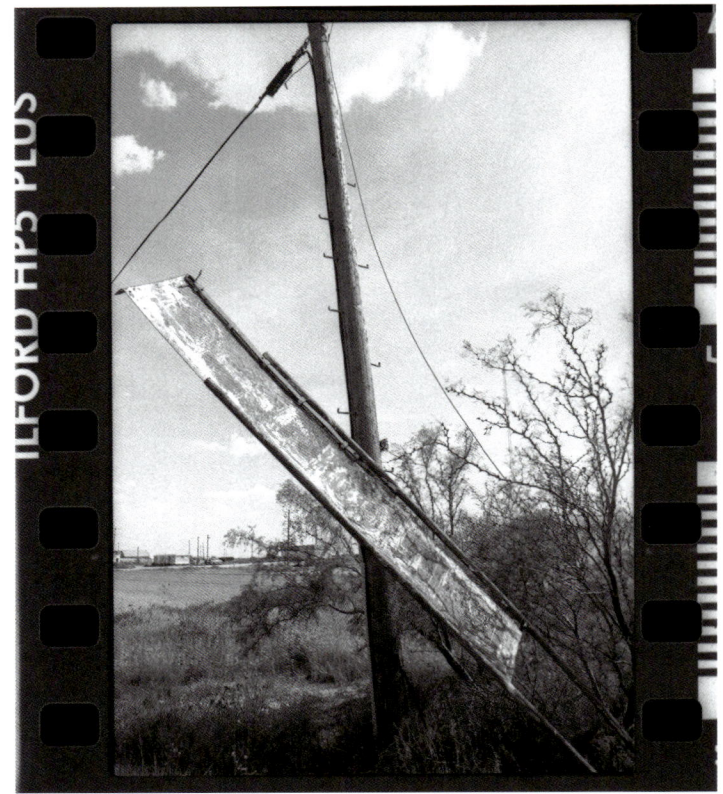

FIGURE 5.6 The Ilford HP5 Plus is a great all-round film that is suitable for use both indoors and out. This can be helpful in decay photography because you may find yourself in different types of lighting situations at the same scene. Abandoned house in Pecos, TX.   **Nikon F90X with 28 mm f/2.8D, 1/1000 @ f/16 ISO 400, Ilford HP5 Plus**

very important if you want your images to match the quality of an image shot with a DSLR.

Color film is similar in construction to black-and-white film, except that instead of one layer of silver halide emulsion the color negative film has three separate layers of emulsion, each of which is dyed one of the three primary colors: red, green, or blue. The emulsion layers are exposed just the same as a black-and-white negative, but during the development process *color coupling* chemicals form a dye cloud. Once bleached and fixed the dyes are rendered as cyan, magenta, and yellow, and remain as a color negative on the substrate.

Note: Current films use more than three emulsion layers with different chemical compounds, but the basic layers are still based on the three-color RGB layer system.

One caveat about using color negative film is that the substrate has a strong orange tint; this is due to the fact that film is ultimately supposed to be printed in a darkroom using chemicals. The orange tint filters out when wet printing, but when scanning the tint remains. Upon inverting the scan, color negatives appear overly cyan and this must be adjusted for by using image-editing software; although some scanner software allows you to make adjustments I find that adjusting the scan in Photoshop yields better results.

To be honest, in this day and age of high-resolution DSLRs, I find that shooting color negative film is unnecessary and ends up being more work than it's worth due to the amount of color correction needed, not to mention the film grain tends to show up even at lower ISO settings. Unless you are having your film professionally processed and printed I recommend sticking with digital for color work. That being said, if you *are* interested in shooting color negative film, here is a list of a few of my favorites.

- **Kodak Ektar 100.** If you're looking for a fine-grained film with colors that pop, this is probably the best film out there. This film doesn't have as much exposure latitude as some other color negative films such as Kodak's Portra series due to its high-contrast properties.

- **Fuji Superia X-tra 400.** This is another relatively high-contrast film with vivid colors. I prefer this to the Kodak Ektar 100 due to the higher speed, which allows better opportunity for handholding the camera in darker areas. This is the best all-round 35 mm color negative film.

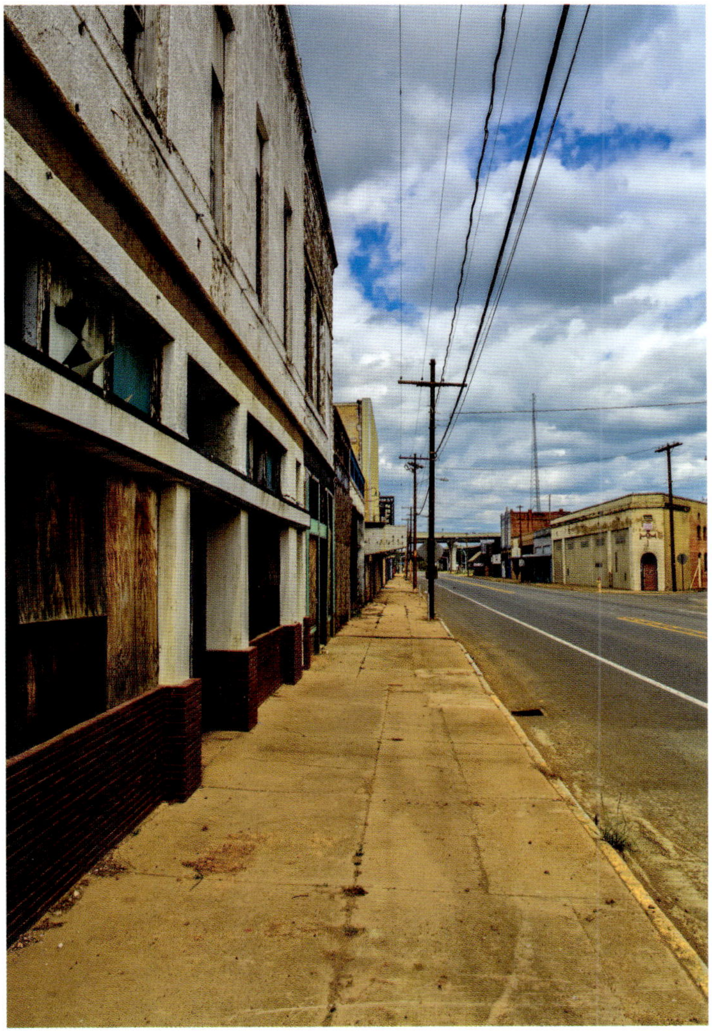

If you prefer a film with more exposure latitude and less contrast, the Kodak Portra series is a very good film. This is a great film for shooting foggy or misty scenes.

Transparency or color positive

This type of film goes by a number of different names; transparency, color positive, color reversal, chrome, or, most commonly, slide film. This type of film is by far the most beautiful of all the films. Slide film innately has a very fine grain, is fairly high in contrast and has excellent color rendition. The downside is that the processing cost is much higher than with color negative film.

The makeup of slide film is very close to that of color negative film, except that the substrate is transparent and the emulsion layers are cyan, magenta, and yellow, and are converted to red, green, and blue during processing.

While slide film produces very fine and richly colored images, the exposure latitude is very unforgiving, meaning you must get the exposure exactly right or you will lose highlight detail, or end up with completely black shadows.

While slides look great (especially when projected), to get a scan that is going to reproduce the slide faithfully a high-quality film scanner is essential. Most flatbed scanners with film adapters aren't adept at pulling the detail from slides, which are typically denser than color negative films. The upsice to scanning slides is that since there is much less grain than color negative film, the color rendition is much easier to faithfully maintain since slide film doesn't have the orange color masking of negative film. A good scan of a medium-format slide will still rival that of a high-resolution DSLR.

FIGURE 5.7 Abandoned house in Arizona. Ricoh KR-5 Super with Rikenon 50 mm f/2. 1/125 @ f/4 ISO 100, Kodak Ektar 100

100 Urban and Rural Decay Photography

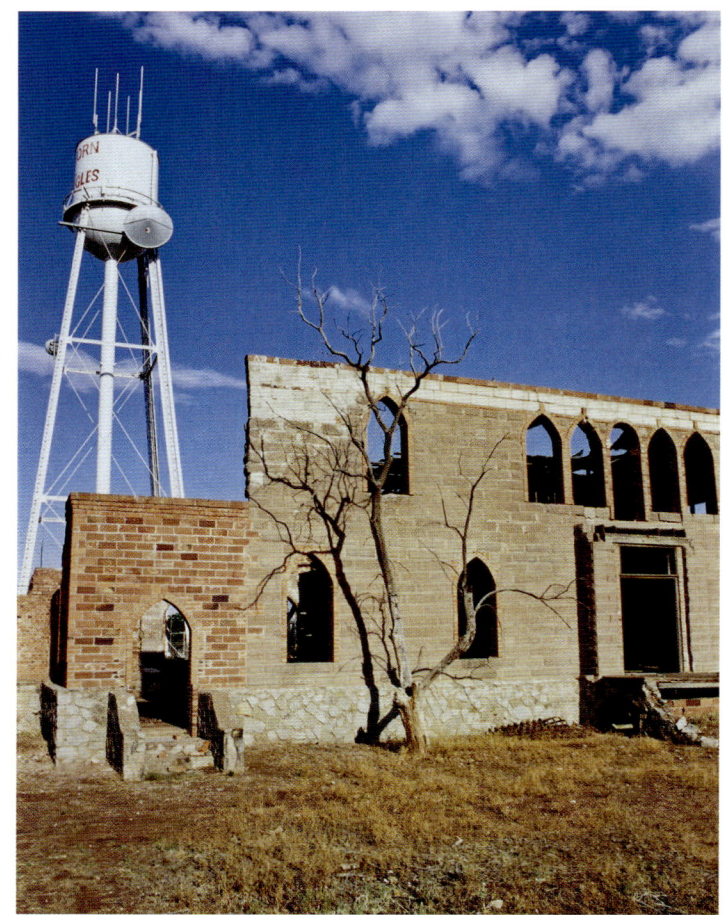

FIGURE 5.8 Van Horn, TX.   Pentax 645 with 80 mm f/3.5. 1/125 @ f/16 ISO 400, Fuji Pro 400H

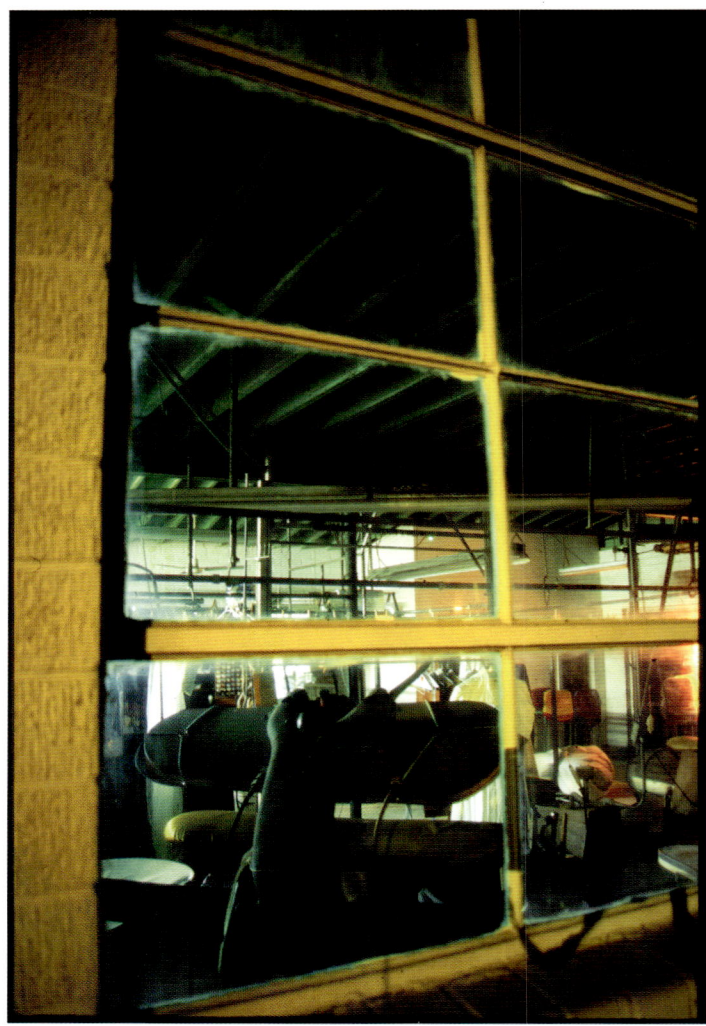

FIGURE 5.9 Former South Congress Cleaners in Austin, TX.   Nikon F90X with 28 mm f/2.8D. 15 sec. @ f/8 ISO 400, Fujichrome Provia 400X

Although slides were the preferred form of publishing and stock photography for many years, slide photography has seen a steady decline as high-resolution digital camera files have largely replaced it. The decline in sales has been so marked that in March 2012 Kodak announced that it is no longer manufacturing slide film at all. As of this writing you can still find Kodak slide film, but supplies are dwindling.

Luckily, there are still some die-hard chrome shooters and Fuji is still manufacturing their two excellent slide films, Velvia and Provia. Velvia is known for its highly saturated colors, while Provia is a little more subdued to accommodate for skin tones. Most photographers agree that Velvia is probably the most beautiful film there is, especially when viewed projected onto a screen.

Slide film is great for decay photography scenes that have bright, contrasting colors.

Instant (Polaroid)

Admittedly, this is a very niche product, but what most people don't know is that instant film is still readily available in this day and age, and the Polaroid cameras that are designed to work with the film are plentiful and available inexpensively from eBay.

Fuji is a company that is dedicated to keeping different films around. Even as Polaroid abandoned their own product, Fuji still continues to make instant film. The film is known as *pack-film* because the separate films for each print are contained in one pack. Each picture has its own negative, paper, and pod. The pod contains the chemicals that are needed to develop the film and photo paper. After the exposure is made you pull a tab that pulls the film between two steel rollers in the camera back that break the chemical pod and distribute the chemicals. After the allotted development time (about 90 seconds) you peel apart the film and you have two halves, the positive print and the negative. Some people refer to the negative as the *goop* side because of the chemical residue from the development pod. The negative is generally meant to be thrown away, but some people hold onto them for scanning after they're dry.

The only cameras that will work with the pack-film are the Polaroid Land Camera "100-series" cameras. These cameras have designation numbers that are in the hundreds, i.e., 100, 200, 300, and 400. Examples of model numbers are 100, 250, 320, 430, etc. You can usually find these cameras on eBay for $40 or less.

Fuji makes two types of pack-film:

- **Fuji FP-100C.** This is an ISO 100 color film. It's relatively slow so plenty of light should be available when using this film or have a tripod handy. This print retains a good amount of detail and scans well.

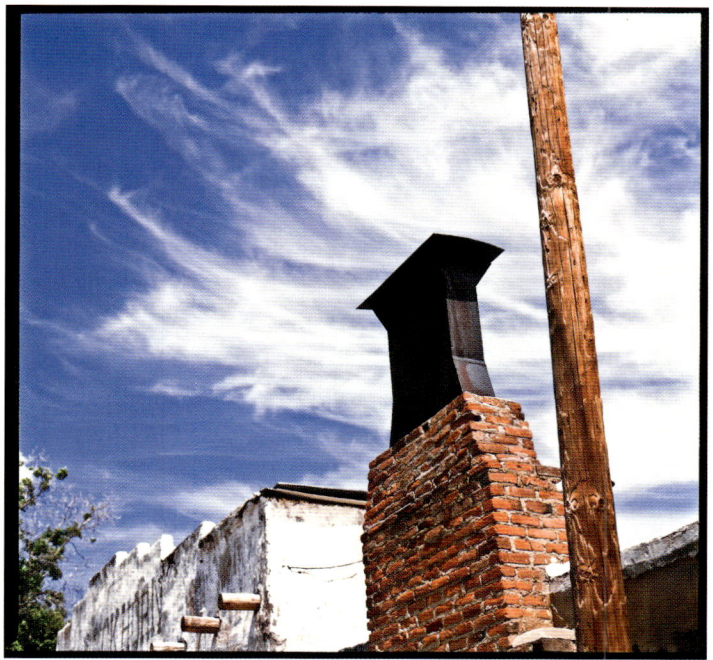

FIGURE 5.10 Piños Altos Opera House in Piños Altos, NM. Bronica SQA-I with 50 mm f/3.5. 1/125 @ f/16 ISO 100 Fujichrome Velvia 100

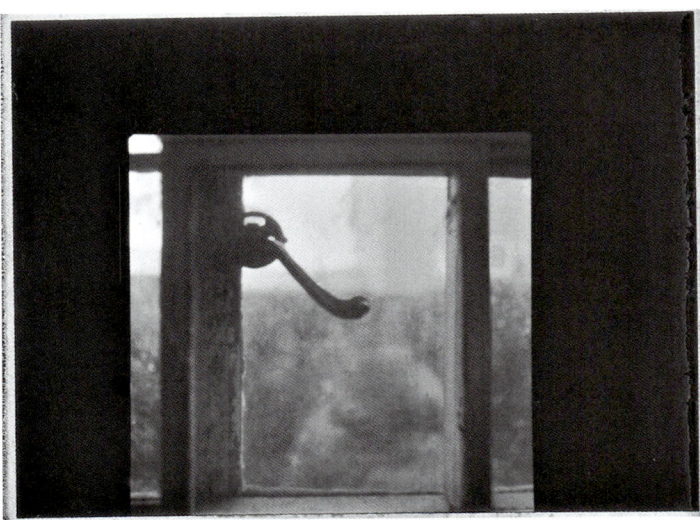

FIGURE 5.11 This image was shot using Fuji FP-3000B Polaroid-type peel-apart pack film. It was shot using a Bronica SQ-Ai using a Polaroid back. As you can see, the medium-format camera only uses a 6 × 6 cm area (same as the negative size). Polaroid backs were initially only used for proofing and checking exposure so that expensive medium-format film wasn't wasted.

- **Fuji FP-3000B.** This is a high-speed black-and-white film. It's great for handholding in darker scenes. The downside to this film is that the print doesn't retain a lot of detail. The upside is that the goop side actually retains a lot more detail that can be brought out when scanned.

Bracketing

One of the things that film photographers do to ensure they get the proper exposure is to *bracket* the exposures. Bracketing is a technique that involves taking multiple shots of the same subject, but varying the exposure settings. Bracketing usually involves taking from three to five shots, one shot as metered and one to two shots underexposed and overexposed.

Film processing at home

There's a bit of a misconception that processing film is somehow expensive and difficult, but nothing could be further from the truth. Processing film at home is a fun and rewarding process. The chemicals are still readily available, the required accessories can often be found used very inexpensively online or at your local camera shop, plus it's lots of fun. Don't get me wrong, when you first start processing film, it can get a little frustrating; it takes quite a bit of practice and attention to detail, but after you get the hang of it, the process becomes second nature.

Most people prefer to process black-and-white film because the process is pretty simple, and black-and-white film has a lot of latitude as far as processing time and temperature are concerned. There's a myth that has perpetrated for years that you can't process color film at home, which is completely untrue. Processing color negative film at home can be done. There are complete chemical kits available to buy relatively cheaply, and the accessories needed are exactly the same as black-and-white film. The differences between processing black and white and color is the different chemicals and the fact that the tolerances for chemical temperature are much more stringent. There are two well-known kits: the Tetanal C-41 kit, available through B&H Photo; and the Digibase C-41 kit, available though Freestyle Photographic Supplies. Since C-41 processing is a little more advanced, I'm not going to cover it here; complete instructions come with the kit.

In any case, as I mentioned previously, film can very easily be melded into your digital workflow with a simple film scanner. There is also something very satisfying about the hands-on approach of processing your own film that is somehow lacking in these days of the near-instant feedback of digital photography.

As I mentioned, black-and-white film processing is a relatively forgiving process when it comes to temperatures and developing times, so if you're new to film processing I recommend starting with black and white before moving on to the color process.

Supplies

Before you get started there are a few things you need to acquire to process your film:

- **Changing Bag.** This is a light-tight bag that allows you to spool your film on the reel. Film cannot be exposed to any light at all or it will be ruined. You can get one at most online photography stores for about $25. Another option is to use a dark room. Personally, I use a closet inside my bathroom that is completely dark (to be sure it's dark, close yourself in and wait for 5–10 minutes. If your eyes adjust and you can see, it's not dark enough).
- **Film reel.** You wind your exposed film on this. There are two kinds, plastic and stainless steel. I prefer the stainless and I've been using mine for over 20 years. These are also about $25 at most online stores. The plastic ones are a little easier to reel the film on, but they aren't necessarily the sturdiest options and tend to need replacing every so often.

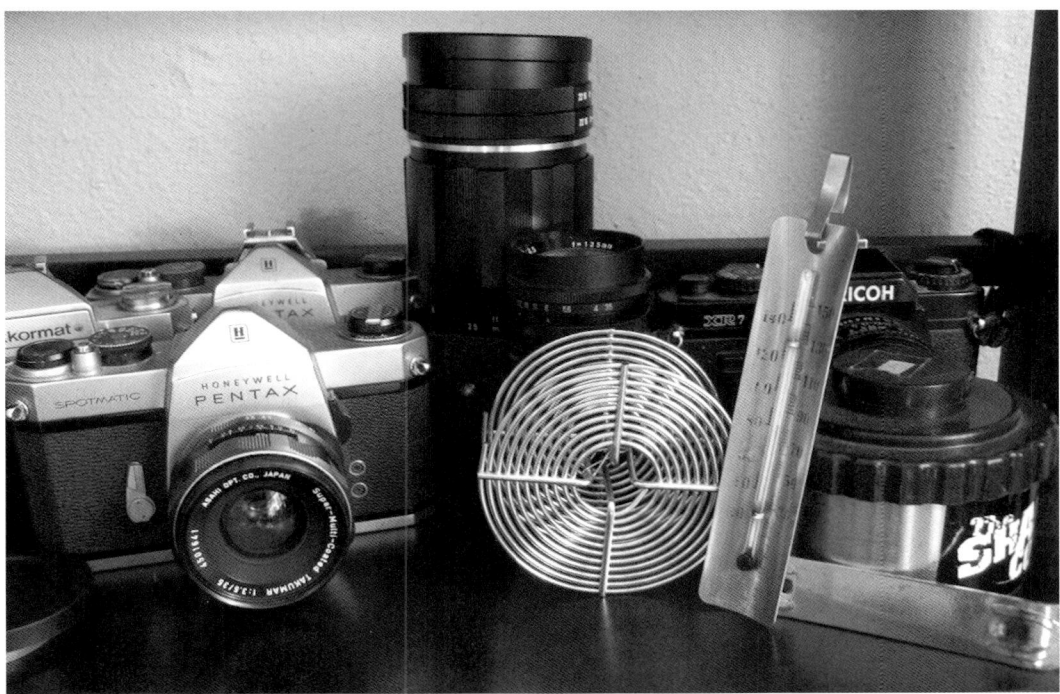

FIGURE 5.12 A sampling of film cameras and developing gear

- **Developing tank.** These are canisters that you put your reel into. They have a light-tight lid that allows you to pour the chemicals in and out. Again, I recommend using stainless steel. These come in a few sizes; the single size for one 35 mm roll, the double for two 35 mm or one 120 roll and the quadruple for four 35 mm rolls or two 120 rolls.
- **Bottle opener.** An old-fashioned bottle opener. This is used to pop open the 35 mm film canister.
- **Thermometer.** Just a regular thermometer will do. You can get one for less than $5. I use a standard chef's thermometer.
- **Measuring cups.** You'll need three measuring cups for mixing your chemicals. While you're at it, a medicine dropper with millimeter measurements is an immense help for mixing up the chemicals.
- **Scissors.** Any scissors will do.
- **Chemical storage bottles.** These are called datatainers. You can get them for about $4 each. They are brown to keep out the light and have areas for you to write on so you know which chemical is in which container. You will need at least two of these, for developer and fixer, possibly three if you use a chemical stop bath.
- **Chemicals.** You need a few chemicals to process. Some people use as many as five different chemicals, but it can be done with only two.
  - **Developer.** This is a must-have. Kodak D76 is the cheapest ($4/liter). I usually use Kodak HC-110 or some discontinued Agfa Rodinal that I have stashed away in the refrigerator. D76 is mixed from a powder form, but HC-110 is liquid, so therefore easier to prepare.
  - **Stop Bath.** I use Kodak Indicator Stop Bath; it's an acidic chemical that stops developer, which is mostly alkaline. Some people simply use water. I recommend distilled water if you go this route.
  - **Fixer.** This is a very important step. The fixer makes sure your negatives hold the image. If the film isn't fixed properly the image will disappear. You can get a liter of Ilford Rapid Fixer for $10. Fixer can be used over and over again.
  - **Hypo Clearing Agent.** This chemical quickly removes fixer residue, shortening rinse time. It's not absolutely necessary and I don't use it.
  - **Photo-flo.** This is what is known as a *wetting agent*; it inhibits streaks and spots when the film is drying. This isn't a necessary step, but I do recommend it.

Loading film

The first thing you'll need to do before getting started is to learn to load the film on the reel properly. Buy a couple of cheap rolls of film from the local big-box store and use these. Don't bother exposing them, just do it right out in the light.

Using the bottle opener, pop off the end of the film canister (the flat side is the easiest) and then slide out the film; try to touch the film only on the edges to avoid contaminating it with your body's natural oils. Feel for the film leader (this is the narrow edge that sticks out of the canister when the film is first opened). Use the scissors and cut this part off. Try to cut as straight as possible.

Next, grab the film with your thumb and forefinger at the edges of the film. With your other hand holding the reel, secure the film under the clip or catch the sprockets on the prongs, depending on which type of reel you have (I prefer the one with the prongs, commonly known as the Hewes reel). Once the film is secured, give it a slight bend by lightly pressing it with your thumb and forefinger, then start turning the wheel and winding the film onto it. Be gentle and let the film be pulled naturally;

don't hold the film too tight. It should reel up rather loosely to allow the chemical to permeate the film completely. If you feel the film bind, just back it up a little and continue the process. After the film is reeled, run your fingers up the sides of the reel; if you feel film protruding it has probably gotten bound up and you will have to re-reel it. Once again, this isn't something you will excel at right away; it takes lots of practice, so don't get frustrated if it doesn't work out the first few times.

Loading 120 film is quite similar, except that the film only needs to be separated from the paper backing, then placed under the clip. Since 120 film is wider and has no sprocket holes it has always been a little easier for me to reel.

After your film has been reeled, place it into your developing tank and place the lid on the tank. You can now turn on the light (remember, film must be loaded in complete and total darkness).

Chemistry and processing

The first thing you need to do is mix up your developer. Developer is best used at room temperature (68°F); higher temperatures cause quicker development time and negatives with more contrast. If using a powdered developer, such as D76, it's best to mix the developer a day ahead of time. Powdered developer must be mixed with hot water to dissolve, so giving it a day or at least a few hours to cool down is recommended. For liquid developers, mix it up according to the directions. Mix it about an hour before you process so t can get to room temperature.

Next you can mix up your stop bath. As with the developer, allow it to sit for an hour or so to get to room temperature. As I mentioned previously, using a chemical stop bath isn't a necessity. It's relatively cheap, so I use it, but you can also use plain water. I recommend using distilled water and letting it sit out at room temperature, or you can use plain tap water at room temperature. The reason I don't recommend tap water is that some cities have hard water, which can leave stains and residue on your negatives.

Now we move on to fixer. This is an essential chemical. Fixer makes the image on your negative stable and removes the unexposed silver halide crystals. This makes the film insensitive. There are two types of fixers, hardening and non-hardening. Either fixer works fine with most films such as Fuji, Kodak, and Ilford because they have hardening agents built into the film to harden the emulsion to make it scratch resistant and more durable. The only contemporary film that I recommend using a hardening fixer with is Efke, which doesn't have a hardening agent added to the film. Fixer can be used over and over again, so if you store it at room temperature you don't have to worry about it much after you mix your first bath until it's depleted. To determine if your fixer is depleted, stick a piece of unexposed film in a small amount of it. If it takes more than 6–8 minutes to clear you should mix up a new batch.

After you have your film reeled and in the tank and your chemicals mixed and at the right temperature, it's time to process. One of the most important parts of processing is agitation. To properly agitate your film you pick up the tank, invert it, un-invert it, and repeat the process for the allotted time. When you're done agitating, tap the tank gently to remove any air bubbles. Then *put the tank down*. Holding the tank in your hands between agitation will raise the temperature of your chemistry (remember, body temperature is around 98.6°F). Now onto the process:

1. **Developer.** Keep in mind that your developer temperature is very important. The best thing to do is leave some water out

to get it to room temperature. Then use hot or cold water from the tap to bring it to 68°F/20°C. Development times vary depending on film type, ISO speed, and temperature. A great resource for almost any film and developer you can imagine is www.digitaltruth.com/devchart.php (they even have an app). Note the developer time and set a timer. Remove the cap from the top of the tank (not the *lid*, just the cap) and pour in the developer. Agitate the film for the first 30 seconds, then for 10 seconds for each minute of development. Dump the developer down the drain (this is eco-safe).

2. **Stop bath.** As I mentioned previously, using a chemical stop bath isn't a necessity. Some folks use water, but I use the chemical type. For the chemical stop bath pour it into the tank and agitate constantly for one minute or longer, preferably two minutes. When using water, fill the tank, agitate for one minute, empty the tank and repeat twice more. That's three minutes of agitation and three rinses.

3. **Fixer.** This is an essential step. Generally, it's best to fix your film anywhere from four to six minutes. What I do to determine the time is to take the cut-off film leader and immerse it in a small amount of fixer and see how long it takes to clear, then add a minute or two to be sure. New fixer requires less time to fix while older fixer takes a longer time to fix. Agitate the film for the first 30 seconds and 10 seconds for each minute thereafter. After you're finished, pour the fixer back into your container. Fixer can be reused numerous times. When the fixer is depleted *do not* pour it down the drain – fixer is toxic to the environment. You can take it to the nearest photo lab or haz-mat place to have them dispose of it for you.

4. **Rinse.** Once your film is fixed, you can expose it to light. Now it's time to rinse the film to make it chemical-free. Take the lid off of the canister and let running water flow over it for at least ten minutes. The water should be about room temperature; if the water is too hot *reticulation* will occur, which is caused by the emulsion shrinking away from the substrate. I rinse my film for at least ten minutes.

5. **Photo-Flo.** This is what is known as a wetting agent. It keeps the water from drying too fast and thus leaving spots. A lot of people don't use it, but it's super-cheap, one bottle lasts forever, and it saves you from cleaning spots off of your negatives, especially if you have hard water. Use about two drops into the tank full of water and *gently* swirl the reel around using your fingers. I emphasize *gently* because if done too vigorously the Photo-Flo will foam up. Swirl this for a few seconds then empty the tank and take the reel out.

You can now take the film from the reel. *Do not* let it touch anything; this avoids transferring dirt or dust to your film. Use film clips or clothespins to hang the film to dry. The easiest way is to use a hanger on your shower rod and hang the film using the clips or pins. Let the film dry for a few hours. *Don't touch it* as you will leave smudges and fingerprint marks. Drying in a dust-free environment is best.

Once it's dry you can cut the film into segments. Make sure you thoroughly wash your hands first or use cotton film-handling gloves, then insert them into negative sleeves, which are available at most photography stores.

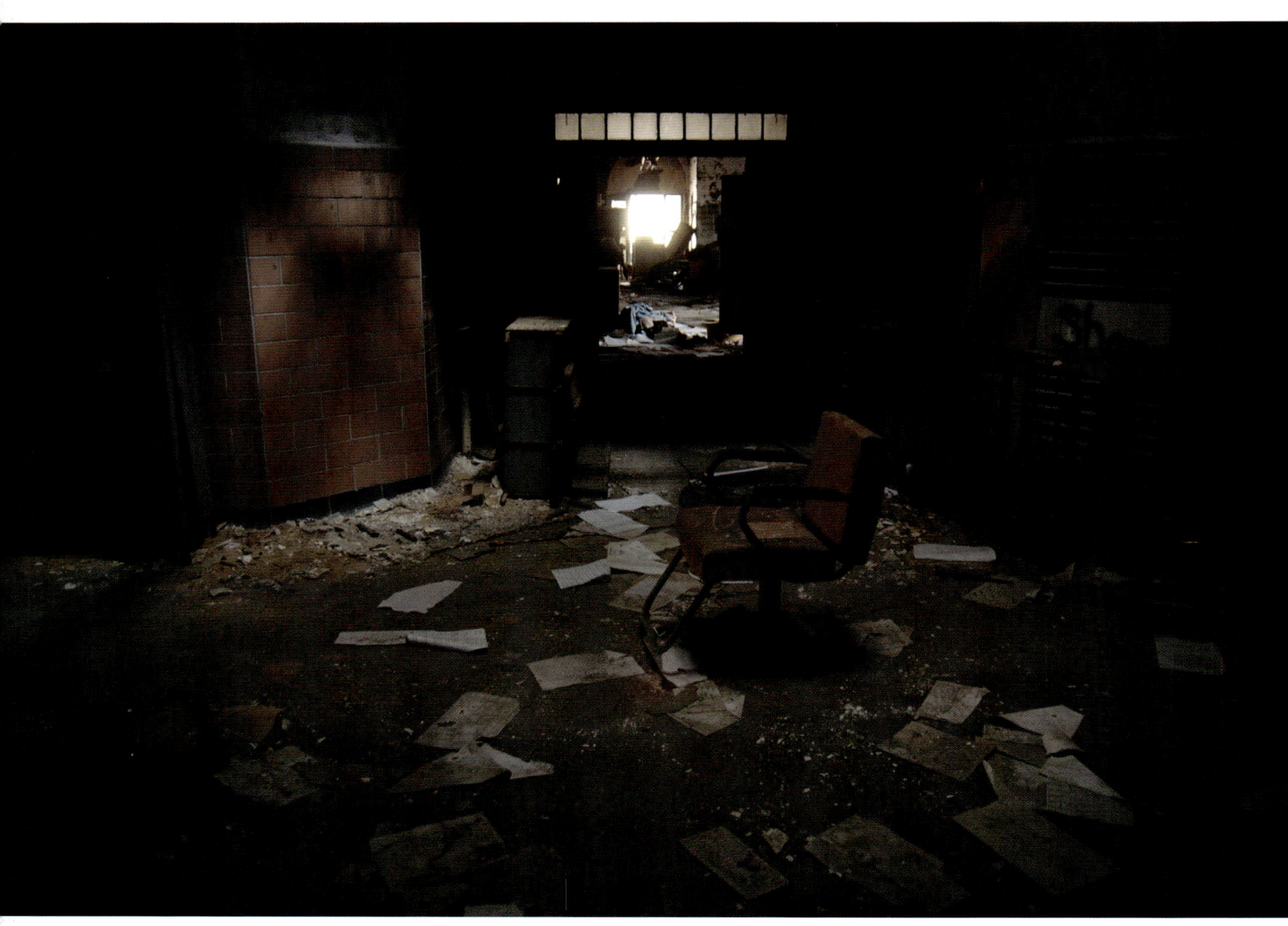

SHOOTING IN LOW LIGHT

Six

FIGURE 6.1 Forest Haven Children's Development Center in Laurel, MD.   **Sony α300 with Tamron 17–50 mm f/2.8 at 17 mm (25 mm equivalent) @ f/2.8 ISO 400. © Chris Folsom**

Why shoot in low light? There's no straightforward answer to this question, but sometimes it's as simple as there's no light in the location that you've chosen to shoot. Even in the middle of the day you may find yourself inside an abandoned structure with no windows at all, or if there are windows, the sunlight coming through them may be dim and filtered through years of dirt and grime, obscuring the light until it's a dull wash.

Shooting at night often adds to the essence of the decay scene. Darkness can lend a feeling of solitude, sadness, or even a bit of horror and scariness to your image. Humans have a visceral reaction to the dark that is embedded deep into their psyche. Images taken in darkness and low light can often draw your viewer in simply because of the innate fear of the dark that pervades most people.

Shooting at night can also provide a sort of outlet for a photographer, a chance to be alone with the camera and the subject, a time to unwind from the stresses of the day with solitude and quiet that isn't usually found during the day.

A fairly significant percentage of decay photography is done in low-light situations, and shooting when the light is low requires some different procedures and also offers opportunities to experiment with different techniques than when shooting with ample light.

Note: Most compact cameras aren't adept at shooting in low light. The maximum shutter speeds are often limited and the small sensor usually creates unusable images due to noise.

When shooting in low light there are some extra tools and accessories that you wouldn't necessarily need in a situation where the light is plentiful that can make the job a little easier. There are also a couple of items that are pretty much essential.

- **Tripod.** When shooting at night this is an absolute necessity. Long exposures are impossible without one. See Chapter 2 for more information about tripods.
- **Cable or remote release.** Personally I find this to be an essential accessory. This allows you to trip the shutter without causing camera shake by pressing the shutter release button on the camera, which results in motion blur when doing long exposures. Most remote releases also allow you to use the bulb function on the camera for exposures over 30 seconds.
- **Vibration-reducing or image-stabilizing lens.** If you don't have a tripod with you (sometimes I'll run across abandoned structures unexpectedly) or if you're in a confined space where using a tripod isn't feasible, having a lens that compensates for camera shake can be an invaluable tool. Unfortunately, a lot of Nikon's and Canon's professional lenses don't have this feature yet, but a lot of their consumer lenses do, and most third-party manufacturers make very good lenses with this feature. These lenses can make a world of difference if handholding the camera is a necessity.
- **Flashlight.** A flashlight comes in handy not only for the obvious reason to help you find your way in the dark, but you can also use it to help you with autofocus, and for light painting, which is discussed later in the chapter. A head-mounted lamp is a good option as it frees up your hands and allows you to see and handle the camera with ease in dark places.
- **Flash.** This isn't a necessity, but you can pop off a flash while doing a long exposure to add some texture and interest to the scene. An expensive flash that's dedicated for your camera brand isn't necessary since you'll be using it off-camera. This is also discussed later in the chapter.

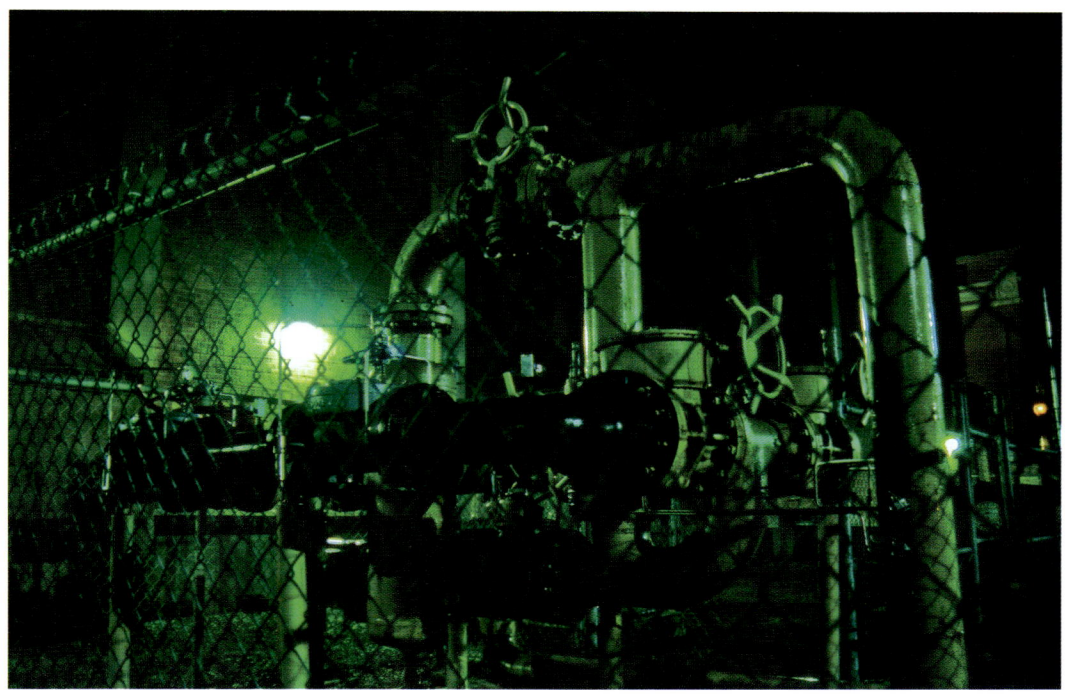

FIGURE 6.2 Shooting this image with daylight-rated film caused the high-pressure sodium light in the background to give off an eerie green light. Although I was able to correct the color in Photoshop, I preferred the color as it was shot. **Nikon F90x with Nikon 28 mm f/2.8D @ f/8 for 30 seconds on Fuji Astia 100F**

Settings

When shooting in low light, how you choose your settings is not only a matter of achieving the correct exposure, but different settings also have different effects on your photography and how the image appears. For this reason it is more necessary to think your exposure settings through before releasing the shutter.

The following sections cover some of the different idiosyncrasies of each setting in the triumvirate of exposure.

ISO sensitivity

The ISO sensitivity setting of a digital camera doesn't make the sensor more sensitive to light, it simply amplifies the electrical signals from the sensor, which are directly proportional to how much light the sensor is exposed to. As the signal is amplified so is the inherent interference that is present in all electronic devices – we call this interference *noise*. For this reason, simply cranking up the ISO setting when the light is low isn't always the best option as it can result in overly grainy images scattered with random specks of color. This is the main pitfall of using

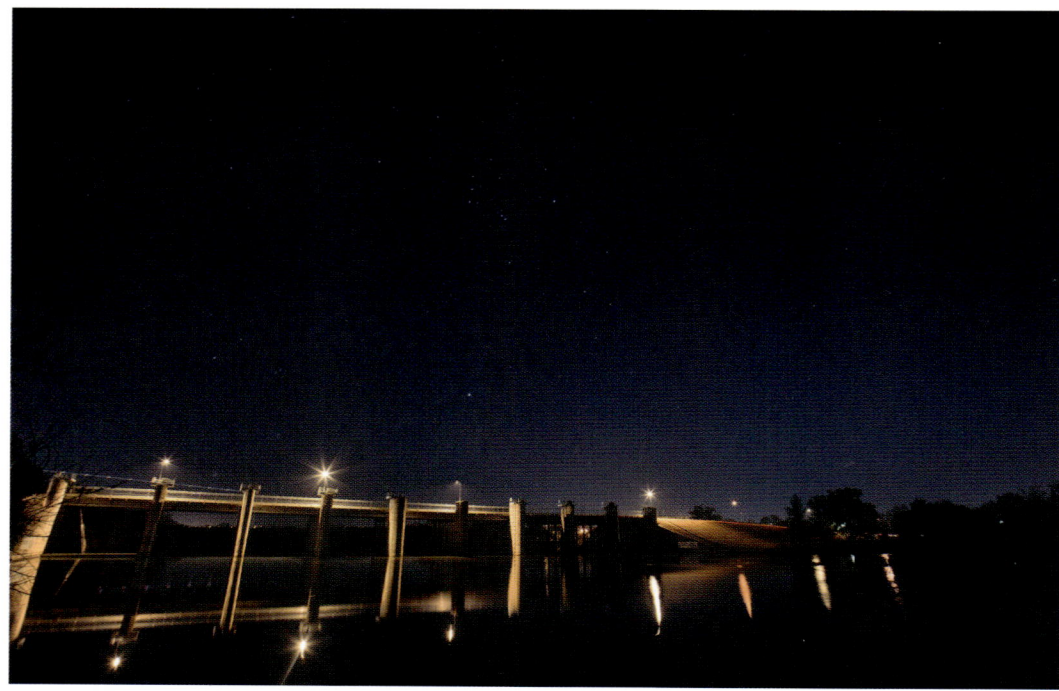

FIGURE 6.3 For this image I used a tripod and a remote release to ensure that my long-exposure images were free from blur caused by camera shake. Nikon D600 with Sigma 17–25 mm f/2.8–4G at 17 mm. 30 seconds @ f/8 ISO 400

higher ISO settings, but sometimes living with noise is a necessary evil.

Generally speaking, to get the best image quality you want to set your camera's ISO sensitivity to the *native setting*. This is the lowest base ISO that your camera can be set to. This is usually around ISO 100–200 depending on the make and model (Leica has an odd base ISO of 160). The native ISO is the sensitivity at which the sensor is designed to function best. ISO settings on most cameras range from ISO 100 to ISO 6400, and some cameras offer extended settings, some to lower sensitivity and some to raise the sensitivity above the highest rated setting, but these settings do not offer optimal image quality. A common misconception is that the lowest ISO (often termed Lo-1 or L/1) setting will offer the best image quality; this is untrue – in actuality this overexposes the image (that is, exposes at the native ISO) and uses in-camera processing to pull back the exposure, therefore reducing your dynamic range. At the opposite end, shooting at the Hi or H settings doesn't actually increase the gain of the sensor, it simply underexposes the image and uses in-camera processing

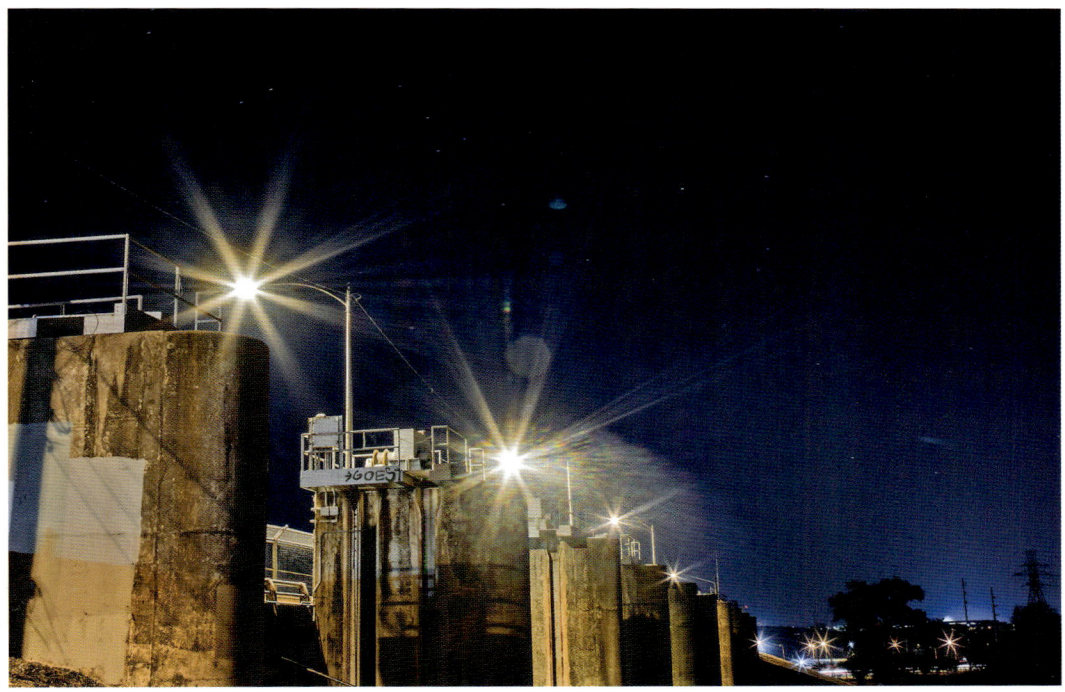

FIGURE 6.4 When shooting at night I try to use as low an ISO setting as I can. High ISO noise is much more difficult to deal with than long-exposure noise. For the most part decay photography comprises non-moving subjects so long shutter speeds aren't a hindrance. Nikon D600 with Sigma 28–70 mm f/2.8–4 DG at 14 mm. 30 seconds @ f/9 ISO 200

to push the exposure, with the result of increased noise. You can do the same thing using a RAW converter's exposure slider.

For night photography using film I don't recommend using fast films. Films rated to ISO 800–1600 (or even 3200) are made for photographing action in low light. Decay photography isn't action oriented, so using a slower film will yield better results image-wise due to the finer grain of the film. If you're planning on handholding your camera or don't want to deal with the trouble of reciprocity, I suggest sticking with digital capture.

Generally I recommend using films rated ISO 100–400. You'll find that these films will produce the best results with fine grain and a wide tonal range.

Shutter speed

Selecting an appropriate shutter speed when shooting in low light is critical. There are two options that you can choose from when selecting a shutter speed for low-light photography: fast or slow. Neither one is correct for every shooting situation.

Your shutter speed selection primarily depends on what effect you want to achieve.

Selecting a fast shutter speed (anywhere from 1/30 or faster) has a few drawbacks. In order to get a fast shutter speed you either need to turn up the ISO sensitivity settings, open up the aperture, or sometimes both. A fast shutter speed allows you to handhold the camera without the fear of blur from camera shake, and freeze any motion in the scene (depending on your shutter speed and speed of the motion), but the pitfalls of having a faster shutter speed are high ISO noise, lack of depth of field due to using a wide aperture, and the possibility of lack of image sharpness due to using a wide aperture (most lenses are sharpest when stopped down about two stops).

Selecting a slower shutter speed (1/15 and slower) has its own drawbacks and benefits as well. First of all, a slower shutter speed allows you to use a lower ISO setting, but in this situation you then run into long-exposure noise; this is most prevalent when doing exposures longer than a second or two. Long-exposure noise is generally more fine and is easier to remedy in post-production, so don't let the thought of long-exposure noise deter you from using long-exposure settings or doing *timed exposures.* Timed exposures is the term that's often used when the exposure settings are longer than can be set on the camera, so a remote release is used to trigger when the shutter open and closes and the shutter time is controlled by the photographer.

Using a slow shutter speed is a double-edged sword. A slow shutter speed will cause blur in your images. This is a good and bad thing. The bad thing is that you can't handhold the camera without getting blur from camera shake, so using a tripod is necessary, but when using a tripod and a long exposure you can capture motion in your image as a blur while non-moving elements of the image stay sharply in focus.

This second kind of motion blur can be used to create an artistic element to your decay photography. Of course, the longer the exposure the more motion blur can be captured, although if the shutter speed is slow enough things can move through the image without being recorded.

Using a long exposure can also allow you to use a flash or flashlight to add to the ambient light of the scene. This is referred to as light painting and is a great tool for adding light to very dark shadow areas, as well as being useful for highlighting specific areas to draw attention or lead the viewer's eye to it.

Also, as mentioned briefly in the previous section, using a longer shutter speed can allow you to get sharper images and deeper depth of field when you stop down the lens aperture.

When buying film you should have an idea of what kind of shutter speed you will likely need for your specific shooting situation. Forethought is one of the keys to successful photography when shooting with film. Having a few different speeds of film or having a couple of cameras loaded with different speed films can come in handy if you find that you need a faster or slower shutter speed to get a desired effect.

Aperture

As you probably know by now, ISO sensitivity, shutter speed, and aperture settings are all combined to create your exposure, and none of these settings can be changed without modifying one of the other settings two settings in order to keep an equivalent exposure.

The relationships of the other two settings in comparison to the aperture setting have been covered in the previous two sections, but to summarize: you can use a wider aperture to reduce the ISO sensitivity setting or to increase the shutter speed. Conversely, using a smaller aperture results in the need

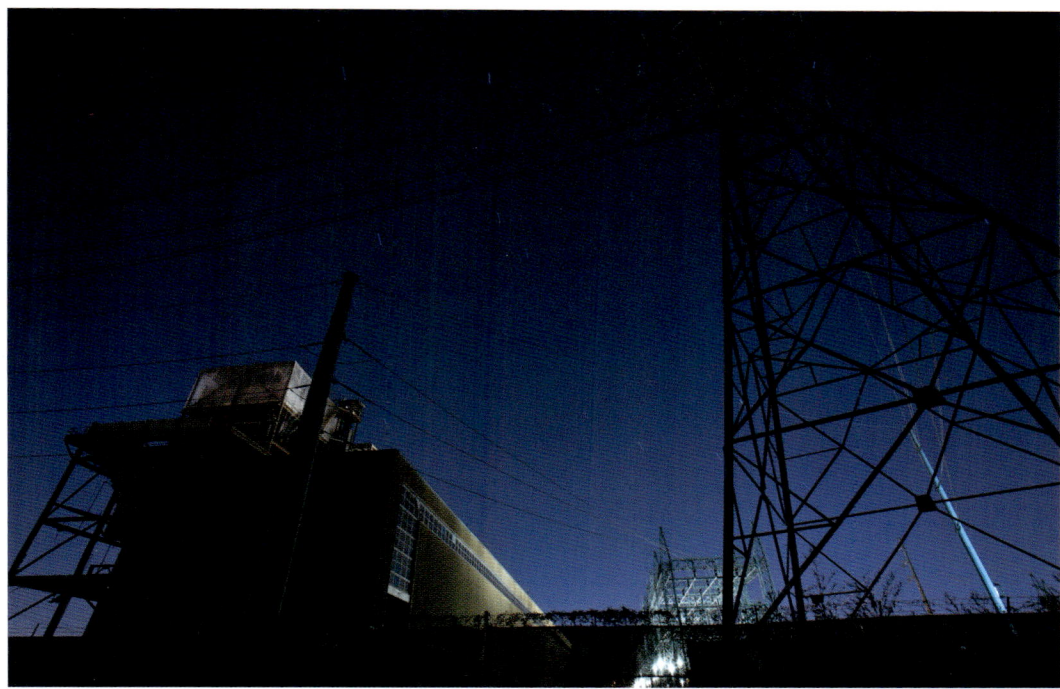

FIGURE 6.5 This image of the Holly Street Power Plant was taken using a remote release to control the exposure. With one press of the button the shutter is opened and a second press closes it. The scene was so dark here that the exposure ran over five minutes. A minimal amount of noise reduction was applied to the image.   Nikon D600 with Sigma 17–35 mm f/2.8–4 HSM at 17 mm, 308 seconds @ f/11 ISO 100

to increase the ISO sensitivity or the length of the shutter speed.

One thing that's often overlooked when selecting an aperture for night photography is how the size of the aperture affects the bright areas of the image. Streetlights or other extremely small and bright light sources are majorly affected by the size of the aperture. When shooting wide open these light sources can be rendered as indistinct blobs, but when shooting with the aperture stopped down these highlights are instead rendered with a star-like pattern due to the diffusion of the light as it enters the lens through the aperture blades. The smaller the aperture the more defined the star pattern is.

Note: The number of aperture blades the lens has determines the number of points on the star.

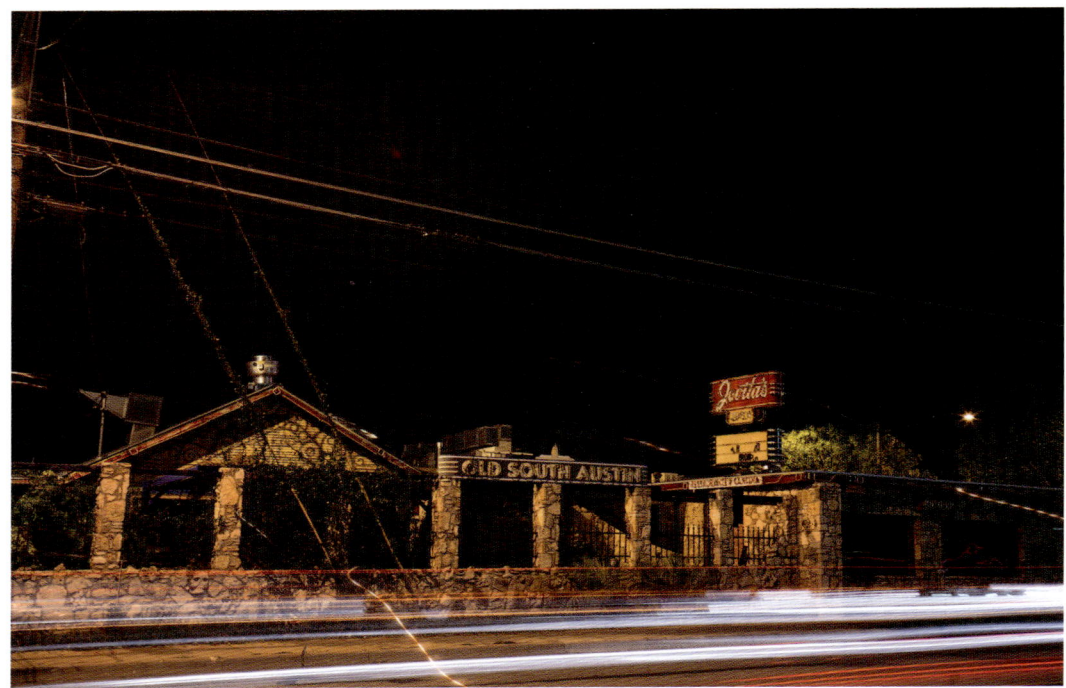

FIGURE 6.6 The long exposure allows cars to move through the scene without being captured in the image; only the lights are bright enough to register on the sensor. You wouldn't know it, but there was also quite a bit of foot traffic through the scene while I was taking the picture. The people moved fast enough that there was never enough light to allow them to show up in the final image. Nikon D600 with Sigma 28–70 mm f/2.8–4 DG at 40 mm. 10 seconds @ f/11 ISO 100

Digital

Shooting digital in low light is a bit different than shooting during the daylight or in a scene where there is plenty of light to make a correct exposure. When shooting digital in the dark you have different decisions to make, such as "Should I use a long exposure and low ISO or a short exposure and a high ISO?" Getting an optimal exposure in low light isn't necessarily more difficult than it is in a brighter setting, but you must expose *differently* to get the best quality out of your images.

Shoot RAW

The first thing you *must* do is shoot RAW. In a well-lit situation you can get away with shooting JPEGS, but in low light you will need all of the tonal information you can get. Recording your images straight to JPEG takes all of the data that your sensor

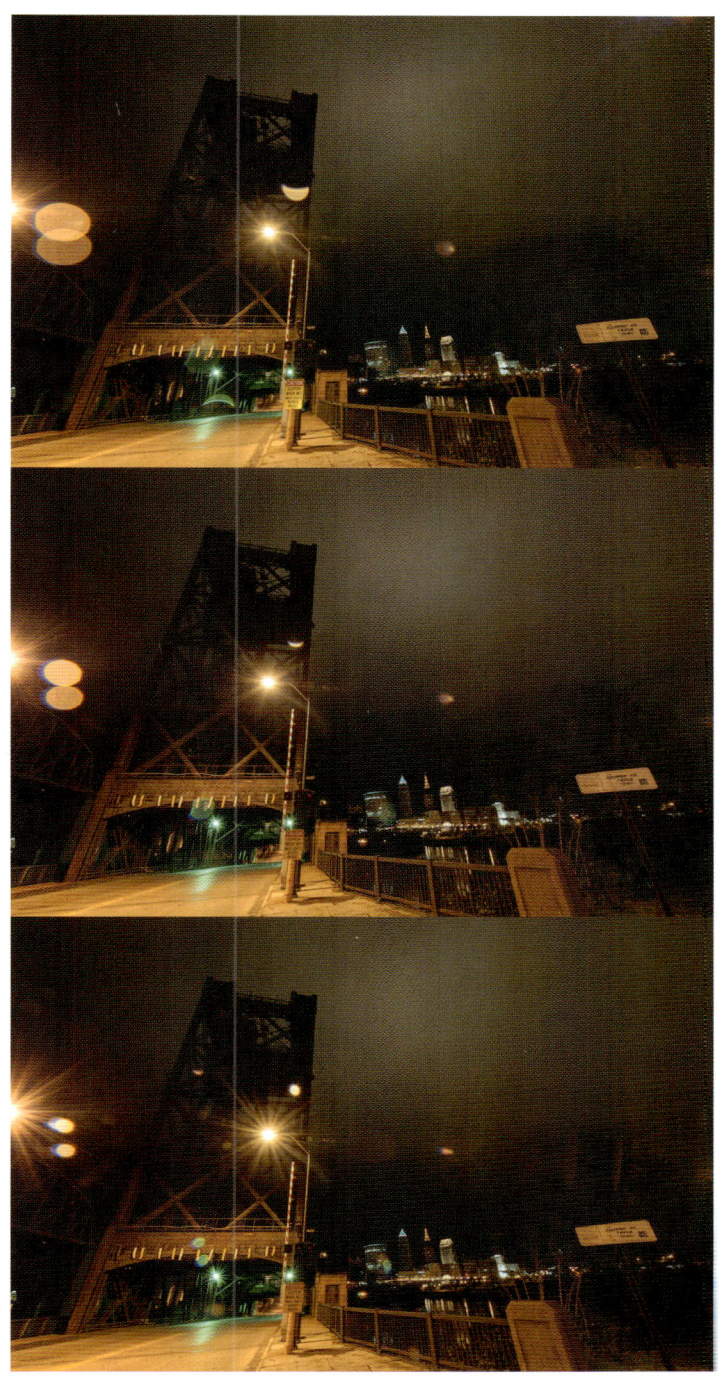

FIGURE 6.7 As you can see in this series of images, the size of the aperture changes the way the highlights and lens flare looks. From top to bottom the aperture settings are f/5.6, f/8, and f/16.   Nikon D700 with Nikon 14–24 mm f/2.8G at 14 mm

captures, uses what it needs, and throws the rest away. That data can never be recovered and if you need to make adjustments your image quality is going to suffer. Added to that, every time you open and close the JPEG file a little more information is discarded and after time the quality degrades even more. The hardest areas for a digital camera to capture detail are shadow areas, and when shooting in low light most of your image is going to be shadow areas, so you need to shoot RAW to preserve every bit of detail each pixel captures.

RAW images capture and retain a wider amount of dynamic range, which makes it easier to control and fine-tune exposures where there is a very wide dynamic range, such as you will often find when shooting decay indoors. Usually you will have a darkened room broken up with rays of bright sunlight streaming in from windows, doors, and cracks. This type of setting is difficult to expose from, but using RAW gives you much more leeway to rein in the highlights than a JPEG file can.

Set your white balance

When shooting in daylight or in a simple well-lit area I usually set my white balance to auto and adjust it in post-processing. When shooting a scene in the dark, especially outside at night, you will come across mixed lighting more often than you will in the daytime. Why setting the white balance is important is because when shooting at night you will need to rely on the histogram more to judge your exposure than you do in brighter situations. If you can get your white balance set as close as you can to what you think your final image is going to be, your histogram will give you a more accurate reading. Since you're shooting RAW you can still do any minor or even major adjustments in post-processing.

Exposure

As I mentioned previously, there are a few options to choose from when shooting in the dark: low ISO and a slow shutter speed; high ISO and a fast shutter speed; or a mid-range ISO setting and a semi-slow shutter speed. Each option has its strengths and weaknesses depending on the situation. I'm going to break down each element of exposure and discuss the strengths and weaknesses of each separately, but first I want to discuss the most important rule of digital low-light photography: expose to the right, sometimes referred to as ETTR.

The origins of ETTR are actually based on an old rule of thumb from film photography: expose for the shadows, develop for the highlights. The idea here is that you capture all of the detail in the shadows, but when processing the film pull the exposure to ensure that highlight detail is retained, therefore maximizing the dynamic range of the film.

When shooting digitally this same principal is followed: by exposing to the right you capture all of the detail you can where the camera sensor is most adept, in the brighter ranges, then when "processing" the RAW file you pull back on the exposure and the result is an image that is tonally rich.

The phrase "expose to the right" refers to the luminance histogram. In a nutshell, the luminance histogram represents the brightness levels of the pixels on the sensor. Pixels that receive more light are represented on the right side of the histogram and pixels that received little light are represented on the left side. For more detailed information on the histogram, see Chapter 4.

To get an optimal exposure for a low-light shot you technically want to overexpose the image. The caveat here is that you must pay close attention to the histogram to make sure that even as you're overexposing the image you do not allow the

Shooting in Low Light 119

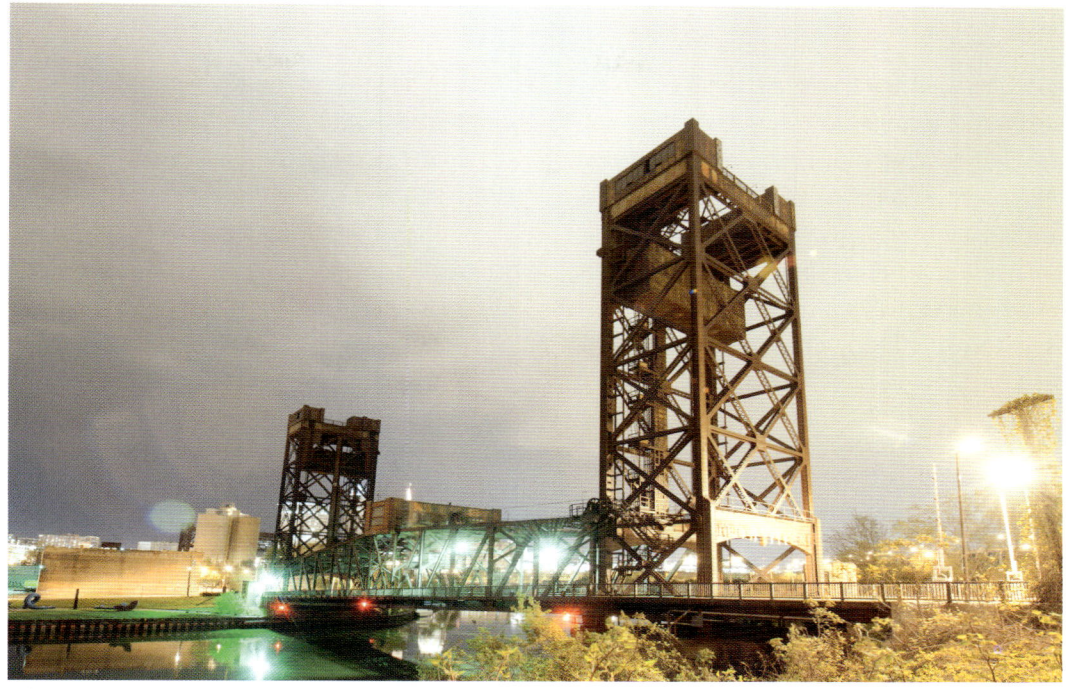

(a)

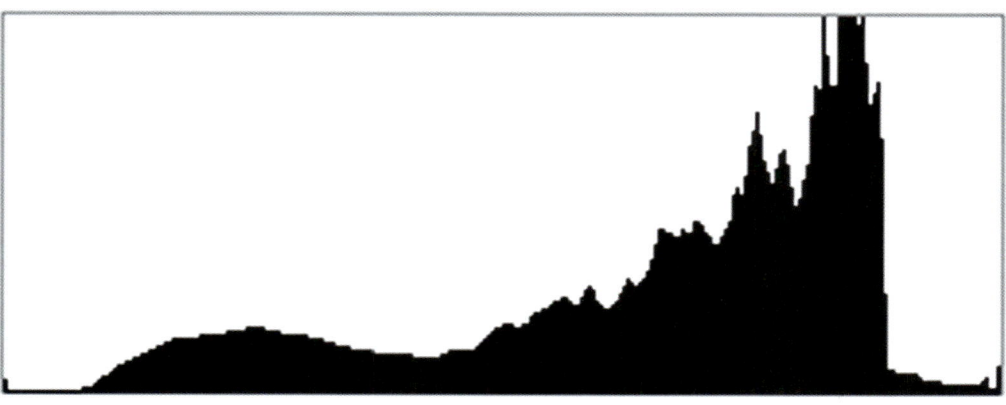

(b)

FIGURE 6.8 (a) For this image I exposed to the right to capture all of the detail in the shadow area. The image is overexposed, causing it to lose a lot of the characteristics of a night-time shot. **Nikon D700 with Nikon 14–24 mm f/2.8G at 14 mm. 30 seconds @ f/9 ISO 200.** (b) This histogram for Figure 6.8a shows that although the image is overexposed, most of the detail is retained in both the shadow and the highlight areas of the image.

highlight detail to clip. You want the histogram to taper off as it gets closer to the edge of the histogram. This ensures that not only do you have adequate detail in the shadow areas, but that you retain detail in the brightest areas as well. In some instances, if there are pinpoints of lights, such as from a streetlight, you will notice a spike running up along the edge of the histogram – this is sometimes unavoidable.

Note: The image review on your camera LCD will appear to be overexposed.

Once you get the overexposed RAW image downloaded onto your computer, you then open it up in your RAW converter of choice (Lightroom, Adobe Camera RAW, Aperture, etc.) and you pull back the exposure slider, again keeping a close eye on the histogram, until the histogram is weighted to the *left*, which is what you want to see for an image shot in low light. As when you're making the exposure you want to be sure that the histogram tapers off as it gets to the edge, indicating that you are retaining detail in the shadow areas. You can then make other adjustments such as color corrections, saturation, noise reduction, etc.

Noise reduction

When shooting in low light, whether at high ISO settings or using long exposures, you introduce what is known as *noise* into your images. Simply put, noise is random specks of color that appear throughout the image, but is generally more noticeable in the shadow areas of the image. There are two types of noise: *high ISO noise*, which is a symptom of the inherent background noise that is present in all electronic devices being amplified when the ISO sensitivity gain is turned up, and *thermal noise*, which is caused by the sensor creating extraneous electrons as it heats up while a long exposure is made.

In addition to the two types of noise, noise also has two different attributes: chrominance noise and luminance noise. Chrominance is the color of the specks of noise and luminance is the size and shape of the specks of noise.

Almost all digital cameras have built-in noise reduction techniques to handle the noise problem. Each type of noise is dealt with in a different way (in-camera at least). For high-ISO noise, the imaging processor inside the camera analyzes the image and reduces the chroma of the noise, resulting in a grain that is free of the colors of the chrominance noise. Once the chroma is reduced, the image processor usually softens the luminance or grain, giving the image a smoother appearance. This often results in the loss of fine detail in the image as well.

The way thermal noise is dealt with is completely different. Thermal noise is handled by what is called a *dark-frame noise reduction*. How this works is that after the camera makes the initial exposure of the scene, a second exposure is made without the shutter opening, the sensor is simply activated for the same amount of time as the initial exposure. The camera's image processor then analyzes the thermal noise data from the dark frame exposure and uses the noise patterns from the dark frame to eliminate the noise from the original exposure.

For the most part, noise reduction is only useful when shooting JPEG files. When a RAW file is created the noise reduction information is stored in the file data but is usually only accessible to the camera manufacturer's proprietary software, like Nikon's Capture NX2 or View NX2, or Canon's Digital Photo Pro or EOS Viewer Utility. When opening RAW files with third-party software such as Adobe Lightroom or Adobe Camera RAW, you can apply the noise reduction on your own. I recommend turning off the noise reduction in your camera settings if you're using third-party software.

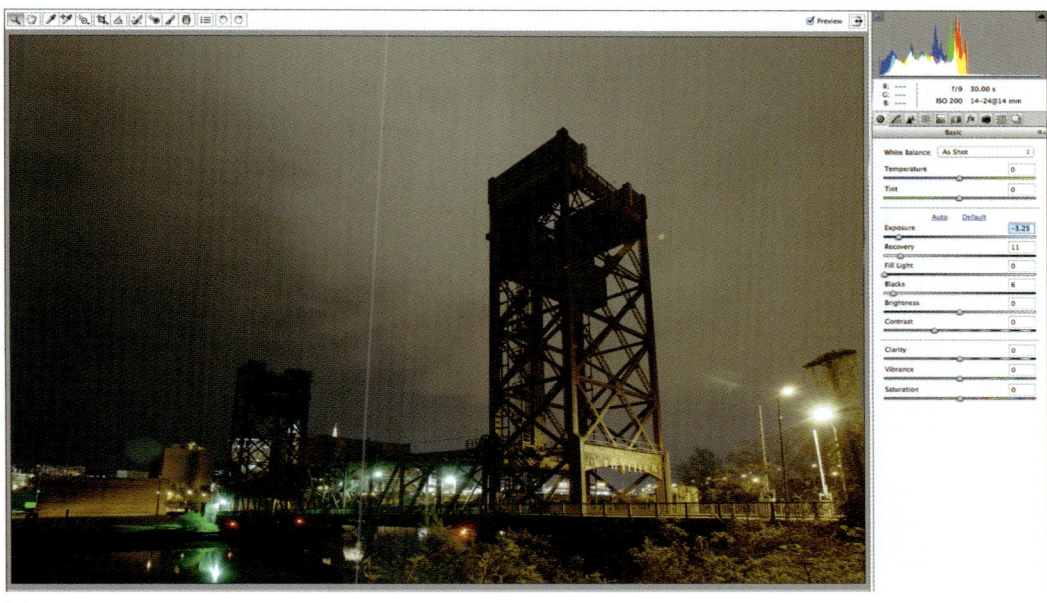

(a)

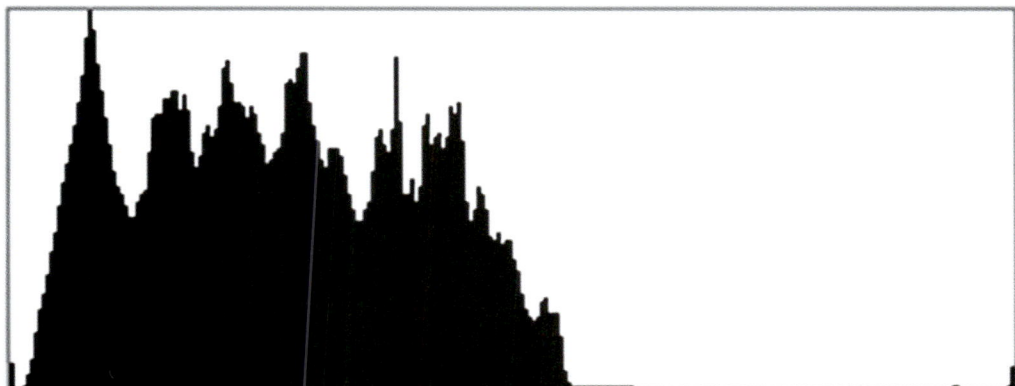

(b)

FIGURE 6.9 (a) Once opened up in Adobe Camera RAW the exposure can be adjusted to bring the image back to a night-time look. **Nikon D700 with Nikon 14–24 mm f/2.8G at 14 mm. 30 seconds @ f/9 ISO 200**, (b) This histogram for Figure 6.9a shows that the image is low-key and mostly dark in tone. The histogram tapers off, showing the image has detail where it needs it without clipping the highlights or shadows

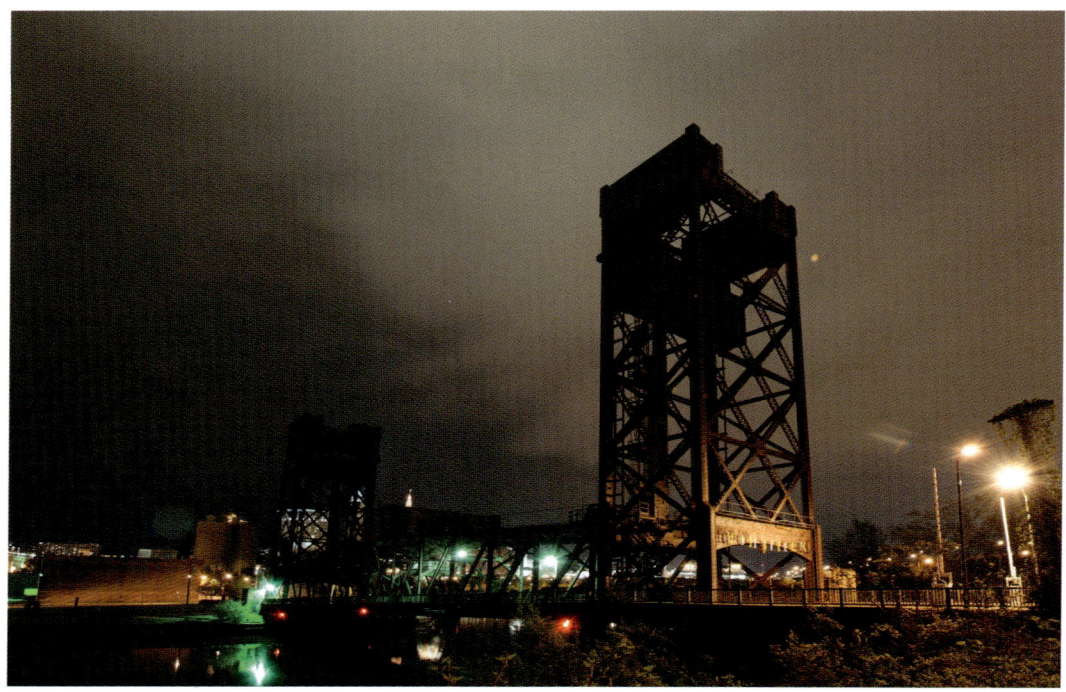

FIGURE 6.10 After reducing the exposure in Adobe Camera RAW this image looks exactly like it did in person.   Nikon D700 with Nikon 14–24 mm f/2.8G at 14 mm. 30 seconds @ f/9 ISO 200

I find that most in-camera noise reduction is very aggressive, leading to soft images that lack fine detail.

Film

Shooting film in low light is not only different than shooting film in daylight, but it's also different than shooting digital in low light.

Probably the most difficult aspect to shooting film at night is that unlike digital you don't have the instant feedback of the image review or histogram available to you. Added to that handicap, there is also the fact that you can't rely on the camera light meter or even a handheld light meter to give an accurate exposure reading. This is due to the fact that most film camera meters are designed to meter for an average setting, and low light is anything but average. Unless you are out in the middle of nowhere on a moonless night, you are likely photographing scenes that have high contrast and a wide dynamic range from very bright pinpoint areas of light, such as moonlight or streetlights, to deep, dark shadow areas.

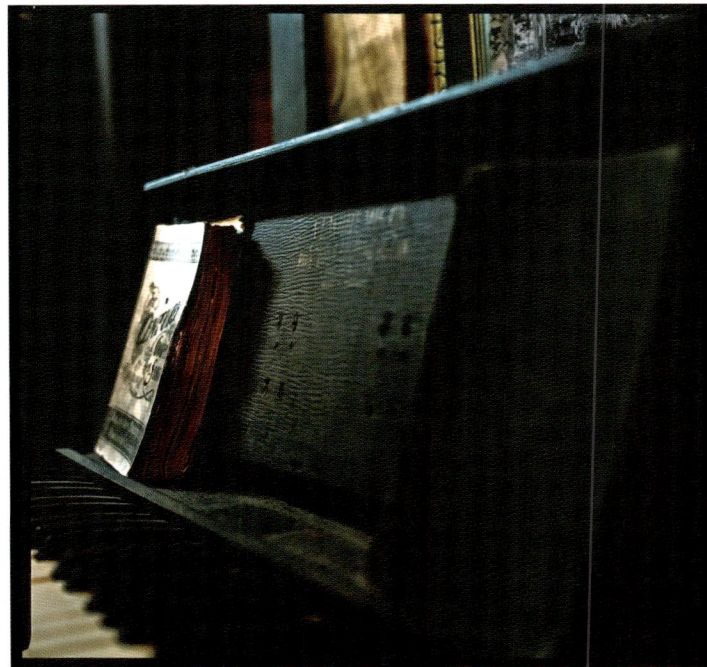

FIGURE 6.11 I find that using slide film gives better image quality when shooting in low light. Despite the lower dynamic range, it has better color reproduction and less grain than color negative films.   Bronica SQAi with Zenzanon 80 mm f/3.5. 1 second @ f/3.5 ISO 400. Fuji Provia 400F

between aperture and shutter speed breaks down. In short, in order to get the exposure indicated on a light meter, you need to add extra exposure time to make up for lost sensitivity.

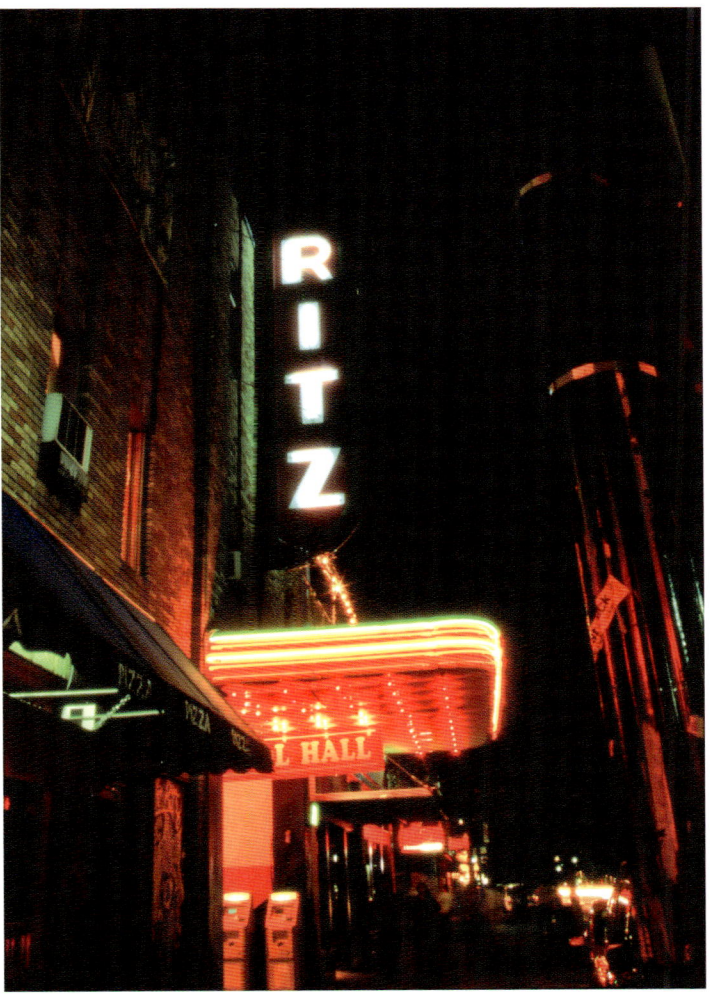

FIGURE 6.12 This shot of the former Ritz Theater pool hall was shot on print film. The quality of a decent DSLR usually beats out the quality of scanned 35 mm print film.   Nikon F90X with Nikon 28 mm f/2.8D. Exposure unrecorded

This brings us back to the ETTR technique I discussed earlier in the chapter. Of course, film has no histogram, so we expose for the shadows and develop for the highlights.

Reciprocity failure

On top of the meter being unreliable, film emulsion grows less sensitive to light as exposure time is increased. This phenomenon is called *reciprocity failure*, which means that as exposure gets longer the reciprocal relationship that you have

TABLE 6.1 Black-and-white film approximate reciprocity corrections

Measured exposure		1 sec.	2 sec.	4 sec.	8 sec.	15 sec.	30 sec.	1 min.
Corrected exposure	Ilford Pan F Plus 50	1.5 sec.	3 sec.	6 sec.	12 sec.	22 sec.	44 sec.	1 min. 30 sec.
	Ilford Delta 100	1 sec.	2 sec.	4.5 sec.	9 sec.	19 sec.	41 sec.	1 min. 33 sec.
	Ilford HP5 Plus	1 sec.	2 sec.	5 sec.	10.5 sec.	24 sec.	54 sec.	2 min. 35 sec.
	Kodak T-Max 100	1 sec.	2 sec.	4.5 sec.	10 sec.	21 sec.	49 sec.	1 min. 48 sec.
	Kodak T-Max 400	1 sec.	2 sec.	4.5 sec.	10 sec.	21 sec.	49 sec.	1 min. 45 sec.

Adding more confusion to the problem of reciprocity failure is that there isn't a standard formula you can use to make up for it. Each type of film and emulsion has different degrees of reciprocity failure. For example, Kodak Tri-X 400 may need to be exposed double the time of Ilford Delta 100, even though it's technically two stops faster. And to even further complicate the problem, when using color film the three different layers of emulsion may each have different degrees of reciprocity failure, which results in color shifts. The good news is that most current color and slide films don't suffer too badly from reciprocity failure. Most current production color films are good for long exposures up to two seconds and any color shift can usually be corrected for once the film or slide is digitized. If you are buying old stock and discontinued film, you should look it up on the internet before shooting, or shoot wide brackets.

Note: Reciprocity failure generally starts with exposures lasting one second or longer, depending on the film.

The main thing you will find when using film for night photography is that a lot of experimentation is required, especially when you reach long exposures. Night photography requires patience and can be a lengthy and time-consuming process.

A few tips for successful night or low-light photography using film are:

- **Bracket.** Exposure bracketing is pretty much a necessity to get a usable exposure, especially when you start out. Once you get used to the characteristics of certain types of films you may not need to bracket.
- **Keep notes.** The only way you will be able to fully understand the different properties of your film and its reciprocity is to keep judicious notes. Write down the type of film as well as record the exposure for each frame. It's also helpful to make a note of the weather conditions. Some film cameras, such as the Nikon N90s, have a data back that records the camera settings for you.
- **Process for low contrast.** If you process your film at home, use a low-contrast technique. This usually involves using a more diluted developing solution as well as cooler temperatures and longer developing times with less agitation.

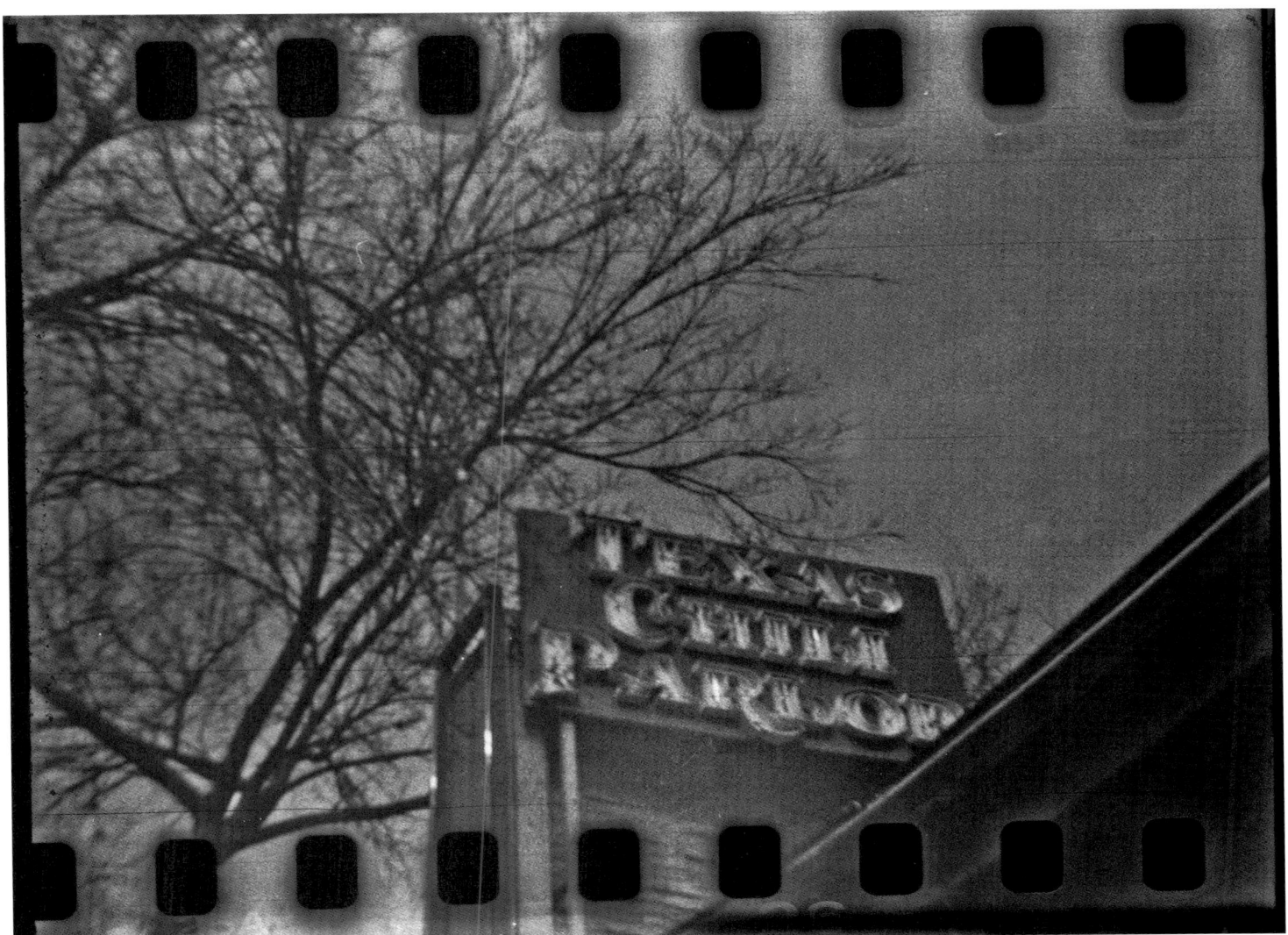

FIGURE 6.13 For this shot taken with a home-made pinhole camera I had to expose an extra-long time to compensate for reciprocity failure. This exposure was approximately 20 minutes long. **Taken with Ilford Delta 100 film**

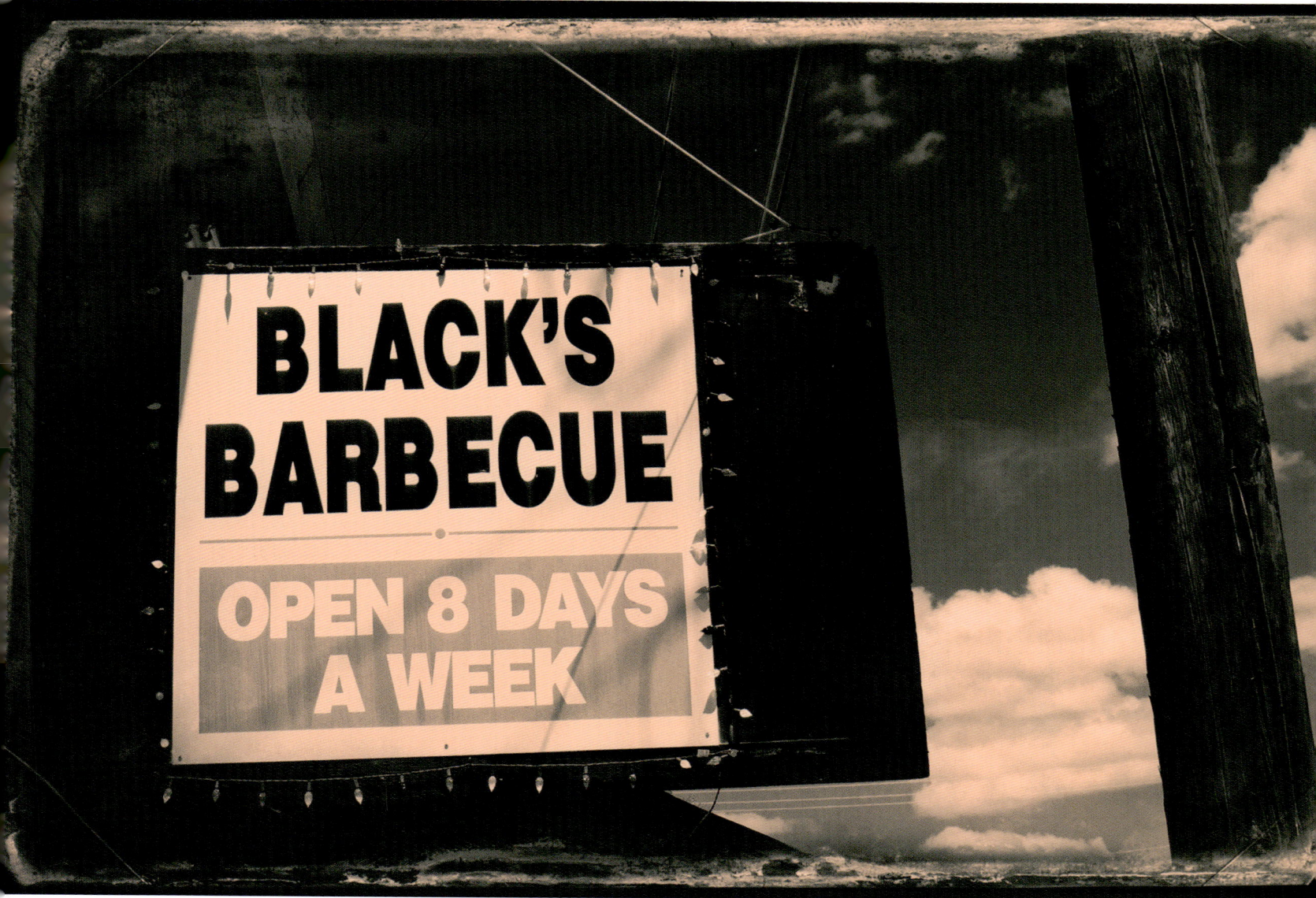

DIGITAL POST-PROCESSING

Seven

FIGURE 7.1 Black's BBQ, Lockhart, TX. Nikon D300s with Nikon 35 mm f/1.8G. 1/500 sec. @ f/11 ISO 200

Although I cover film photography in a few places throughout this book, it's to be understood that most photographers are going to be approaching this subject from a digital perspective; therefore this chapter isn't going to cover darkroom tips and techniques, but most of these tips can also apply to film that has been scanned to create a digital file.

Post-processing is a highly individual process and many people use different methodologies when it comes to getting their images exactly how they envision them in their mind prior to actually taking the photograph. Some folks may try to get the perfect shot in-capture and use a JPEG straight from the camera, or some, such as myself, prefer to shoot RAW images so that there is room for tweaking and fine-tuning.

If you ask 100 photographers you're likely to get 100 different answers about how post-processing should be done. Some photographers like to take a hands-on approach and control every facet of the image from the overall tone all the way down to the minutest details, such as pinpointing areas of noise reduction and shadow and highlight recovery, sometimes spending hours editing a single image to perfection.

Other photographers like to take the approach of using filters, actions, plug-ins, or special software to achieve the look they desire. This can be a quicker way to arrive at your goal or vision, but can still be painstaking. There's no right or wrong way to approach image editing or post-processing.

In addition, editing and post-processing can be very specific for each different job. I have a different workflow for shooting concerts than I do with weddings, and this goes for my decay photography as well. This is primarily because with concerts and weddings I have a high volume of images that need to be processed, so the workflow must be streamlined and there are different things that each client needs.

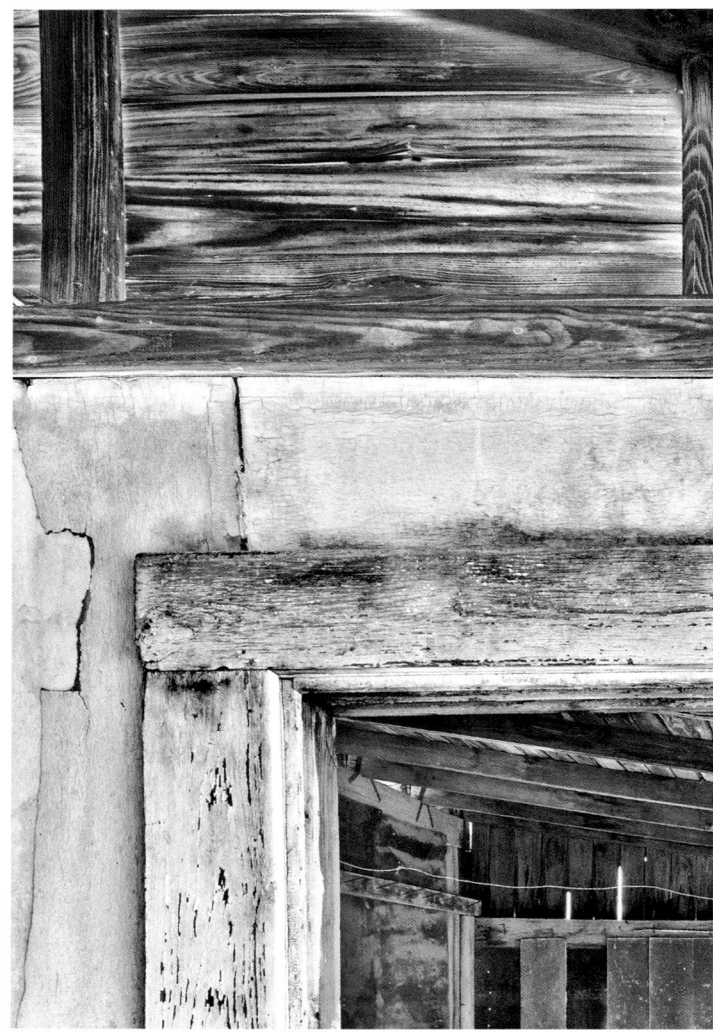

FIGURE 7.2 Window frame and wood in east Austin, TX. This photograph took quite a bit of time and editing in Photoshop CS6 to get the most detail into the final image. There were many adjustment layers for localized tonal adjustment and to maximize the contrast of the wood grain on the top with the plaster of the wall I created a separate layer, inverted the image to a negative, and used a layer mask to reveal the original positive of the lower part of the image. **Nikon D800 with Nikon 28–70 mm f/2.8 at 70 mm. 1/60 sec. @ f/8 ISO 400**

Unless you're shooting for a magazine article or a similar assignment, and you have an art director telling you exactly what they expect the image to look like, the processes you choose are likely to be highly dependent on your own personal tastes. You may spend minutes or hours developing your images.

One of my favorite things about this type of photography is that it is very personal, and each image you select can be processed any number of ways, depending on your individual taste or even your mood at the time. Sometimes, I'll spend hours working on an image only to decide that I don't like the image at all and I'll scrap it. Sometimes I'll take an image, do a minor adjustment to the white balance or contrast, and it will be done in a matter of minutes. Once in a while, even after several years, I'll go back and revisit images that I've shot and find images I'd skipped over or I'll process images in different ways. Such is the art of decay photography. It can be ever-evolving as you grow as a person and a photographer.

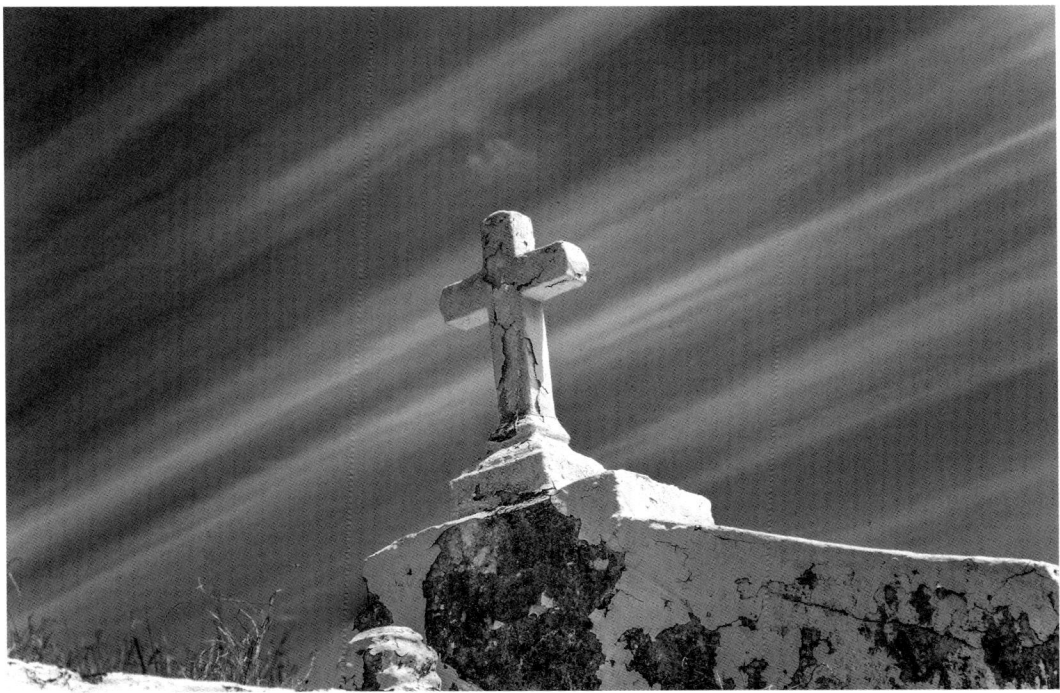

FIGURE 7.3 Detail of mausoleum with sky, New Orleans Cemetery #1. In this image I used the black-and-white adjustment layer in Photoshop CS6 to convert to black and white. I used the sliders to adjust the blue sky to make it appear darker, similar to what you would see when using a red filter shooting black-and-white film.   Nikon D60 with Nikon 18–55 mm f/3.5–5.6 at 55 mm (82 mm equivalent). 1/640 sec. @ f/5.6 ISO 100

Finding the keepers

After returning home from a day of shooting, you're more than likely to have hundreds of images on your memory card, and in this day and age of digital photography, where high-resolution cameras are the norm and most photographers shoot many variations and angles of the same subject, you can easily end up with hundreds of gigabytes worth of files in a very short time, especially if you shoot RAW files for more flexibility in post-processing. Just as an example, the RAW files from my 36 MP Nikon D800 are on average about 34 MB per image – less than 30 images and I amass about 1 GB of image data. In one location I can easily fill up a 16 GB memory card. In short, you can fill up a lot of hard drive space in a very little time.

The first step you should take is what I call *file management*, or more simply, finding the keepers. This means getting rid of any unusable images. This doesn't mean you should get rid of all of the images you're not drawn to straight away, but literally get rid of the *unusable* images. Although an image may not appeal to you at first, if it has nothing that renders it completely useless you may want to hold onto it, because as I mentioned previously you may go back later and find something in the image that does appeal to you. The reason for this file management is to rid your hard drive of any extraneous unusable files that are simply going to take up storage space while the files may never even be opened. This is a good habit to get into, not only in your decay photography, but also in your everyday photography workflow. Keeping your hard drive free of superfluous images helps you maintain a more organized hard drive.

The first thing you should do when clearing out unusable images is to look for extremely over- or underexposed images. Keeping image detail in the shadow and highlight areas is one of the most important goals in any type of photography. If there is no hope of retrieving detail in any of your photographs, especially from a RAW file, then you should delete them (of course, if these are images you bracketed for an HDR you should keep them).

The next thing to check for is critical focus. If the image is completely out of focus or if the focus isn't sharp on the central subject of the composition, then there is no reason to keep the file. Critical focus isn't always readily apparent, so if there is any doubt as to whether or not the image is tack sharp where it counts, then you should zoom in and look at the image at 100 percent zoom to be sure. If the image isn't in critical focus, delete it.

The next step is to take a look at the composition. If you have multiple images of the same subject that are similarly composed, shot from the same angle, exposed properly, and focused correctly, there's no need to keep these files as they are unnecessary duplicates. Pick the image you like best and keep that file.

Once you have weeded out all of the images that you're not going to use, it's a good idea to rename the keepers so that they are easily searchable. Your naming conventions may vary, but as a default I generally use the name of the place, my initials, and a file number. For example, my filename may be, McMaynerberryPrison_JDT_001.jpg. I also place them in a folder with the name of the location, with subfolders with the dates on them in case I happen to visit the same place multiple times. Again, this is just an example of how I do it; there are any number of ways to do it, depending on what is easiest and makes the most sense to you.

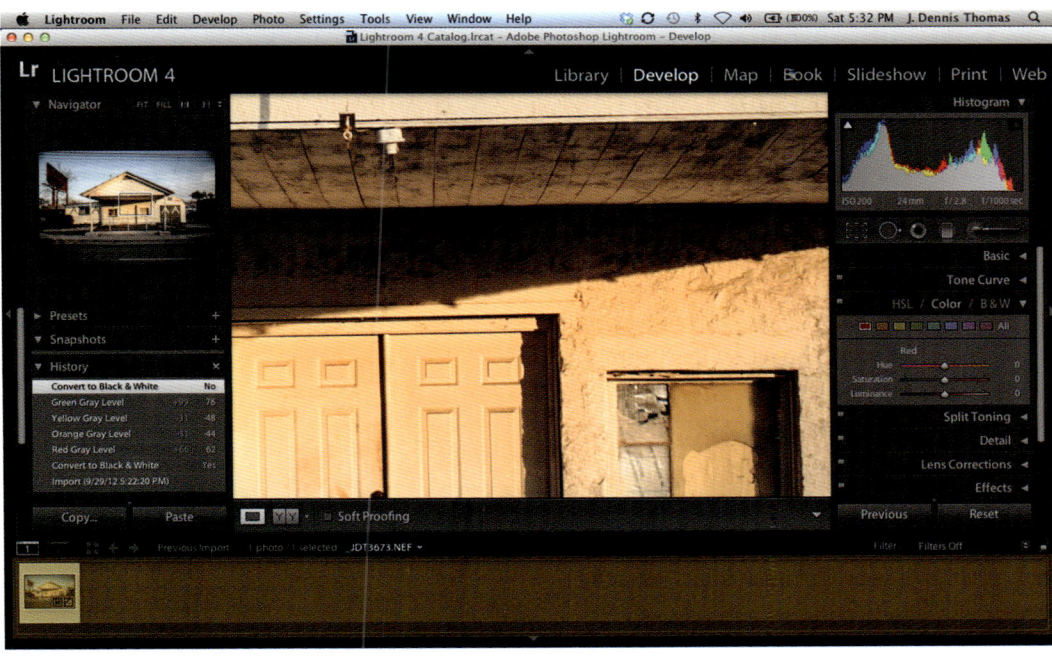

FIGURE 7.4 Using Lightroom, I view the image at 100 percent to check for sharpness

Metadata

An often-overlooked aspect of the digital image editing workflow is adding metadata information. Essentially, metadata is data about data, or in a less cryptic explanation, metadata is information about a digital file. Pertaining to digital imaging and photography, metadata is used for a number of different applications. First there's the standard EXIF data that is written to the file automatically as the image is recorded. EXIF stands for exchangeable file image format. This is the specific information about the image: the filename, the exposure mode, lens information, metering information, exposure, and ISO settings, etc.

The other type of metadata is the IPTC metadata. This is information that you can add using editing software such as Lightroom or Photoshop or other programs specifically made for adding or editing metadata, such as Exif-O-Matic. IPTC is the acronym for International Press Telecommunication Council, which is the protocol used in international news agencies for exchange of news data for different types of media. Right about now you're probably thinking "I'm not a member of the press, what does all this have to do with my decay photography?" Well, IPTC metadata can be used for things other than communication between press agencies. Lots of useful information can be added to your images, such as the photographer's name, copyright information, subject name, location, image title, keywords, and more.

This information is helpful to have attached to your file because it not only establishes you as the photographer and copyright owner of the image, but small things such as keywords are extremely helpful for you as the photographer for searching through images at a later date. You can do a search for the keywords associated with the image and quickly pull up the photos using Adobe Lightroom or Bridge, rather than trying to remember where you saved certain files. This becomes increasingly important as time passes, because when you start amassing a large number of images, finding certain ones can start to become a little difficult.

Adobe Lightroom and Bridge allow you to edit and store metadata templates so you can speed up the process by having information such as your name, email, copyrights, etc. stored so it can quickly be applied and any additional information specific to the images can be added as needed. You can also use Lightroom to automatically add metadata from a template as it imports your images.

Figure 7.5 is a screenshot of a typical metadata template that I use for most of my images. I keep the information I provide pretty basic. I leave personal information out of the metadata since these images may be posted to the web and anyone who can access the image can view the EXIF data with minimal effort. The information I add is as follows.

- **Creator.** Add your name as the person who initially created the image.

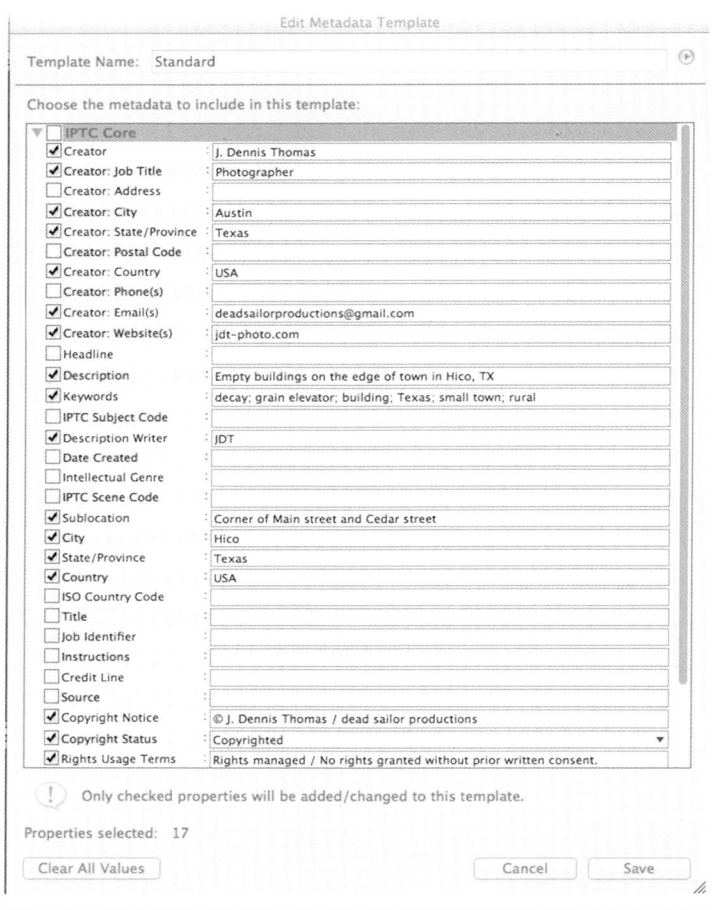

FIGURE 7.5 The Edit Metadata Template in Adobe Bridge

- **Creator: job title.** Add the job you had in creating the image (being the photographer).
- **City/state/country.** This information is optional, but you can put your current area of residence here.
- **Creator: email.** Adding your email address can be helpful for people to contact you if they find your image in a search and wish to license it for usage.

- **Creator: website.** This information isn't 100 percent necessary, but if a person comes across your image and wants to look at more of your work they can easily find your web presence.
- **Description.** Here you add some brief commentary pertaining to the image.
- **Keywords.** These are specific words that describe details and aspects of the image. These can be used to search for images on your hard drive at home and can also help people looking for images on the web and can lead to image sales. Examples of keywords can range from the subject, the location, type of photography, overall color of the image, and more.
- **Description writer.** This is optional; I put my initials here to indicate that I filled out the information in the metadata template.
- **Sublocation.** This is a field to be added at your discretion. This could be a specific location, such as a building name or street intersection.
- **City/state/country.** The locale where the image was taken can be added here.
- **Copyright notice.** Add your name and/or business name here as the copyright owner of the image.
- **Copyright status.** There are three choices in the field: copyrighted, public domain, and unknown. According to the Federal Copyright act of 1976 your images are copyrighted to you at the moment you click the shutter, so this field should always read "copyrighted."
- **Rights usage terms.** This field is where you spell out the usage rights for your images. Unless you have granted someone else permission to use the work, you should include here "No rights granted without prior consent." This lets people know that the image isn't free to use. If you wish to make your image available for free use, you can simply use a Creative Commons license. See creativecommons.org for more information about this.

Tonal adjustments and color correction

Rarely is an image perfect straight out of the camera. This is why I'm a big proponent of photographing in RAW. Most images need to be tweaked a bit to get the most out of them, whether it's a matter of a simple white balance, a minor color adjustment, contrast adjustments, or major tonal corrections involving recovering lost detail from shadows and/or highlight areas of the image.

I don't adhere to any one photo editing software, nor do I endorse any particular one over any others, so I'm not going to get into specifics on any single type of software. There are many great options out there for editing and processing RAW images. Adobe Lightroom is probably the most used application these days for most photographers. It's a very powerful tool for editing, browsing, and cataloging images and isn't overly expensive. Adobe Photoshop was once the best option, but has become a bit overkill for general editing, although it can't be beat for serious heavy editing involving retouching, layers, and more. Apple's Aperture is very similar to Lightroom and is also relatively inexpensive and well regarded. For very basic and intuitive editing, Apple's iPhoto is available for Mac users, and Photoshop Elements is a much simpler form of Adobe's Photoshop. For free software that supports most RAW formats, Google's Picasa is a good alternative to paid software. One thing is for certain, even the most basic RAW converter, such as Nikon's ViewNX and Canon's Digital Photo Pro, has tools that enable you to make changes to the white balance and exposure adjustments for tonality.

Start with assessing the white balance. If it looks good, leave it alone, but generally it needs a little tweaking to add a bit of blue or amber to cool it down or warm it up, or to add a bit of green or magenta to get rid of a color cast. The reason to do this first is that white balance, especially if the change is drastic, can affect the actual tonal range of the image and will change the histogram. If the white balance is seriously off you can start by clicking the white balance tool on a neutral area. Areas of white, black, or gray all work well, as long as any of the white or black areas aren't at the extreme edges of brightness or darkness. Click around on a few different things until you find a setting that is pleasing.

Next, take a look at the image's exposure. Do this not only by looking at the image, but also by looking at the histogram. The histogram in your RAW editor is going to be more accurate than the one you can view on your camera monitor because it

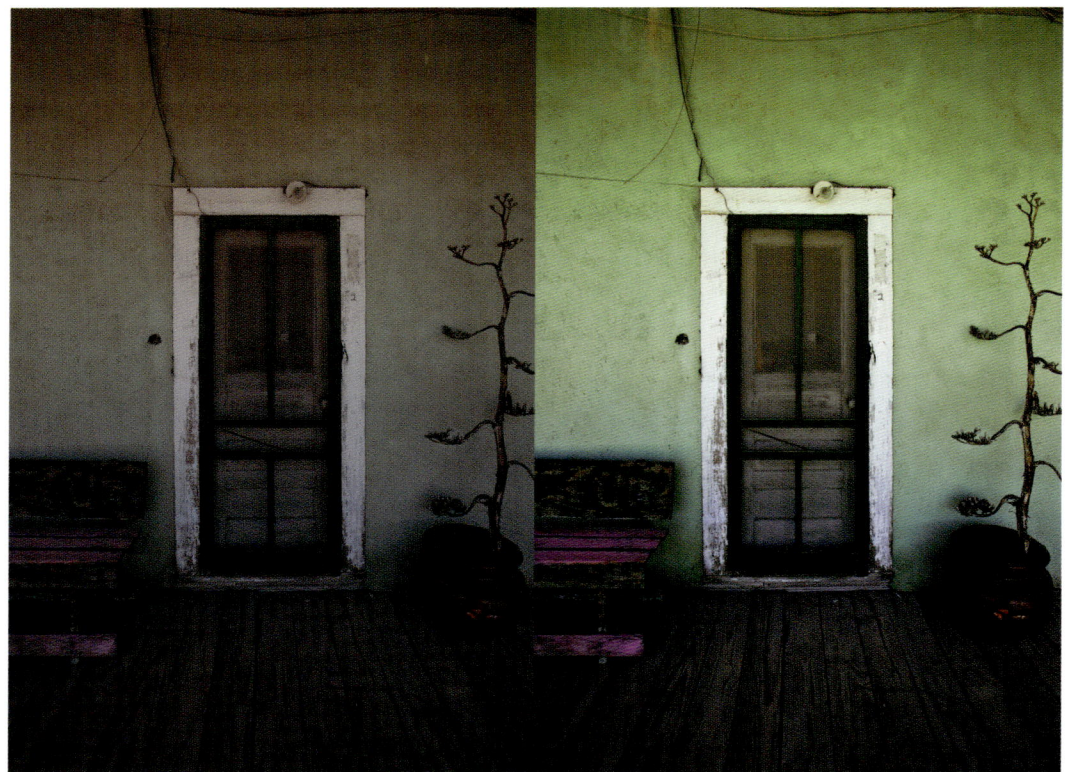

FIGURE 7.6 The image on the left was taken straight from the camera; as you can see, it's flat with very low contrast. The same image, on the right, after adjusting the exposure level, adding some contrast, and boosting the saturation, is more vibrant and tonally rich. **Nikon D600 with Sigma 17–35 mm f/2.8–4 at 20 mm. 1/20 sec. @ f/3.2 ISO 400**

will reflect the 12- or 14-bit RAW file, not the 8-bit JPEG preview your camera shows during the image review. The RAW converter histogram will also likely reflect changes in real time, so pay close attention to it. This will tell you whether or not your shadows and/or highlights are clipping, and if one of the red, green, or blue channels is clipping as well.

After assessing the exposure, it's time to determine what needs to be done tonally to get the most out of your image. Generally, the contrast will need to be boosted. You can do this in any number of ways: by doing a levels or curves adjustment, or by using any number of sliders in your RAW conversion software. Pull back the exposure slider a bit if there are out-of-control highlights. I use this method because the highlight recovery sliders often take out too much contrast and can sometimes even add a gray tint. To brighten up the shadows the fill light slider (or equivalent tool) usually works wonders on bringing out lost shadow detail.

Black-and-white conversions

As mentioned in Chapter 5, black and white is a great look for decay photography. It adds abstractness to the imagery and can lend a stark contrast to your decay photographs. Removing color from your images allows the viewer to focus more on the subject and content of the image rather than the interplay between the different hues in the image. Forms, shapes, lines, and textures all take center stage when you have an image that isn't filled with colors to distract the viewer. Black-and-white photographs also lend a timeless quality to your images and hearken back to past eras.

Tip: Images taken at high ISO settings or long exposures that have excess noise are often made usable by converting to black and white.

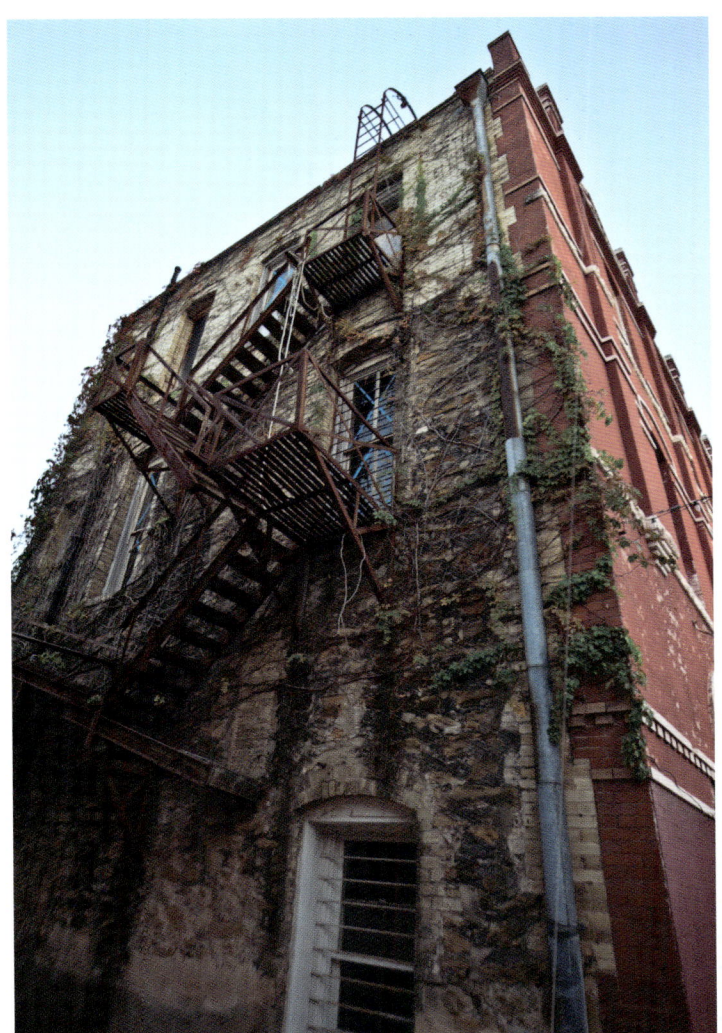

FIGURE 7.7 The "as-shot" white balance setting for this image was leaning toward the blue side. Using the eyedropper/white balance tool in Adobe Lightroom 4, I clicked on the white of the windowsill, which warmed up the image and gave a truer white balance to the photo. **Nikon D600 with Sigma 17–35 mm f/2.8–4 at 20 mm. 1/20 sec. @ f/3.2 ISO 400**

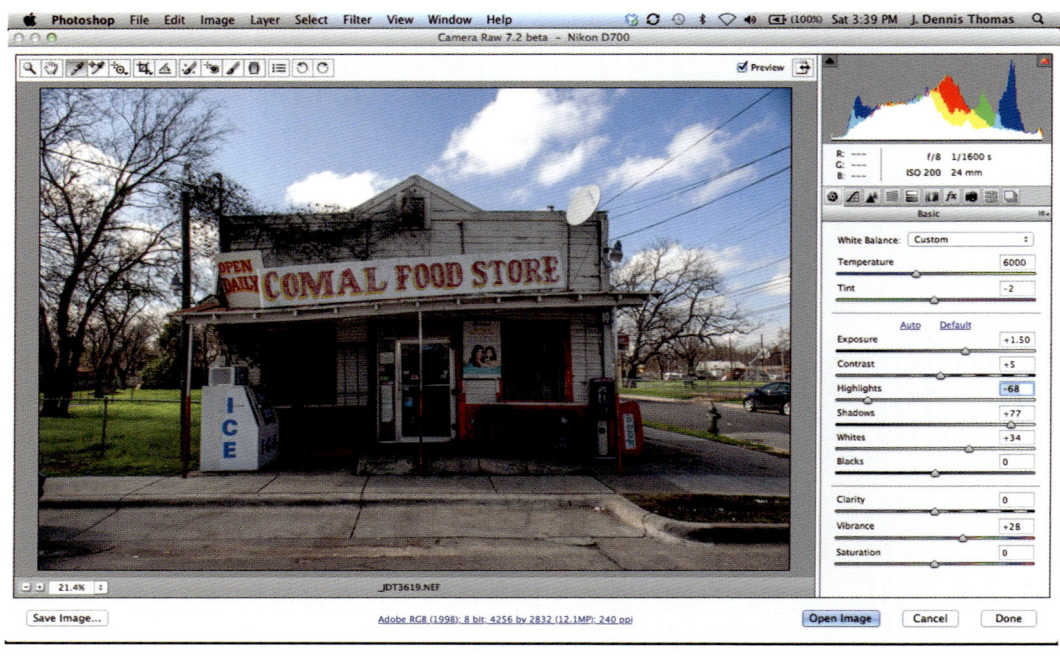

FIGURE 7.8 Adobe Camera RAW allows you to adjust the white balance, exposure, and even make lens corrections all at once. The user interface is intuitive and easy to understand

So the question remains, *when should I convert to black and white?* The answer is quite simple: *when color doesn't add anything to the image.* As simple as this sounds, there are some thought processes to go through. You may come across scenes of bright color that make the image come alive, but sometimes you may also find that an area of color takes the attention off the subject, thereby detracting from the essence of the photo. Converting to black and white removes the distraction of color and draws the attention back to the subject. Scenes with relatively low contrast or scenes that are tonally similar without much color variation are good candidates for black and white.

There are many different options to consider when deciding to convert your images from color to black and white. There are programs designed specifically for black-and-white conversions, such as Nik Silver Efex Pro, Topaz B&W Effects, and Alien Skin Exposure, or you can make the conversion using adjustment layers in Photoshop or presets in Lightroom. Simple editing programs like Photoshop Elements and iPhoto offer easy one-click solutions to your black-and-white conversions.

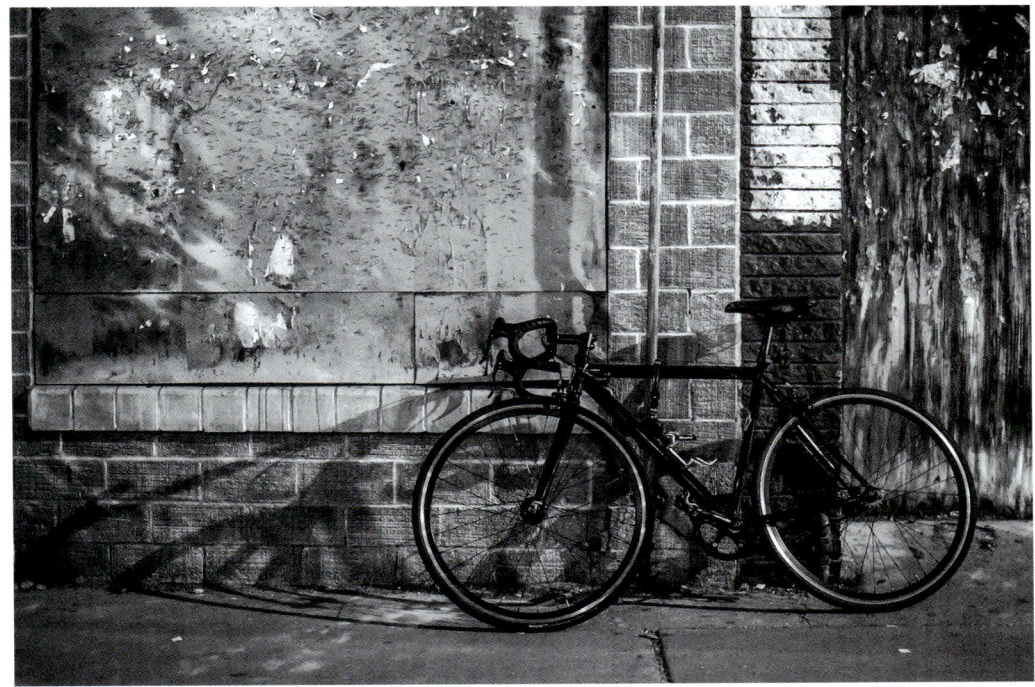

FIGURE 7.9 This composition didn't have anything to offer in the color spectrum since it was dark and the only light source was a yellow sodium vapor light. I captured this straight to JPEG using the camera's Black and White setting. **Leica M8 with Voigtländer 28mm f/2 Ultron. 1/20 sec. @ f/2 ISO 1250**

Tip: If you come upon a scene you know you will be converting to black and white, consider changing your Picture Control (Nikon) or Picture Style (Canon) to monochrome. This allows you to preview what your image will look like even when shooting RAW.

Probably the most convenient way is to do the conversion right in the RAW conversion software, this is a non-destructive conversion since it only saves the black-and-white information as a sidecar file in the original RAW file, so you can go back and adjust the settings at any time. Doing the conversion in Lightroom 4 or Adobe Camera RAW allows you to convert the image to grayscale, and then you can adjust the luminosity of the different color tones in the image, which gives you a lot of control. This is one of the most precise ways to do a black-and-white conversion.

Probably the easiest way to do it is to use a Photoshop plug-in. One of my favorites is Alien Skin Exposure. This program emulates different black-and-white film types, such as

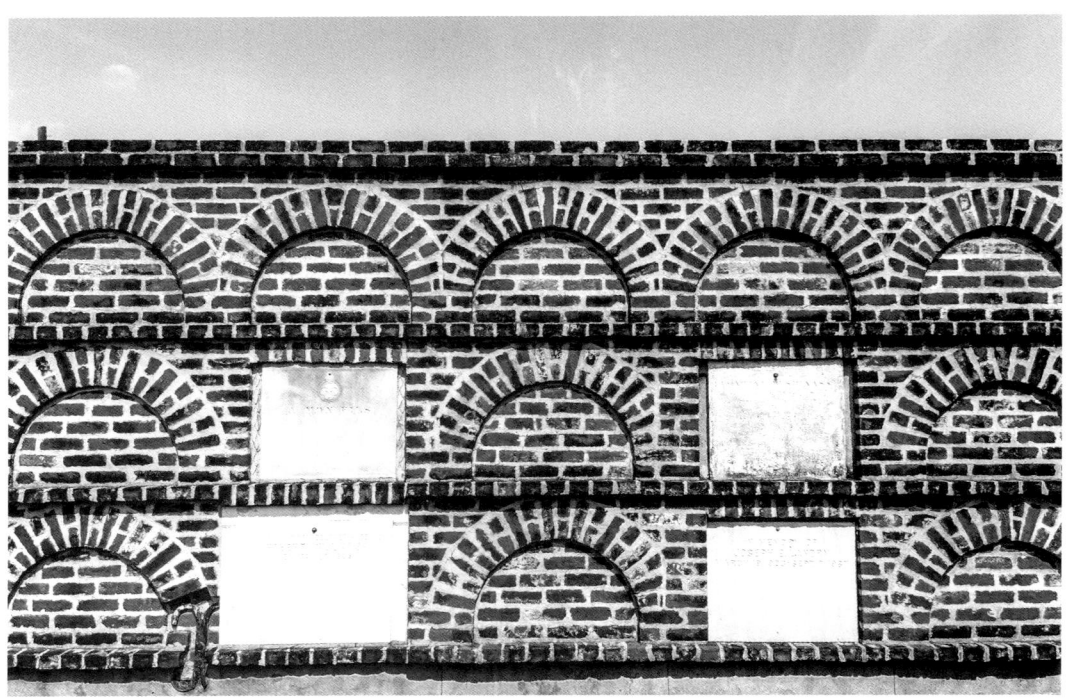

FIGURE 7.10 This image taken of tombs in New Orleans Cemetery #1 is more about texture and pattern than color, which made it the perfect candidate for a black-and-white conversion. Converted using Photoshop's black-and-white adjustment layer. **Nikon D60 with 18–55 mm f/3.5–5.6 at 18 mm (27 mm equivalent). 1/500 sec. @ f/11 ISO 100**

Ilford Delta and Kodak Tri-X, by converting your image to grayscale and adding grain, texture, and contrast. You can fine-tune the conversion by using individual sliders.

Another great program for black-and-white conversion is Nik Software's Silver Efex Pro. This is a very comprehensive package for doing black-and-white conversions. You can control almost everything. You can do localized contrast and grain adjustments by using control points, and you can also view side-by-side comparisons.

Color conversions

Converting your images to monochrome isn't the only choice you have when editing your decay images. Purposely altering the colors to get a unique effect is a common practice.

Color conversions can range from a simple subtle desaturation to drastically altering the hue and contrast of the image to create a completely unrealistic effect. A lot of color conversions are done to emulate the look of a certain type

Monochrome

While all black-and-white images are monochrome, not all monochrome images are black and white. Even in the early days of photography, before color film was invented, photographers played with color by toning their images. The toning of images was initially done by replacing the metallic silver of the emulsion on the paper with another chemical compound, the most common being sepia (silver sulfide) and selenium (silver selenide). The toning process had its beginnings not as a way to add color to a black-and-white print, but as a way to make the image more stable to add longevity to the print. Other toning options are gold and platinum, or iron and copper, the latter two of which actually reduce the stability of the print, diminishing its longevity.

Another monochrome variant is the cyanotype, which gives the image a bluish hue. These days you can make a monochrome image of just about any color using image editing software, or in some cases in-camera image editing.

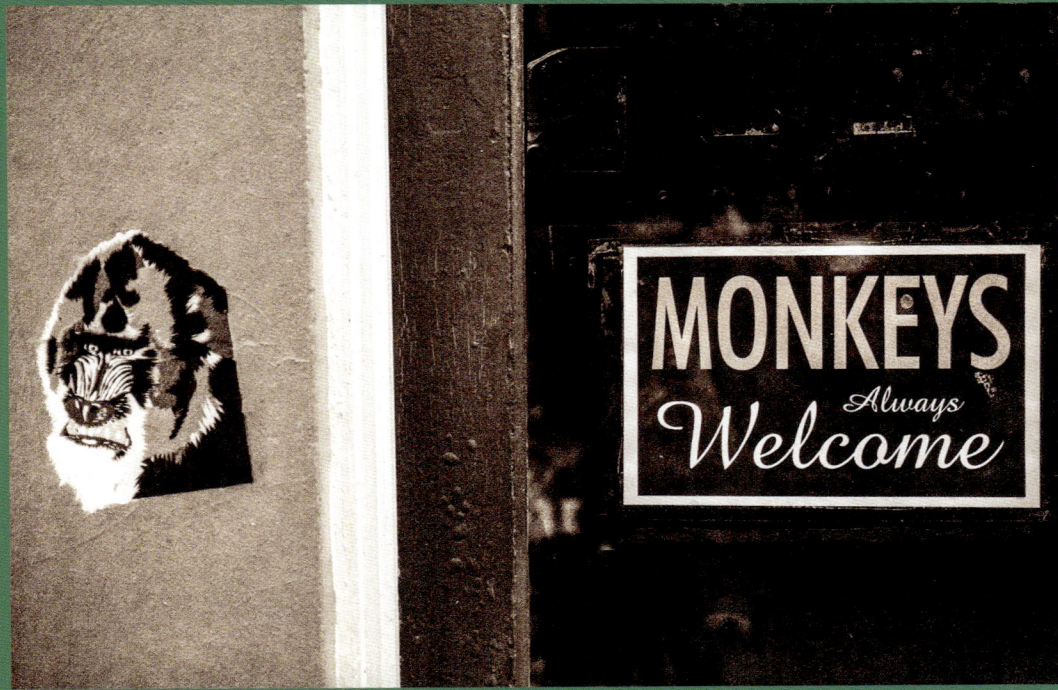

FIGURE 7.11 For this image I added a little sepia toning in Photoshop to warm it up and give this rather contemporary shot a bit of vintage flavor. Nikon D700 with 35 mm f/1.8. 1/160 sec. @ f/1.8 ISO 3200

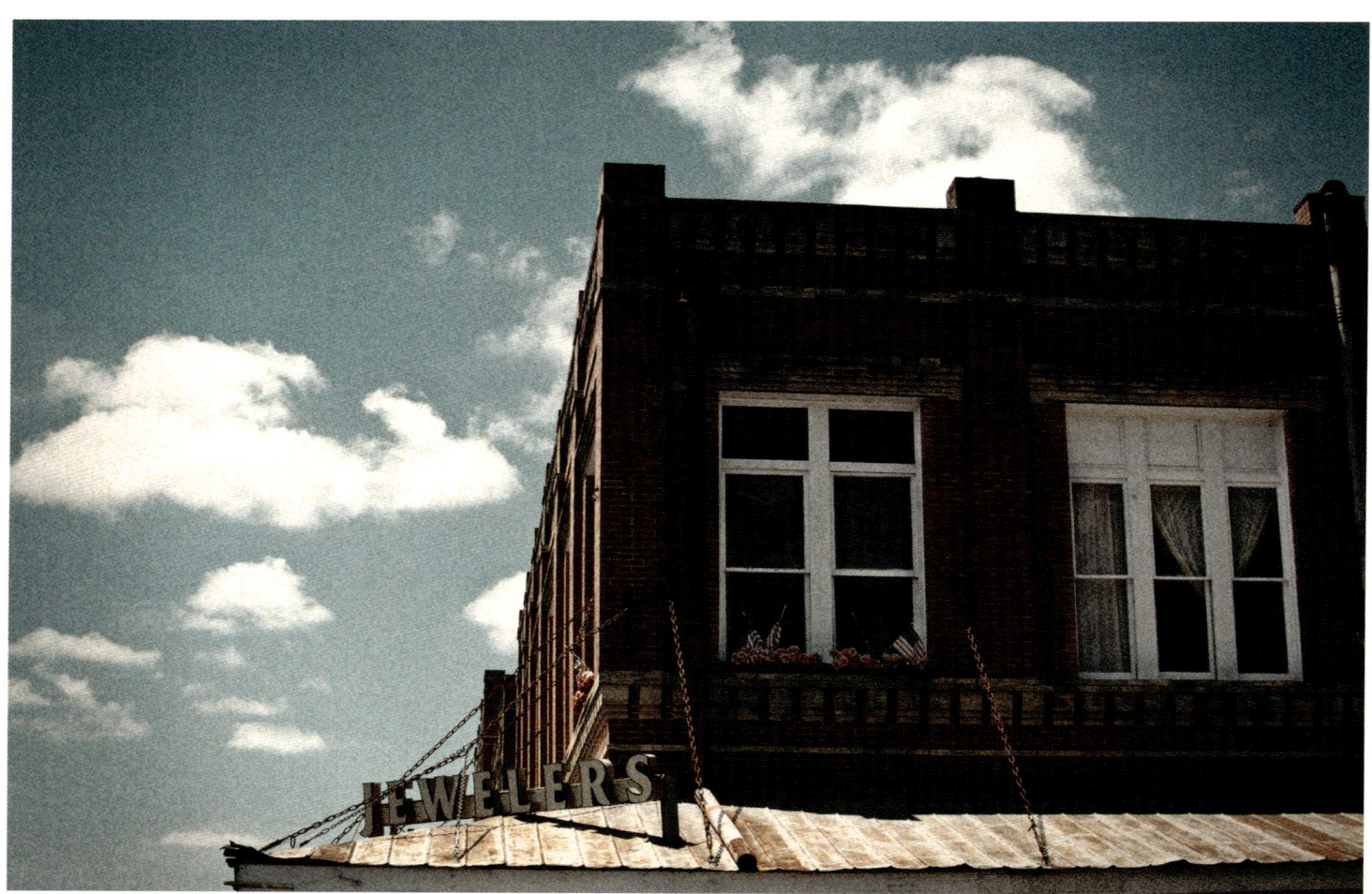

FIGURE 7.12 Using Alien Skin Exposure I converted this shot of a building in downtown Lockhart, TX to simulate Polachrome, Polaroid's now-extinct instant slide film. **Nikon D300s with 35 mm f/1.8. 1/320 sec. @ f/10 ISO 200**

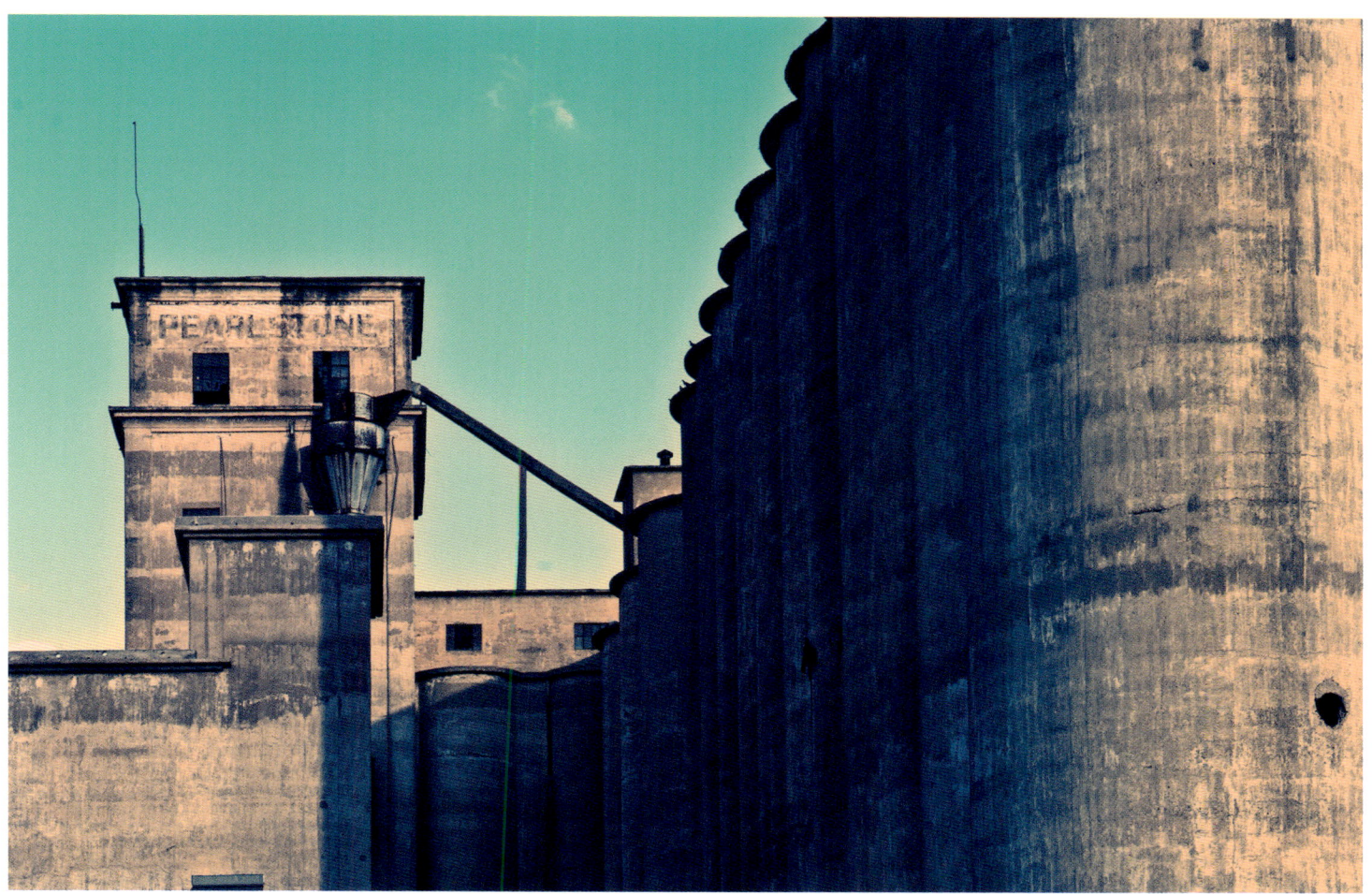

FIGURE 7.13 For this digital cross process shot of the Pearlstone building in Dallas, TX I opened the image in Photoshop and used a curve adjustment layer to approximate the effect of cross processing Agfa Optima slide film. Nikon D700 with Nikon 28–70 mm f/2.8D. 1/320 sec. @ f/10 ISO 560

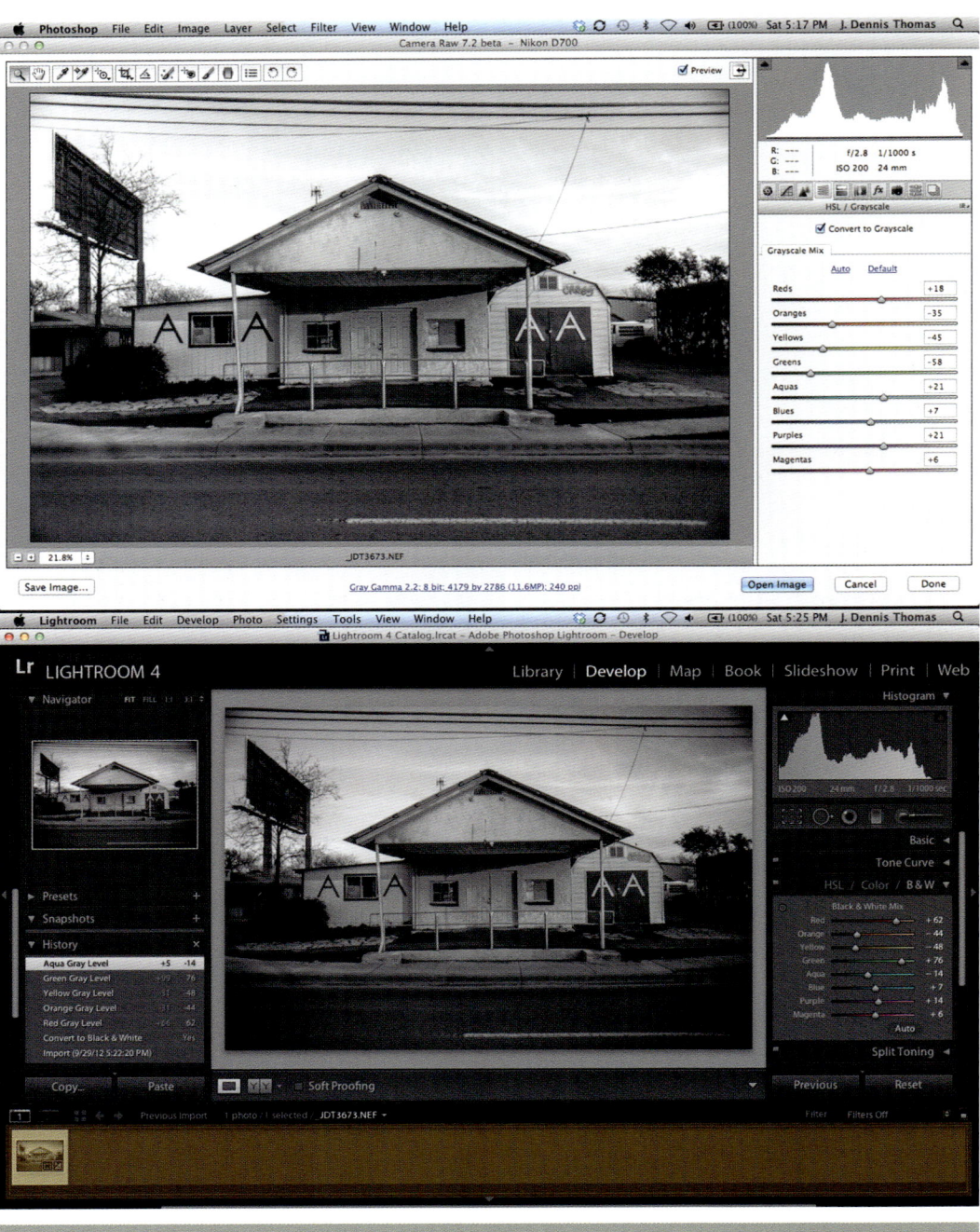

FIGURE 7.14 Adobe Camera RAW and Lightroom both have a black-and-white conversion option. Using the color sliders (right side) you can control the luminosity of the different colors in the image, allowing you to do very final tonal adjustments when converting. Lightroom also has presets for one-click black-and-white conversions

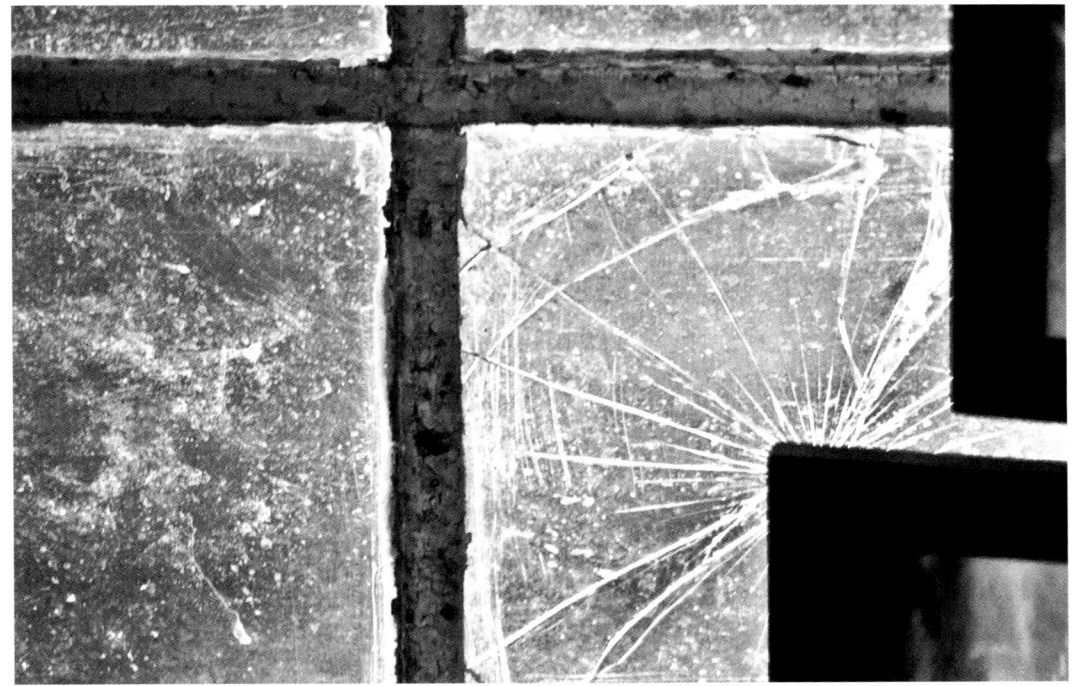

FIGURE 7.15 I converted this image to black and white using Nik Silver Efex Pro. I added quite a bit of sharpness and grain and increased contrast for a distressed "grunge" look. **Nikon D800 with Nikon 80–200 mm f/2.8D at 200 mm. 1/15 sec. @ f/2.8 ISO 1000**

of film, such as Kodachrome or Velvia. For these types of conversions software is usually employed. The software team has evaluated the different types of films for color, contrast, and grain, and when the filter runs the image is transformed to emulate that certain look. As with black-and-white conversions, the best product that I can recommend for color film emulation is Alien Skin Exposure. It's a simple plug-in that works with Photoshop or Lightroom. You can click on the presets and use them as-is, or you can use the controls to fine-tune your images to get any look you can think of. Nik Color Efex Pro is another great program; it's a little more involved and gives you greater control over the outcome of your images.

Another common color conversion practice stems from a film photography technique called *cross processing*. Cross processing, sometimes referred to as X-pro, is the result of developing negative film in chemicals meant for slide film (C41 to E6) or developing slide film in the chemicals for negative film (E6 to C41). This causes the films to take on unusual color cast and higher than normal contrast. The results are fairly unpredictable, but certain films are known to have definite

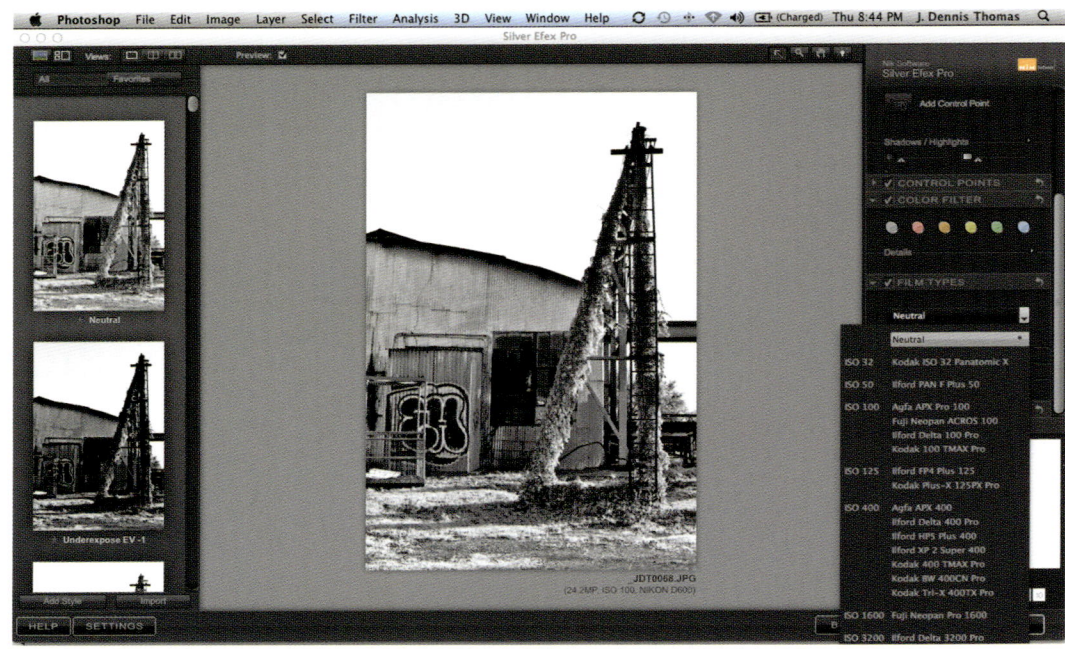

FIGURE 7.16 Dedicated black-and-white conversion software, like Nik Silver Efex Pro, offers presets that convert your images to black and white while simulating the characteristics of different types of film stocks. Simply select the film type from the drop-down menu on the right and click to apply

color properties due to their particular emulsions. You can do this type of color conversion by using the aforementioned software or by using presets in Adobe Lightroom or Photoshop.

For Photoshop and Lightroom users there are also lots of presets and actions available to download on the internet. Some are free, created by photographers for anyone to use, and some come in bundles that you have to pay for. A quick search for *cross processing actions* or *cross processing presets* will bring up some results.

TtV: melding film and digital

Through the viewfinder, better known as TtV, is a little-known technique that caught my eye about six years ago. This technique is almost the marriage of digital and film photography since it uses two different cameras to create a unique image: one digital camera and one film camera (most often a cheap TLR with a discontinued film format). The premise is very simple: take a digital camera and shoot the

Frames and borders

To add some distinction to an image, some photographers like to add frames or borders to their images. These frames can make an image look like a vintage print, or sometimes the borders are made to look like film edges or emulsion. In some cases the borders can emulate an effect from a certain camera like a Holga or Lomo. These effects are available in some Photoshop plug-ins like Alien Skin Exposure or onOne Software's PhotoFrame. One caveat to using frames is to not overuse them – that is to say, don't use a frame on every image. Overuse will make your images look gimmicky and take away the impact of the frame effect.

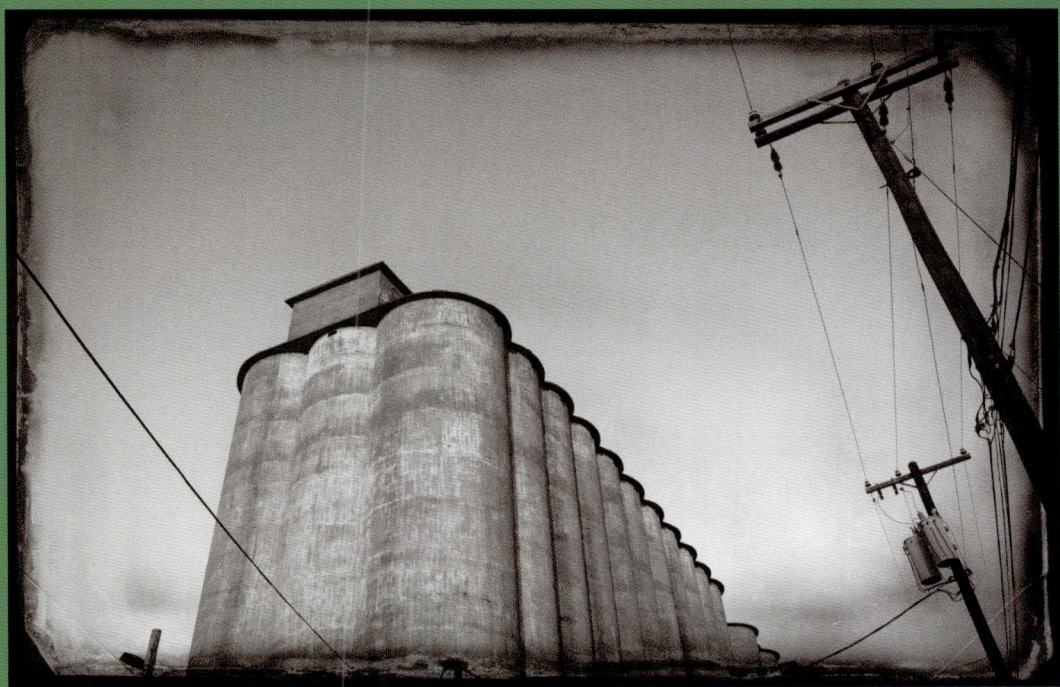

FIGURE 7.17 For the photograph of these grain elevators, I used Alien Skin Exposure and applied the Daguerreotype – Sepia – Black Frame filter to give the appearance of a vintage daguerreotype. **Nikon D700 with Nikon 28–70 mm f/2.8D. 1/320 sec. @ f/10 ISO 400**

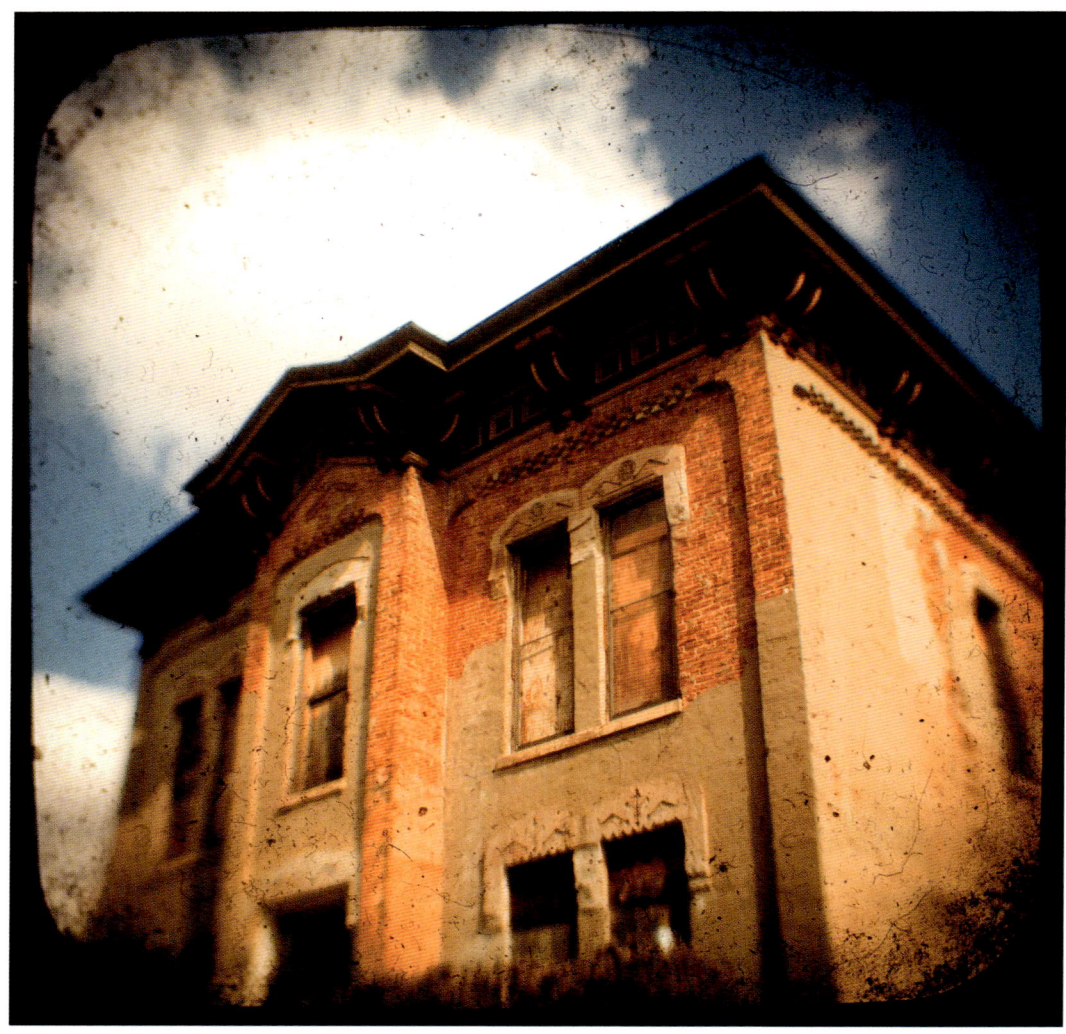

FIGURE 7.18 House of Jaguars TtV. Canon Digital Rebel XSi with a EF-S 60 mm f/2.8 macro 1/1000 @ f/2.8 ISO 400 through an Anscoflex viewfinder. © Connie Toebe

Digital Post-Processing 147

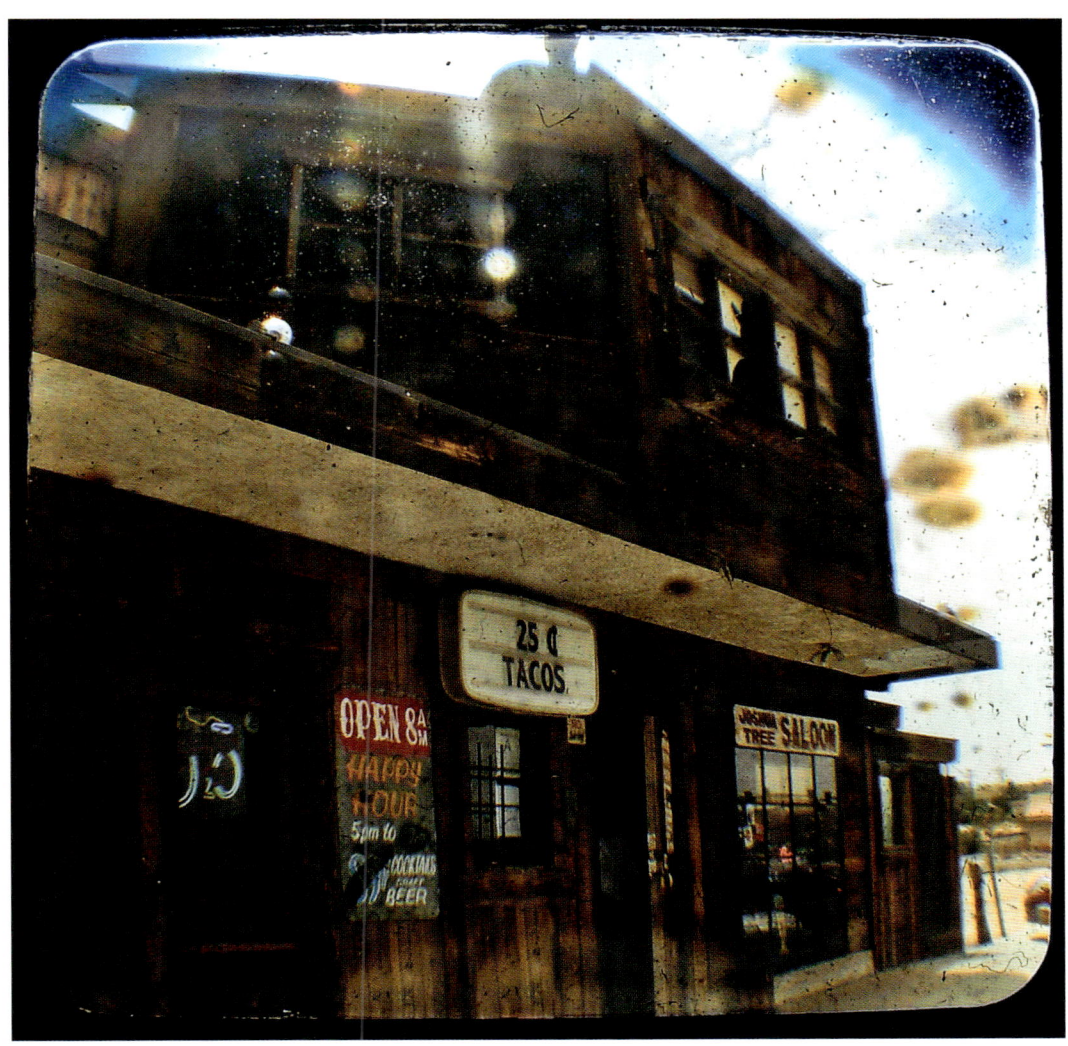

FIGURE 7.19 Joshua Tree Saloon TtV.   Nikon Coolpix L5 1/420 @ f/5.4 ISO 79 through a Kodak Duaflex IV viewfinder

148　Urban and Rural Decay Photography

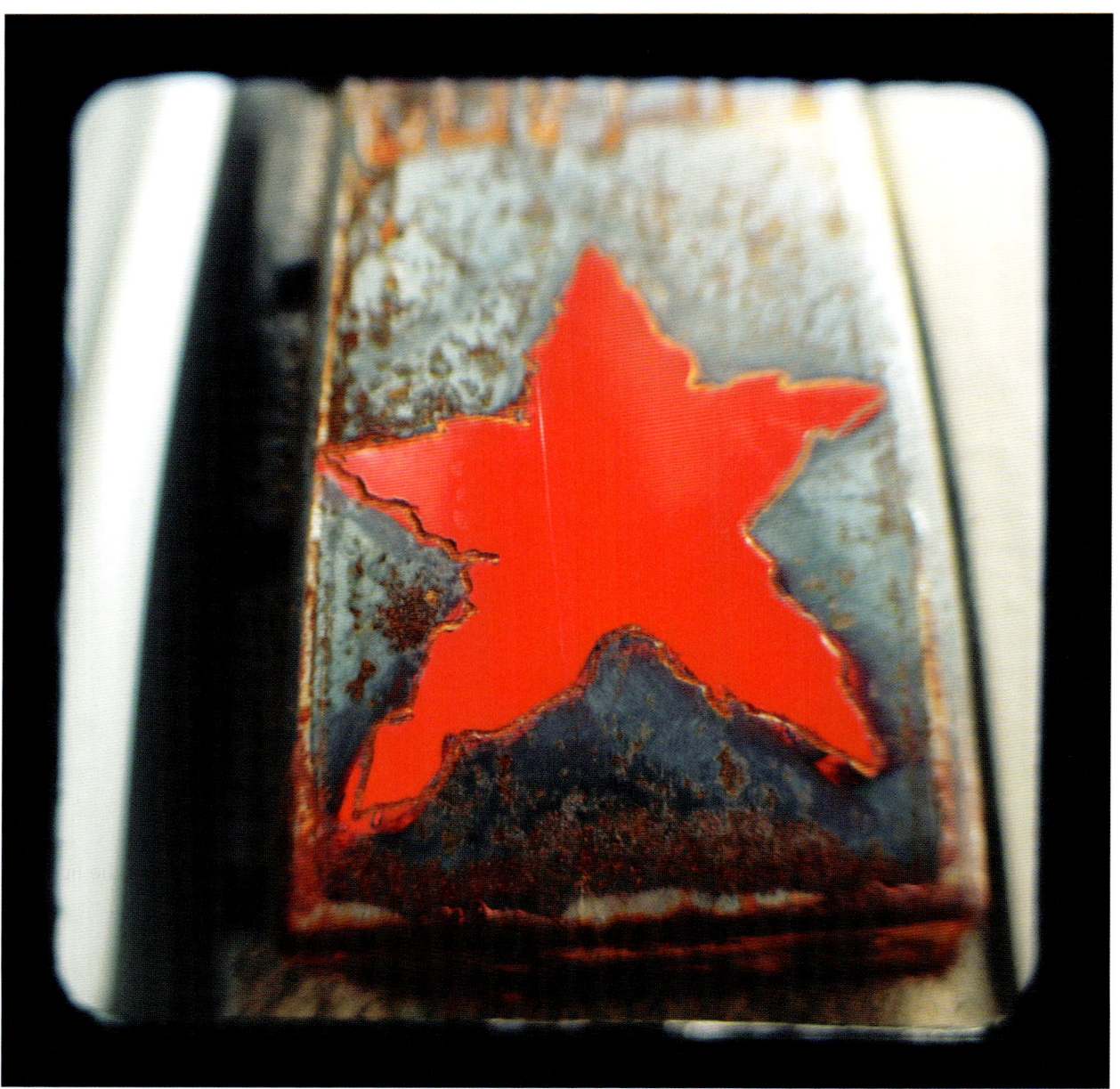

FIGURE 7.20 Old Red Star TtV.　　Pentax *ist D 1/80 @ f/5.6 ISO 200 through a Kodak Duaflex viewfinder. © Russ Morris

cameras are often coated with dust, dirt, fungus, and general crud, which adds a great lo-fi effect to the images that really lends itself well to decay photography. Some photographers, however, are known to dismantle the old film cameras to clean them out for clearer images.

Many different types of cameras have been used for this technique, but by far the most popular is the Kodak Duaflex models. If you like the technique and are interested in learning more about it, there's a great tutorial at www.russmorris.com/ttv

Getting started in TtV is a fairly easy process requiring just a few pieces of equipment. All you need is a DSLR, a macro lens, and an old camera (preferably a TLR with a waist-level viewfinder). A macro lens is preferred over a traditional lens because it's easier to handle the TtV cameras when you can keep them relatively close together. You can then simply point the top camera (digital) at the bottom camera (film), focus on the image in the viewfinder and shoot. Another option, which is the method I prefer, is to use a small compact digital camera as your top camera. This is much more manageable to handle in my opinion.

You will find that you will get better results with your TtV when you block extraneous light from coming between the top and bottom cameras. TtV photographers have dealt with this issue in many different ways, building what have now become lovingly known as "contraptions" to block the light. There are many different ways to do this, but the most popular is the *smokestack* method as outlined in Russ Morris' TtV tutorial. Some people make very simple contraptions and some like to get more elaborate and make a real project out of it. I made a relatively complex contraption for one of my cameras using a flash bracket that allowed me to attach both cameras together, as well as a flash for added effects.

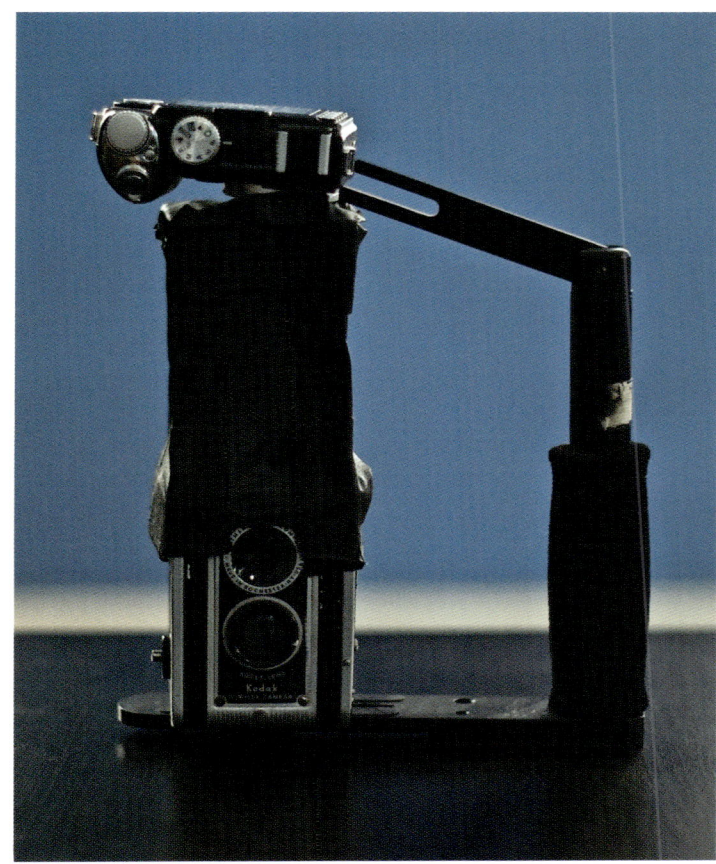

FIGURE 7.21 This is my Nikon P500C and Kodak Duaflex TtV setup with a homemade contraption rigged with a flash bracket. This allows me to not only hold the TtV cameras together, but also to add an additional flash component as well if needed

picture through the viewfinder of an old film camera, hence the name *through the viewfinder*. This is a wonderful technique that breathes new lives into old cameras and creates a very distinctive look because no two cameras have the same anomalies in their viewfinders. The viewfinders of these old TLR

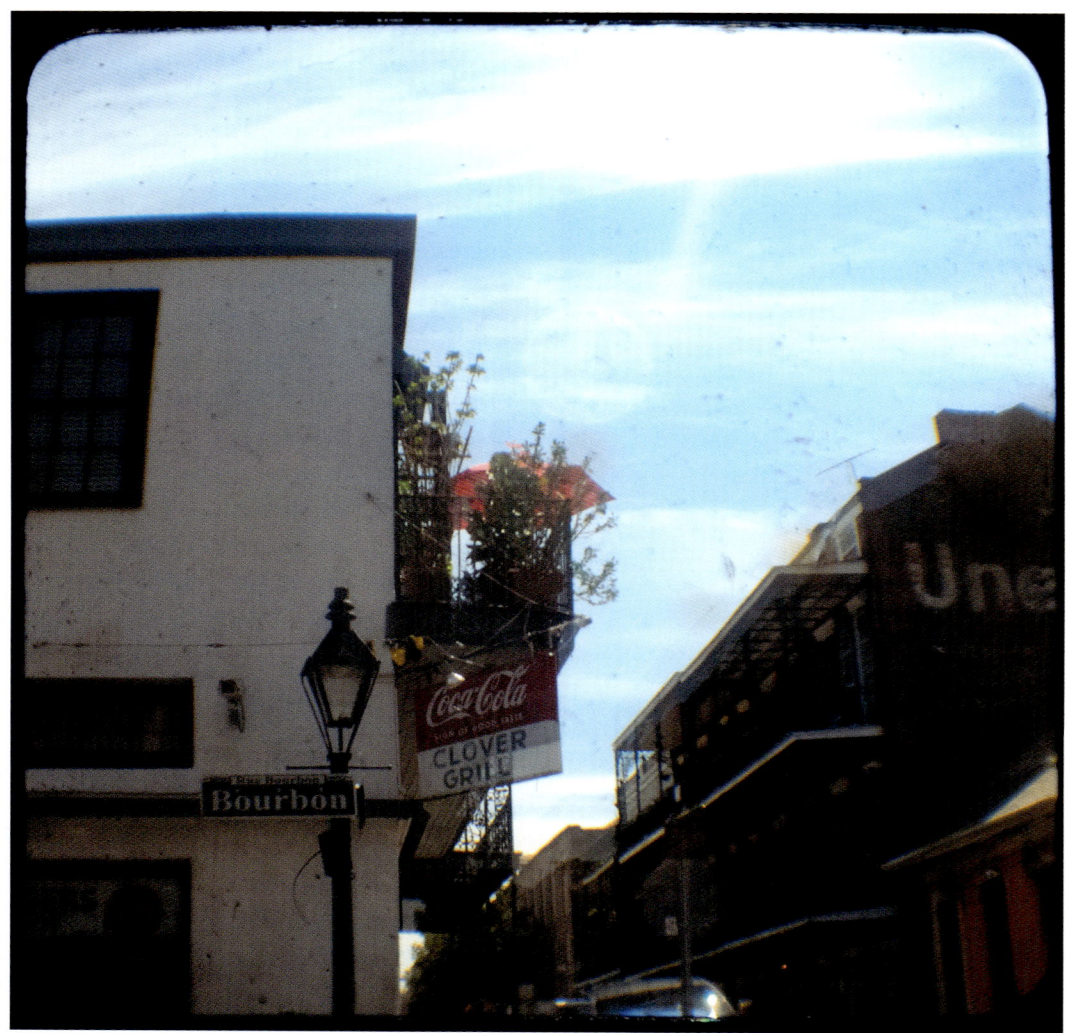

FIGURE 7.22 Clover Grill at the corner of Bourbon and Dumaine in New Orleans. **Nikon D60 1/2500 @ f/5.6 ISO 800 through a Kodak Duaflex IV viewfinder**

Take a look at the TtV group on Flickr and search through the "contraptions" discussion thread. I think you'll be amazed at the cool and inventive things that people have done to make their TtV contraptions.

Of course, in these days of Photoshop, digital imaging, and smartphone apps, you can easily apply a TtV filter to any digital photo that you take, but doing actual TtV is a fun project that creates images unique to each camera; there won't be a million iPhone photos out there with your TtV camera's unique fingerprint. It's also a great conversation piece when you're out in public.

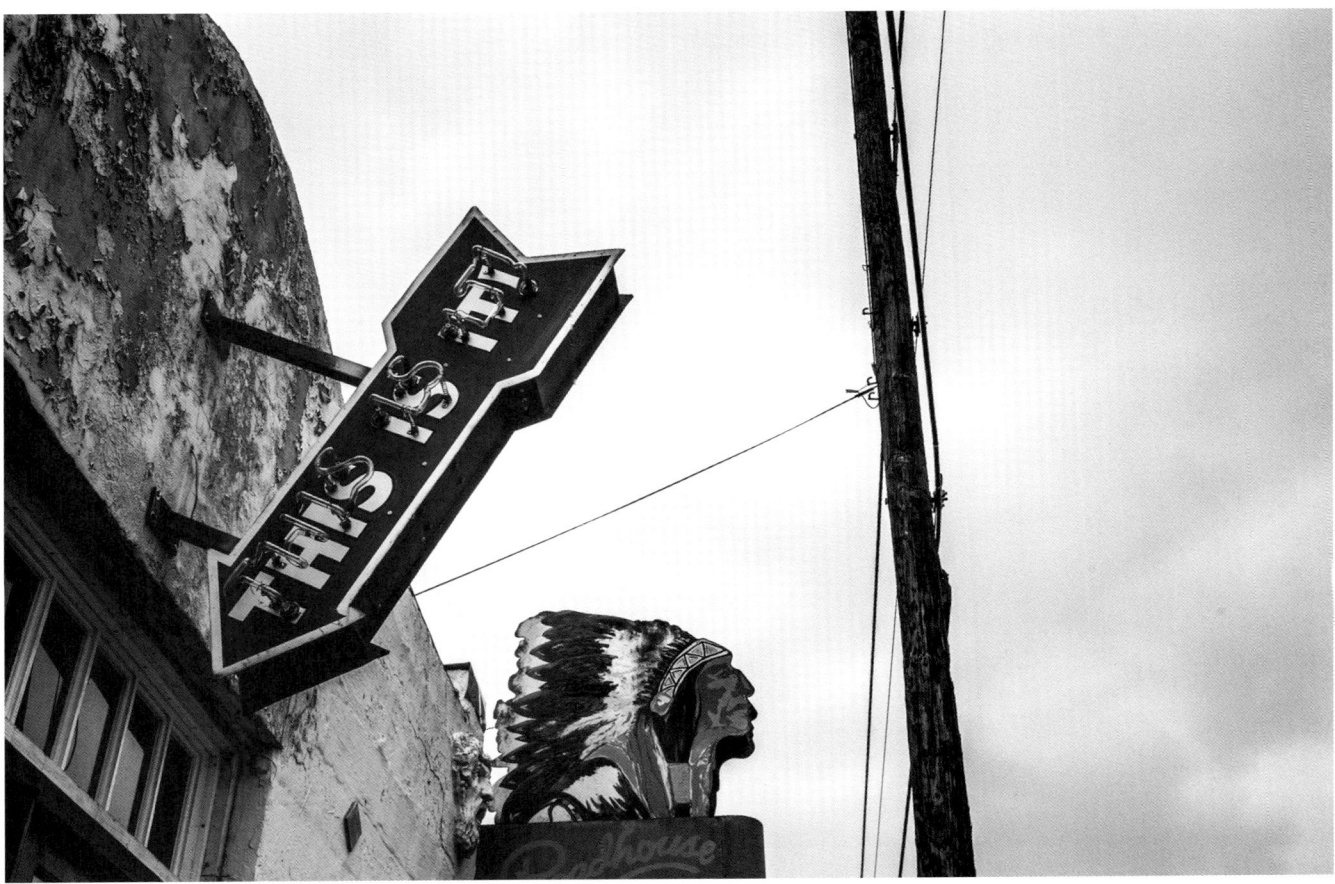

FIGURE 7.23 Sign shop in Austin, TX.   **Leica M8 with Voigtländer 28mm f/2 Ultron. 1/125 sec. @ f/8 ISO 160**

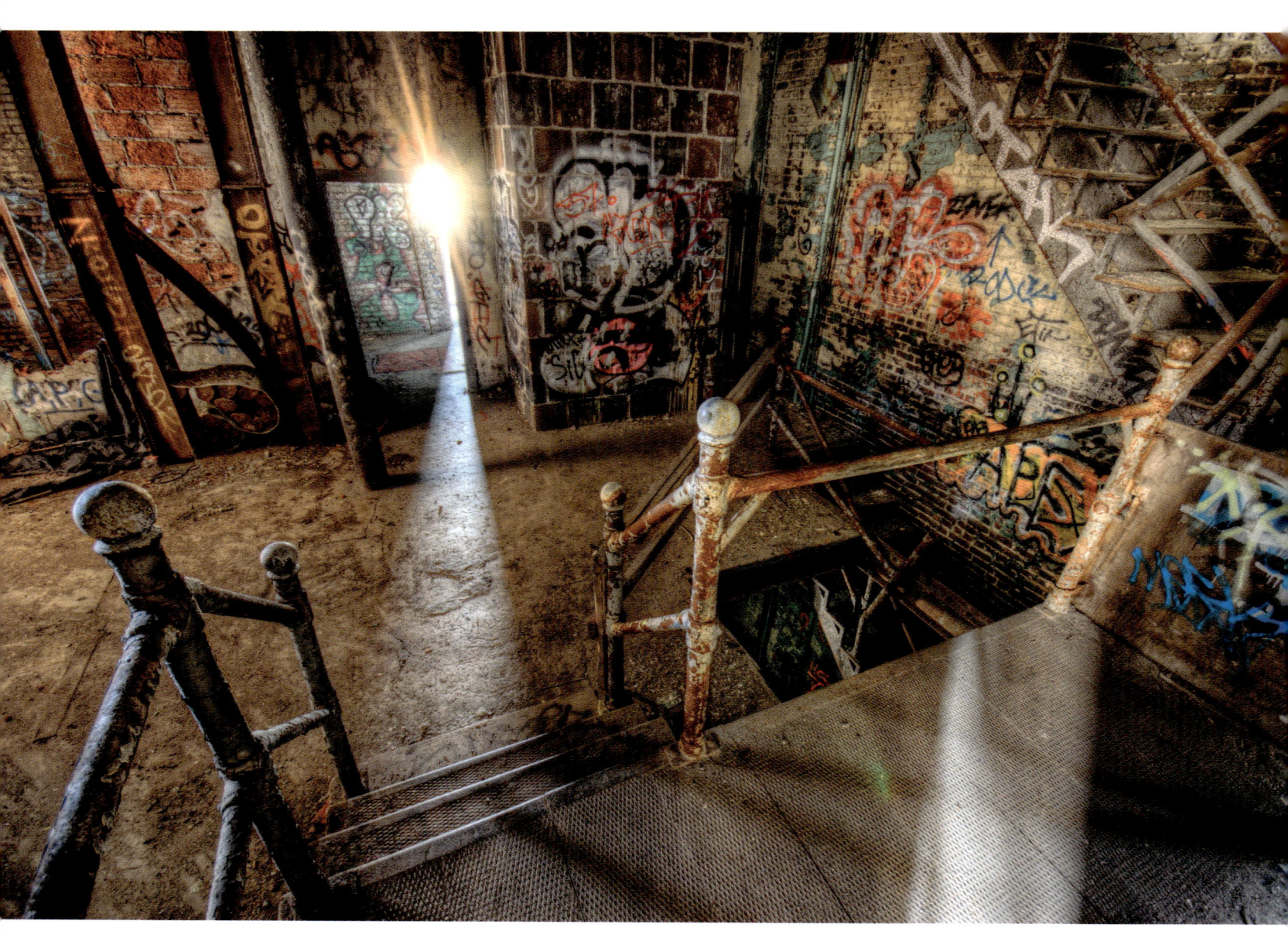

HIGH DYNAMIC RANGE

Eight

FIGURE 8.1 Image © Eric Constantineau

High dynamic range imaging (or HDR as it's most commonly known) is a technique that allows you to expand the dynamic range, or the latitude of brightness, of your images beyond what can actually be captured by your camera's sensor. The maximum dynamic range of a typical decay scene can often surpass the capabilities of a camera sensor to effectively reproduce the full gamut of luminosity of the scene. Therefore, taking more than one exposure and combining them together allows you to attain an image that spans a wider dynamic range and enables you to capture detail in the brightest highlights and darkest shadows.

Today, HDR is usually done with special software, but it can be done manually in Photoshop very easily, and in fact HDR has existed in some form since about 1850. French photographer Gustave Le Gray, who was quite famous for his seascapes, would shoot two negatives, one exposure for the sky and one exposure for the sea, and combine the two separate negatives to create one print that combined both exposures to capture all of the detail of the scene (today a photographer would just use a graduated neutral density filter to achieve the same effect.)

Later on, as photographic technology progressed and film could record a wider dynamic range, "HDR" was performed by processes called *dodging and burning.* This involved exposing different parts of the photographic paper for different times. For less exposure, the photographer would use a tool to block the light for a period and to for more exposure the photographer would use a different tool to increase the exposure on a certain spot. This technique involved quite a bit of trial and error, but resulted in prints with a relatively wide gamut of luminosity.

So where does HDR fit in for decay photography? Well, it's useful in many ways. For one, decay photography is often done outdoors and is very similar to landscape photography, which often has a wider range of luminosity than the camera can capture. HDR can bring all of the tones into a single image that appears more accurate to what the eye sees. Another situation where HDR comes in handy is when you're photographing inside an abandoned building where the only light is coming from the windows. Usually the light from the windows is so much brighter than the shadow areas that both highlight and shadow detail can't be captured in one exposure – HDR helps here, too. Lastly, HDR imaging can create hyper-real or surreal otherworldly looks to images and is often used as an artistic effect.

Doing a search on the internet will quickly reveal that quite a few photographers feel that HDR and decay photography go hand in hand simply because the technique adds a more vivid feel to images, can enhance the decaying aspect and even add a somewhat horrific or menacing feel to an already ghastly subject.

Bracketing

Today most photographers use digital images to create HDR photographs. The key to getting a successful HDR image is *bracketing*. Bracketing is the term that photographers use for taking a series of shots using different settings. There are a number of different types of bracketing (exposure, focus, flash, white balance, etc.), but for HDR purposes exposure bracketing is used.

For the best results at least three bracketed images should be taken. One at metered exposure, one underexposure, and one overexposure. Some photographers use five or more images. For most purposes five exposures captures more than enough dynamic range to create a successful HDR image (one metered exposure, two underexposures and two overexposures).

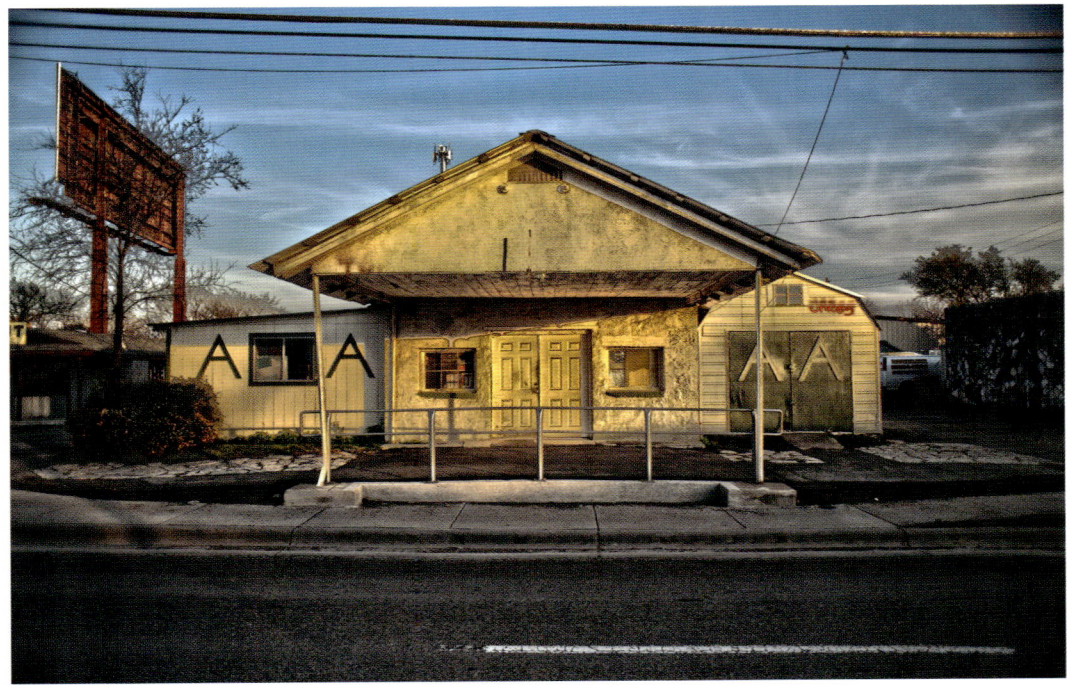

FIGURE 8.2 This image of a decaying old building in Austin, TX was processed using Photoshop CS6 Merge to HDR Pro. Using the 16-bit option the image was tone-mapped to add color saturation and shadow and highlight detail to the initially high-contrast scene. **Nikon D700 with Nikon 24 mm f/2.8D Three bracketed exposures @ f/2.8 ISO 200**

Most photographers that I know that do a lot of HDR imaging recommend shooting RAW files at two stops apart for each exposure.

Note: I have run across a few photographers that shoot HDR in JPEG. If you decide to go this route it's best you use five or more shoots exposed one stop apart.

Remember, when shooting for HDR the images need to line up perfectly, so using a tripod is almost a necessity. I have gotten successful HDR images by shooting in a burst while my cameras is set to auto-bracketing, but not all cameras feature auto bracketing; if your camera doesn't you will have to bracket manually and a tripod will be absolutely necessary.

Another thing to remember is that you want the images you are going to composite to have the same depth of field, so using the same aperture setting is advisable. You can bracket like this two different ways: by adjusting the shutter speed or by adjust the ISO. You will yield the best HDR results by adjusting the shutter speed since higher ISO settings will result in images with more noise in them. Exposure bracketing by

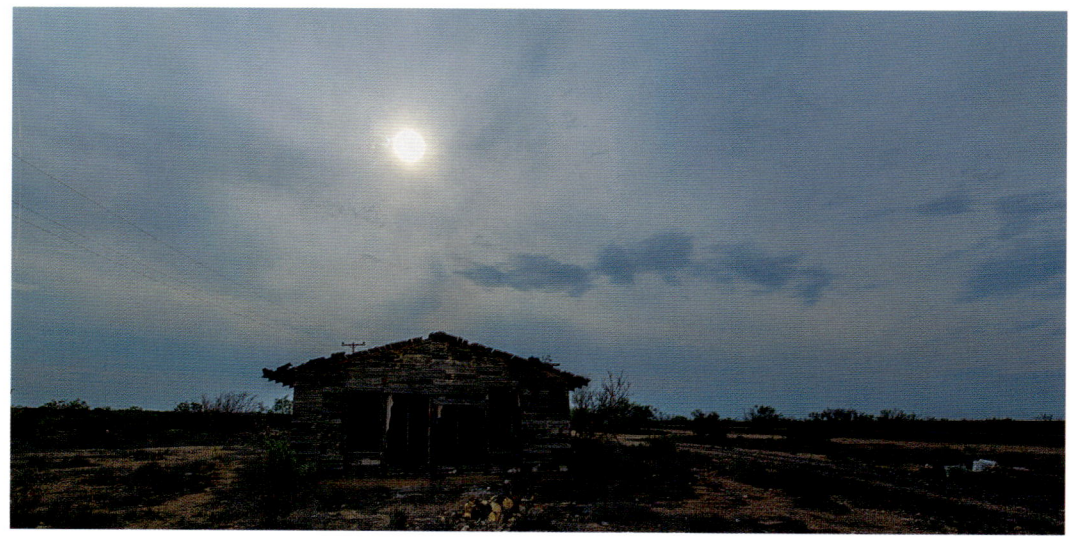

FIGURE 8.3 Abandoned shack in west Texas. The bright sun backlighting the scene in the frame proved to make this a difficult shot to accomplish. I bracketed five exposures at two-stop intervals to get all of the dynamic range of the scene that I could.   **Nikon D800 with Nikon 14–24 mm f/2.8G at 14 mm. f/8 ISO 100**

shutter speed is recommended for most subjects, but keep in mind that if there is any movement in the scene it will be rendered with a ghost-like quality (ghosting). The best advice is to try to stick to static subjects, and if you're shooting outdoors try to shoot on a day with no wind.

Although strict HDR purists don't recommend this method, I've had success in the past by taking one RAW file and adjusting the exposure and saving between two and five 16-bit TIFF files. You can do this if you don't have a tripod handy or if there is a substantial amount of movement in the scene, such as a windy day, or a beach or lake scene. You do, however, want to be sure that your shutter speed is fast enough to freeze all motion in the single RAW file.

Manual layer blending

This method was one of the first methods used to create an image with a high dynamic range. These images are realistic looking and don't necessarily reflect the type of images that most photographers have in mind when they hear the term HDR. For these types of images you make three exposures: one for highlights, one for mid-tones, and one for shadows. Using Photoshop you create a file with three layers for each exposure and use layer masks to paint in areas that need tonal adjustment. This method is similar to dodging and burning in a traditional dark room.

Tone mapping

When most people hear the term HDR, what they usually picture is an HDR image that has been tone-mapped. The problem with HDR image files is that they contain a vast amount of dynamic range! Now this probably sounds counter-intuitive to you, but this is actually a drawback because the devices or the medium photographs are usually viewed on actually have *less* dynamic range than even your camera sensor is able to capture. What happens when your images are converted to HDR is that in order to compress the high dynamic range of the image to fit into a space that has a relatively low dynamic range, such as a computer monitor, photographic paper, or even the pages of this book, is that the image comes out flat and lacking contrast.

When most people think of HDR they think of bright images with lots of contrast that seem to jump right off the screen or the paper. That's where tone mapping comes in. Instead of adjusting the dynamic range of the whole image to fit into the limited space of the monitor or print, tone mapping makes local changes to the brightness and contrast of each area of the image. Of course, this is a simplified explanation of what goes on, because tone mapping requires the computer to run many complex algorithms and different programs have different algorithms and different ways to run them.

Note: Some newer models of cameras have an HDR function built in. This usually involves the camera taking two or three shots automatically and blending them in-camera. It's a pretty handy feature, but it lacks the control and fine-tuning that you can do in post-processing.

The subject of HDR imaging is a highly polarized one within the photographic community. You'll find that most photographers

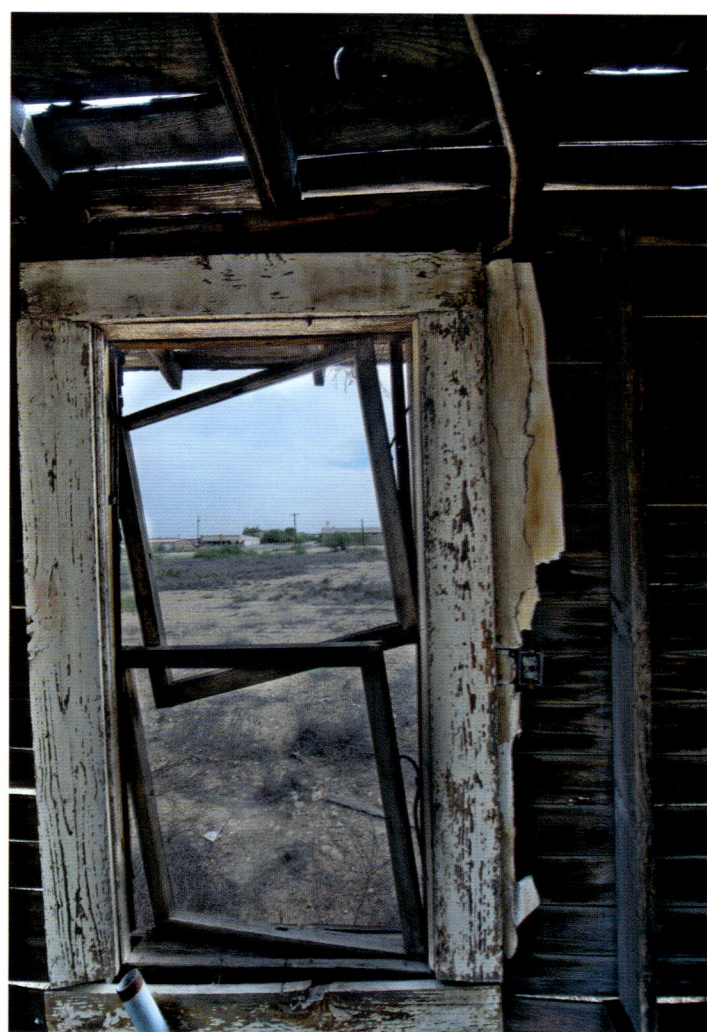

FIGURE 8.4 Looking out of the window in Dryden, TX. For this image I simply made two exposures from one RAW file, one for the relatively dark indoors and one for the bright outdoors. I combined the two images by layering the files and using a layer mask to reveal the detail in the window. **Nikon D800 with Nikon 14–24 mm f/2.8G at 14 mm. 1/60 sec. @ f/8 ISO 100**

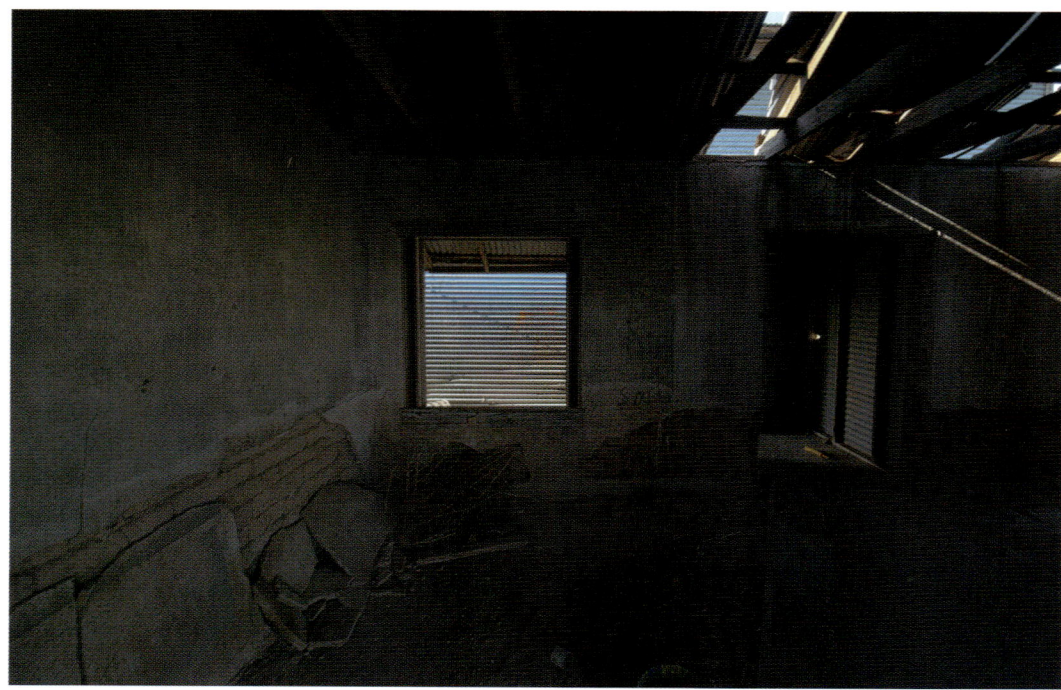

FIGURE 8.5 This is what an image looks like after merging to HDR, but before tone mapping. This 16-bit image file contains all of the luminosity data of five merged images, but is compressed in order to make it viewable on low dynamic range media

either claim to love it or vehemently oppose it. Some photographers think it's a great artistic technique, not unlike applying a filter in Photoshop, but a lot of photographers take exception to the overly saturated colors and hyper-realistic or even surrealistic look that tone mapping can give an HDR image (a common term is *over-cooked*).

The truth is that neither faction is right. It's up to you as the photographer to decide what is right for your own personal images. Tone mapping can be very subtle and preserve just the right amount of shadow and highlight detail. On the other hand, tone mapping can also be applied very heavily, giving the image an unrealistic look that can sometimes be quite garish. Personally, I like the HDR effect to be as subtle as possible. If you're going for a more surreal look I suggest you take your time and really look at the image. Overdoing the tone mapping can cause various artifacts in your HDR images.

Some of these artifacts are:

- **Halos.** This is the most common issue I see, especially with people who are new to HDR photography. This is where an

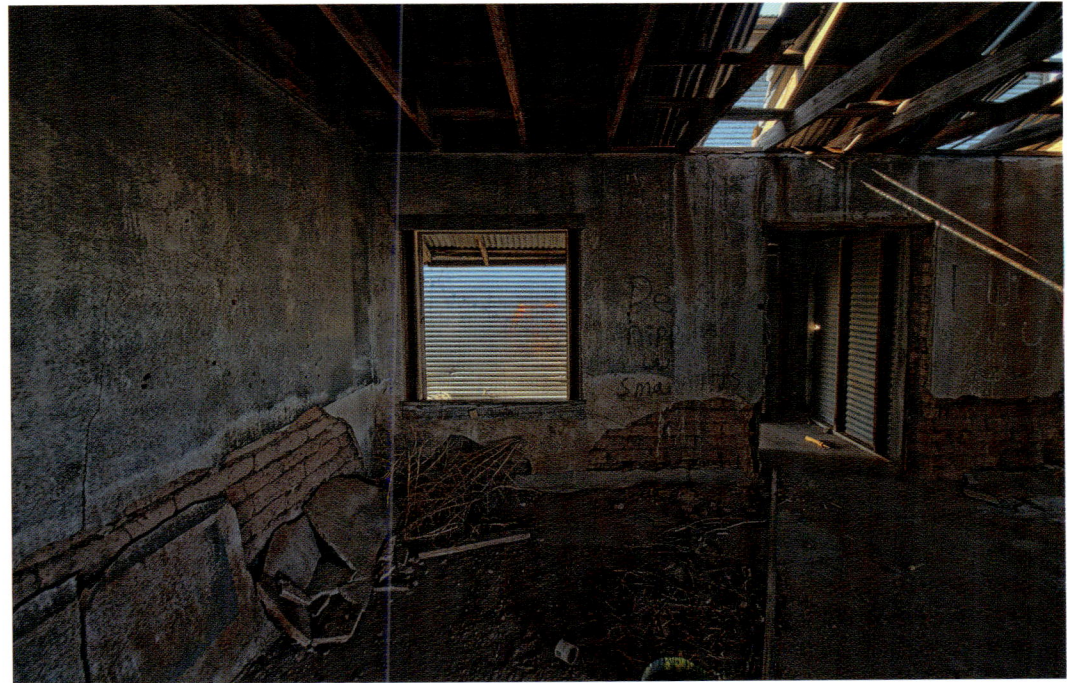

FIGURE 8.6 Here is Figure 8.5 after running it through the Topaz 5 tone mapping. Here I added a little contrast to bring out the details and saturation to make the colors as bright as they appeared in real life

area of high contrast and low contrast meet. Here you will notice that the area appears to have a bright glow around it. This typically happens when the tone mapping is overdone.

- **Excess noise in the shadow areas.** One of the reasons HDR is done is to increase dynamic range, but without adding noise to the shadows. In this situation the noise is amplified by over-sharpening the image detail.
- **Oversaturated colors.** This is another very common ailment in HDR photography. While sometimes adding saturation will make the image pop, a lot of times it tweaks the colors too much, resulting in unappealing and unnatural-looking images.
- **Dark clouds.** This is less of a problem, but it does tend to get overdone quite a bit. Adding some texture and darkness to clouds can result in a dramatic effect, but easing back can make your images more natural.
- **Over-sharpening.** Oftentimes the desire to add detail to the image results in over-sharpening. At this point every tiny detail in the image is visible and results in an image that becomes quite hard to view because the detail contrast

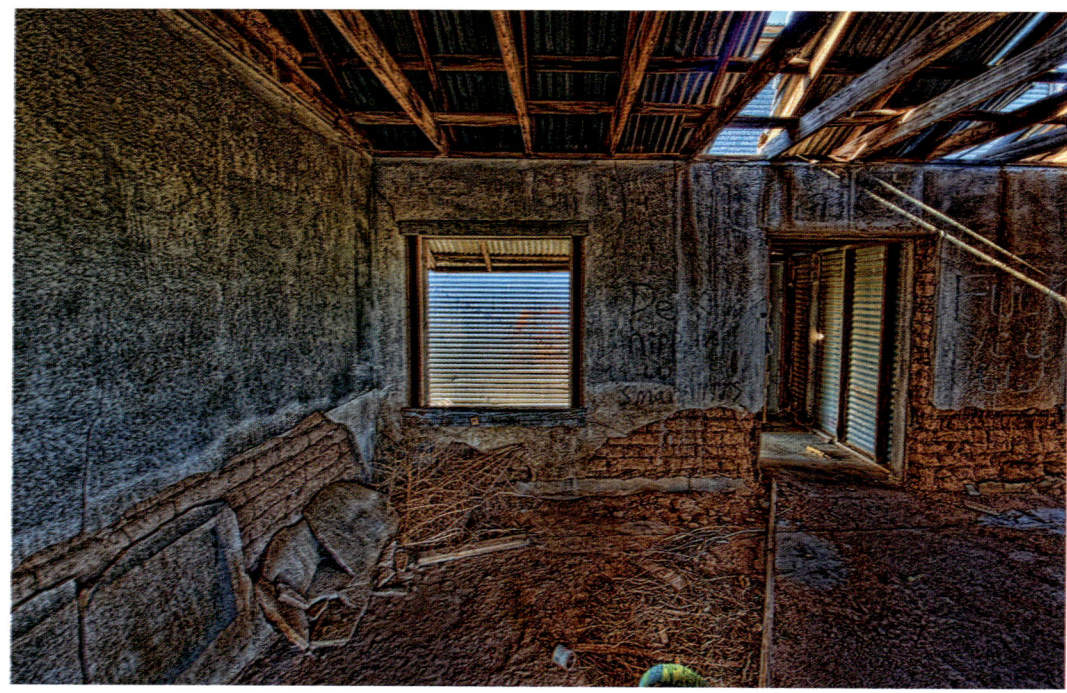

FIGURE 8.7 This is another tone-mapped version of Figure 8.5, but this version has been processed much more extensively. As you can see, the contrast and details have been highly boosted, resulting in a hyper-realistic image with dramatic detail. The saturation has also been applied liberally, resulting in a cartoonish or painting-like image

detracts from the subject, making it hard for the viewer to decipher what the image is.

The key to making a successful HDR image is to know where to draw the line and also knowing when to use it and when not to. Some photographers, especially when first discovering HDR, tend to use it too judiciously, sometimes relying on it as a crutch to make bland images more interesting. Before deciding to create a tone-mapped HDR image, decide whether the scene actually needs it. This can even be evaluated before the shutter release button is pressed. Is the scene high contrast? When the optimal exposure is made, are there blocked up shadows, blown out highlights, or both? Check the histogram. Exposing to the right and pulling the exposure back in camera RAW may be all the image needs to have the full gamut of dynamic range.

Exposure blending

Very similar to the manual technique I described earlier in the chapter, this technique takes a number of bracketed images and fuses them together, blending parts of the images together to balance highlights, mid-tones, and shadows so that an image with increased dynamic range is produced. This image contains detail in the bright highlight areas and the shadow areas, as well as having well-defined mid-tones.

What's different about this technique is that a computer program, which runs an algorithm similar to that of tone mapping, automatically does it for you. The great advantage to exposure blending images is that they are much more realistic without the artifacts that tone mapping can produce.

While the idea behind exposure fusion has been around for centuries, only in the last few years have software engineers been adding this feature to their programs. Software such as Photomatix and HDRtist Pro both incorporate exposure

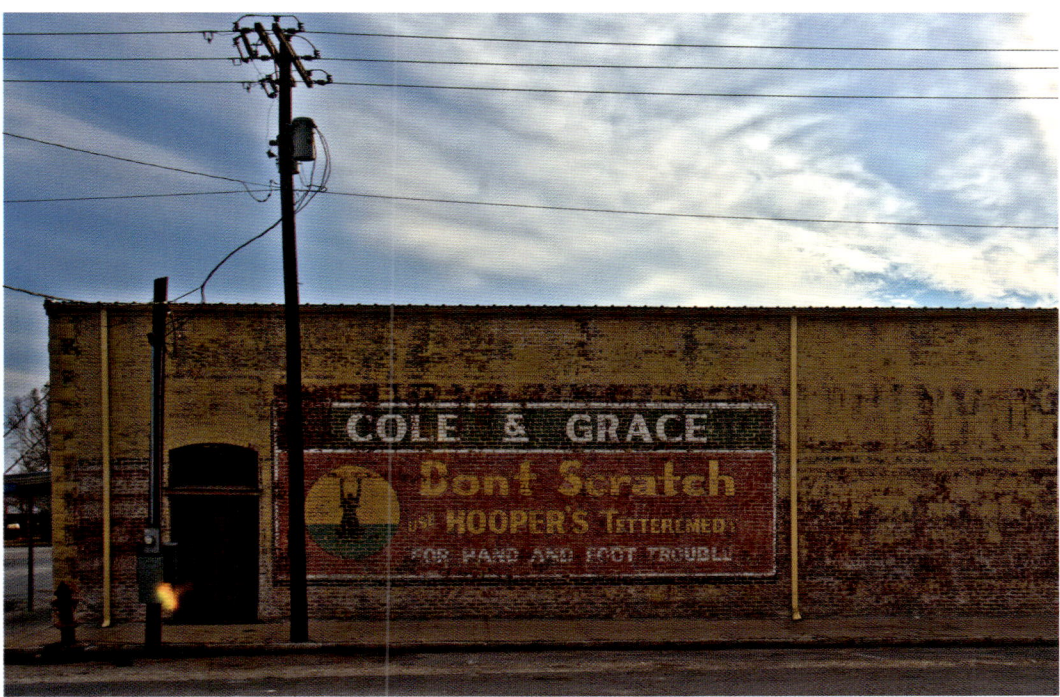

FIGURE 8.8 This image of an old general store in Hico, TX (reportedly home to outlaw Billy the Kid) was processed using the Photomatix exposure fusion process to create a realistic HDR image

blending (or exposure fusion in Photomatix vernacular) into their software.

Software

There are quite a few options out there when it comes to merging photographs for HDR, exposure blending, and tone mapping. There is no one perfect program for this type of imaging, but there are plenty of options available to you, no matter what your skill level or needs are.

Each type of software uses its own proprietary algorithms to make calculations, and each one has different interfaces, some more user-friendly than others. Almost all of the software that's available has free trials, so you can try each one out before you actually buy the program.

Photoshop

Beginning with Photoshop CS2, Adobe has featured the Merge to HDR option. It wasn't highly regarded by many HDR photographers because there was no option for tone mapping, which meant you had to use another standalone program or a plug-in. When CS5 was released Photoshop had fixed this with Merge to HDR Pro, which provides a tone mapping dialog box that appears once Photoshop has finished merging your bracketed images. This feature is also available in the newest version of Photoshop CS6.

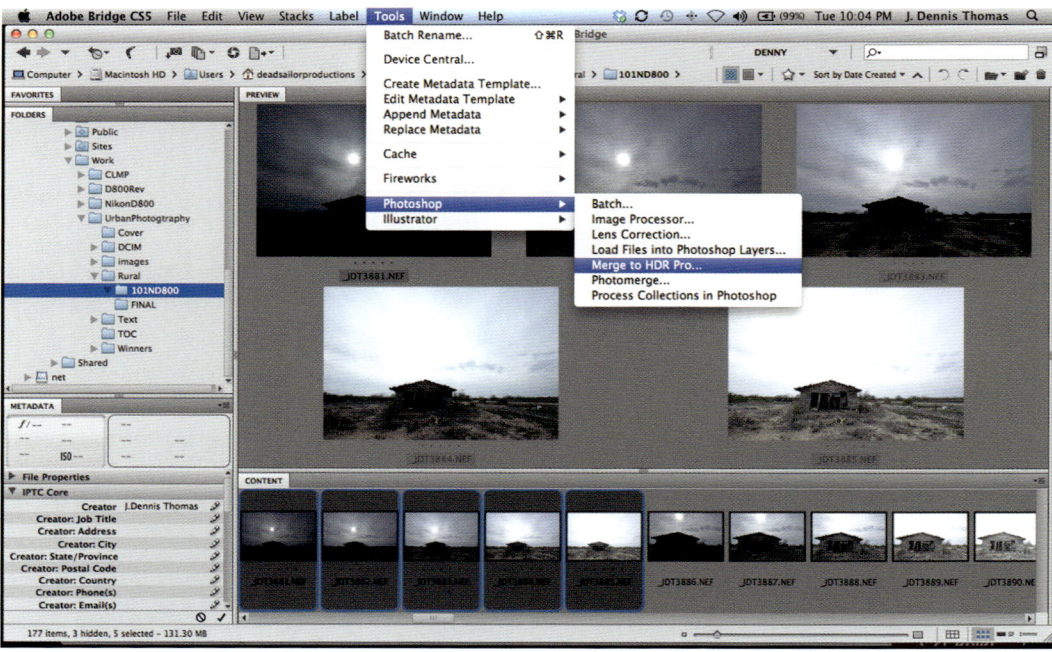

FIGURE 8.9 The Merge to HDR Pro feature in Adobe Photoshop CS5

Photoshop can also store the HDR images as a 32-bit floating point file, which allows you to adjust the luminance values, as opposed to a 16- or 8-bit non-floating point in which the luminance is fixed. You can later use this 32-bit f le for tone mapping using other software. To take advantage of the Merge to HDR Pro tone mapping option you must select the 16-bit option (this isn't the same as a 16-bit non-floating point image because the 16-bit option only applies to output here).

Merge to HDR Pro also has a great feature that automatically aligns images and reduces ghosting from images that may have had camera or subject movement. Personally, I use Photoshop's Merge to HDR Pro for most of my HDR imaging and toning. I already own Photoshop so I didn't need to buy extra software to create HDR images.

Photomatix

A company called HDRsoft created Photomatix. From what I know, it was one of the first HDR imaging programs available to the general public. Photomatix is available as a standalone program or for use as a Photoshop plug-in, meaning you can use the Merge to HDR Pro feature in Photoshop and use the Photomatix tone mapping features without exporting the image out of Photoshop.

Because Photomatix was there at the beginning of the HDR craze, it remains one of the most popular HDR programs and is used by most photographers that I know who do a lot of HDR imaging. Photomatix has a very powerful tone mapping interface and also allows you to do exposure blending, or Exposure Fusion as they call it.

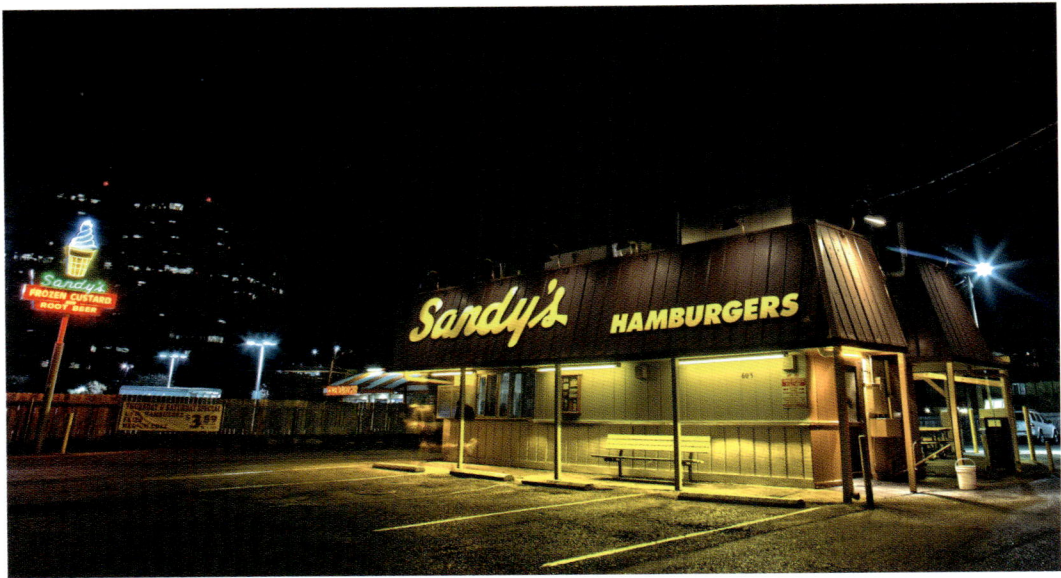

FIGURE 8.10 Sandy's Hamburger's in Austin, TX processed using Photoshop CS5 Merge to HDR Pro

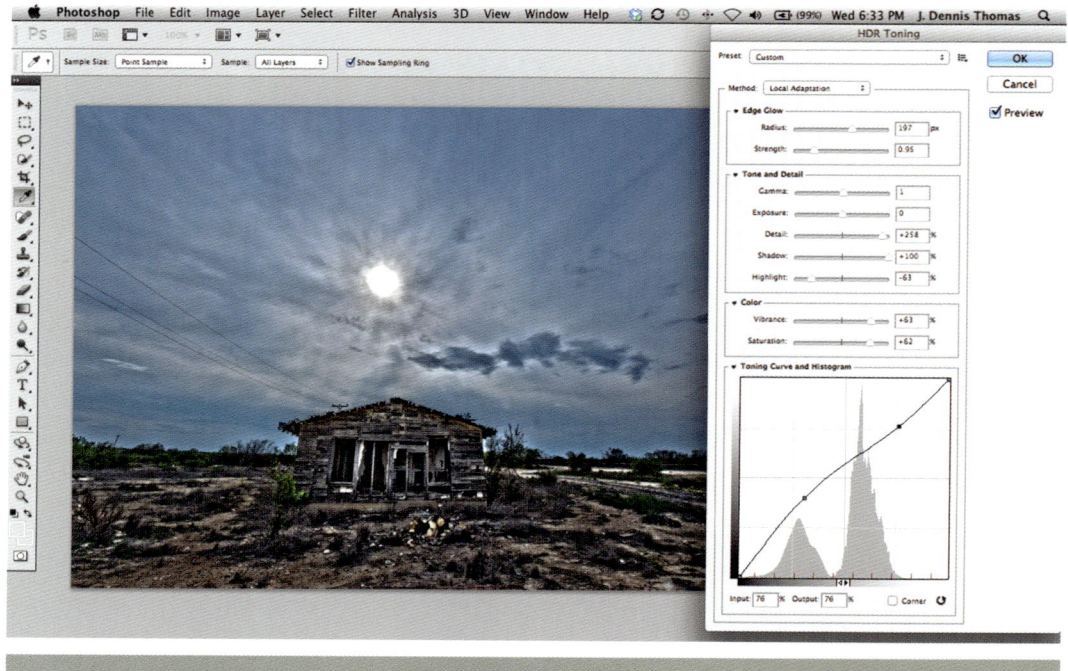

FIGURE 8.11 The HDR Toning dialog box in Photoshop CS5's Merge to HDR Pro feature

Photomatix is available as a fully functioning free download with the caveat that a watermark is placed on images processed and saved with it. You can also upgrade to Photomatix Pro with all of the features, or Photomatix Essentials for basic HDR imaging.

Topaz

Topaz Labs is a software company that specializes in Photoshop plug-ins. They offer a plug-in called Topaz Adjust, which allows you to adjust exposure and color as well as tone mapping controls. Topaz also enables you to select a single image and add HDR and tone mapping effects, but it works best when used in conjunction with Photoshop's Merge to HDR Pro 16-bit files.

The interface slightly resembles Adobe Lightroom, but it's kind of quirky and doesn't offer the most intuitive interface for making adjustments. I find that Topaz is a little ham-fisted in its approach and it takes a little more time to get a usable image than some of the other offerings.

HDRtist

HDRtist by Ohanaware is a Mac-only application and it's probably the simplest one to use. You can drag and drop your image right

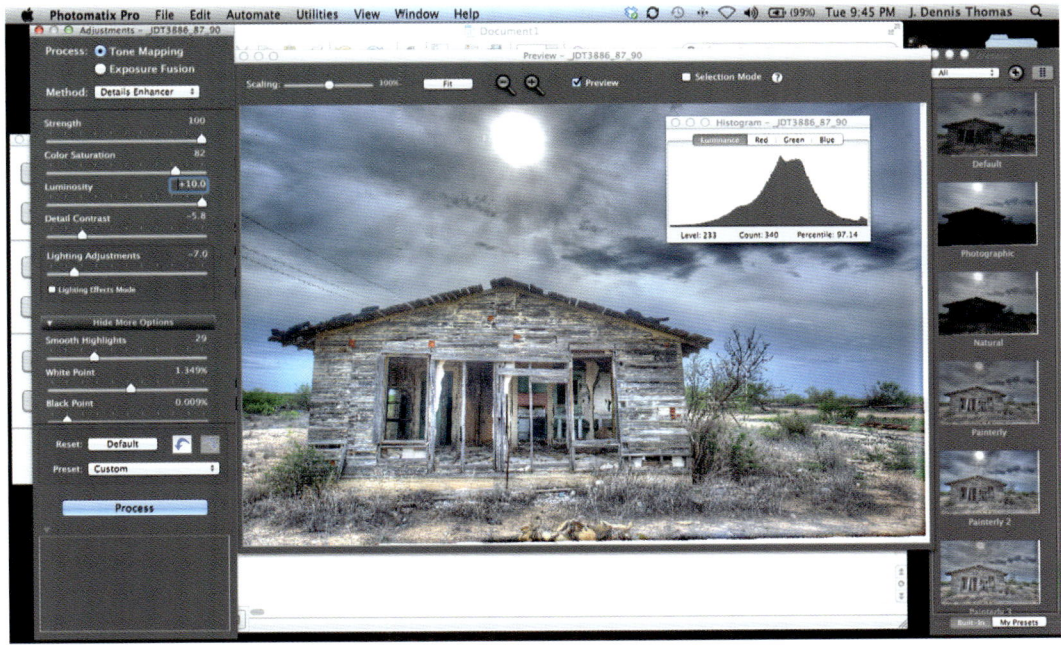

FIGURE 8.12 The Photomatix Pro standalone application

into the interface to start the process. There are, however, two *very* different versions. The free version, simply called HDRtist, only has one adjustment, strength. The free version is free for a reason – it's not very good. Unless your images are perfectly lined up you will see obvious ghosting and the images pretty much come out soft and almost plastic looking. As you can see in Figure 8.15, it's not a very attractive look. Upgrading to HDRtist Pro, however, gets you a much more flexible program that offers both tone mapping and exposure blending options. I find the exposure blending works especially well.

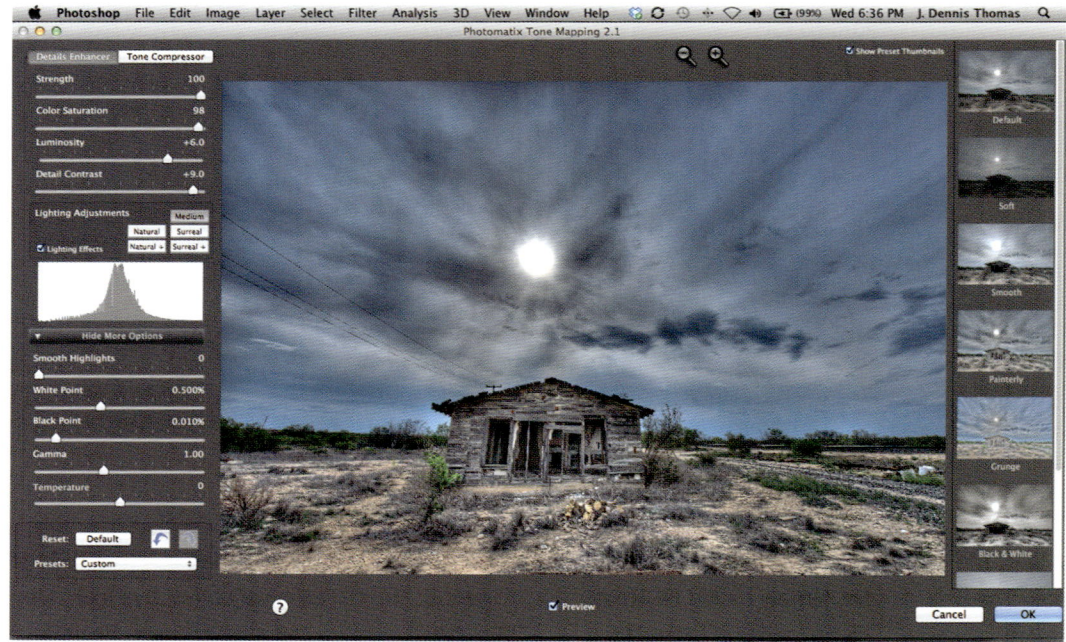

FIGURE 8.13 The Photomatix Pro Photoshop plug-in

High Dynamic Range 167

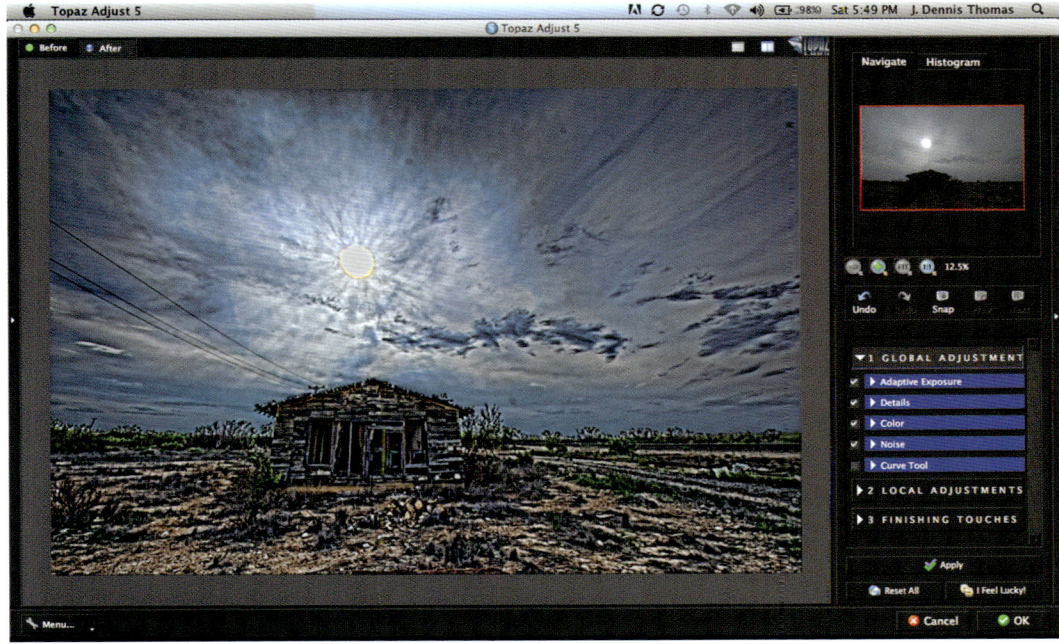

FIGURE 8.14 The Topaz Adjust 5 Photoshop plug-in

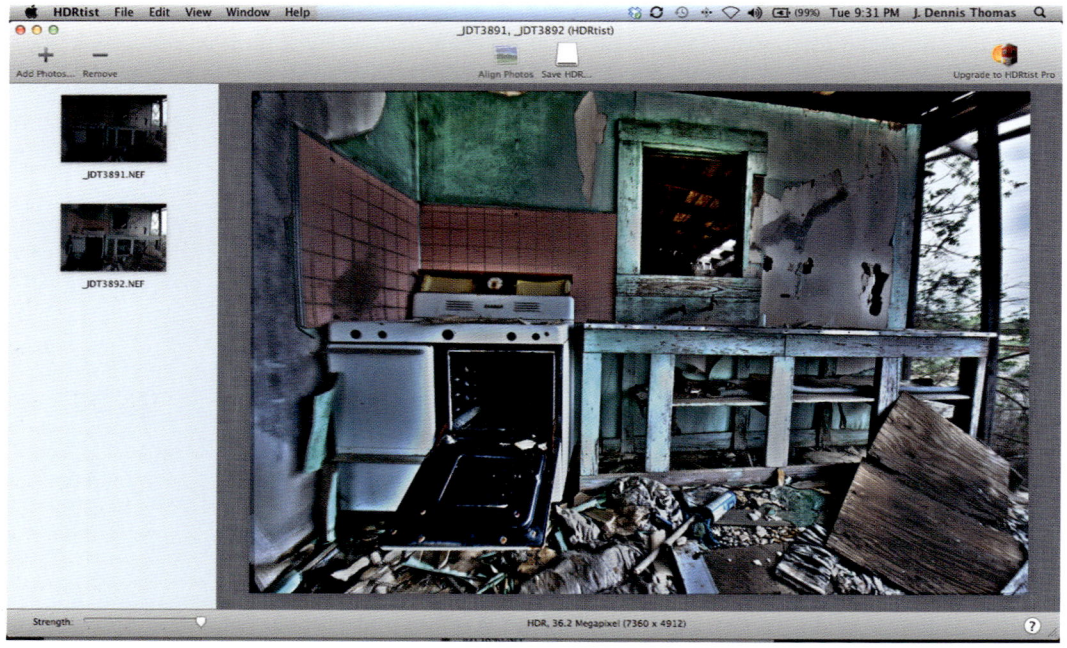

FIGURE 8.15 HDRtist free version interface

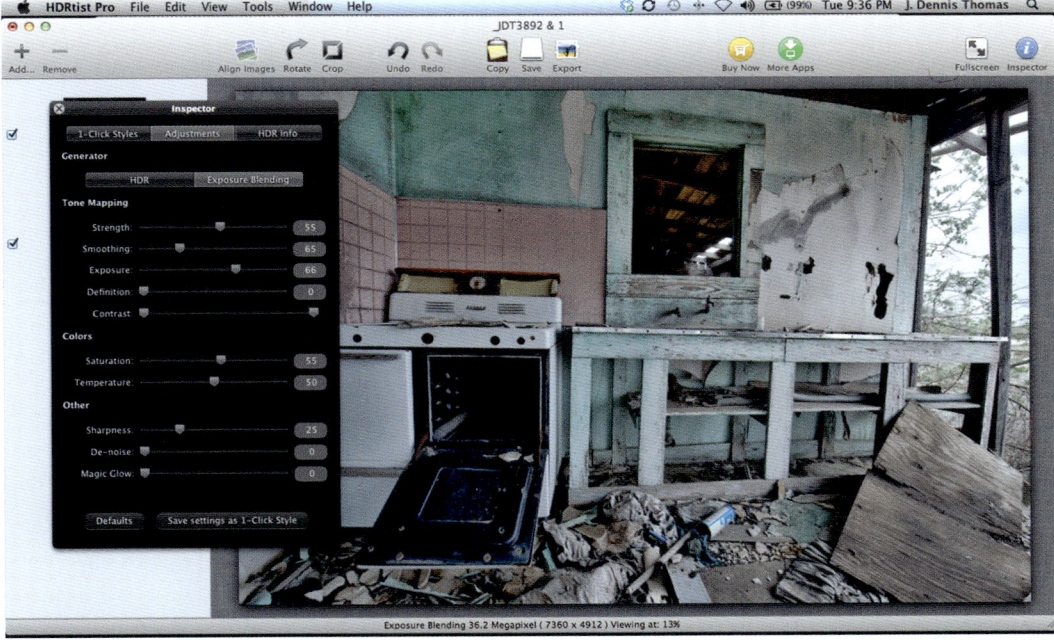

FIGURE 8.16 HDRtist Pro version interface

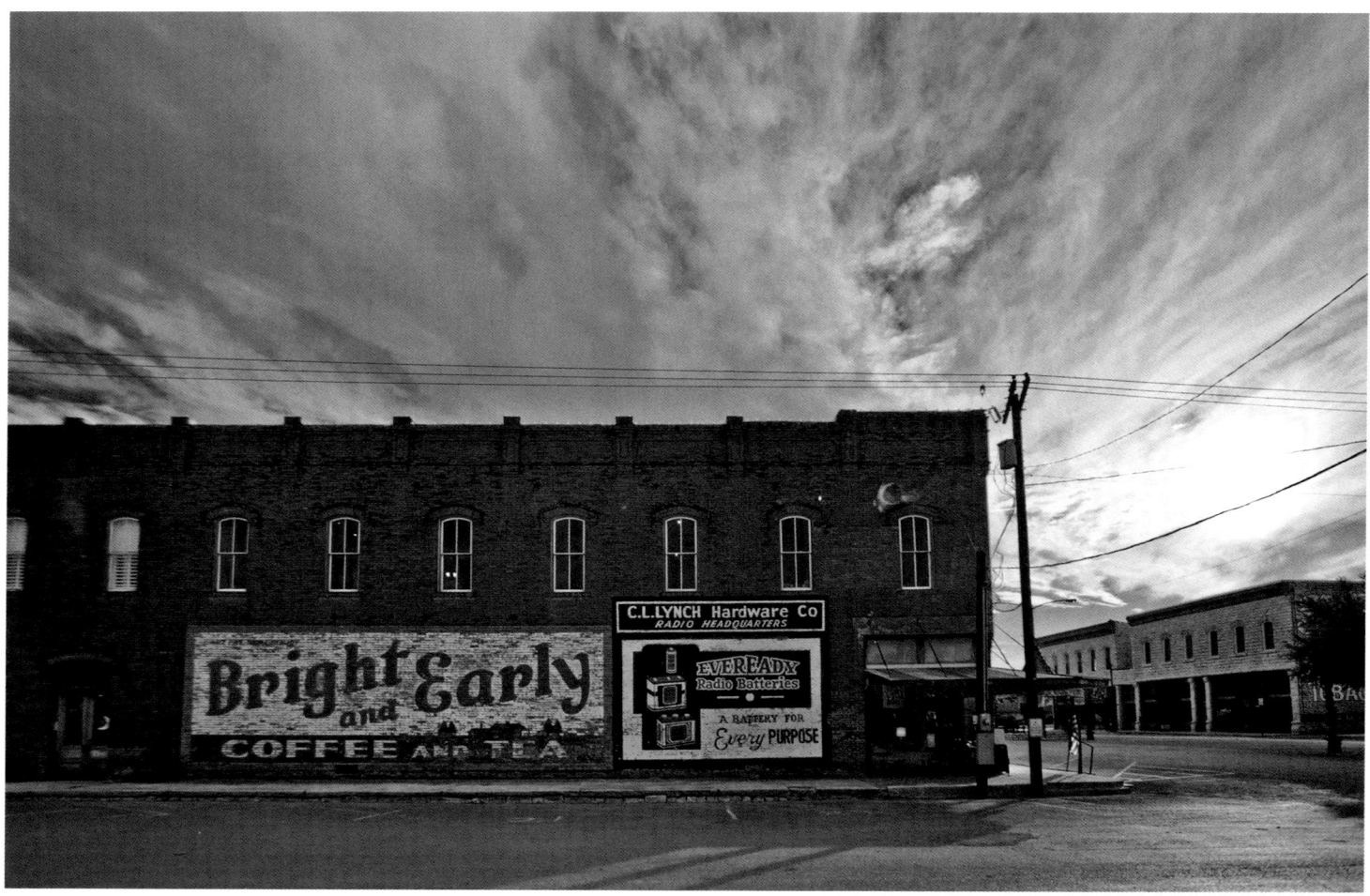
FIGURE 8.17 HDR images don't have to be in full color; they can be just as eye-catching when converted to black and white.

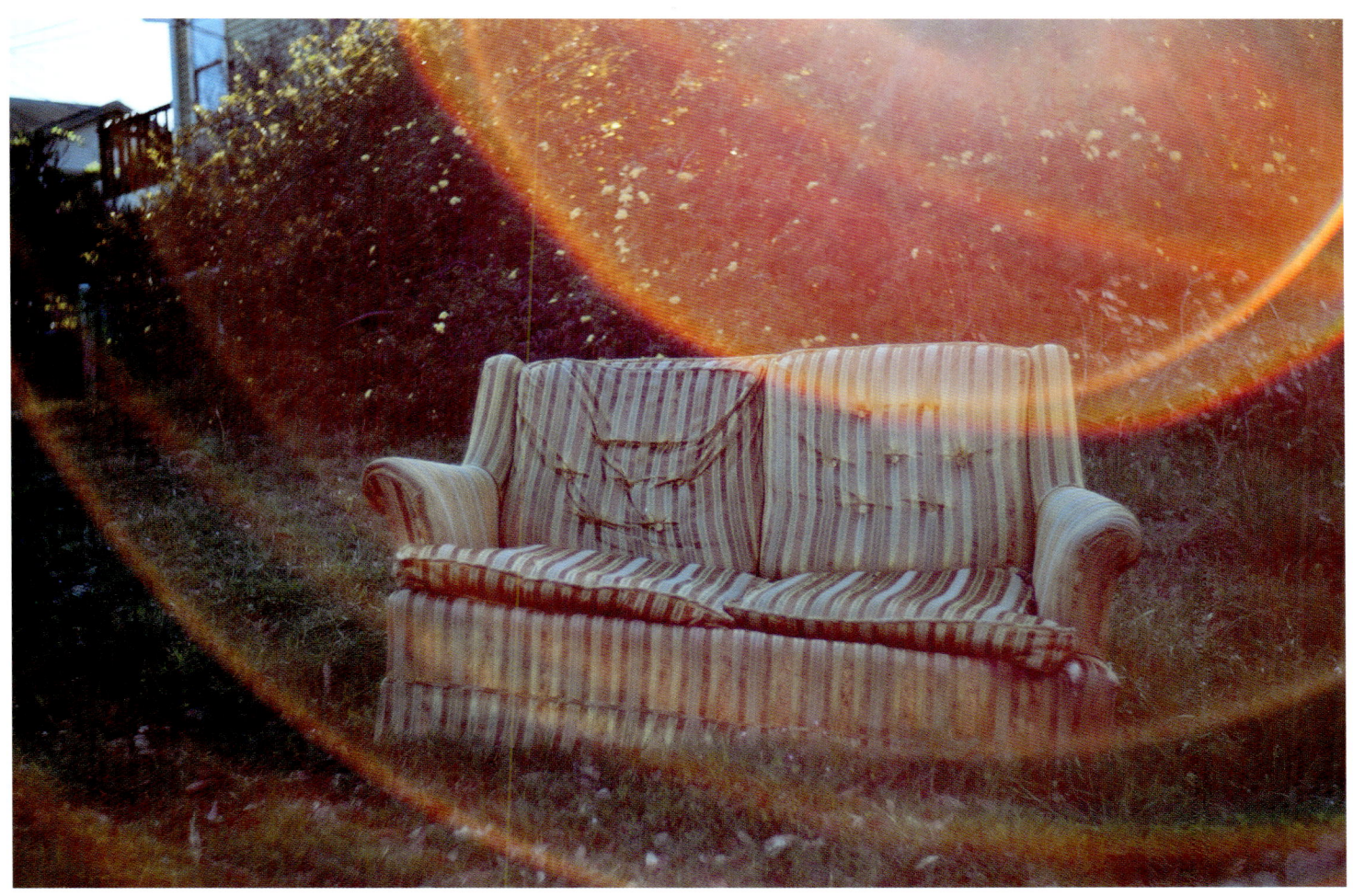

FIGURE 8.18 The Love Seat - 78704.   Leica M8 Voigtländer 35mm f/1.4 Nokton Classic SC. 1/4000 sec. @ f/1.4 ISO 160.

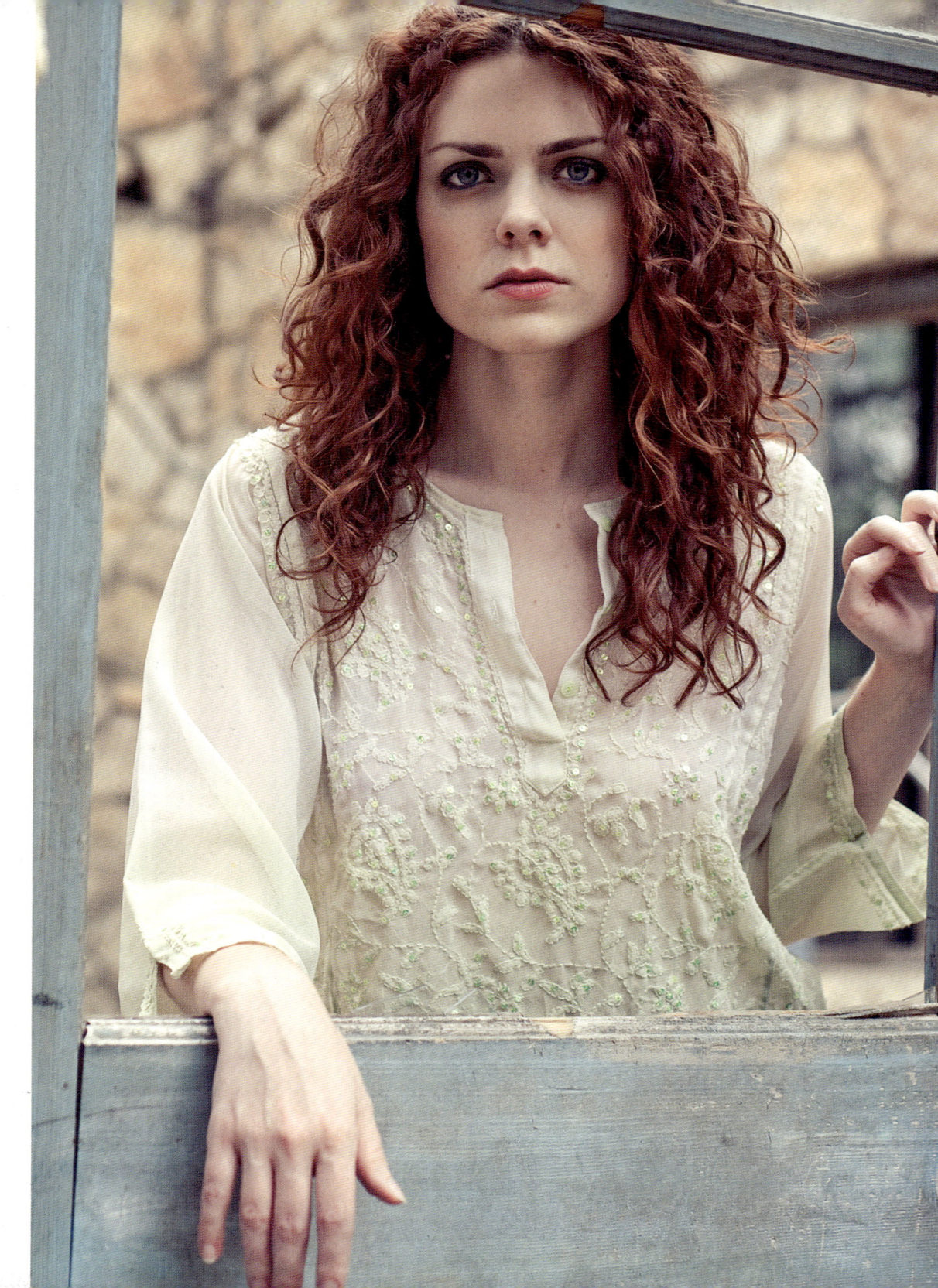

DECAY PORTRAITURE

Nine

Scenes of decay make great locations for interesting portraiture. **Nikon D300 with Nikon 50 mm f/1.8D (75 mm equivalent). 1/250 sec. @ f/2.5 ISO 250. © Julian Humphries**

There's very little information out there in regards to doing portraiture in this specific style, so I decided to include this information here. Although this may not be considered decay photography in the truest sense of the definition, including some elements of decay into portraiture is something that advertising and fashion photographers have been doing for a long time. Placing an object of beauty in the midst of a scene of deterioration is an effective counterpoint and therefore accentuates the allure of the subject. There's something inherently appealing about the dichotomy of vivaciousness and decay — perhaps it's the underlying fear of aging that makes us fascinated by these types of images. In any case, urban and rural landscapes make great locations for portraiture.

Gear and settings

Decay portraiture shares many traits with traditional portrait photography, but obviously the location plays a more important role in the composition. In a sense, this type of photography is more in line with environmental portraiture, as the background invariably figures more prominently in the photo than in a typical portrait. One of the main differences is that the use of aperture to control depth of field is more of a consideration when shooting in decay locations. Generally in portraiture a wider aperture of f/1.4–2.8 is desirable to achieve a shallow depth of field to allow for definitive separation of the subject and the background. When shooting decay portraits, using a smaller aperture can be more effective so you can establish location to portray the decay feel and ambience in your image. I generally prefer a mid-range aperture (f/4–5.6) that renders background out of focus just enough that you can make out what the background is, but it's not so sharp that it begins to compete with the subject. The key is to find the right balance with the subject and background focus.

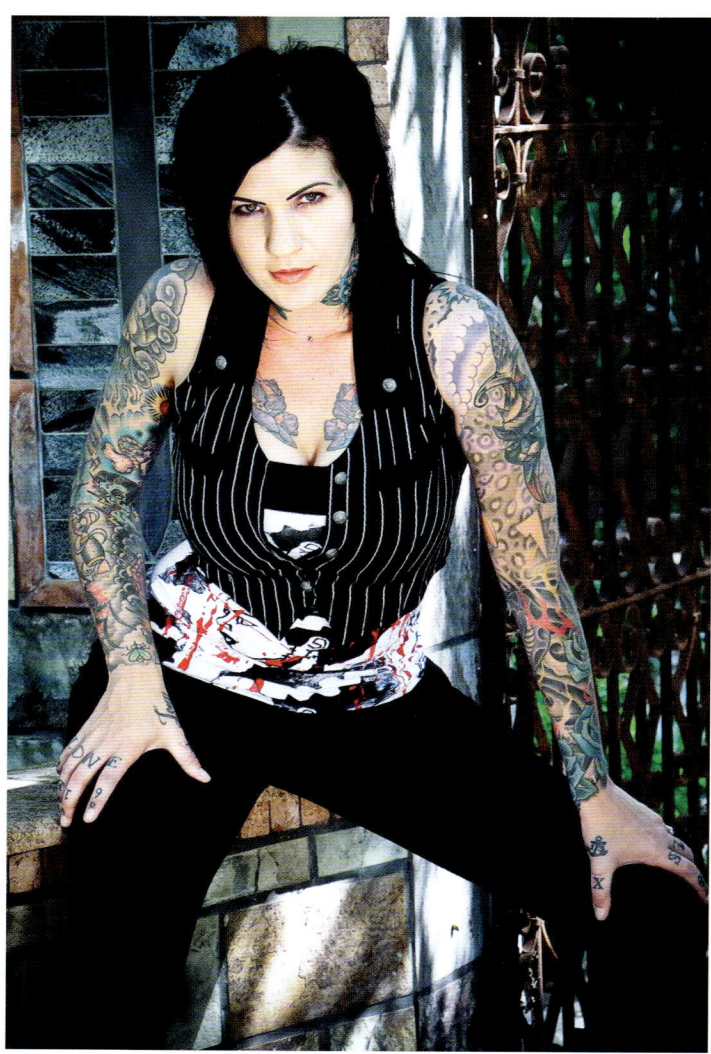

FIGURE 9.2 Using a mid-range aperture setting allows you to achieve just the right depth of field. Nikon D90 with Nikon 18–105 mm f/3.5–5.6G at 105 mm (157 mm equivalent). 1/125 sec. @ f/5.6 ISO 500

Another difference from traditional portrait photography is the type of lens and focal length that is typically used. For most portrait photography a normal to short telephoto lens (50–85 mm) is the norm since portraits are generally composed relatively tight, and longer focal lengths compress and flatten the features of a model. When shooting in the decay environment using a lens with a shorter focal length helps to establish the location by providing an increased depth of field and allowing a looser crop that shows more of the background.

Keep in mind that there are no hard-and-fast rules to follow when photographing portraits in decay settings. I recommend being flexible when shooting these types of photos, and varying both focal length and aperture settings. You can often create more interesting images when you don't confine yourself to a set of rules and allow yourself to be more innovative by playing fast and loose with the rules. This type of photography really lends itself well to experimentation.

Tip: One cool thing about photographing portraits in decay settings is that there is *usually an abundance of props you can use to make the subject more compelling.* Don't forget to look around for interesting things to add to the composition as you're scouting for locations to shoot in.

Lighting tips

As with any type of portrait photography, you can approach the subject of lighting in a number of different ways. You can come at it from a simple perspective and use available light for a natural look, or you can tackle it from a more ambitious direction and use additional external lighting to create a studio-like effect out in the field. With each of these types of lighting options there are different techniques you can use to

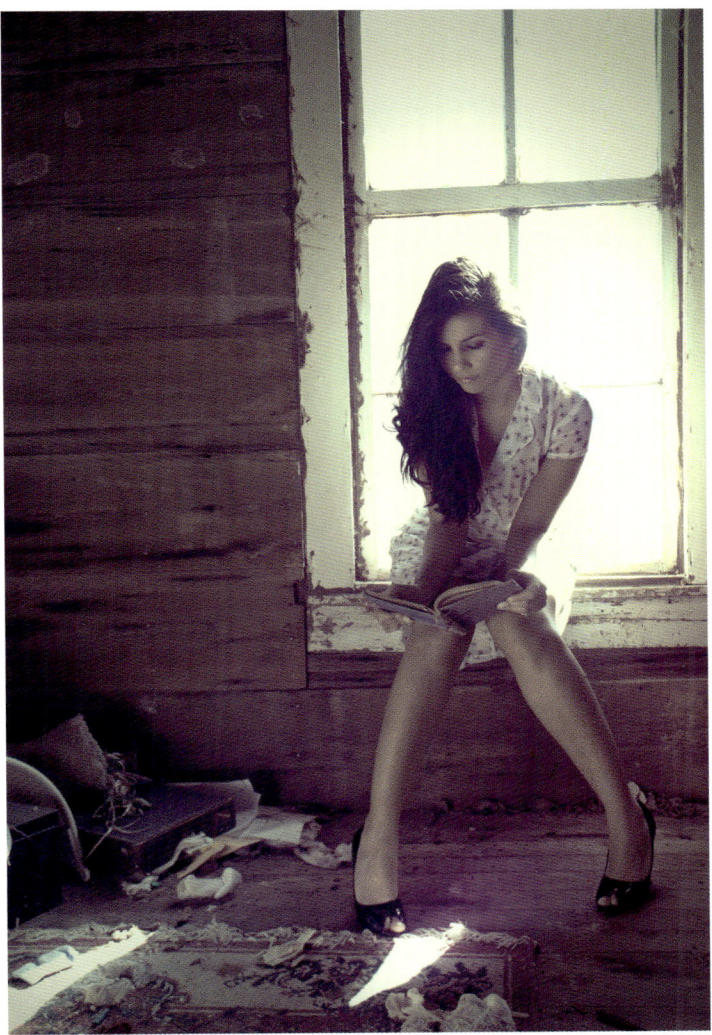

FIGURE 9.3 Using a relatively wide focal length and a loose composition highlights both the model and the decay setting. Nikon D300 with Nikon 18–70 mm f/3.5–4.65 at 27 mm (33 mm equivalent). 1/100 sec. @ f/5.6 ISO 500. © Julian Humphries

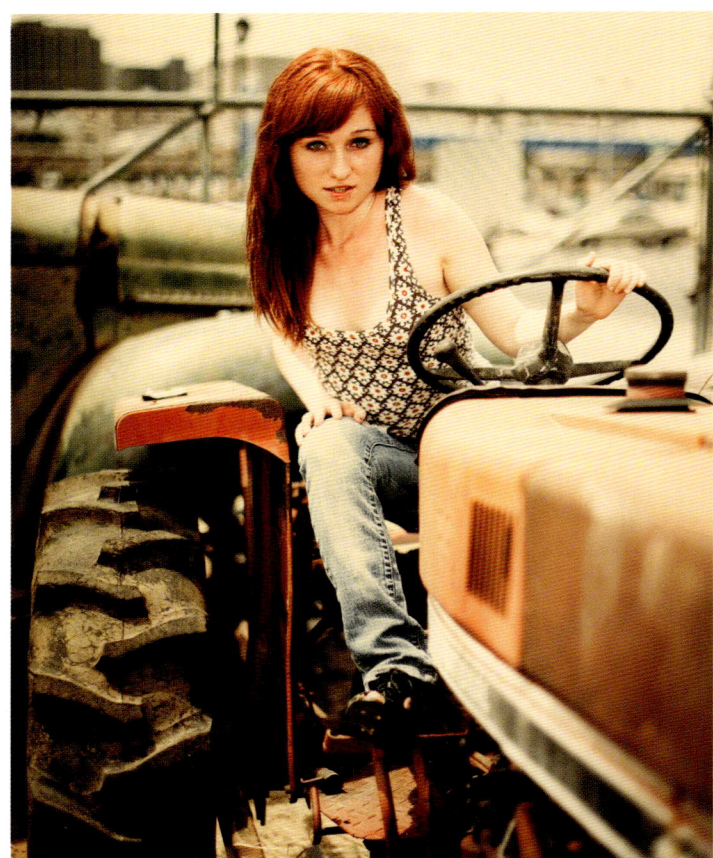

FIGURE 9.4 I had the model use this rusty old tractor as a prop while photographing in a small junkyard that used to be in downtown Austin. Nikon D700 with Nikon 50 mm f/1.4G. 1/8000 sec. @ f/1.4 ISO 200

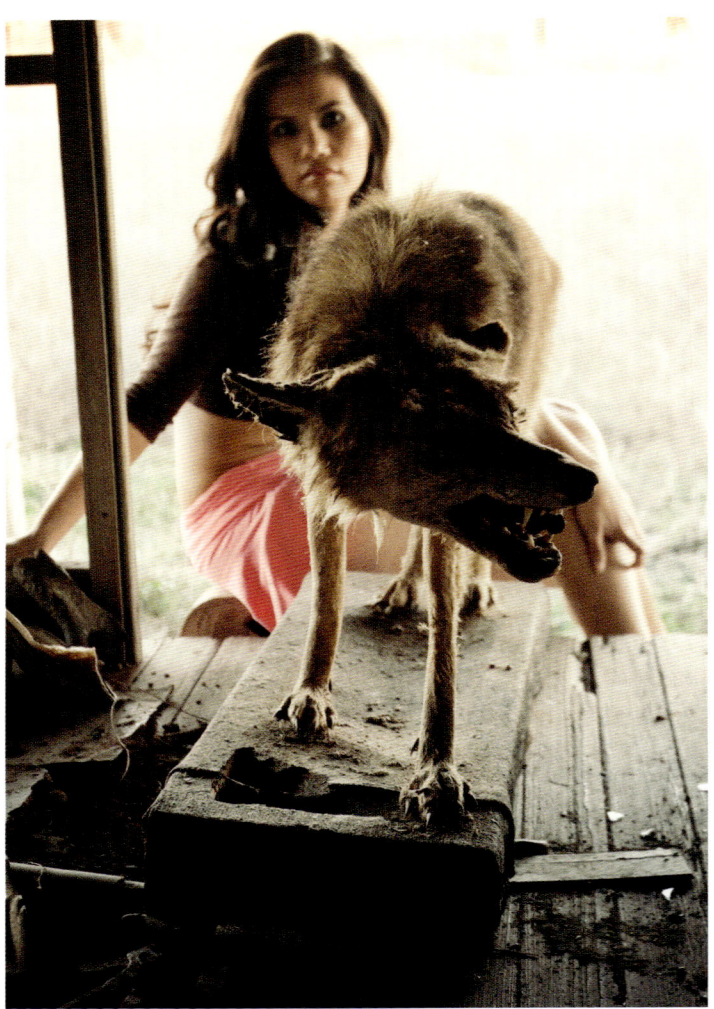

FIGURE 9.5 In an interesting twist, here the prop becomes the main subject while the model takes a backseat. Don't be afraid to bend the rules to create an unconventional image. Nikon D300 with Nikon 18–70 mm f/3.5–4.5G at 40 mm (60 mm equivalent). 1/100 sec. @ f/4.5 ISO 1600. © Julian Humphries

create dramatic effects to enhance the image so it accentuates both the model and the background.

In Chapter 3 I talked a little about the *quality of light* – hard light and soft light. When shooting portraiture these same principles come into play and are even more important when it comes to lighting people. This is mostly due to the fact that the

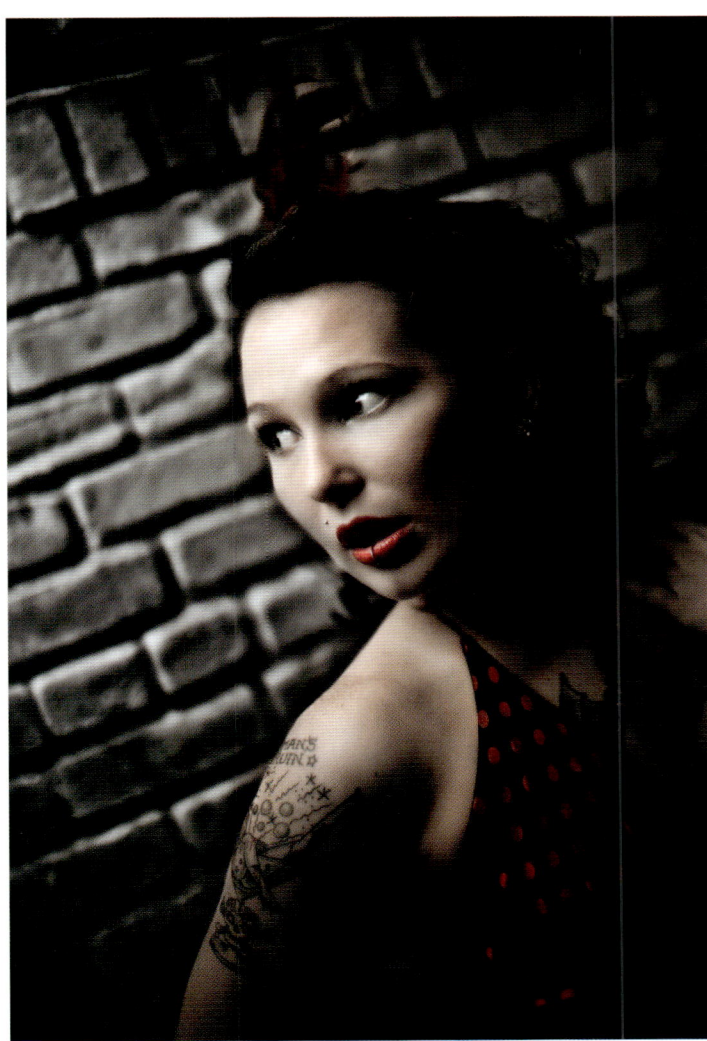

FIGURE 9.6 I used an external flash with an umbrella to create studio-quality lighting in a back alley in downtown Austin. Nikon D700s with Nikon 50 mm f/1.4G, 1/60 sec. @ f/1.4 ISO 200

perfect light for your decay scene isn't necessarily going to be the perfect lighting for your portrait subject. The good thing about lighting people is that there's a lot more flexibility. With large subjects, such as buildings, you are limited to whatever light is on hand or by the size of the subject. You can wait to shoot at a different time of day or wait for different weather conditions, but by and large you are at the mercy of the world. Shooting at night or indoors you can add some illumination with additional light sources such as flashlights or strobes, but you are limited by the amount of light that is feasible to provide without having loads of lighting gear at your disposal.

When lighting for portraiture, if using available light you can easily modify the light using an inexpensive reflector or diffusion panel, you can move your subject easily if the direction of the light isn't striking your fancy, or you can completely change locations without too much of hassle if it comes to that.

Soft light and hard light

Soft light is typified by having diffused edges and light shadows. Soft light is generally the preferred lighting for portraiture. The shadow edges are very subtle, causing the shadow areas to blend seamlessly into highlights. Soft light seems to wrap around and envelope the model and allows your subject's facial features to be portrayed smoothly. Soft light is very flattering, which is why it is generally used more than hard light when lighting for people. Soft light can make your decay portraits seem moody, which can work to soften the effect of a harsh background or, in some cases, add a ghostly effect to a background that may be more ethereal in nature. Rural scenes typically benefit more from soft light.

Sometimes soft light can lack the dramatic effect that one might need to portray the subject in an edgier atmosphere. Hard light is typified by well-defined shadows that break up the highlight areas, which delineates features and accentuates details in both the model and the background. Urban settings are great candidates for hard lighting. This can give the scene a decidedly gritty feel that emphasizes the hard lines and angles that characterize a run-down, inner-city vibe.

High key and low key

Another factor to think about when shooting portraits is *key*. In simple terms, the key is defined by the brightness of your image. There are two basic *keys* in photography: high key, which is exemplified by bright lighting, playing up the highlight areas with little in the way of shadows and mid-tones; and low key, which is characterized by dark, high-contrast lighting with most of the image content being in the darker mid-tone and shadow area.

High-key images are just on the verge of being overexposed, or in some cases may even contain overexposed areas. These types of images tend to feel more light and airy, but can still carry a mysterious look due to the subject matter in the background.

Low-key images are much darker, which tends to lead to a more dramatic and moody effect. The high contrast between the dark and light areas creates more depth in the image that helps lend a more dimensional feel to the portrait.

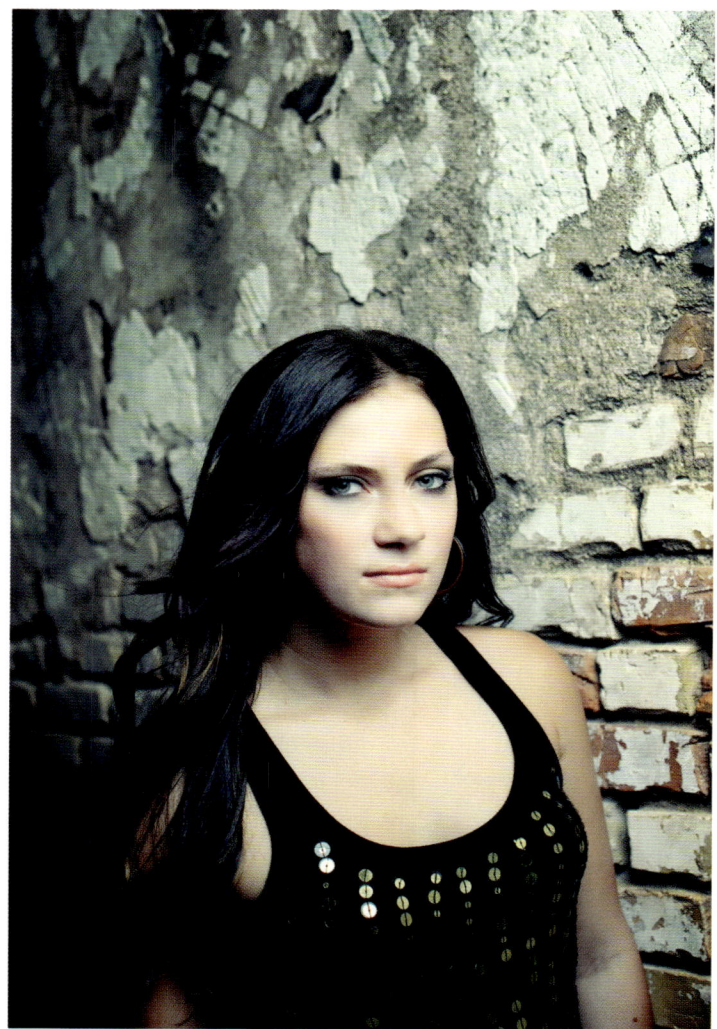

FIGURE 9.7 For this urban portrait I used close lighting to create a soft but directional light. Nikon D700 with Nikon 50 mm f/1.4G. 1/60 sec. @ f/4 ISO 400

Direction

The direction of your light is also a key factor to consider when setting up a shot. There are three main types of lighting direction: front, side, and back. These are pretty

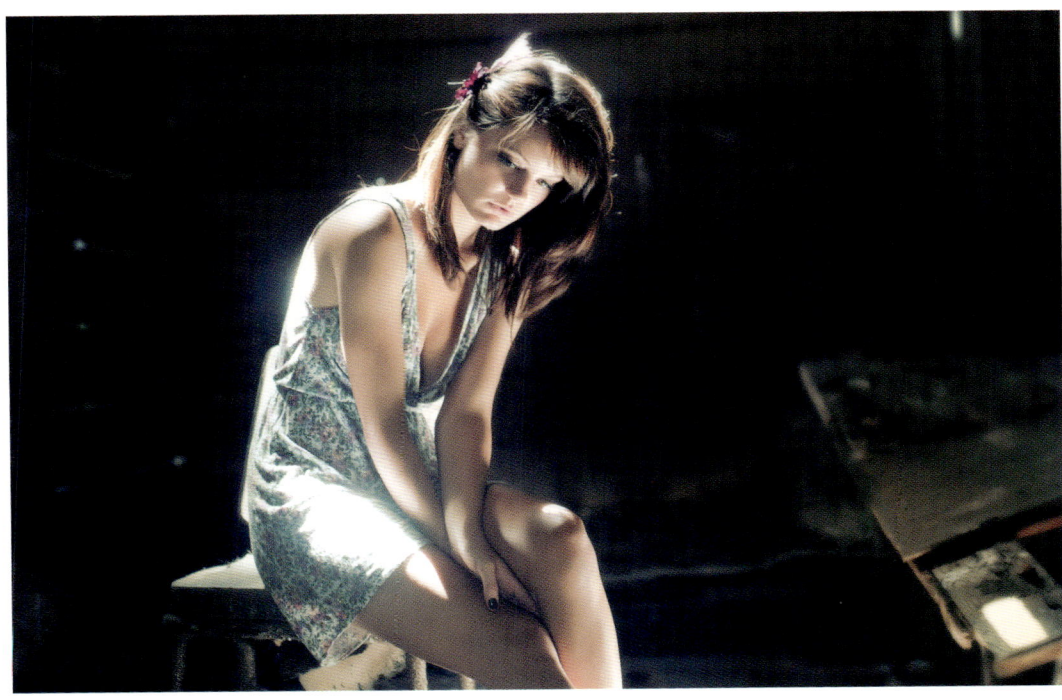

FIGURE 9.8 This image combines both hard and soft light. The hard light shining through the cracks of the structure onto the model combined with the soft light of the background creates a distinct ethereal effect. Nikon D300s with Nikon 50 mm f/1.8D (75 mm equivalent). 1/80 sec. @ f/3.2 ISO 800. © Julian Humphries

self-explanatory as far as where the light source needs to be located in regards to the subject.

Front light is the most common type of light. As the name suggests, the light source is in front of the subject and lights it very evenly. This type of light gives very little shadow area and while it can be good for a nice evenly lit portrait, it can lack the depth and drama that may be needed for decay photography.

Side light is probably the best type of light to use for portraits with a decay theme. Lighting your subject from the side emphasizes depth by adding more shadows and revealing texture. Your light source can come in anywhere from a 30° to 90° angle.

Back light is one of the least used types of light, but when photographing portraits in a decay setting it can be one of the strongest types of lighting when it comes to portraying your subject with a dramatic flair. Spot metering is the best way to determine exposure for back light. Exposing for the shadows is a great way to get an interesting high-key image, and exposing for the highlight areas will give your images a darker, low-key look.

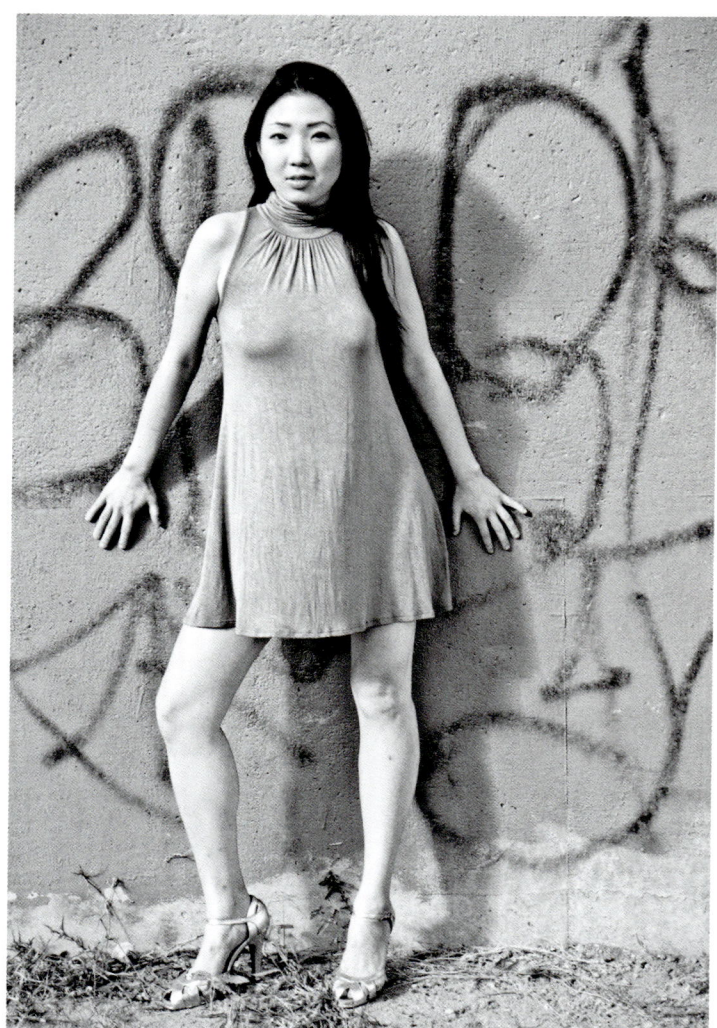

FIGURE 9.9 High-key images are bright with very little mid-tone and shadow values. Nikon D300 with Tamron 17–50 mm f/2.8 at 50 mm (75 mm equivalent). 1/160 sec. @ f/2.8 ISO 100

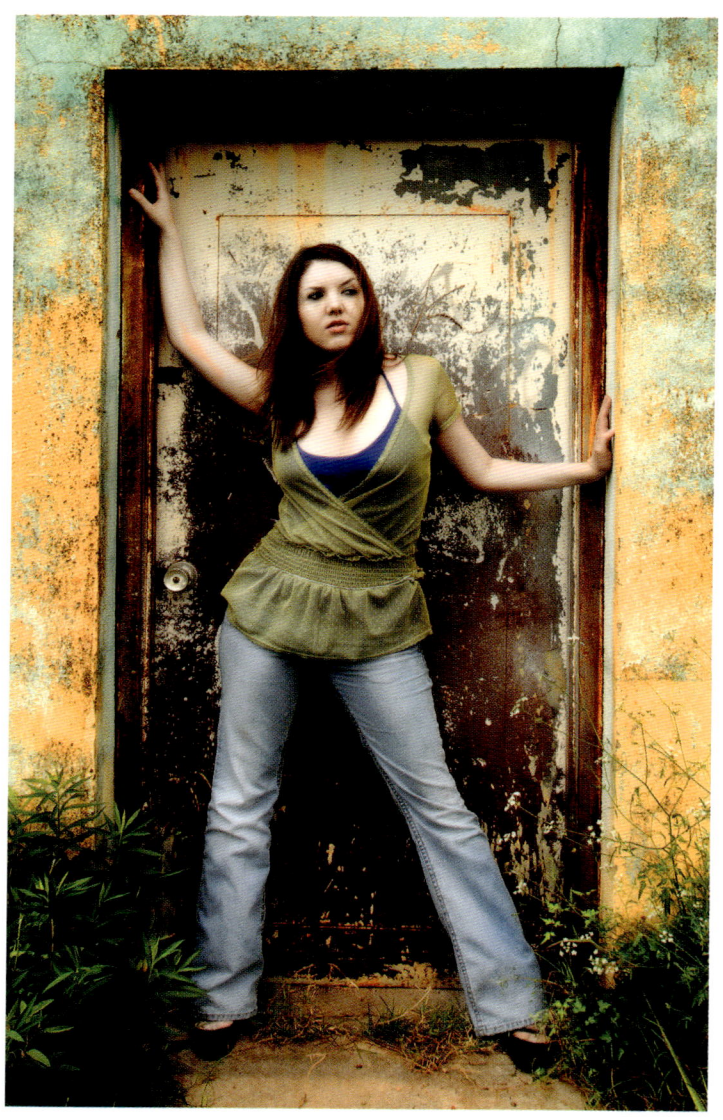

FIGURE 9.10 This image is front lit. To compensate for the lack of dramatic light, I accentuated the composition by using a brightly colored background. Nikon D200 with Nikon 18–70 mm f/3.5–4.5G at 22 mm (33 mm equivalent). 1/160 sec. @ f/6.3 ISO 100

Available light

The easiest way to go about shooting decay portraits is to use whatever light is in the scene, often referred to by photographers as available light. Shooting outdoors is obviously going to give you more available light to work with than shooting indoors, because in the majority of cases the indoor scenes are going to be rather dim unless there is an abundance of window light.

For good, soft portrait light it's usually advisable to keep your subject out of the direct sunlight. Placing your subject in the shade is a good option. Although you want to place your subject out of the direct light, it's a good idea not to get too far undercover or away from the light source or you will lose any directionality of light. While you want a soft light, keep your subject close enough to the light so you can still see the direction from which the light is coming.

An excellent way to achieve soft yet directional lighting is by using window light. Simply place your subject near a window with a reasonable amount of light. The light filtering through the glass is perfect for flattering portrait light.

External light

When photographing in low light, whether indoors or out, you're going to need an external light source if you want to shoot portraits. There are two kinds of external light sources: continuous and flash. Considering that most decay scenes are likely to not have any source of power, using continuous light isn't going to be a viable option unless you plan on hauling in a generator or a heavy-duty battery power supply. The better option is to use small portable shoe-mount flashes. These are extremely light and very powerful for their small size.

While you can simply slide your flash into the hot-shoe and use the auto mode to shoot away, you're not going to get the best results. Your images will be lit directly from the front, resulting in harsh, unflattering light. I don't recommend this approach at all. The easiest way to start out lighting using a shoe-mount flash is to use it on-camera, but to swivel the flash head away from the subject and *bounce* the light from the flash off the ceiling or an adjacent wall. The reflected light is scattered and softened, resulting in a much more pleasing effect than straight-ahead flash.

If you're more serious about crafting professional-looking decay portraits, you need to look into using off-camera flash. Most cameras and dedicated flash units these days are equipped with the ability to do wireless flash, which allows you to take the flash and use it remotely, placing it anywhere you like and controlling it from the camera using a commander. Some cameras have a commander flash option built-in, while others require an additional commander unit. Research your specific camera make and model for more information.

You can put together a bare-bones, easily portable portrait lighting kit for a couple of hundred dollars at the most. If your camera has a built-in flash that works as a wireless commander, all you need is a remote flash, an inexpensive light stand, and a light modifier such as a diffusion dome or, more ideally, a small umbrella. You can create professional-looking portraits with one simple off-camera flash.

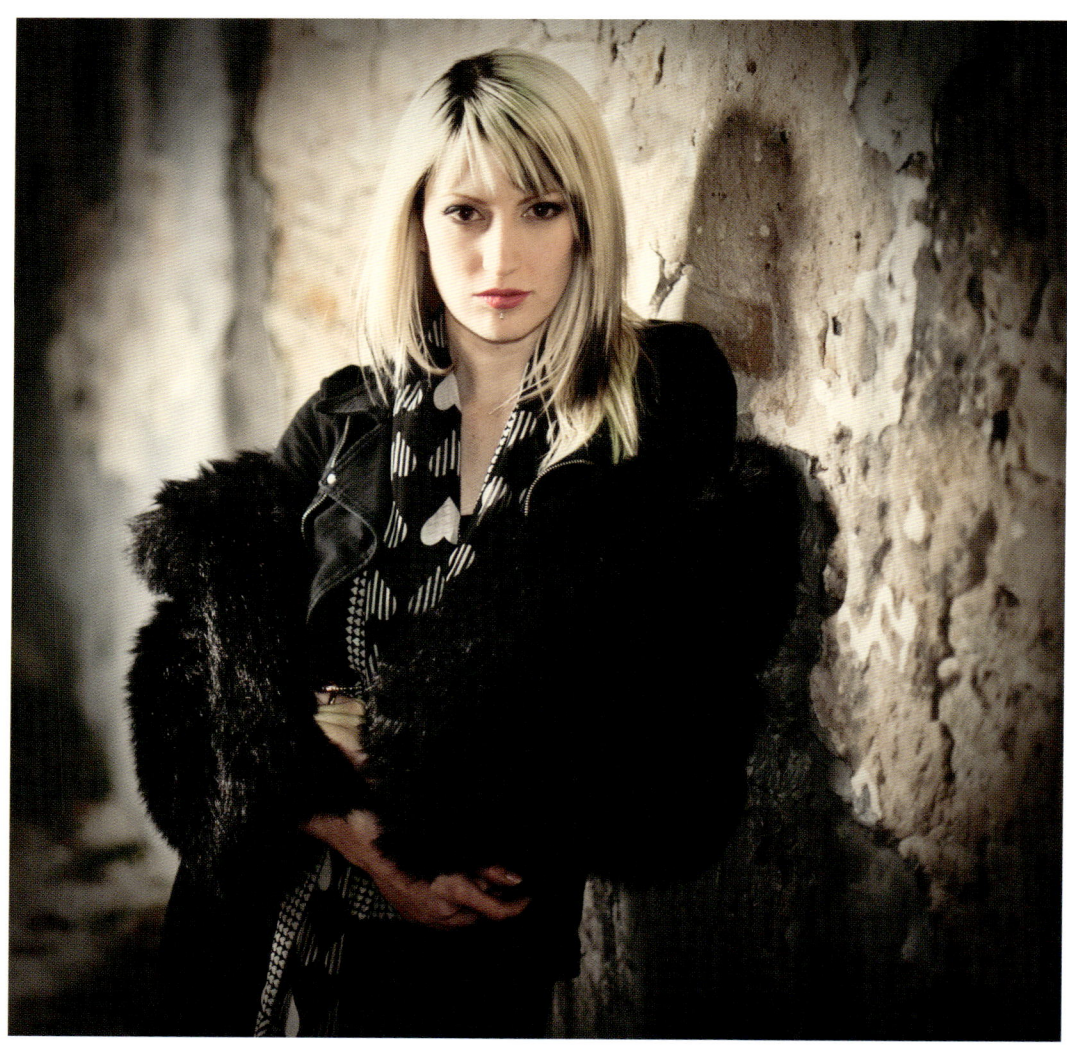

FIGURE 9.11 In this image I used my off-camera light kit, consisting of one Nikon SB-900 flash with an umbrella. I used side lighting to create a dramatic low-key image. **Nikon D700 with Nikon 50 mm f/1.4G. 1/60 sec. @ f/1.4 ISO 200**

Index

A/D (analog-to-digital) converter 73–4
Adams, Ansel 46
Adobe Bridge 132
Adobe Camera RAW 87–9, 120
Adobe Lightroom 33, 87, 120, 131–3, 136–7, 143–4, 164
Adobe Photoshop 22, 87, 98, 131–3, 136–7, 144–5, 151, 154, 156, 162–4
Adobe Photoshop Elements 133, 136
Alien Skin Exposure 136–7, 143, 145
aperture (or f/stop) 77–8
    low light shooting 114–15
Apple iPhoto 31, 151

balance 51–2
baLens 84
black-and-white conversions 135–8, 143
black-and-white film 94
    anti-halation layer 94, 95
    latent image 95–6
    light-sensitive emulsion layer 94–6
    substrate layer 94
    types 96–7
bracketing 124, 154–6
burning 154
Burtynsky, Edward 5

cameras
    APS-C 22, 24
    compact 32
    cost 22
    full frame vs crop sensor 22–6
    mirrorless 32–3
    modifying 28
    point and shoot 32
    rangefinders 26
    second-hand 75
    SLRs and DSLRs 22, 33
    TLR 26–8
    toy 26, 28
Canon 22–3, 39
Canon Digital Photo Pro 120, 133
Canon Picture Style 137
CCD (charge coupled device) 72–3
chemicals for processing 104
    developer 104
    fixer 104
    hypo clearing agent 104
    photo-flo 104
    stop bath 104
chemistry and processing
    developer 105–6
    fixer 106
    photo-flo 106
    rinse 106
    steps 105–6
    stop bath 106
chrominance 84, 87–8, 120
circle of confusion 79
clouds 159
CMOS (complementary metal-oxide semiconductor) 73
color 56, 58
color conversions 138
color correction 133–5
color negative 97–9
color oversaturation 159
complementary color 58
composition and technique 46
    angles 67, 68
    balance and symmetry 51–2
    color 56–8
isolating the subject 60–1
leading lines/patterns 52–5
light 46–9
rule of thirds 49–50
textures 55–6
contraptions 149, 151
counterweight 51
crop factor 23
cross processing 141–4
cyanotype 139

dark-frame noise reduction 120
decay photography
    background 2
    description of 2–3
    importance of documenting 6
    key photographers 3–6
    legal issues 16–20
    meaning of 2
    rural 10–11
    safety issues 13–16
    urban 7–10
depth of field (DoF) 79
digital photography 72
    exposure 76–81
    histograms 81–3
    low light shooting 116, 118, 120
    noise/noise reduction 84–8
    sensors 72–6
    shooting RAW 83
    white balance 83–4
digital post-processing see post-processing
dodging 154
DSLR (digital single lens reflex) 22, 33
Dutch (Deutsch) angle 67
dynamic range 76

eBay 22, 28
Efke film 97
EOS Viewer Utility 120
ETTR (exposed to the right) 118, 123
Evans, Walker 4
EXIF (exchangeable image file format) 131, 132
ExpoDisc 84
exposure 46, 76–7
    aperture 77–8
    blending 161–2
    bracketing 124
    combination of settings 77
    depth of field 79
    ISO sensitivity 80–1
    low light shooting 118, 120
    shutter speed 80
    stops 77
    timed 114

Farm Security Administration (FSA) 4
file management 130
film 94
    low light shooting 122–4
    processing see processing at home
film types 94
    black-and-white negative 94–7
    color negative 97–9
    instant (polaroid) 101–2
    transparency or color positive 99–101
flashlight 110
Flickr 28, 31–2
focal length 24, 79
frames and borders 145
Fuji FP-100C film 101
Fuji FP-3000B film 102
Fuji Neopan 100 Acros 96

Fuji Superia X-tra 400 film 99
full frame 24, 26

geo-tagging 33
Golden Hour 47
Google Picasa 133
GPS 33

halos 158–9
HDR (high dynamic range) 22, 33, 76, 154
   bracketing 154–6
   dodging and burning 154
   exposure blending 161–2
   software 162–5
   tone mapping 157–60
HDRsoft Photomatix 163–4
HDRtist 164–5
high-speed film 84–5
histograms 81–3
Holga 28

Ilford Delta 138
Ilford Delta 100 film 96–7
Ilford HP5 Plus film 97
IPTC (International Press Telecommunication Council) 131–2
IS (Image Stabilization) 39
ISO sensitivity 77, 80–1
   high ISO noise 85–6
   low light shooting 111–13
isolate the subject 60–1
   add something different 61
   fill the frame 61, 64
   perspective 61
   selective focus 61
   selective lighting 61

Johnson, Kelly 60
JPEG 83, 116, 118, 156

kelvin 83–4
key 178
KISS (Keep It Simple, Stupid) 60–1

Kodachrome 143
Kodak 100
Kodak Duaflex camera 149
Kodak Ektar 100 film 98
Kodak T-Max film 97
Kodak Tri-X 138
Krages, Bert, *Legal Handbook for Photographers* 19

Lange, Dorothea 4
latent image 95–6
leading lines 52, 54
legal issues
   photographer's rights 18–19
   trespass 16–17
lenses 33–4
   cost 33
   focal length and aperture 34
   image-stabilizing 110
   interchangeable 34
   IS, VR, OS, VC 38–40
   mid-range, standard, normal 37
   telephoto 38
   vibration-reducing 110
   wide-angle 35–7
light
   available 181
   back 179
   external 181
   flash light 47
   front 179
   for portraiture *see* portraiture
   quality of *see* quality of light
   side 179
Lo-1 or L/1 setting 112
Lomo 26
Lomo LC-A 28
Lomo Sprocket Rocket 28
low light shooting 110
   cable or remote release 110
   digital 116–20
   film 122–4
   flash 110
   flashlight 110

night time 110, 113, 115, 122–4
   settings 111–15
   tools and accessories 110
   tripod 110
   vibration-reducing or image-stabilizing lens 110
luminance 84, 87–8, 120

manual layer blending 156
metadata 131
   EXIF data 131
   IPTC data 131–2
   template 132–3
Micro Four Thirds (M43) 32–3
monochrome 139
Morris, Russ 149
motion blur 114
MPs (megapixels) 74–5
Mydans, Carl 4

native setting 112
negative space 51
Niépce, Joseph Nicéphore 2
night photography 110, 113, 115, 122–4
Nik Color Efex Pro 143
Nik Silver Efex Pro 136
Nik-D-Fine 88
Nikon 22–4, 33–4, 39, 75, 80, 83
Nikon ViewNX 120, 133
No Trespassing signs 9–10, 11, 16–17
noise 84–5, 111
   chrominance and luminance 84, 87–8, 120
   excess in shadow areas 159
   high ISO noise 85–6, 120
   long exposure 86, 114
   reduction 86–8, 89, 120
   thermal 120

Ohanaware 164–5
onOne Software PhotoFrame 145
OS (Optical Stabilization) 39
over-sharpening image 159–60

pack-film 101
patterns 54–5
Photomatix 163–4
pixels 73–4
Polaroid 101–2
Polaroid Land Camera "100"-series 101
portraiture 174
   available light 181
   direction lighting 178–9
   external light 181
   gear and settings 174–5
   high key and low key 178
   lighting tips 175–81
   props 175
   soft light and hard light 177–8
post-processing 128–9
   black-and-white conversions 135–8
   color conversions 138
   color correction 133–5
   file management 130
   keepers 130
   metadata 131–3
   tonal adjustments 133–5
   TtV technique 144–9
processing at home 102–3
   chemistry and processing 105–6
   loading film 104–5
   low contrast technique 124
   supplies 103–4
processing supplies 103
   bottle opener 104
   changing bag 103
   chemical storage bottles 104
   chemicals 104
   developing tank 104
   film reel 103
   measuring cups 104
   scissors 104
   thermometer 104
pushed film 84–5

quality of light 46
   available light 47–9

clouds 48
hard light 46–7, 49, 177–8
night light 48
soft light 47, 49, 177–8
sunlight 47–8

rangefinders 26
RAW files 83–4, 116, 118, 120–2, 128, 130, 133–7, 142, 155–6, 160
low light shooting 116, 118
reciprocal rule 39–40
reciprocity failure 123–4
resolution 74–5
Riis, Jacob 3
Rothstein, Arthur 4
rule of thirds 49–50
rural decay
description of 10
finding subjects for 10–11
russmorris.com/tv 149

safety
cell phones and flashlights 15–16
clothing 14–15
dangerous elements 13

health issues 14
injuries 15
Seagull 26
sensors 72
analog to digital 73–4
CCD 72–3
CMOS 72–3
dynamic range 76, 77
resolution 74–5
size 76
settings for low light shooting 111
aperture 114–15
ISO sensitivity 111–13
shutter speed 113–14
shadow edge transfer 47
shooting in low light see low light shooting
shutter speed 80
low light shooting 113–14
Sigma 23, 39
silver halide crystals 95–6
slide film 99–101
SLR (single lens reflex) 22
medium-format 25
smartphone apps
Flickr 32

Hipstamatic 31–2
Instagram 31
Photo55 32
Plastic Bullet 32
smartphones 29, 31
smokestack technique 149
Sony Steady Shot system 39
spot metering 179
symmetry 51–2

take only pictures, leave only footprints 19
Tamron 39
technique see composition and technique
textures 55–6
thermal noise 120
timed exposures 114
TLR (twin lens reflex) 26, 144, 149
tonal adjustments 133–5
tone mapping 157–60
tone mapping artefacts
dark clouds 159
excess noise in shadow area 159
halos 158–9
over-sharpening 159
oversaturated colors 159

toning of images 139
Topaz Adjust 164
Topaz B&W Effects 136
toy cameras 26, 28
Diana 28
Holga 28
Lomo LC-A 28
Lubitel 28
tripods 40–1, 110
TtV (through the viewfinder) 144–9

urban decay
description of 7
disregarding *No Trespassing* signs 9–10
finding subjects for 9

VC (Vibration Compensation) 39
Velvia 101, 143
Vergara, Camilo José 5–6
VR (Vibration Reduction) 39

white balance 83–4, 118

zone of acceptable sharpness 79
zoom vs prime 34